Delinquency in Three Cultures

DELINQUENCY
in Three Cultures

Carl M. Rosenquist
and
Edwin I. Megargee

PUBLISHED FOR THE HOGG FOUNDATION FOR

MENTAL HEALTH

BY THE UNIVERSITY OF TEXAS PRESS

AUSTIN AND LONDON

Standard Book Number 292–78415–5
Library of Congress Catalog Card Number 70–89627
Copyright © 1969 by the Hogg Foundation for Mental Health
All Rights Reserved

Type set by G&S Typesetters, Austin
Printed by The Steck-Warlick Company, Austin
Bound by Universal Bookbindery, Inc., San Antonio

To our wives,
HELEN B. ROSENQUIST
and
ANN P. MEGARGEE

FOREWORD

When the Hogg Foundation for Mental Health embarked upon a major program of research grants to scholars and scientists in 1955, an area of immediate concern was the lack of knowledge about social and cultural factors and their influence upon human behavior. Late that same year, the Third Interamerican Congress of Psychology was held in Austin, Texas, making it possible for a number of psychologists, psychiatrists, and related social scientists from Mexico City to meet for the first time with psychologists, anthropologists, and sociologists from The University of Texas. Common interests in cross-cultural research were quickly discovered, leading to a series of small international conferences and the launching of several research programs that are still continuing. One of the most significant collaborations to emerge from these exchanges involved Professor Carl Rosenquist, a sociologist with long-standing interests in criminology, and Professor Hector Solis Quiroga, a distinguished lawyer and sociologist from Mexico City. Although other pressing duties prevented Solis Quiroga from active involvement in their cross-cultural study of juvenile delinquency after the first two years, his contributions were sufficiently significant to ensure the success of the study in Monterrey as well as San Antonio.

Designing and conducting a cross-cultural investigation with the scope and complexity needed to provide definitive answers to important questions about delinquency and culture proved to be no small feat. With great patience and skill, Professor Rosenquist and his associates elicited the cooperation of schools, courts, reformatories, government authorities, and, most important, the three hundred teenagers themselves in this searching study of delinquency in three cultures. Rosenquist developed and refined a number of the psychological techniques employed in the study, a significant undertaking in itself. Several years were needed merely to collect the information from interviews, psychological testing, and medical examinations of both delinquent and nondelinquent boys from Anglo and Latin cultures in San Antonio and from Mexican culture in Monterrey. Two more years were required to sift through the countless bits of data before the findings began to take shape.

Shortly after all the information had been collected and a preliminary analysis had been completed, Professor Edwin Megargee joined The University of Texas faculty as a clinical psychologist, fresh from several years of working with juvenile offenders in California. At the same time, Rosenquist retired from his faculty position and moved to California. Megargee agreed to carry the project through to completion, and a close collaboration developed between the two social scientists. Responsibility for the final analysis of the data and preparation of the manuscript, including the review of the literature, the description of the three cultures, and the interpretation of the findings, rests largely upon Megargee.

The book that has resulted from this fruitful collaboration is much more than simply a technical report of the primary investigation. The extensive scholarly research and theoretical formulations dealing with a wide range of important issues in personality, society, and culture constitute major contributions in their own right. When added to the significant empirical findings of their cross-cultural study, the result is a definitive work that should stand as a major treatise for many years to come.

WAYNE H. HOLTZMAN

ACKNOWLEDGMENTS

A project of this magnitude and duration cannot be accomplished without the help of many people. It is indeed a pleasure to be able publicly to express our gratitude to these people.

First and foremost, we wish to thank the Hogg Foundation for Mental Health and its codirectors, Robert Sutherland and Wayne Holtzman. While the financial support provided was of course indispensable, the interest, advice, and encouragement of the Foundation staff were no less essential to the successful completion of this project.

The contribution of Hector Solis-Quiroga was also indispensable, for it was he who was the prime mover in arranging for the collection of data in Monterrey. Without his assistance this would not have been a cross-national study. We also owe a major debt of gratitude to the school and correctional court officials in Bexar County, Texas, and Monterrey, Nuevo León, Mexico, who provided the subjects and facilities in which data collection could take place, as well as to the 300 boys who served as subjects in the study. We are also grateful to the officials of the Travis County Juvenile Court who provided subjects and space for developing and pretesting the psychological tests used in this study.

Professor and Mrs. James A. Forrester played a central role in the data collection in San Antonio, as did Dr. Luis Lara-Tapia in Monterrey. Among those who helped collect the data were Elie Arnaud, Marjorie and Lindy Burgess, Sam Buchanan, Josephine Claudio, Mrs. Kay Downing, K. R. Jones, M.D., Mrs. Bob Matocha, Edmundo

Rague, M.D., Carl John Rosenquist, M.D., Mrs. Eleanor Russell, Mrs. Mollie Sadler, and Mrs. Paul Saunders.

The primary job of test scoring was done by Mrs. Helen B. Rosenquist. Among those who assisted her by translating and typing test material and tabulating data were Mrs. Ann C. Hardy, Mrs. Ann B. Mangum, Maria Ortega, Francisca Paz, Henry Pocock, Carlos Rodriguez, Mrs. Lyle Speck, and Mrs. Mildred Trevor.

In the data analysis phase, the advice and assistance of Professors Earl Jennings, Quinn McNemar and Robert K. Young were most helpful. Mrs. Beth Mitchell assisted in the computation and the library research.

Final preparation of the manuscript was facilitated by the editorial assistance of Mrs. Elizabeth Byrne. Mrs. Etelka Lynn, of the Hogg Foundation, helped take care of innumerable details. The early drafts of the manuscript were typed by Sylvia Jacobson and Penny Bledsoe, and the final draft by Betty Bobenia and Dottie Driskill. The constructive criticism and comments of Marvin Wolfgang, Luis Lara-Tapia, Rogelio Diaz-Guerrero, and, especially, Wayne Holtzman were of great help in writing the final report.

To all of these individuals and organizations, as well as to any others we may have failed to acknowledge specifically, we wish to express our sincere thanks.

C.M.R.
E.I.M.

PERMISSIONS

DELINQUENCY IN THREE CULTURES

"Personality and Delinquency," by H. C. Quay, in *Juvenile Delinquency*, edited by H. C. Quay. 1965, Van Nostrand.

Profile of Man and Culture in Mexico, by S. Ramos (translated by P. G. Earle). 1962, University of Texas Press.

Spanish Harlem, by P. S. Sexton. 1966, Harper and Row.

"Ways of Life," by E. H. Spicer, in *Six Faces of Mexico: History, People, Geography, Government, Economy, Literature and Art*, edited by R. C. Ewing. 1966, University of Arizona Press.

Principles of Criminology, seventh edition, by E. H. Sutherland and D. R. Cressey, published by J. B. Lippincott Company. Copyright © 1966 by J. B. Lippincott Company.

Symonds Picture-Story Test, by Percival M. Symonds (New York: Teachers College Press), copyright © 1948, Teachers College, Columbia University.

CONTENTS

PART I

The Problem and Its Background

CHAPTER 1

INTRODUCTION TO THE STUDY

Police and FBI statistics are notoriously unreliable sources of data on crime rates. A change in the method of reporting data, a crackdown by a new administrator, or expanded facilities in the local detention center can all contribute to spurious increases in the number of reported crimes. Even allowing for such inaccuracies, however, there can be little doubt that the incidence of detected crimes by juveniles has been steadily rising in the last decade and has outstripped the increase in the juvenile population (Wirt & Briggs, 1965).

This growth in the rate, as well as the absolute number, of crimes has been accompanied by considerable public concern and the demand for new programs of prevention and treatment. However, it is difficult to alter or prevent a phenomenon that we do not understand; since most scholars agree that our understanding of juvenile delinquency is still less than perfect, it is obvious that additional research is necessary. This was recognized explicitly by the Ninetieth Congress in the Juvenile Delinquency Prevention Act of 1967: ". . . to support the research for knowledge about delinquency in order to develop methods for and the capability of dealing with and preventing it."

Few dispute the notion that knowledge is desirable. However, when we ask what sorts of knowledge are most desirable, we are clearly inviting an argument. Nevertheless, by adopting some procedures and rejecting others, every empirical investigator makes implicit value judgments about the sorts of knowledge that he feels are desirable enough to be worth months or years of work. The first such judgment made by the present investigators was that it was worthwhile to spend several years of effort doing research on delinquency. This may seem to be a trivial decision at first glance, but, as those who have done such research know all too well, it is a more difficult decision than it appears. Everyone agrees that scientific knowledge of delinquency is desirable, but many question whether it can be attained because of the numerous research problems it involves.

A typical problem is the basic one of definition. Who is a delinquent and who is not? If we define a delinquent as someone who breaks the law, we are then confronted with the problem of how to classify the youth who commits an illegal act but is not caught, tried, or convicted. This is about as easy to resolve as the question of whether the tree falling unheard in the forest makes any noise. The problem becomes even thornier when we examine the "delinquent" act, for we soon are confronted with the most ancient of philosophical dilemmas, the difference between right and wrong. What of the person who breaks an immoral law? Can we really regard as criminals the German arrested for sheltering a Jew in 1935, the Negro arrested for sitting in at a segregated lunch counter in 1960, or the Mexican-American arrested for attempting to unionize the Rio Grande farm workers in 1967? What of the person who breaks the law unintentionally or the person who intends to commit a crime but is accidentally prevented from it by forces beyond his control?

One solution to the problem of definition is to ignore these insoluble philosophical dilemmas and simply let the courts decide what constitutes a crime. This leads to further problems, however, because the law states that an act may be a crime for some people but not for others. No matter what he does, a young child or a person who is "insane" cannot be considered a criminal under modern Western law. An adolescent may be arrested for being on the streets after 10:00 P.M., for buying a drink, or for not going to school—behavior that is perfectly acceptable for an adult. A man who has intercourse with an underage girl can be convicted of statutory rape in most jurisdictions, but not a woman who has intercourse with an underage boy. Thus, age, sex, and mental condition of the perpetrator all play a role in determining whether or not an act is considered criminal. Moreover, the researcher must face the fact that in all likelihood race, socioeconomic status, and political influence often determine which youths who commit a crime are actually arrested and brought before a court. Because of these factors almost any operational definition of delinquency that an investigator may use is open to criticism from some quarter. By "willfully and knowingly" deciding to conduct a study of delinquency (whatever that is) the present investigators were affirming their conviction that despite the many problems it is still possible to obtain worthwhile data on the subject.

Given the decision to do research on delinquency, further value judgments dictated the nature of the research. Surveying the literature, it was apparent that many individual studies of delinquency had been conducted and many hypotheses regarding the nature and causes of delinquency had been offered. However, much of this research seemed overly narrow. Investigators in one discipline too often overlooked relevant variables because they happened to fall within the territory staked out by someone from another discipline or by someone from a different theoretical orientation within the same discipline. It would be natural, for example, to suppose that nutrition, intelligence, and socioeconomic status might be closely interrelated variables that could influence delinquency. However, if the physician, the psychologist, or the sociologist separately examines only the one variable that clearly falls into his specialty, such interrelationships will be overlooked. This is not to say that narrow studies are worthless. On the contrary, they constitute the building blocks from which theories can be constructed. But unless narrow studies are supplemented by broader investigations that relate the data in one domain to the results being obtained in another, the field is apt to suffer from scientific provincialism and premature rigidity.

Several broad studies of delinquency have been conducted over the years; the investigations by Healy and Bronner (1936) and the Gluecks (1950) are but two classic examples. However, even these investigations, which displayed commendable breadth in the range of variables examined, have shown unfortunate narrowness in other respects. Many of these early studies were exploratory investigations, and the investigators often neglected to relate their findings to the observations of other scholars or to use their data to test different theoretical positions. These studies were also culturally narrow. The investigators typically compared delinquents and nondelinquents

in one location or in a single subcultural group and failed to replicate their investigations in other locales or among other groups. As
a result, a large body of information has grown up about the characteristics of lower-class urban delinquents in the Northeastern
United States, but little effort has been made to determine whether
the findings obtained can be generalized to delinquents in other
nations, to delinquents in different subcultures within the United
States, or even to delinquents from the same general subculture
who live in other regions of the United States. Yet, before broad
programs of delinquency prevention or treatment can be undertaken,
it is obviously necessary to know whether the San Antonio delinquent resembles the Boston delinquent, or if the Mexican-American
delinquent has the same problems as the Anglo.

The present investigators, therefore, felt that what was needed at
this stage was broad research to determine the generality of the
existing data and theories. It was decided to conduct a cross-cultural,
cross-national investigation comparing the differences between delinquents and nondelinquents in three cultural groups: Anglo-
Americans and Mexican-Americans in the United States, and Mexican nationals in Mexico. To prevent disciplinary narrowness, it was
decided to collect a wide range of data, including measurements of
sociological, psychological, and physiological variables.

If research on delinquency is beset by methodological problems,
they pale into insignificance compared with the problems involved
in cross-national research. Problems of sampling and of obtaining
the cooperation of school and correctional authorities are difficult
enough in one locale; the difficulty increases geometrically when two
locales in two nations are used. Procedures must be found that are
appropriate for not one but three sets of customs, and the responses
must be evaluated according to the cultural context. The mere process of having to translate materials from English to Spanish and
back again creates many difficulties. Nevertheless, the investigators
felt that the potential advantages to be gained from using the cross-
cultural method outweighed the difficulties. Whiting (1954, pp. 52–
53) has discussed some of these advantages as follows:

The advantages of the cross-cultural method are twofold. First, it en-
sures that one's findings relate to human behavior in general rather than
being bound to a single culture, and second, it increases the range of
variation of many of the variables . . .

Furthermore, the cross-cultural method, by studying cultural norms, holds individual variation constant. Psychological studies of individuals in a single society do just the opposite, in that cultural norms are held constant and individual variations studied. A combination of these two methods should supplement and correct each other in the development of a general theory of human behavior.

Northern Mexico and the Southwestern United States offer a unique laboratory for such research. This vast semiarid region was originally settled by Mexicans whose folkways and physiology represented a mixture of Spanish and Indian ancestry. North Americans, or "Anglos," started migrating to the area north of the Rio Grande 150 years ago. Following the Texas Revolution, this territory became part of the Republic of Texas and was later annexed to the United States. Thus, a dominant Anglo culture was superimposed upon the indigenous Mexican culture, and a Mexican-American culture that borrowed from both traditions developed.

Consequently, the American citizen of Mexican descent differs significantly from American citizens whose cultural roots are in other lands. First, he lives in an area in which his people were the first settlers and in which the North Americans are the newcomers. Secondly, unlike other ethnic groups, the American of Mexican descent lives immediately adjacent to the Old Country so his cultural roots have been nourished by continued direct contact with the traditional culture. Frequent visiting and fairly easy immigration, both legal and illegal, have been made possible by a relatively permissive border policy. Moreover, the bracero program admits thousands of Mexican agricultural workers to the United States on a temporary basis each year. As a result, the Mexican-Americans of the Southwest have maintained their cultural distinctiveness to a much greater extent than have most immigrant groups in the United States.

Anglos living in San Antonio, Mexican-Americans living in San Antonio, and Mexican nationals living in Monterrey, Nuevo León, Mexico, represent three points on a continuum of cultural and physical dissimilarity to the residents of the Northeastern United States who have served as subjects for most of the previous psychological, sociological, and biological research. By conducting parallel investigations comparing juvenile delinquents and nondelinquents in each of the three cultures, the generality of much of the previous work could be tested, as well as certain theories of the nature and cause of delinquency. Since Anglos and Mexican nationals are both members of dominant cultural groups, their patterns could be compared with those obtained by other investigators who have studied dominant groups in other areas. The Mexican-Americans represent a minority group that, while similar in culture and physique to the Mexicans, is living as a relatively unassimilated minority in a city dominated by the Anglos. This group could be used to test certain theories that attribute delinquency to cultural conflict.

In addition to allowing the cross-cultural generality of various observations to be determined, it was hoped that the inclusion of a wide range of sociological, psychological, and physiological variables might allow the present investigators to determine the interrelationships among many factors that are often studied separately. For example, let us assume that in a given cultural sample the delinquents manifest more bitterness and feelings of deprivation on the psychological tests than do the nondelinquents. If they also come from homes where the divorce rate indicates there has been more marital discord, or if the medical examination suggests more physical neglect, then we might interpret these feelings of deprivation as being appropriate and realistic. On the other hand, if these feelings are not accompanied by any indication that the delinquents have suffered more physical or emotional privation, then it might suggest that these attitudes reflect intrapsychic reality, which in turn might imply that, for this group, programs aimed at changing the personality would be more effective than those aimed solely at the milieu.

In order to evaluate the procedures and interpret the results of the present study, it will be necessary for the reader to have an acquaintance with the major theories and findings in the area of delinquency and to have a general understanding of the three cultures. The next two chapters are devoted to providing this background. In the chapter that follows, some theories and data regarding juvenile delinquency are briefly sketched. In Chapter 3 the cultures are described in somewhat greater detail. Then, in Chapter 4, the problem addressed by the present study will be defined more sharply in the light of the background material.

The next section, consisting of nine chapters, will constitute the bulk of this report. Chapter 5 will describe the general methodology of the study, including the factors governing the selection of the sites, the method of sampling, and a general description of the various tests and measurements that were employed. The remaining eight chapters will present detailed discussions of each of the specific sets of data. The first of these chapters, Chapter 6, will discuss the sociological data. The next six chapters, Chapters 7 through 12, will present the data regarding each of the individual psychological assessment devices. The final chapter in this section, Chapter 13, will discuss the results of the medical examination. In each of these chapters the format will be roughly the same. The chapter will begin with a detailed discussion of the literature regarding a given procedure. For example, while a brief overview of the research on the differences in tested intelligence of delinquents and nondelinquents will be presented in Chapter 2, this literature will be discused in detail in Chapter 7, at which point methodological problems will be examined and the relevance of the findings for various theoretical viewpoints pointed out. Following the review of the literature, the detailed methodology used with each measure will be described and the results presented. Each chapter will then conclude with a discussion of the results and their implications in the light of the review of the literature and the results already reported in earlier chapters.

The concluding section of the book will consist of two chapters in which the broad expectations presented in Chapter 4 will be evaluated and the many diverse findings will be integrated, insofar as possible, into a coherent whole and in which the implications for theory, future research, and action programs will be discussed.

Summary

This book presents a cross-cultural, cross-national study of the sociological, psychological, and medical differences between delinquents and comparison groups of nondelinquents in three cultures. In the present chapter the potential contributions of such a study to the literature on delinquency were discussed. Despite the fact that research in the area of delinquency is plagued by a number of methodological difficulties, including the problem of even defining what is meant by delinquency, the increasing rate of juvenile crime makes such research imperative. Much research to date has been of limited value because disciplinary narrowness restricted the range of variables investigated and obscured their possible interactions. The generality of many investigations is also an open question because few have been systematically repeated in different cultures or subcultures. Despite the methodological problems, cross-cultural research on delinquency using a broad range of variables appears to offer the best chance to determine the generality, reliability, and interrelations of the findings and theories in the literature.

In Northern Mexico and Southwestern United States, peoples from two distinct cultures, each with its own language and traditions, have settled. In each country the dominant culture has continued in relative purity, while among American citizens of Mexican descent there has been a continued conflict between Old Country and Anglo values. This area thus offers a unique laboratory in which the generality of many observations and theories of delinquency—sociological, psychological, and physiological—might be studied.

CHAPTER 2

JUVENILE DELINQUENCY: Theory and Research

In this chapter, the data that have been collected regarding juvenile delinquency will be briefly reviewed, along with the theories that have been proposed to explain these observations. This section is intended as a brief overview and not as a detailed survey. The reader who wishes further details on a given theoretical position or empirical study should consult the primary source material or one of the more detailed secondary sources, such as Cavan (1962), Quay (1965a), Robison (1963), or Vold (1958).

Two broad types of theoretical positions have been delineated in the present chapter. The first group includes all those theories that attribute delinquency to some innate constitutional factor. Some of these theories suggest that delinquency itself is inherited; others hypothesize that delinquency stems from some innate intervening variable, like biological inferiority or defective intelligence. The second group of theories places the primary emphasis on environmental variables. Within this broad group, some theorists place primary emphasis on the action of social forces, while others prefer to discuss individual psychodynamics.

Theories of Innate Inherited Characteristics as Causes of Delinquency

The earliest and most enduring class of theories consists of those that attribute delinquency to some innate characteristic of the individual. These theories, like those of Freud and Darwin, grew out of the biological determinism of the nineteenth century. Some regarded criminal tendencies themselves as being inherited; others attributed criminality to some intervening innate trait, like defective intelligence. These theories have probably had more empirical testing using larger samples than have any other class of criminological theories. Sample sizes frequently have run into the thousands. However, as is often the case in human genetic research, these investigations have been hindered by sampling problems, and, in some cases, by problems of measurement. Consequently, none of these theoretical positions can be considered established, despite the large masses of data that have been collected. Given the modern *Zeitgeist*, which is predisposed toward environmental causation, these theoretical positions have been rejected by most criminologists.

THE LOMBROSIAN HYPOTHESIS

One of the earliest constitutional theories was that of Cesare Lombroso (1835–1909), who hypothesized that the criminal, who often behaves in a savage fashion, is in fact an "atavistic reversal" or throwback to a more primitive form of man. Lombroso suggested that this hypothesis could be tested by comparing the physical characteristics of criminals and noncriminals. If the criminal were indeed such a throwback, Lombroso predicted he would have more primitive somatic characteristics or "stigmata," such as a low sloping forehead, than would the noncriminal. Accordingly, Lombroso made numerous anthropological measurements of Italian criminals and soldiers and reported that he had found a higher incidence of such peculiarities among the criminal samples.

In the present century, extensive investigations of Lombroso's hypotheses have been made by Goring (1913) and Hooton (1939b). Goring concluded that his investigation offered no support for the Lombrosian hypothesis; Hooton, who criticized Goring's procedure, felt that his own findings supported the Lombrosian position. Most modern criminologists, who share a strongly environmentalist orientation, criticize Lombroso's and Hooton's methods and cite Goring to prove that the Lombrosian position is untenable. The present writers agree that, because there are so many drawbacks to the sampling procedures used by Lombroso and Hooton, their conclusions cannot be accepted. At the same time, we feel that an equally rigorous analysis reveals similar flaws in Goring's study. Therefore, we feel that the best conclusion regarding the Lombrosian hypothesis is the Scotch verdict, "not proven."

THE CRIMINAL AS A BIOLOGICALLY INFERIOR ORGANISM

Many of the environmentalist criminologists who accept Goring's work relatively uncritically seem unaware of the fact that, while he rejected Lombroso's theory, he nevertheless maintained that criminality was the result of innate physical and mental inferiority. The hypothesis that the criminal is an inferior organism also has been put forth by other writers who have observed that delinquents tend to be less healthy than nondelinquents (Burt, 1944). The evidence on this matter, however, is rather contradictory. As we shall see in Chapter 13, a number of studies have found no significant differences between the physical fitness of delinquents and nondelinquents; in fact, some have even found the delinquents to be somewhat superior.

THE RELATION BETWEEN DELINQUENCY AND BODY TYPE

Constitutional psychiatrists like Kretschmer and Sheldon have suggested that there is a close link between physique and temperament. Sheldon (1949) devised a procedure for rating individual physiques and applied it to a sample of 200 young men who had gotten into various types of trouble with the law. As a result of this investigation, he concluded that physical inadequacy is a basic cause of crime and that eugenics offers the best long-term solution to the crime problem. Sheldon's theories have been strongly criticized and the methods he used in his research have been challenged. Sutherland (1951) reanalyzed Sheldon's data, using what he felt was a more meaningful criterion of delinquency, and found no significant differences between the seriously delinquent and the nondelinquent boys. The Gluecks (1950, 1956) found that mesomorphs (boys with muscular builds) were overrepresented in their delinquent sample, while ectomorphs (boys with slender, linear physiques) were underrepresented. This finding would appear contrary to the theory that delinquents are physically inferior. While the predominance of mesomorphs could be attributed to some genetic factor that causes both delinquency and mesomorphy, an environmental interpretation that muscular boys are more likely to be rewarded for aggressiveness and thus develop more antisocial habits is equally tenable and probably more parsimonious.

DELINQUENCY AS A RESULT OF GLANDULAR MALFUNCTION

Another physiological theory of delinquency was the hypothesis that crime resulted from emotional disorders produced by malfunctions of the endocrine glands (Schlapp & Smith, 1928). While in some individual cases it is clear that disordered or criminal behavior has resulted from endocrinological malfunctions, most endocrinologists agree there is no evidence to justify regarding endocrinological disorders as a major explanation for criminal behavior (cf. Ashley-Montagu, 1941; Hoskins, 1941).

DELINQUENCY AS THE RESULT OF MENTAL DEFICIENCY

Still another physiological theory was the hypothesis that innate mental deficiency was the basic cause of crime and delinquency. This theory reached its zenith from 1915 to 1930 when standardized intelligence tests were being developed. Investigators like Goddard and Kuhlman examined numerous prisoners with the new tests and reported that a large proportion of them were "feebleminded." Later research demonstrated that this was an erroneous conclusion stemming from the fact that the new tests had not been adequately standardized for use with adults. Reanalyses of the data did not indicate that an extraordinarily high percentage of the inmate population was mentally retarded (Vold, 1958).

While the notion that mental deficiency is the cause of delinquency has been dispelled, research does indicate that delinquents as a group do score significantly lower on standard intelligence tests than do nondelinquent groups. Typically, delinquents do poorest on tests stressing the verbal and conceptual abilities, which are rewarded in a school setting, and best on nonlanguage or performance tests. Poor language skills and reasoning ability naturally make for poorer performance in school and increase the likelihood of difficulties in adjusting to the school situation; difficulties in adjusting to school in turn can result in educational retardation and a greater relative deficiency in conceptual skills. Thus, while the overlap between the IQ scores of delinquents and nondelinquents demonstrates that innate mental deficiency is not the primary cause of delinquency, it is also clear that learning disabilities, particularly in the verbal area, could be a significant factor in many individual cases.

Theories of Environmental Factors as Causes of Delinquency

Most contemporary theories of delinquency emphasize environmental factors such as the family, the neighborhood, or the school, as the primary causes of delinquency. One large group of theories views most delinquency as the normal behavior learned in a deviant subculture. The primary goal of many of these theories, most of which have been proposed by sociologists, is to explain how the deviant subculture comes into existence. A second large group of theories views most delinquency as a symptom of individual personality disorder. The theorists who favor this approach are primarily psychoanalysts and psychologists who focus on sources of neurotic conflict within the individual's family.

Despite their different emphases, these diverse theories seek to account for and synthesize the same basic body of knowledge. Therefore, before summarizing some of these theoretical positions, we shall present an overview of findings regarding the delinquent's background and personality that they seek to explain.

 Modal Environmental Patterns

Cole and Hall (1966, p. 437) have summarized the data regarding the delinquent's home environment as follows:

A "delinquent" environment consists . . . of three main elements: a home in which parents are unsuccessful economically, are of not more than average native ability, are of undesirable personal habits, and are of questionable morality, who are ineffective in discipline, unable to furnish emotional security, and inclined to reject their delinquent child both before and after his misdeeds; a neighborhood that is devised for adults, quite without safeguards for children, largely without safe outlets for emotional and social life, and full of unsatisfactory models and conflicting standards; and a school that tries to make scholars out of nonacademic material and sometimes furnishes teachers who are too rejective in their attitudes.

Let us examine some of these environmental factors more closely.

The Delinquent's Family

There can be little doubt that the delinquent usually comes from a more adverse family milieu than do his nondelinquent peers (Peterson & Becker, 1965). His parents are much more likely to be criminals themselves, to be alcoholic, or to suffer from serious physical ailments, emotional disturbances, or mental retardation. His home is more likely to be broken by illegitimacy, desertion, or divorce; even in the intact home there is often separation from the mother during the early years. Within the home the child is more frequently exposed to antisocial behavior, and there are fewer restrictions on his early participation in activities normally reserved for adults, such as smoking, drinking, and sexual relations.

Because the father is often unable or unwilling to support the family, the delinquent child's home is likely to be poverty stricken, with all the frustrations that poverty entails, such as overcrowding, lack of privacy, and inadequate food. Both parents and children are likely to be tired, bitter, and discouraged; this often results in intrafamilial bickering and squabbling.

The delinquent child is likely to suffer from emotional as well as physical deprivation. The delinquent's parents, preoccupied by their own problems, reject dependent behavior by their child. Punishment is likely to be harsh and punitive, erratic and inconsistent. Aggression against the parents is rarely tolerated, although aggression against other children may be encouraged. The latter pattern is particularly noteworthy in view of the typical delinquent's pattern of emotional expressiveness. While many observers have stated that the delinquent usually expresses his feelings more directly and with fewer inhibitions than the nondelinquent, this is only partly true. The delinquent is much less reluctant to express hostility or resentment; however, he is more reluctant to express tenderness, dependency, or any other emotion that could be construed as a sign of weakness. This pattern could well have its roots in family patterns that discourage dependency but partly reward aggression.

Within the family, the relationship between the delinquent and his father is quite likely to be poor. Often the father is absent from the home, but even when he is present or there is a father surrogate, such as a stepfather, unconcealed animosity often exists between father and son. Such a situation naturally makes it difficult for the son to form a good masculine identification.

The importance of certain family patterns was demonstrated by the Gluecks' research, in which five familial factors were found to be closely associated with the occurrence of juvenile delinquency. These factors, which the Gluecks' research suggests characterize the homes of about 90 per cent of the delinquents they have studied (Glueck, 1960), include overstrict or lax discipline by the father, unsuitable or only fair supervision by the mother, indifference or hostility on the part of either or both parents, and a lack of integration or cohesiveness in the family. Subsequent research has indicated that discipline by the father, supervision by the mother, and cohesiveness of the family are the most important of these factors (Craig & Glick, 1963).

Cavan (1962, p. 125) has summarized what has been learned about the delinquent's family as follows:

In comparison with families of nondelinquent boys, delinquency-prone families as a group have a greater proportion of rejecting or harsh parents, parents who impress their sons as indifferent to their welfare, parents who are erratic or lax in discipline, or who offer little for the sons to admire or emulate. Delinquency-prone families are more likely than other families to be broken (for some delinquents there is no family at all), with the female-based family a common type in some groups. The delinquency-prone family frequently is financially dependent on outside assistance or public relief; when the mother is employed it is usually at occasional jobs. There is evidence that an accumulation of unfavorable factors increases the likelihood that the boy will become delinquent and also that he will become a recidivist. However, some unfavorable factors can be balanced against favorable ones—for example, the effect of the harsh father may be neutralized by the loving mother. Thus families differ as to the number and combination of favorable and unfavorable factors.

The latter point regarding the interaction of positive and negative factors is worth special emphasis. Before attributing too much causal significance to these familial patterns it is also wise to recall that the relationship between many such factors and delinquency could be, at least in part, an artifact of police practices. Lower-class poverty areas are patrolled more intensively than upper-class residential areas. The complaint made to the police about a lower-class perpetrator is more likely to be made to the parents of the upper-class boy. If two boys are apprehended by the police for the same offense, the boy from an intact home with concerned, responsible parents is more likely to have his case handled unofficially; the boy from a broken home with hostile, indifferent, or criminal parents would be more likely to be sent to an institution where he could receive the supervision and guidance apparently lacking at home. Since most research uses adjudicated delinquents, at least some of the observed family patterns could be artifacts of the judicial process.

The Delinquent's Neighborhood

The incidence of reported juvenile delinquency is significantly higher in some areas than in others. The cities have higher per capita rates than the suburbs, and the suburbs, in turn, have higher rates than rural areas (Short, 1966). Within most cities it is possible to distinguish high- and low-delinquency areas. Shaw and McKay (1942) have shown that, while the overall rate of juvenile court cases per 100 boys in Philadelphia was 5.6, the range was from 0.0 in the lowest area of the city to 22.6 in the highest; similarly, Cleveland was found to have a city-wide rate of 8.9 with a range from 0.6 to 37.7. Obviously, an area in which there are 37.7 court cases per 100 boys must differ significantly from an area in which there is less than 1 case per 100.

Generally, it has been found that these high-delinquency areas fall into three types: (1) run-down residential areas in which businesses are being established, (2) industrial or manufacturing areas, and (3) areas with a highly unstable population (Garrison, 1965). In such areas there is also a higher incidence of other social problems, such as poverty, suicide, adult crime, mental illness (Short, 1966), and, more recently, rioting (National Advisory Commission on Civil Disorders, 1968). These areas are characterized by low rents, educational underachievement by adults and children, poor or inadequate recreational facilities, a lack of organized activities for adolescents, and overcrowding and congestion (Garrison, 1965).

It was once thought that there was little or no social organization in such slum areas. However, the work of Whyte (1955), Short (1965, 1966), and others has indicated that these areas are not *disorganized* but *differently* organized. Whereas the primary institutions in a low-delinquency area might be the family, the school, and the church, in the delinquent area they appear to be "the gang, the hangouts, drinking, parties in the area, and the police" (Short, 1966, p. 436). According to Short (1966, p. 437):

The relation between institutions of this sort and delinquent behavior goes much beyond the contact they afford between illegitimate "purveyors of pleasure" and their potential clientele, however. It is in such settings that much behavior occurs which is disruptive of both the larger social order and the local community because of threats to basic values of life and property. Of particular concern are episodes of violence which result in serious injury, death, or property destruction, the threat of which is ever present in situations ranging from the shifting liaisons of common-law marriage to even less formally structured quarter parties,[1] poolhalls, and street corners.

In a high-delinquency area there are few of the external inhibitions against deviant behavior that are to be found in more stable communities. Families in the urban slum do not know one another as they do in smaller, more integrated communities. It would be difficult for a small-town boy to get in a street fight without his parents learning about it from concerned neighbors. In the city slum, however, adults witnessing such an incident would be less likely to know the boy's parents or to report the fight to them.

Schisms are rife within the slum. People from vastly different backgrounds are thrown together, the single common denominator being that they were unable to obtain better housing. There may be ill feeling between members of different ethnic or racial groups. In the absence of understanding, there is suspicion; in the absence of community good will, hostility. There is little cooperation and few shared child-rearing values.

Because his home is crowded and his mother may have to work during the day without being able to afford the luxury of a baby-sitter, the developing child is likely to spend a great deal of his time in the street. There the child sees adults gambling, buying drugs, pimping, and propositioning. While most parents are concerned over this atmosphere (Sexton, 1966), they are realistically afraid to do anything about it. Law enforcement is left to the police, but, as alien intruders, even honest police can do little.

The child growing up in a high-delinquency area has few positive adult models to emulate. The adult who does achieve legitimate success moves out of the slum, leaving the failures behind. The most

---

[1] A quarter party is a party at which guests pay a quarter to get in and a quarter for each drink. They are given to make money and are crowded, noisy affairs in which fights are frequent (Short, 1966).

successful people the slum child sees are likely to be the bookie or the gangster.

Thus, the high-delinquency area maximizes the temptations for illegitimate behavior and minimizes the external inhibitions. Indeed, actual pressure may be applied to engage in delinquent activities. "Bopping clubs" (street fighting gangs) need recruits, and the "coolie" (nongang member) who does not want to join may be subjected to the "draft," in which he is beaten until he sees the value of gang membership (Salisbury, 1959).

In a milieu like this, the adolescent, along with everyone else, is engaged in what is literally a battle for survival. The environment places a premium on aggressiveness, on living for the moment without worry over past or future, and on the ability to get as much as possible of what little there is for oneself (McCandless, 1967). Such a tough, egocentric, cynical attitude is naturally conducive to delinquent behavior.

The Delinquent's School

From the time that he is six until well into his teens, the delinquent or predelinquent boy is forced to spend a major part of each weekday confined in the school. Garrison (1965, p. 425) has summarized the attitude of many delinquents toward school as follows:

> The delinquent's attitudes toward school are heavily charged with hate and hostility; they change schools frequently; truancy is frequent and habitual; leaving school as soon as the law will allow is the rule; membership in special classes for atypical students is more often observed; they seem to enjoy little feeling of belonging in the classroom; they rarely participate in volunteer extra-curricular activities; they tend to be the bullies on the playground, and they take their frustrations out on school property.

It is not surprising that school is anathema to the delinquent boy. He usually enters the first grade deficient in those qualities necessary for school success, such as the ability to delay gratification, patience, polite decorum, respect for authorities, abstract conceptual skills, and well-developed habits of work and discipline. Consequently, he is apt to be a slow learner and a disruptive influence in the classroom. As he falls behind the other students he becomes increasingly bored and frustrated and soon he is locked into a year-long power struggle with his teacher. While the school may be as poorly adapted to him as he is to it, almost invariably it is he who must alter his ways to meet the school's demands; rarely is the school flexible enough to change its patterns to meet his needs.

Given this stalemate, it is only natural for the child to seek escape. It is not surprising that truancy is often the first delinquent act to come to the attention of authorities. Absence from classes compounds his educational problems. One study of 345 institutionalized delinquents indicated that the median level of retardation was five years in reading and six years in arithmetic (Eckenrode, 1949). The goal of both delinquent and teacher is often the boy's removal from the classroom; if he makes enough difficulty he may be suspended and perhaps exempted from school. This "solves" the school's problem by passing it along to the community employment bureau, which must find work for an unskilled, uneducated boy, or to the Welfare Department, which must support him if no work can be obtained. With no job and no school to occupy his time, it is often not long before idleness leads to trouble, and the police and the probation department are added to the list of agencies involved. Usually, their first move is to attempt to get the boy back into school and so the cycle continues.

ENVIRONMENTAL FACTORS AS AN EXPLANATION FOR JUVENILE DELINQUENCY

Sociologists and psychologists[2] have both tended to look to environmental as opposed to genetic factors for the cause of juvenile crime. The questions they seek to answer and the variables upon which they have focused have naturally varied from one discipline to the other. The sociologists have mainly addressed themselves to the problem of why juvenile crime is more prevalent among certain social groups, such as the poor, the immigrants, and the slum residents, and have sought the answers in terms of social factors, such as the economic cycle and the conflict of different cultural groups. Psychologists have focused on the individual in an attempt to answer why one person in a given social group becomes delinquent while another from similar circumstances does not, and to determine

[2] "Psychologist" is used here as a generic term for all those who study individual as opposed to group behavior; in this sense it includes not only psychologists but also psychiatrists and psychoanalysts.

what function delinquent behavior serves within the individual's personality structure. To answer these questions they have focused on detailed analyses of the histories of individual delinquents and have placed primary emphasis on early childhood experiences and disturbed family relationships. While sociologists have tended to regard delinquency as normal behavior in an abnormal social situation, psychologists have been more apt to interpret delinquency as a symptom of psychopathology.

The Economic Cycle as a Cause of Crime and Delinquency

Sociological theories have attributed delinquency to a variety of social forces, including the economic cycle, the neighborhood, subcultural mores, the problems of adolescence in Western culture, and group conflicts. One of the earliest theories sought to explain delinquency or crime in terms of fluctuations in the economy. In the nineteenth century, von Mayr demonstrated a positive correlation between the fluctuations in the price of rye and the changes in the rate of certain crimes in Bavaria from 1836 to 1861. However, Wiers found a negative association, using data collected in Detroit from 1921 to 1943 (Vold, 1958). A number of other scholars have also investigated the relationship between the economic cycle and the crime rate, with equally contradictory results. The theory that poverty causes crime is intuitively appealing, particularly in the wake of widespread rioting and looting by the residents of poverty-stricken urban ghettos. However, this notion cannot account for middle-class or white-collar crime. Even among the poor it is debatable whether poverty causes crime directly or exacerbates other conditions that are conducive to delinquency, such as overcrowding, disease, and broken homes.

Deviant Subcultural Values as a Cause of Crime

According to another group of theories, what is normal behavior for some groups in society is rejected as criminal by members of the dominant middle-class culture. One of the earliest theorists in this group was Thorsten Sellin (1938), who focused on how such differences in conduct norms could lead to crime among certain subgroups. His classic example was a Sicilian immigrant who was incredulous when he was arrested for murdering the 16-year-old boy who had seduced his daughter, "since he had merely defended his family honor in the traditional way" (Sellin, 1938). Sellin recognized that differing conduct norms cannot explain all crime in our society and that other social, psychological, and physiological factors also play a role. The leveling effect of mass communications media in the last decade, coupled with the decline in immigration, has undoubtedly done much to lessen the disparity between the values of different cultural groups.

Miller (1958) has analyzed what he believes to be the focal concerns of the lower class. According to his analysis, the lower-class person is concerned with trouble, toughness, smartness, excitement, and autonomy. These focal concerns of the culture are seen by Miller as being conducive to the generation of gang delinquency. This conception differs from Sellin's in that, instead of a basic disagreement as to what is right and wrong, the subculture is seen as having values that lead to behavior both cultural groups would probably classify as wrong.

E. H. Sutherland's (1939) "differential-association" theory also falls into this general classification. According to Sutherland, much delinquent behavior is simply learned from imitating delinquent models. Thus, a high-delinquency area is perpetuated as each successive cohort of teenagers is initiated into delinquent activities by the cohort ahead of him. The forcible recruitment of gang members through the "draft" would be another form of cultural transmission (Salisbury, 1959). Sutherland indicated that delinquency originated in the subculture through cultural conflict that resulted from social disorganization.

Delinquency as an Adolescent Crisis

Another group of theorists has focused on the problems confronting the adolescent in Western society, suggesting that delinquency may result from the problems associated with this period of development. Erikson (1950) has hypothesized that the critical conflict in early adolescence is between "ego identity" and "role diffusion" as the adolescent, faced with a changing body and ambiguous cultural expectations, strives for some definition of himself. In the course of this crisis he may experiment with various roles and behaviors, including delinquent behavior. Bloch and Niederhoffer (1958) have pointed out how the ambiguity of the adolescent's role in Western society during the long period when he is physically mature but economically dependent can lead to rebellious and delinquent behavior.

Social Conflict and Delinquency

Another broad class of theories attributes delinquency to the conflict of social forces. One of the first such theorists was Robert Merton (1957), who noted that, while everyone in American society is expected to achieve status and material success, many lower-class boys find the legitimate paths to wealth blocked. This conflict between approved goals and the lack of approved means may result in a state of "anomie," or normlessness, in which the ends become more important than the means. This state is conducive to delinquency and crime, according to Merton's analysis.

Cloward and Ohlin (1960) adopted and embellished Merton's theory, adding to it elements of Sutherland's differential-association approach. Like Merton, Cloward and Ohlin pointed to the disparity between the goals that lower-class children are expected to adopt and the inadequacy of the means available for their attainment. "Faced with limitation on legitimate avenues of access to these goals, and unable to revise their aspirations downward, they experience intense frustration; the exploration of nonconformist alternatives may be the result" (Cloward & Ohlin, 1960, p. 86). During this period of exploration differential association plays a crucial role. A lower-class boy, frustrated by his inability to achieve wealth and status through legal means, will be more likely to turn to crime if he knows a successful professional criminal who might give him an opportunity to run numbers. If there are no such illegitimate opportunities available, then youths may be guided to the "conflict subculture," in which status is won through acts of violence, or the "retreatist subculture," which features the use of drugs.

Some critics think Merton's theory implies that juvenile delinquency is much more goal directed and rational than is actually the case. Both Merton's and Cloward and Ohlin's analyses have also been criticized for exaggerating the importance of social class while minimizing the importance of individual, familial, racial, and ethnic factors, and for overlooking the fact that much delinquent behavior is fun and may be caused by nothing more than a desire for excitement (Caldwell, 1965).

Albert Cohen (1955) also stresses the conflict between middle-class and lower-class cultural expectations. The primary arena for this conflict, according to Cohen, is the school, in which the lower-class child is expected to behave according to middle-class standards and compete on middle-class terms. No matter what they do, many lower-class children find themselves faced with rejection and failure in this middle-class world. Therefore, they rebel and seek status among their peers, forming subgroups in which the middle-class value system is turned upside down. Thus, the delinquent subgroup comes to prize aggressiveness, sexuality, and malicious vandalism and to scorn conformity, self-control, or intellectualism.

George Vold (1958) has shifted the focus from the conflict of social forces to the conflict of special interest groups. He has pointed out that crimes associated with disputes between labor and management or the efforts by civil rights groups to desegregate public facilities are not the product of the social forces or individual personality disturbances usually associated with crime. While Vold certainly does not hold that all crime is the byproduct of such intergroup conflicts, he does maintain that the importance of this factor has been underestimated in other theoretical approaches.

Individual Psychopathology as a Cause of Delinquency

Psychologists have focused more on the psychodynamics of the individual, and, as is usually the case, closer examination reveals myriad complexities that are overlooked in the broader study of large groups. The primary contribution of the psychologist has been the revelation of the role that unconscious motives may play in delinquent behavior. Most psychological theorists hold that delinquent acts are multiply determined. A boy who commits a rape may be motivated by the desire for sexual gratification, but the psychologist's microscope is also likely to reveal that unresolved hostility against his mother, repressed fears of girls, and unconscious doubts regarding his own masculinity also played a role in determining this behavior.

Most of the psychologists who have written about delinquency have shared a psychoanalytic frame of reference. While these investigators specialize in the detailed analysis of individual cases, they have noted some patterns that have recurred often enough to be worthy of comment. Sigmund Freud (1957) suggested that some offenders are driven by a sense of guilt that precedes and causes the antisocial behavior. For example, a child who feels guilt over masturbation may seek punishment by clumsily committing some crime for which he is certain to get caught. Adelaide Johnson (1949) focused on the role parents may play in unconsciously encouraging their children's delinquencies in order to satisfy their own repressed antisocial desires. Kate Friedlander (1947) described several neurotic patterns that may produce delinquent behavior, including acting out fantasies and using delinquent acts to satisfy unconscious aggressive desires.

The importance of neurotic motives in determining delinquency is a matter of some controversy. Typologists have typically reserved separate categories for neurotic and "normal" delinquents (Alexander & Staub, 1962; Hewitt & Jenkins, 1946; Kvaraceus, 1958; Reiss, 1952). There is still disagreement, however, over what proportion of the delinquent population should be classified as "disturbed" and what proportion as "normal"; much depends on the definitions employed.

Definitional problems also impede research on the issue, for defining delinquency is simple compared with the problem of defining normality. If the investigator regards delinquency as a basic symptom of neurosis, it is obvious that little can be accomplished. A less circular approach has been to look for accessory symptoms, such as enuresis or nail-biting; another has been to measure delinquents on various personality tests. Investigations such as these have demonstrated a higher incidence of signs of personality disturbances among delinquents than among nondelinquents (Glueck & Glueck, 1950; Hathaway & Monachesi, 1953; Healy & Bronner, 1936). However, the data from such studies have not indicated that all delinquents are disturbed, unless the definition of disturbance is stretched so far beyond its normal limits as to lose all meaning.

A number of investigators have abandoned the attempt to determine the proportion of disturbed and normal delinquents and have turned to the task of studying the etiologies of different sorts of crimes and the incidence of more homogeneous delinquent subtypes (Quay, 1965b). Data collected by Kvaraceus (1958), for example, suggest that middle-class delinquents tend to be more disturbed than lower-class delinquents. Megargee (1966c) has focused on assaultive offenses and has demonstrated that some extremely assaultive offenders are undercontrolled, while others paradoxically appear overcontrolled. Informal observations suggest that the rate of psychological disturbance is higher among delinquents who commit certain offenses, such as arson, than among delinquents arrested for other offenses, such as auto theft. Research also indicates that the rate of disturbance is higher among delinquent girls than delinquent boys (see Konopka, 1966).

Control and Containment Theories

Some sociologists have focused on both individual personality variables and social factors in their efforts to account for delinquent behavior. Reiss (1951) has suggested that delinquent behavior results from a failure of both social and personal controls. In the absence of strong external social controls, the individual's internal inhibitions (conscience or super ego) can prevent antisocial behavior. Similarly, when the individual's internal inhibitions are below average, strong social sanctions, such as the presence of a policeman, can often deter the undercontrolled individual.

Reiss tested his theory by studying factors associated with recidivism, using cases from the Cook County Juvenile Court. He obtained data supporting his contention that personal and social controls interact. As might be expected, his findings indicated that, of the two, the personal controls were more effective than the social controls in curbing delinquency.

Nye (1958) has also focused on social factors that might contain or control delinquent tendencies. He differentiated four types of social control: (a) direct controls from discipline or punishment, (b) internalized controls, or conscience, (c) indirect controls, which stem from the individual's desire not to disappoint his parents or loved ones, and (d) the availability of alternative means of achieving goals. Nye maintained that the family is the primary agent of control, although controls can also be exercised by institutions, such as the school or a church, as well as by peers and significant adults, such as teachers or national heroes. In his research using high school students who admitted engaging in illegal behavior, Nye has attempted to identify the familial factors conducive to the development of controls.

While Nye felt that deficient social control was the factor underlying most crime and delinquency, he has been careful to point out that social controls could not account for all types of delinquency. He specifically stated that his theory did not account for compulsive or neurotic crime or the socialized crime learned in a delinquent subculture.

Reiss' and Nye's emphasis on the interaction of personality and the social setting contributed to Walter Reckless' development of "containment" theory. Reckless (1961) hypothesized that a favorable self-concept acts as an insulator against the pressures toward deviance found in a social environment conducive to delinquency. A favorable self-concept comes about primarily from being reared in a nurturant milieu, such as a family setting with affectionate, interested, well-socialized parents. Reckless also posited the existence of an "individual factor" that may facilitate or impede the development of a positive self-concept. He described environmental factors from which this individual factor may develop, but the possibility of innate differences, such as individual differences in temperament or arousal thresholds, is implicit in his formulation. Like Reiss, Reckless specifically stated that his containment theory does not apply to acting-out neurotics or to psychopaths.

Multiple-Factor Theories of Juvenile Delinquency

Many theorists are coming to favor what has been called a "multiple-factor" approach, in which it is specifically recognized that many different individual and social factors can interact to produce criminal behavior. A typical list of factors can be found in Table 1.

This approach has been subjected to strong criticism, however, by theorists like Cohen, who has written, ". . . a multiple factor approach is not a theory; it is an abdication of the quest for a theory" (Cohen, 1962, p. 78). Opponents of multiple-factor approaches feel that there is a tendency to describe each observed case as being unique so that there are no general laws or testable hypotheses. A related objection is that multiple-factor theorists seem to explain each case on a *post hoc* basis. The present writers, who lean toward an eclectic approach, feel that, while the exact combination of factors in each individual case may well be unique, this does not mean that a relatively few general explanatory principles cannot be used. For example, it is well established that childhood encephalitis is often followed by severe conduct disorders; indeed, this relationship is as lawful as any we have in the area of delinquency (Brill, 1959). It

Table 1

Factors Associated with Delinquency*

Heredity		
	1.	Bad family stock—incidence of feeblemindedness, insanity, epilepsy higher than in families of nondelinquents.
	2.	Defective mentality—average IQ of delinquent groups is 85 to 90 instead of 100. (However, about two thirds of all delinquents are of normal or above-normal mentality.)
	3.	Specific inability to handle verbal symbols, resulting in slow progress in school.
	4.	Unusual vitality, drive, and energy, resulting in restlessness, overactivity, and aggressiveness.
Home		
	5.	Poverty and crowding in home.
	6.	Delinquency and crime among parents or other siblings.
	7.	Home broken by death, separation, divorce, desertion, or prison term.
	8.	Lack of emotional security, high degree of tension in home; lack of emotional stability in parents.
	9.	Lack of proper or uniform discipline.
	10.	Rejection of child by parents, neglect of child, lack of interest in his activities.
School		
	11.	Poor work in school; one or more retardations.
	12.	Dislike of school.
	13.	More or less truancy.
	14.	Rejection by some of the teachers.
Neighborhood		
	15.	Existence of many criminal models in the neighborhood.
	16.	Lack of adequate supervision and protection.
	17.	Lack of adequate outlets.
	18.	Exposure to low or conflicting adult morals.
	19.	Exposure to minority conflicts.
Resulting Personality Traits		
	20.	Feelings of inferiority, insecurity, and rejection.
	21.	Constant frustration and development of deep hostility.
	22.	Emotional immaturity.
	23.	Aggressive drives turned toward parents, school, and society.
	24.	Identification with criminal models.
	25.	Emotional satisfaction found in antisocial groups.
	26.	Strong impulses, uninhibited by conscience.

* From L. Cole and I. N. Hall, 1966, p. 438.

would be patently absurd to attribute all delinquency to this syndrome; it would also be erroneous to have a general theory of delinquency that neglects to include such illnesses as one of the factors that may lead to delinquency.

Another criticism of multiple-factor approaches is the implicit assumption by some multiple-factor theorists that the factors contributing to delinquency can be combined in a simple additive fashion. To oversimplify this position, a boy who had encephalitis and a criminal father, both factors that had been found to be criminogenic, would be twice as likely to become delinquent as a boy who had encephalitis and a noncriminal father. However, such oversimplification is not as prevalent in the ranks of multiple-factor theorists as the critics assume. Indeed, most multiple-factor theorists feel it is the single-explanation theorists who underestimate the complexity of juvenile delinquency.

An example of the problems associated with an oversimplified outlook can be found in the literature on assaultiveness. As long as assaultiveness was regarded as a simple unidimensional phenomenon caused by excessive hostility and inadequate controls, it was difficult if not impossible to discriminate assaultive from nonassaultive criminals on standard psychological tests with any degree of accuracy (Megargee, 1964b, 1966c; Megargee & Cook, 1967; Megargee & Mendelsohn, 1962). With the demonstration that at least two distinctly different personality types were involved in extremely assaultive offenses, one characterized by excessive inhibitions and the other by inadequate inhibitions, it was possible to move ahead and devise instruments to assess the factors involved in the two types and improve prediction considerably (Megargee, 1965; Megargee, Cook, & Mendelsohn, 1967). It was concluded from this research (Megargee, 1964a):

It is apparent that even within the relatively simple category of aggressive behavior there are vast differences in personality patterns among the people who engage in such behavior. If we expand the horizon to include the whole panorama of illegal behavior subsumed under the heading of "crime," ranging from dope peddling to income tax evasion, from safe-cracking to homosexuality, from sit-ins to murders, the futility of finding a single cause or a single cure can be seen.

Summary

Theories and research regarding juvenile delinquency were reviewed in this chapter. A number of theories have been proposed that attribute delinquency to some innate characteristics of the individual. These theories include the hypothesis that the delinquent is an atavistic throwback to some more primitive form of person, the notion that delinquency is the result of innate biological inferiority, the hypothesis that innate defective intelligence causes delinquency, and the theories that delinquency stems from the physical constitution or from defective endocrine glands. While many data have been collected in an effort to establish these theories, the interpretation of these studies has been hindered by problems in establishing proper controls and by difficulties in obtaining reliable measurements. It was concluded that, while such factors as defective intelligence or sickliness might be important in individual cases, the research literature did not support the hypothesis that any one of these factors could be regarded as a necessary or sufficient explanation of delinquency.

Theories and data relating delinquency to environmental factors were also examined. The "typical delinquent" usually was found to come from a lower-class home with a below-average standard of living. His family usually was less cohesive and well integrated than that of the nondelinquent, and, if the home was not actually broken, it at least had less warmth and mutual respect among the various family members. Discipline was likely to be erratic or extreme and the parents were more likely to be disturbed or criminal themselves. As a result, the delinquent was characterized by problems in identification, excessive aggressiveness, bitterness, authority acceptance, and egocentrism.

The delinquent's neighborhood was also found to lack the external controls existent in more stable areas. It was likely to be overcrowded, dirty, and lacking in recreational resources. Not only were neighbors unlikely to aid in socializing the child, but they also often provided negative models by engaging in delinquent or criminal behavior. Schisms and ill will among members of different ethnic groups were common and sometimes found expression in gang warfare or civil disorders.

The delinquent child was found to be poorly prepared for the demands made by the middle-class school. Typically, the school was unable to meet his needs and he was unable to adapt to the school. Frustration and academic failure often led to antipathy and to authority conflicts. As a result, the delinquent was frequently educationally retarded.

Sociologists have typically attempted to account for delinquency by describing the action of various social forces. Among the factors sociological theorists have pointed to are the effects of the economic cycle, deviant values learned from others within the neighborhood, and problems engendered by society's failure to provide consistent expectations for the adolescent in our culture. Several theorists have focused on the social conflict experienced by the lower-class boy who is expected to achieve success in the middle-class school and in work but is unable to do so.

Psychologists have typically engaged in detailed analyses of individual cases. Delinquency has been seen by them as a symptom of neurotic conflicts and disturbances caused by a number of conscious and unconscious needs. While most scholars concede that neurotic conflicts can cause delinquency, there is disagreement over the proportion of cases with such an etiology. Current research is attempting to determine the origin of certain subgroups of delinquents instead of trying to resolve the question of the importance of psychopathology in causing delinquency as a whole.

A number of theorists are adopting eclectic or multiple-factor approaches. While some critics reject multiple-factor approaches as unscientific, the present writers maintained that this is not necessarily a valid criticism.

CHAPTER 3

THE THREE CULTURES

In this chapter the modal personality patterns and typical mores of lower-class Anglo-Americans, Mexicans, and Mexican-Americans will be examined. Since many readers will be unfamiliar with some of these cultural patterns, they will be described in more detail than was the phenomenon of delinquency. The reader who is already familiar with a culture may prefer to review the summary that follows the detailed description.

In writing brief descriptions of modal personality patterns it is impossible to avoid a certain amount of distortion. The first source of distortion comes from emphasizing the typical patterns, resulting in a rather stereotyped picture in which the many individual variations are overlooked. When contrasting the cultures, on the other hand, we have emphasized the differences at the expense of the similarities. Thus, we have devoted more attention to the fact that the Mexican family is more authoritarian than the Anglo-American than we have to the important fact that in both cultures the children live with the parents. The reader should thus bear in mind that these descriptions will underemphasize the differences between individuals within a culture and also underemphasize the broad similarities among the three cultural groups.

In the empirical investigation, nondelinquents who lived in the same neighborhoods as the delinquents were selected for the comparison groups. As we shall see, this generally limited the subject population to members of the lower class, sometimes referred to as the working class. As such, they lived in the poorer areas of San Antonio, Texas, or Monterrey, Nuevo León, Mexico. Their fathers generally worked at menial or semiskilled trades, if they were employed at all. In describing the cultural folkways we shall therefore focus on the characteristics of the lower-class members of the three cultures.

Before turning to an examination of these cultures, a preliminary definition of the three groups will be attempted. This will be more general than the operational definition to be offered in the presentation of the empirical study. To define the three cultural groups, it is first necessary to define *la raza*[1] or "the race." According to Madsen (1964, p. 15), "This term refers to all Latin-Americans who are united by cultural and spiritual bonds derived from God. The spiritual aspect is perhaps more important than the cultural." This mystical quality of *la raza* transcends political allegiances. A member of *la raza* may be a citizen of any nation; similarly, a non-Latin immigrant to Mexico may become a Mexican citizen but he will never be a member of *la raza*. In this transcendance of political ties and organized religious affiliations, a Latin American is a member of *la raza* in much the same way that a Jew is a member of the "Jewish people." In both cases there is shared an ancient cultural heritage with religious overtones; moreover, both groups regard themselves as a suffering chosen people.

The first cultural group we shall define consists of lower-class citizens of the United States who are not members of *la raza* and who therefore do not share in the Spanish-Indian culture of Northern Latin America. The term we shall apply to this group is "Anglo," a term commonly used in the Southwest to denote any non-Mexican. While "Anglo" implies that the people are of Anglo-Saxon stock, this is not necessarily true. In some parts of the Southwest anyone who is not Indian or Latin is Anglo (McWilliams, 1949), and in some studies anyone without a Spanish surname is considered an Anglo, whether he is of Oriental, European, or African ancestry. (According to this latter criterion, the liberator of Chile, Bernardo

[1] See glossary for definition of terms.

O'Higgins, who was most decidedly a member of *la raza*, would be classified as an Anglo.) Despite the fact that "Anglo" is thus an anthropological barbarism, it is preferable to other labels, such as "gringos," which is derogatory, and "whites" or "Americans," which imply that Mexicans are not white or American.

The second cultural group consists of those lower-class residents of the United States of Mexican extraction who are members of *la raza*. These people may or may not be United States citizens. A number of labels have been used to identify this group. Terms like *la raza*, *chicanos*, or *chulos* are acceptable to the group but have little meaning for most readers. On the other hand, the term "Spanish-American" underemphasizes the importance of their Indian heritage, while "Mexican-American" seems condescending. "Spanish-speaking people" is inaccurate because some people of Mexican ancestry do not speak Spanish and many "Anglos" do (McWilliams, 1949). The phrase "Americans from Mexico" is inoffensive but awkward, as well as inaccurate, since the majority are not from Mexico but are native-born United States citizens. In fact, since the members of *la raza* arrived in the Southwest long before the first Anglos, they understandably resent any hyphenated terms that imply they are the newcomers.

With full knowledge of the inadequacies of the term, we have chosen the label "Latins" to designate this group. One advantage of this label is that it is more discriminable and less awkward than "Mexican-American" or other hyphenated terms. Moreover, it appears to be less offensive, since members of *la raza* use the term to identify themselves, as in the case of the LULAC (League of United Latin American Citizens). The designation "Latin" must not obscure the fact that most of the cultural traditions of the San Antonio "Latins" that set them apart from the dominant "Anglo" culture are associated more with the Mexican and Indian cultures of the Southwest than with the cultures of South America and Spain.

The third cultural group in the study consists of lower-class members of *la raza* who are residents of Mexico. This group will simply be labelled "Mexicans."

The lower-class Anglo culture will be described first, followed by a description of the lower-class Mexican culture. Since the Latin culture blends elements of both, it will be described last.

I

LOWER-CLASS ANGLO CULTURE

Family Patterns

The original stereotype of the lower-class family's child-rearing practices was that they were generally harsher than those of the middle class. However, the findings of a 1946 study by Davis and Havighurst were in sharp contrast to this picture. Contrary to expectations, they found that the lower-class parents were significantly more permissive than the middle-class parents. This set the stage for a number of investigations of lower-class family patterns.

Kohn (1959) found that parents of both classes shared a common core of values but that, while lower-class mothers were concerned with compliance to external authority, middle-class mothers attempted to develop internal standards of conduct in their children. A major difference was the role of the father. In the lower-class family the father was viewed as the disciplinarian but otherwise remained less involved with child-rearing.

Maccoby, Gibbs, et al. (1964) found that upper-lower-class mothers were stricter and more severe in toilet and sex training and allowed their children less freedom to aggress against parents than did upper-middle-class mothers. They were also more inclined to use physical punishment and were colder and less demonstrative than the middle-class mothers. The upper-lower-class parents were less affectionate toward one another and agreed less on how to rear the children; the mother was more likely to be critical of the father. However, the lower-class father was no less involved than his middle-class counterpart. Some bias may have resulted from using only intact families, since the least involved fathers may have deserted.

Father absence is likely to be as significant a determinant of personality in the lower-class home as are any specific child-rearing practices. There is little doubt that father absence as a result of illegitimacy, separation, desertion, divorce, death, or institutionalization is substantially more prevalent in the lower socioeconomic strata (Miller, 1959). Ironically, the provision in many welfare codes that the unemployed or sporadically employed father must be out of the home before the mother can apply for assistance has probably exacerbated this problem.

In reviewing the literature, both Becker (1964) and Caldwell (1964) found that most studies conducted in the 1950s agreed with the findings of Maccoby, Gibbs, et al. (1964). However, Caldwell pointed out that most studies investigated the upper-lower class and few studied the lower-lower class. An exception was a study by Wortis, Bardach, Cutler, Rue, and Freedman (1963), who traced the child-rearing practices of 250 Negro mothers of premature babies from the children's birth to age 5. While this study used Negro subjects, it is likely that similar patterns could be found among Anglos in comparable circumstances. The parents were interviewed when the children were 2½ and 5 years old. Of the employed fathers in this sample, 89 per cent were engaged in manual or unskilled labor. In 67 per cent of the families the annual income was less than $3900 during the period 1959–1962, and 29 per cent of the families were supported in whole or in part by public relief. The environment was quite different from that of the typical middle-class child. In 20 per cent of the households there were no toys of any description; in 52 per cent no one read or told stories to the child. Only about half the children lived with both natural parents; 38 per cent lived with the mother alone and 8 per cent lived with neither parent. Since almost all the mothers worked as domestics or in factories, their children had spent significant amounts of time being cared for outside the home by parent substitutes. Wortis et al. noted that not infrequently these parent substitutes lived in other states, so that there was no contact with the mother. Wortis et al. found that at age 2½ the mean number of mother figures per child was two, and that 25 per cent had known three or more mother figures.

In child-rearing, the primary concern appeared to be the mother's convenience. The mothers were permissive, in that there was little pressure for early weaning or toilet training and the young child was permitted to grow and develop at his own pace. However, there was frequent corporal punishment—often with a strap. The mothers themselves appeared subdued, apathetic, and unhappy, and 8 per cent were described as seriously depressed. One third used negative terms in describing their children and 4 per cent expressed extreme dislike or antagonism toward them.

When their children were five, 47 of the mothers were interviewed, using Sears' interviews, which were rated using Sears' techniques. Many of the findings were similar to those of Sears', with the mothers being rated as having low permissiveness for dependency, aggression toward the parents or sex, and little warmth or esteem for the father. There was a high incidence of disagreement between parents on child-rearing, and severe punishment was the rule. A much higher percentage of the mothers (60%) encouraged their children in aggression against neighborhood children, which Wortis et al. felt was quite realistic if their children were to survive in the neighborhood.

Thus, Wortis et al. found that the lowest-class child was exposed to more rejection, coldness, authoritarianism, social disorganization, and deprivation, both material and emotional, than are most middle-class children; he was also under less pressure to develop faster, so that he could grow at his own pace. However, this could also lessen achievement motivation. The investigators concluded that these children were being molded to "enter the class of the least-skilled, least-educated, and most-rejected in our society" (Wortis et al., 1963).

EFFECTS OF FAMILY PATTERNS

Some of the personality characteristics that have been observed in lower-class men can probably be traced to these familial patterns. As we might expect, lower-class children perceive their parents as being harsher and more punitive than do middle-class children. They apparently view authority figures in general and parents in particular as unreasonable, severe, repressive people who offer them little in the way of warmth or companionship. As a result, they comply rather rigidly with externally imposed rules (Mussen, Conger, & Kagan, 1963). However, Maas (1951), on the basis of interview data, noted that lower-lower-class children who have such rigid hierarchal relationships with their parents were blocked from communication and seemed to feel afraid, rejected, and unworthy. Maas (1951, p. 147) stated:

> Fear of parental authority and its explosive anger mutes the child until he explodes in similar manner or redirects his hostile aggressions, as well as his tender feelings toward siblings or other contemporaries. With them, he may become either a prototype of the bully, status and power seeking —or an ever-submissive follower.

Since the mother is frequently the breadwinner in the lower-class home, she is often the dominant figure in the family. Such maternal dominance can be of vital importance in determining whether or not sons identify properly with their fathers. If the father is not the dominant figure, there is much less likelihood that the son will identify with the masculine role, and maladjustment and psychopathology can result (Clausen, 1966; Payne & Mussen, 1956; Yarrow, 1964). This is particularly likely when the mother assumes a derogatory attitude toward the absent father or toward men in general. In fact, it has been hypothesized that the excessive delinquency rate among lower-class boys may be the result of boys reared in female-dominated households seeking proof of their masculinity (Miller, 1958). Whether or not this is the case, there appears to be little doubt that difficulties in identifying with the father are associated with delinquent behavior in boys (Bandura & Walters, 1959).

Miller (1958) has described six areas that are of focal concern in lower-class culture: trouble, toughness, smartness, excitement, fate, and autonomy. Pearl (1965), summarizing the literature, has stated that most studies have found the following factors to characterize lower-class personality structure: a poorer self-image, a greater sense of powerlessness, a more fatalistic attitude toward life, a lack of future orientation, a greater potential for impulsive acting out, more anti-intellectualism, less verbal ability, more primitive conceptual ability, and unrealistically high aspirations mixed with more depressed expectations. Sexton (1965), in her review, touched on many similar areas and added some new ones. Her sources indicated that members of the lower-lower class are more anti-intellectual, are more reluctant to participate in voluntary associations, feel powerless and insecure, and have a strong preference for the familiar; they are authoritarian, intolerant, pessimistic, and insecure. Moreover, they tend to be misanthropic and cynical, distrustful and extra-punitive toward others. The family is patriarchal in orientation, and toughness is valued. The members tend to be slow in establishing social relationships with others and when they do, the relationships are typically with neighbors. On the brighter side, the lower-lower-class individual is reported to have closer ties with kinfolk, although family life is less stable.

Sexton (1965) has reservations about the generalizations she found in the literature. For the most part the statements are accurate but quite one-sided in their "downbeat" emphasis on the negative. She protests (Sexton, 1965, p. 176):

> Strangers do have a false image of East Harlem. They tend to see only negatives. There are more negatives in East Harlem than in most neighborhoods, but there are also many positives—the children, the variety, the simplicity and directness of life, the natural warmth and generosity of many people, and the struggle that makes life meaningful as well as grim. Though East Harlem's residents are housed in symmetrical boxes, the people are not all standarized and prepackaged. They are diverse, colorful, expressive, and often profoundly individualistic.

In the sections that follow, we shall examine some of these characteristics of lower-lower-class culture in more detail. We shall start with a survey of some of the modal personality patterns that have been observed, and then discuss factors that influence academic and vocational success, such as achievement motivation, ability to delay gratification, and aspiration level. In the final section we shall examine the lower-class male in his peer group.

Modal Personality Patterns

AGGRESSION

Most scholars agree that members of the lower class are more inclined to express their aggressive feelings directly and in a more extreme verbal or physical fashion than are middle-class individuals of the same age (McCandless, 1967). Several factors enter into this. It has been well established that frustration breeds aggressive feelings (Dollard et al., 1939). Since there is little doubt that lower-class life is more frustrating, we can therefore infer a higher than ordinary level of aggressive drive.

The second factor entering into aggressive behavior is the amount of inhibitions against aggressions that have been learned. McCandless has pointed out that aggressive behavior probably is highly rewarded in many lower-class homes, in which one must literally fight for his share of the available food. Also, it will be recalled that Wortis et al. (1963) believed aggression was fairly adaptive in the world in which their lower-lower-class subjects lived. Thus, members of the lower class have little reason to learn strong inhibitions against expressing aggression.

SEX

As in the case of aggression, members of the lower classes appear to have relatively few inhibitions against the direct expression of sexual drives. This was exemplified in Kinsey, Pomeroy, and Martin's (1948) study of male sexual behavior. These investigators divided their sample into three class groups on the basis of total education. The lowest group had eight years or less of schooling, the middle group had nine to twelve years, and the highest group had one year of college. The incidence of premarital intercourse reported by the subjects in the highest group was markedly less than that reported by the subjects in the other two groups. By age 15, 57 per cent of the subjects in the lowest group had experienced premarital intercourse, in contrast to only 15 per cent of the subjects in the highest group. By age 21, 84 per cent of the lowest group had had premarital intercourse, as compared with 49 per cent of the highest group. The data regarding marital and extramarital intercourse also showed that more direct sexual activity was reported by the lower-class subjects. However, as might be expected, they used indirect or substitute outlets, such as masturbation or petting to climax, less often than the higher-class groups.

It is not surprising that there should be more overt aggressive and sexual behavior among lower-class males. In the crowded living conditions of the slums the child's exposure to sex and aggression is typically early and direct. Fights and sexual exploits are frequently bragged about by older male identification figures. While some have interpreted this as a seeking of masculinity in a female-dominated world, the fact that aggressive and sexual adventures are among the few readily available forms of inexpensive entertainment should not be overlooked. As Miller (1958) has pointed out, excitement or relief from boredom through thrills and adventures is one of the focal concerns of lower-class culture.

DRINKING AND DRUGS

Drinking assumes an important role in lower-class life (McCandless, 1967). Life in the ghetto is confining to the body and the spirit. The tavern offers both a physical and a spiritual escape from the stuffy crowded flat that more than one family may share. Escape comes not only through getting drunk, but also through the exciting sexual or aggressive adventures that may start in a bar. While the tavern is not ritualized into lower-class Anglo life the way the *cantina* is in Mexican or Latin cultures, nevertheless, it is an important institution. Among some members of the lower class, drugs have replaced alcohol as an escape device. However, the use of narcotics is a more isolated retreatist pattern than drinking.

FATALISM

Members of the lower class are inclined to be fatalistic, feeling that no matter what one does it makes little difference. The lower-class person has little faith in the future or in his ability to alter his circumstances (McCandless, 1967), and he is apt to agree with such statements as, "When a man is born, the success he's going to have is already in the cards so he might as well accept it and not fight against it" (Mussen, Conger, & Kagan, 1963, p. 379). It does not require great psychological insight to see that it is ego enhancing for the ghetto resident to believe that fate rather than individual worth determines who shall get ahead, just as the person in comfortable circumstances likes to believe that success comes as a result of personal effort and ability. Given the differences in the range of opportunities in which they can display personal ability, perhaps both are correct in their perceptions of their worlds.

Miller (1958) has pointed out that associated with this fatalism is a strong belief in luck, both good and bad, as a major factor influencing life. Consequently, it is not surprising to find that lower-class individuals may be more inclined to attempt to change their lot by gambling on sporting events or the numbers than by investing their money in the capitalistic tradition. Investment or saving requires an unwarranted faith in the future and it also lacks the important element of excitement. Semimagical rituals may be also performed to guard against bad luck or to bring about good luck.

MASCULINITY; TOUGHNESS

A number of writers have commented on the lower-class male's pervasive masculinity. It is extremely important for him to be regarded as a tough and manly person who will not shrink from a verbal or physical duel, who can conquer women, and who remains cynical, brave, and unsentimental (Miller, 1958). In many respects he has taken the stereotyped Hollywood image of the gangster of the 1930s and has made it his ego ideal.[2]

Some writers have sought an explanation for this pattern in the female-dominated households so common in lower-class society. As we have noted elsewhere, it is difficult for a youth to achieve an adequate masculine identification in the absence of an admirable father figure. According to Miller (1958, p. 9), "Since women serve as a primary object of identification during pre-adolescent years, the almost obsessive lower class concern with 'masculinity' probably resembles a type of compulsive reaction-formation." In partial support of this hypothesis, Miller points to the great concern over homosexuality that pervades the lower class.

Even if the lower-class man does have a chance to learn the proper masculine role and to establish an adequate identity, economic forces may prevent him from assuming this role. Steady jobs are scarce for an unskilled man, particularly if he is over 40 or a member of a minority group. Unskilled lower-class women, on the other hand, have less difficulty obtaining work and frequently become the breadwinners. Bored and deprived of his masculine identity as a worker, the unemployed lower-class man may have to seek it through toughness. He may drink too much and then assert his authority over his wife by beating her. He may even leave the family, since they would be better off financially without him. Any of these reactions hinders his sons' efforts to establish an adequate masculine identity.

AUTHORITARIANISM

Several writers have indicated that there is greater authoritarianism in the lower class. At the same time others have commented on the lower-class man's quest for autonomy and independence. It appears that the overt posture of toughness, independence, and freedom from constraints masks an inner dependency. Miller (1958) has commented on how lower-class people will adamantly say, "I can take care of myself!" while in their actions they seek out highly restrictive environments with stringent external controls, such as the military, hospitals, and correctional institutions. Tuma and Liv-

2 As we shall see, this aspect of lower-class culture is similar to the Mexicans' and Latins' concern for *machismo*.

son (1960) present evidence that lower-class boys are more compliant with authority in the home, in the school, and with peers, a finding consistent with the parental insistence on respectability noted by Kohn (1959).

The concept of authoritarianism developed by Adorno et al. (1950) has a similar duality. According to their formulation the authoritarian personality assumes an attitude not only of superiority toward those whom he considers to be beneath him, but also of servility toward those above. It is perhaps not surprising, then, that lower-class individuals tend to have elevated scores on the California F scale, which measures this trait (Sexton, 1965, p. 177).

The F scale was originally designed to measure intolerance, and it is well established that the economically frustrated lower-class Anglo is likely to be more prejudiced against minority groups than are middle-class Anglos (Stagner, 1961). Indeed, this fact is often used to buttress the "scapegoat" or displacement theory of prejudice. The combination of a relatively high level of authoritarianism and a predisposition for aggressive acting out suggests that the lower-class person would be overrepresented among extremist groups like the Ku Klux Klan or the Black Panthers.[3]

The authoritarian person also tends to be egocentric or ethnocentric, viewing the world with little understanding of the viewpoint of others. Issues tend to be seen in absolute, black-and-white terms with little tolerance for ambiguity or for cultural relativism.

Morality Development

Morality in the present context refers to the way in which a person judges a given act, rather than to individual value systems. Piaget has studied the development of ethical judgment by asking children to judge the guilt of other children who do various naughty things. He has noted a fairly uniform series of stages in the criteria children use. Younger children rely strongly on the judgment of authority figures, while other children decide for themselves. Younger children are also more likely to judge an act by its consequences instead of

[3] Once again, it should be pointed out that saying an excessive proportion of the membership of such groups comes from the lower class does not mean that more than a fraction of the people in the lower class belong to such groups.

considering the intention of the perpetrator. Thus, the young child will see accidentally breaking two cups as worse than deliberately breaking one cup; if a child tells a lie and is caught and punished, the young child is inclined to view this as a worse offense than telling a lie that goes undetected (Flavell, 1963).

Mature moral judgments in this context require relativism and flexibility. A given act can be judged only in context and not on an absolute basis. From our discussion of authoritarianism, we would expect that the lower-class child might lag behind the middle-class child in this form of moral development.

Investigators who have applied Piaget's techniques to children from different strata of society have obtained data that are generally consistent with this expectation. Kohlberg (1964) found that middle- and lower-class children moved through the same sequence of developmental stages, but that the middle-class children developed mature moral judgments more rapidly and progressed further. Boehm (1962) found that middle-class children developed the distinction between the intention of an act and its actual outcome earlier than did lower-class children. On the other hand, he noted that the lower-class children showed peer reciprocity (i.e., viewing a lie told to another child as being just as wrong as one told to an adult) and independence of adult judgments earlier than did the middle-class children. This latter finding is somewhat unexpected in the light of the lower-class child's supposedly greater authoritarianism.

The data from numerous sources thus show that there are differences between some of the typical personality characteristics found in middle- and lower-class Anglo cultures. For the most part, these are differences in emphasis or degree, and usually there is tremendous overlap among the members of the different classes. Prejudice, authoritarianism, masculinity, and the like are by no means unique attributes of the lower class; however, these traits do appear to be more prevalent in lower-class culture. The first exposure that the child has to a different set of values usually comes when he enters school. With this in mind, we shall now examine the lower-class child in the school setting and discuss some of the attributes that are most directly related to academic and, later, vocational success and achievement.

Academic and Vocational Adjustment

The conflict between the middle- and lower-class worlds comes to its peak in the arena of the school. Here, teachers, agents of the middle class who are specifically charged with perpetuating middle-class ideology, find themselves confronted with the lower-class child's alien viewpoint (McCandless, 1967). While some teachers approach the lower-class child with sympathy and understanding and try to adapt the school environment to meet his needs, others insist with missionary fervor that it is the child who must adapt to the school. If the child is unwilling or unable to make the required changes, he finds himself sentenced to ten years' confinement in an institution where each day impossible demands will be made of him and he will be subjected to punishment and ridicule when he fails. It is little wonder that many rebel against school and drop out as soon as it is legally possible.

This negative school experience often results in the child's being unprepared to compete effectively in the job market place. In part, the school problem and the later vocational problem are the result of inadequate development of verbal and other skills. In part, they are the result of personality patterns that are not suited to the environment of the school or the job, although they may be excellent for enabling one to survive in the slum (McCandless, 1967). We shall examine each of these factors in turn.

ACADEMIC SKILLS OF THE LOWER-CLASS CHILD

School performance is the best measure of the academic skills of lower-class children. A number of studies have shown that lower-class children get lower grades and fewer academic honors than peers from higher social strata. Moreover, they are less popular, participate less in extracurricular activities, and are regarded more negatively by their teachers (Douvan & Gold, 1966).

Performance on standardized "intelligence" tests is a more objective if less direct measure of the ability to perform well in school. A number of studies have demonstrated that lower-class children and adolescents do poorly on standardized "intelligence" tests like the Stanford-Binet and Wechsler Intelligence Scale for Children (WISC) (Cropley, 1964; Goodenough, 1928; Johnson, 1948; McGehee & Lewis, 1942; Terman & Merrill, 1937).[4] The difference in mean

[4] "Intelligence" is placed in quotes to emphasize the fact that these tests meas-

IQ between the highest and lowest class groups is often as much as 20 IQ points (Goodenough, 1928; Terman & Merrill, 1937). Since research with these tests has conclusively demonstrated their validity as a measure of the ability to do well in conventional middle-class schools, there can be little doubt from these data that lower-class children as a group are less able to compete effectively in such settings.

The relatively poor performance of lower-class children on standard "intelligence" tests is probably due in large part to deficits in the verbal and linguistic skills that are important in the conventional classroom. We have already noted that the lower-class child is more likely to express himself motorically than verbally, and there is evidence that, even during the first five years of life, upper-class children are superior to lower-class children in all aspects of language development (Mussen, Conger, & Kagan, 1963, p. 239). In Cropley's investigation of the "intelligence" test performance of upper- and lower-class 10 and 12 year olds, he found significant differences in Verbal IQ but not on Performance IQ on the WISC.

If the child gets off to a poor start in the early grades, this often marks the beginning of a steady downward spiral. It is almost impossible to learn social studies or fractions in the sixth grade if one has not mastered reading or arithmetic in the second grade. This is documented by the fact that the mean IQ in many ghetto schools decreases steadily with increasing grade level (Sexton, 1965). Thus, the longer he is in school, the less able the lower-class child is to compete academically with his middle-class peers. All too often the result for both pupils and teachers is a frustrated deadlock.

Sexton (1965, p. 56) has quoted some comments by sixth-grade children and their teachers that dramatically demonstrate the feelings and atmosphere in the lower-class schoolroom.[5] One student complained:

---

ure the ability to perform certain mental operations that are related to the skills demanded in the middle-class school. Lower-class children may do poorly on these tests but still demonstrate other sorts of intelligent behavior. Thus, in the case of the culturally deprived child, a low IQ indicates a specific academic disability and is not necessarily a sign of basic mental deficiency.

[5] While Sexton's subjects were Puerto Rican, the comments probably apply to Anglo classrooms as well.

I think the teachers should treat us better, you know. We're young, we don't hardly know nothing. You know, when you tell them something, they say, "Where'd you get that strange story or something." You tell them the truth but they don't believe you or nothing. But I think it's not the teacher's fault. It's up to you. True.

Another was more sympathetic with the teacher's plight:

Suppose you were the teacher and you explained something and I said, "I wasn't listening" and you explained it again, and I wasn't listening again. You would get mad, right? Some of the kids are real bad. Some of the teachers don't know how to hit kids. You hit with a ruler. You should see the Catholic school. You talk to somebody and the sister she tell you to stand up and she takes the ruler and she hits you real hard two times on each hand.

A teacher described her perception of the situation as follows (Sexton, 1965, p. 58):

Things just don't make an impression on these children. We haven't found the way to teach them For some reason they don't relate to school. The reason is that their whole culture is different. The only way to teach them is to repeat things 25 times unless for some reason it means something to them. They are not motivated at home. They can't learn unless they see the specific reason for doing something.

MOTIVATION OF THE LOWER-CLASS CHILD

One problem is that what is taught in school is often quite irrelevant to the lower-class child's life. This was dramatically demonstrated in a film entitled *Marked for Failure*, a report on a Harlem school produced by National Educational Television. The film shows a reading lesson in which lower-class youngsters struggle in an attempt to read a story about two middle-class Anglo children visiting their grandmother in the country. In the story, doting parents feed the children an ample breakfast and dress them in warm garments. Then, arms filled with toys, the children are driven to their grandparents' farm, passing through a lovely countryside full of animals, sailboat-dotted lakes, and happy, friendly people. While this tale is being read aloud, the camera scans the world these students walk through on their way to school—cold, dirty, ugly, filled not with trees but prostitutes, pimps, pushers, and hungry men sleeping in doorways.

The curriculum is not the only aspect of school that is irrelevant to the lower-class child's needs and interests. It has been well established that humans learn best when they are rewarded for learning. In the school system the rewards that are distributed are intangible and abstract—grades, praise, and the like. Moreover, they frequently come long after the behavior that is being rewarded. While the middle-class child may thrive on a delayed, abstract reward system, this is not true of the lower-class child. For him, an immediate tangible reward is much more effective. Research has shown that while middle-class children will work at a task just to succeed, the performance and achievement motivation of lower-class children increases markedly when a material reward like money is introduced (Levine, 1966). It is interesting to speculate on what the effects would be if some of the dollars spent on educational retraining programs like the Job Corps were used to provide nickels for lower-class children who had completed their daily assignments. In any event, the data indicate that the present rewards used in school settings have less reinforcement value for the lower-class than the middle-class child.

The essence of educational motivation is the willingness to forego immediate pleasure, such as playing ball or hanging around with the gang, for greater pleasures in the future. Such a future orientation is much more characteristic of the middle than the lower class. The lower-class child has learned that he who eats his candy today has a piece of candy, while he who saves it for the future is likely to have it stolen. Investing a great deal of time and effort in education requires a faith in the future that may be unrealistic for the lower-class boy who, despite his education, may still have difficulty obtaining a job. The junior author recalls a lower-class Negro student who, after much sacrifice, obtained a degree from a major university, only to discover that the best paying job he could find was passing out towels in the men's room of a local hotel. Hollingshead's study of Elmtown's youth (1949) demonstrated how the young people from the higher social strata were given first preference in the job market, while the lower-class youths had to take what jobs (if any) were left over. Levin (1949) has pointed out how class-related personality factors rather than abilities in the conventional sense are required for many jobs:

In terms, therefore, of the relationships between given occupations and their common class status, certain attitudinal and belief requirements may be expected to be associated with the various occupations. It would not even be rash to assume that many of the emotional and personality requirements of various occupations are fundamentally based on class status factors and not on job requirements, as such. Thus, the professional is expected to appear, behave, feel and think quite differently from the semiskilled worker or unskilled worker.

Thus, even the tangible reward of a better job someday may be absent. This is perhaps less true than it once was as companies attempt to improve their images, but every lower-class citizen knows of people who failed to improve their lot despite a good education. Indeed, he may well be more aware of them, for the failures remain in the neighborhood as a continual negative example, while the ones who succeed move out, disappear, and are easily forgotten.

The attitude of lower-class parents has been underrated in the literature. A myth has grown up that lower-class parents are completely opposed to education. However, Meddinus (1962) found no difference between lower- and middle-class adults on an Attitude toward Education test. The loss of jobs through automation has convinced many parents that they should have remained in school, and they therefore want their sons to do so. These parents may have quite negative attitudes toward the school administrators and school personnel, which teachers have mistakenly interpreted as meaning that they are opposed to education. P-TA attendance is less frequent in the lower class. This does not necessarily indicate a lack of interest; as one mother pointed out, she would like to go to the meeting at the school but unless she stays home at night the rats bite the baby. While lower-class parents may want their children to succeed in school, the lower-class family pattern is not optimal for inducing high achievement motivation in the children. Such family patterns as maternal dominance, father absence, and lack of warmth are detrimental to the development of achievement motivation (Douvan & Gold, 1966).

Thus, to succeed in school, the lower-class child must be able to overcome initial handicaps in the skills that make for school success; cope with a negative attitude on the part of some teachers and peers; be willing to sacrifice immediate pleasures, such as the income that could be derived by dropping out and going to work; and place his faith in the eventual rewards of an education, despite the fact that he knows of others who have obtained an education and have failed to improve their lot. It is surprising that so many do overcome these obstacles and complete school.

VOCATIONAL ASPIRATIONS OF THE LOWER-CLASS YOUTH

Since occupation is the chief criterion of socioeconomic status, it is perhaps redundant to note that the heads of lower-class families occupy poorly paid, unskilled, and undesirable jobs, if indeed they are employed at all. But what of their sons? Do they have the same goals that the middle-class youngster has? Or do they set their sights lower?

Generally speaking, while there is no perfect correspondence between socioeconomic status and educational and vocational aspirations, it can be said that the higher the socioeconomic status the higher the absolute aspiration level (Borow, 1966). This holds even when IQ is controlled. A good example is the comparison of the aspiration level of upper-class and lower-class young men in "Elmtown" reported by Hollingshead (1949). Business or the professions were aspired to by 77 per cent of the upper-class boys, but only 7 per cent of the lower-class youths; only 3 per cent of the upper-class boys wanted to become clerks and another 3 per cent chose crafts, while 10 per cent of the lower-class boys wanted to do clerical work and 14 per cent hoped to become craftsmen. The greatest discrepancies were found in the "trades and services" and "undecided" categories. Only 1 per cent of the upper-class boys wanted to enter the trades and services, in contrast to 25 per cent of the lower class; moreover, only 3 per cent of the upper-class boys were undecided, in contrast to 41 per cent of the lower-class sample. Thus, in contrast to the upper classes, the young men of the lower class had a lower level of vocational aspiration and much more indecisiveness regarding their vocational plans.

It is, of course, natural that the socioeconomic level of the family should influence the vocational choice of the son. We have already noted that the lower-class boy is often handicapped in school. Lacking an adequate education and often having learned to dislike anything associated with writing, reading, and arithmetic, the school dropout's range of choices is drastically limited. Those who do succeed in getting an education usually have little contact with successful people in higher-status jobs whom they could use in an intangible way as models and in a tangible way as sources of information about vocational opportunities. Although the lower-class boys may do well in school, school counselors who regard such goals as unrealistic may discourage them from attempting to enter professions requiring extensive education.

In studying lower-class aspirations, it is therefore necessary to distinguish between what the lower-class boy would do if given the opportunity and what he believes he can do in actuality. A study by Stephenson (1955) indicated that the aspirations of lower-class boys were not too different from those of their middle-class peers; however, the actual occupational plans were much lower.

Douvan and Adelson (1958) studied the occupational mobility represented by the aspirations of 14-to-16-year-old boys whose fathers' jobs were in four groups: professional, white collar, skilled manual, and unskilled manual. Each boy's aspiration was classified as upwardly mobile, stable, or downwardly mobile, depending on whether it was of higher, equal, or lower status than his father's. Of the boys in the lowest class, 84 per cent were upwardly mobile; this was higher than the proportion of upwardly mobile people in the skilled-manual class (58%) and in the white-collar class (46%). (None of the professional-class boys could be upwardly mobile, but only 67 per cent were stable, while 33 per cent were downwardly mobile.) This study demonstrated that when the direction, as opposed to the level, of aspiration is considered, lower-class boys were not less ambitious than middle- or upper-class youths.

A particularly interesting study of relative aspiration level was performed by Sherif and Sherif (1965). Like many investigators, they determined the occupational aspirations of samples of upper-middle-, lower-middle-, and lower-class youths. They found, as expected, that the goals and desired income level were highest in the higher classes. However, they next took the additional step of asking each boy what weekly income he felt would be required to provide a bare subsistence and what he considered to be a comfortable income. They found that the conception of what was required for comfort also increased with social class. When the mean aspiration level and the mean conception of what was required for comfort were plotted together, it was found that for each class the income that was hoped for exceeded the income perceived as necessary for comfort by an equal amount. Thus, while the absolute aspiration level increased as a function of class, the relative aspiration level was constant.

These studies indicate that, while lower-class youth may appear to be less ambitious than middle-class young men, their aspirations, relative to what they perceive as being realistically attainable, are not significantly different. This implies that if the realistic level of attainment could somehow be increased, the level of aspiration would rise accordingly. The junior author's experience with Job Corps youth indicates that, while there are vast individual differences, this is often the case. The success of programs like the GI Bill, which brought higher education into the reach of many who had never before been able to consider it, further supports the notion that lower-class aspiration levels can often be raised by increasing the available opportunities.

In generalizing about lower-class aspirations, however, it would be a mistake to overlook the magnitude of individual differences. The Sherifs (1965), in inquiring about the educational goals of the youths in their samples, found a great deal of heterogeneity among the members of the lower class, with bimodal distributions the rule. They concluded (Sherif & Sherif, 1965, p. 321):

> These findings have led us to suspect that some theorists on lower class life may have overlooked the actual diversity within lower class settings. . . . We suggest that generalizations about the characteristics and values of a class or ethnic grouping must specify carefully what values are involved, and how widely they are shared, before referring to distinct "subcultures" in different settings.

Peer Relations of the Lower-Class Boy

As an Anglo boy moves from childhood to adolescence, his relations with his family become progressively less important relative to his relations with his peers. Being popular and well thought of is of incalculable importance to the adolescent Anglo, and this applies to the lower-class youth no less than the middle-class boy. However, the lower-class boy is apt to find more obstacles in the path of gaining social acceptance. We have already noted that he is more likely to be rejected by his teacher. He is also more likely to be unpopular with his middle-class peers. Glidewell, Kantor, Smith, and Stringer (1966), reviewing sociometric studies from 1934 to the present, concluded that two basic tendencies were found. The first was for a child to be chosen most often by children in the same social class, and the second was for out-of-class choices to be directed upward rather than downward. Thus, the higher the class, the greater the acceptance; the lower the class, the greater the likelihood of being unpopular.

This was demonstrated in Hollingshead's study of Elmtown's youth (1949). Young people in Elmtown classified their peers as "the elite," "the good kids," and "the grubbies." As the name implies, someone who was regarded as "grubby" was not socially acceptable and was rejected. No one in the two highest classes, I and II, was regarded as "grubby," and only 1 per cent of those in Class III were so labelled. However, in Class IV, 20 per cent were regarded as "grubby," and in the lowest class, Class V, 85 per cent of the students were rejected as "grubby."

Some investigators have attempted to determine whether it is social class per se or class-related behavior that determines sociometric choices such as these. Others have attempted to decide whether middle- and lower-class individuals value the same sorts of behavior. The evidence generally seems to indicate that choices are made on the basis of class-related behavior and that there are some significant class differences in the traits that are valued (Glidewell et al., 1966).

One of the most thorough studies was that of Pope (1953), who analyzed data collected by the Berkeley Institute of Human Development to determine whether high- and low-status boys and girls differed in the traits they valued. He found significant class differences. Restless, attention-getting, aggressive behavior was much more acceptable to the lower-class than the higher-class boys. The tough, assertive lad, although not necessarily well liked, nevertheless exercised considerable influence among the lower-class boys. He was also likely to date more frequently. The higher-status boys did not approve of such traits, and among them the "ladies man" was more likely to be gentlemanly and conforming. Whereas the lower-class leader was apt to be tough and dominant, the upper-class leader was more good-natured and could take a joke.

In both class groups the friendly, outgoing, sociable boy who was masculine and good at games but not overly aggressive was well thought of. But, while the high-status boys expected a certain amount of decorum and conformity in the classroom and at dances, these qualities were not stressed by the lower-class boys. Indeed, the good student who got along well with teachers and adults was likely to be rejected by his lower-class peers.

Pope's data suggest that in a homogeneous lower-class environment, lower-class values guide group popularity. However, Hollingshead's data suggest that when a tough, cocky lower-class youth enters a school dominated by the middle class and in which middle-class standards prevail, he is likely to be rejected as "grubby." This is most apt to occur in high school, which, being larger than elementary school, is more likely to bring together boys and girls from both sides of the tracks. Such rejection and exclusion from the social life of the school can be a significant factor influencing the lower-class student to drop out.

If a sizable number of lower-class students are in a predominantly middle-class school, they may band together and form their own clique. These cliques can, as we shall see in the next chapter, foster delinquent or antisocial behavior. Cohen (1955) has suggested that such groups, to emphasize their disdain for the middle-class students who are rejecting them, may in turn reject middle-class standards and prize the very traits of rebellious nonconformity and violence that are most threatening to the middle class. The only other alternative may be to accept middle-class standards and with them the middle-class appraisal of oneself as an unacceptable, "grubby" individual.

Summary of Lower-Class Anglo Cultural Patterns

Research on lower-class Anglos has concentrated on exploring the differences between lower-class and middle-class cultural patterns. Lower-class life is characterized by inadequate income, inadequate housing, poor health conditions, and low morale. Possibly because of this strain, the lower-class family is more likely to be broken than the middle-class family; however, even in the intact home the mother is often the breadwinner, since there are more jobs available for unskilled women than for unskilled men. This can result in adjustment problems for lower-class boys who do not have an adequate masculine figure with which to identify. The toughness and excessive masculinity of the lower-class male may be one result.

Lower-class life tends to be more competitive in that there is less to go around. Hence, assertiveness is rewarded more than passivity, and immediate consumption is favored over delayed gratification that often depends on an unwarranted faith in the future.

Compared with middle-class Anglos, members of the lower class have generally been found to have fewer inhibitions against the expression of overt aggression or sexuality. They tend to be restless and bored and seek excitement even though it may get them into trouble with the law. Representatives of the middle class, such as police and teachers, are often viewed as alien intruders. The pressures of lower-class life may result in a greater tendency to seek escape through the use of liquor or drugs and also through increased psychopathology, such as psychoses or depressions.

Members of the lower class are also more authoritarian. Although they reject dependency on a conscious basis, they may seek out highly structured authoritarian milieus.

Many problems arise when the lower-class child enters the middle-class school, for there is frequently little mutual understanding between pupils and teachers. The home environment has often failed to prepare the child with the motivation, skills, and habits that are rewarded in the school, and an initially poor adjustment is likely to result in the child's falling progressively farther behind the norms for his age group. The lower-class child is also likely to be rejected by middle-class schoolmates. While the lower-class child may aspire to upward mobility, his vocational plans reflect the limitations on his opportunities that exist in the culture.

II

LOWER-CLASS URBAN MEXICAN CULTURE

Historical Forces: The Fusion of Indian and Spanish Cultures

Although the United States and Mexico share the same continent and both were European colonies that revolted and became independent, significant differences in the history and the development of the two countries have helped to shape their present cultural differences.

As every North American schoolboy knows, the area that was to become the United States was first occupied by colonists from the

Protestant countries of Northern Europe. They carved out a rather insecure beachhead along the Atlantic seaboard, subjected to pressure from the French to the North, the Spanish to the South, and the Indians allied with France and Spain to the West. The English came to be the dominant force in the colonies, bringing with them a tradition of a strong yeoman class, dating back to the Magna Carta, which was to be the forerunner of the American middle class. Separation of Church and State, freedom of religion (within limits), free enterprise, and free individuals were among their strongest values. These traditions found expression in the Declaration of Independence, the United States Constitution, and the Bill of Rights after the eighteenth-century War of Independence.

Throughout the nineteenth century, the United States pursued an expansionist policy toward the west that resulted in the virtual extermination of the relatively weak and loosely organized Indian tribes that had formerly occupied the territory. By the end of this period the United States was a powerful, confident, and highly industrialized nation with a strong middle class. There was complete separation of Church and State, and the pre-existing Indian cultures had been replaced by a modified European culture.

Mexico, however, had a far different history. When Córdoba discovered Mexico a century before the Pilgrims were to land in Massachusetts, he found a land already occupied by strong, highly developed civilizations. Yucatán, where he first landed, was occupied by the Mayan civilization. Due west the Zapotecs and Mixtecs shared the hills of the present state of Oaxaca, while in the central Valley of Mexico the Aztecs held sway. The pyramids of Mexico, larger than those of Egypt, today bear mute witness to the Indians' technological and architectural ability, while the Aztec calendar with its eighteen 20-day months followed by a five-day New Year's ritual was in many ways superior to the European calendar that has replaced it.

Unlike the Indians of the United States, the Mexican tribes were large and well organized. The Aztecs, in particular, had a strong central government that was closely allied to an intricate religious system. Tenochtitlan, their capital, had massive well-constructed buildings and a population of 300,000. Only by alliances with some of Montezuma's restless vassals was Cortes able to win mastery over the Aztec empire in 1521 (Ewing, 1966; Vaillant, 1950).

The Spanish brought with them an authoritarian form of government that was closely allied to the Roman Catholic Church. Unlike the English, the Spanish rarely brought their families with them to the New World and usually did not establish colonies of settlers. Their primary goals were to subjugate the country and convert the natives. This they did through a combination of military force, the establishment of civil government, and widespread missionary activities. They intermarried and cohabited with the natives, and a caste system sprang up with the *peninsulares*, or native-born Spanish, at the top, the *criollos*, American born of pure Spanish blood, next in the peck order, followed by the *mestizos* of mixed Spanish and native ancestry, and, last and least, the Indians. However, even the lowliest Indian who converted to Christianity (as all did) was considered a rational human being. His rights were protected by law, and in the Court of the Indians he could, theoretically if not always in practice, obtain legal redress against even the highest *peninsular*.

In the years following the Mexican wars of independence from 1811 to 1821, this caste system broke down and the nation became primarily *mestizo*. While it is still possible to distinguish between Indians and *mestizos*, this is more on the basis of culture and language than on the basis of race or genetics (Spicer, 1966). In the remote Zapotec villages of Oaxaca, where no Spanish is spoken, villagers of mixed ancestry are to be found, just as in the cities, among people competely *mestizo* in culture and language, there are people of pure Indian ancestry.

Thus, the Indian, instead of being exterminated, as in the United States, was joined by the Spanish, and the two cultures amalgamated to produce what is now Mexican culture. In many ways the sixteenth-century Aztec and Spanish cultures were ideally suited for such a merger. In both there was a central monarch holding sway over a vast dominion, the Hapsburg Holy Roman Emperor, Charles I, in Madrid, and the Aztec emperor, Montezuma, in Tenochtitlan. In both there was a semifeudal system with semiautonomous local authorities owing allegiance to the central government. In both there was a strong Church-State alliance, with civil and military policy dictated in large measure by religious needs, as determined by the priests. In both cultures there was also a preoccupation with pageantry, blood, and violence. The symbolic sacrifice of Christ in the Mass was supplemented by the burning of heretics by the Inquisition and the bullfights and cockfights in Spain; human sacrifice, by fire in the worship of Huehuetéotl, the Fire God, and by tearing out the heart in most other ceremonies, was a central feature of Aztec worship. Both nations were imperialistic warrior nations in which a man could improve his rank through military exploits. However, the Aztecs were more democratic, with local leaders selected by the tribes and national leaders by councils of representatives.

Land was owned in common by the Aztecs and there were no personal fortunes. This was a major difference from the Spanish system, yet it made the merger even easier, since title to property simply shifted from one abstract owner, the tribe, to another, the Spanish king, with little change in the lot of the individual.

In both cultures the parents raised the children, and in both there was an initial period of childhood indulgence followed by a period of stricter child-rearing in which the duties of male and female were taught and practiced. In both societies women were considered inferior to men, although among the Aztecs women did have the right to property and redress in the courts (Hayner, 1942; Vaillant, 1950). In both societies girls were raised to be modest, respectful, and obedient. Unmarried girls were expected to be chaste and wives were expected to be faithful to their husbands; husbands, on the other hand, were not expected to be faithful to their wives.

Thus, the two cultures were sufficiently similar so that fusion was relatively easy. This is not to say that the Conquest was a peaceful melding. There was considerable bloodshed and individual Indians were reduced from free warriors to virtual slaves. However, the similarity of basic cultural institutions and premises and the policy of the Spanish toward the Indians made possible an integration of the European and Indian cultures that was never achieved in the United States. As a result, despite regional, social class, rural-urban, and Indian-*mestizo* differences (Edmonson, 1957), there is still a fundamental cultural unity that all Mexicans share to some degree.

The Family

Despite regional and class differences, there is substantial agreement throughout Mexican culture on the proper way to raise a child. As Maslow and Diaz-Guerrero (1960) put it, while the North American parent must consult a book written by some authority, each Mexican parent knows that he is the ultimate authority. Therefore, he is able to handle any decision quickly, confidently, and consistently. Moreover, since the parent's child-rearing goals and methods are shared by all, the child is confronted with a uniform, consistent set of demands and expectations.

The first basic premise of the Mexican family is the unquestioned supremacy of the father (Diaz-Guerrero, 1955, 1965; Hayner, 1942). While he may be physically absent much more than his North American counterpart, psychologically he is ever present. Even in his absence, his word is law. Rather than competing with her husband, the Mexican wife devotes her life to following his wishes, maintaining his authority with the children, and treating him like visiting royalty if he should honor the home by his presence (Maslow & Diaz-Guerrero, 1960). As the *jefe de la casa*, or boss of the household, he receives respect and unquestioning obedience. Children defer to their father's authority, and this respect continues even after the child has reached maturity. In the extended family the grandfather is the unquestioned ruler; even the grown sons defer to his judgment, and his decision is final (Spicer, 1966).

The father's duty to his children is to raise the boys to be manly and the girls to be feminine and to intercede between the family and the outside world. The traditional urban Mexican home is built with a heavy door and barred windows facing the street; family life goes on within the hidden confines of the patio. So, too, the Mexican family is turned inward on itself, revolving around the self-sacrificing, tender presence of the mother. Siblings play with and care for one another rather than playing with neighborhood children their own age.

The father sallies forth from this bastion to do business with the world to ensure his family's welfare and protection. When his business is done he may return to the home. However, he is more likely to spend his evening with his male friends at the club or *cantina*, or he may visit his mistress in the *casa chica* (little house), which he maintains apart from the *casa grande* (big house), in which his wife resides. While the lower-class Mexican may not be able to afford the luxury of one or more *casas chicas*, he is nonetheless likely to be as promiscuous as his means allow. This is his primary way of proving his virility, which, as we shall see, is an overriding concern of the Mexican male.

The Mexican mother's role has been described by Diaz-Guerrero

(1955) as one of total self-sacrifice and abnegation. She is expected to devote herself completely to her husband and children, in that order. In her person she must embody the ideal of pure, holy femininity: all loving, all pure, and all forgiving. Emotionally deserted by her husband, she devotes herself to her children and wins from them a lifelong devotion and fidelity that no one, including their eventual spouses, will ever be able to supplant.[6]

As a mother, she is worshipped. As a wife, she is idealized and protected. However, after the initial courtship, in which she is wooed with romantic poetry, evening serenades, and sidelong glances at church, her husband is apt to berate her for not being as good as his mother was. He is unlikely to treat her as a sex object in the same fashion as he does his mistress. For the Mexican man, sexual relations with the mother of one's children are not quite right. Moreover, he is afraid that if he should teach her the pleasure of sexuality, she might grow to enjoy sex and become an easy victim of the predatory men who are constantly seen as lurking to seduce the unwary woman (Diaz-Guerrero, 1955).

Walled within the home, the Mexican mother raises her children with tenderness and authority. While the husband lays down the overall guidelines of domestic policy, he does not want to be bothered with the day-to-day details of what happens in the home; it is up to the mother to see that his wishes are carried out.

The first goal of child-rearing is to teach the children obedience, respect, and politeness. During the first two years the infant is showered with affection by all—father, mother, and godparents—but nonetheless he is still taught respect. For example, from the time Manuel learns to say his first words he is trained that, when he is asked his name, he should not reply simply, "Manuel," but "Manuel, *a sus órdenes,*" or "Manuel, *mande usted,*" (Manuel, at your command) (Diaz-Guerrero, 1955).

Second only to filial respect and obedience is the goal of raising manly boys and feminine girls. It is difficult to overestimate the importance of masculinity in Mexican culture. Male children are not simply preferred, they are regarded as essential. According to Diaz-Guerrero, unless a family already has at least two or three boys, the

---

[6] Diaz-Guerrero (1955) found that 95 per cent of the Mexican men he queried agreed with the statement, "To me the mother is the dearest person in existence."

birth of a girl is considered a tragedy. Indeed, the virility of the father who sires only girls will probably be doubted, and nothing can be more threatening to the Mexican male.

Once boys are born, they are indoctrinated in manliness. Any feminine tendencies to play with dolls instead of soldiers or to imitate mother in the household tasks are stamped out. Rough, hardy, aggressive games, often at the expense of sister's tranquility, are encouraged. The boy must be courageous and never run from a fight. Nevertheless, he must obey his father. He must be a man, but not as much of a man as his father.

In adolescence, the boy turns to sexuality, for "during adolescence the sign of virility in the male is to talk about or act in the sex sphere" (Diaz-Guerrero, 1955, p. 412). He seeks girls—one who embodies his mother's virtues whom he can idealize and admire and others with whom he can enjoy sexual relations. The greater his sexual successes, the greater the respect in which he will be held by his fellow males. Indeed, all achievement comes to be linked with sexuality, and the person who is a success in any manly endeavor is said by his fellows to have large or well-placed sex organs (Diaz-Guerrero, 1955; Hemingway, 1932; Ramos, 1962). The importance of sexuality is illustrated by Gomez-Robleda's (1948) finding that 34 per cent of the Mexican men he surveyed indicated that sexuality and eroticism were their primary interests in life.

One of the male adolescent's primary responsibilities is to aid in the protection of his mother and sisters. Just as boys are raised to be masculine, so the girls are raised to be feminine. The family and the school work together toward these twin goals. The Minister of Public Education once stated: "The ideal of education is to make the woman more feminine and men more masculine, or in different words, education should enable the boy and girl to refine or emphasize the characteristics of their sex instead of obscuring, nullifying or substituting them . . ." (Maslow & Diaz-Guerrero, 1960, p. 234).

While middle-class *mestizo* girls may seek further education and aim at a career, the daughters of the lower-class and conservative upper-class families typically complete their education with the sixth grade (Hayner, 1942). Excessive education or a career are thought to masculinize a girl, and a competitive, achievement-oriented girl will be criticized.

The girl who leaves school devotes herself to helping her mother and learning the household skills she will need when she is married. Meanwhile, her brothers guard her honor as fiercely and as vigorously as they assault the honor of the neighbors' daughters. By the age of 15, about half the lower-class girls are married, formally if they can afford it and informally if they cannot (Hayner, 1942). While in the past, marriages were arranged by the parents, it is now more common for the young people to select their own mates and then seek parental approval of the match. Today some couples may marry even if the parents should disapprove.

In Monterrey the proximity of the United States and the industrial economy have contributed to a weakening of these traditions. The residents of Monterrey are called the "Yankees of Mexico," and the old customs are adhered to less strictly than they are in the more isolated rural villages to the south.

EFFECTS OF THE FAMILY PATTERNS

To a large degree the Mexican child-rearing practices accomplish their major goals. According to Maslow and Diaz-Guerrero (1960, p. 228):

> The visitor to Mexico soon notices that Mexican children behave differently from American children. The general impression is that the Mexican children are better behaved, more polite, more helpful. They seem to get along well with adults, enjoying their company, trusting them, obeying them, respecting them, and showing no overt signs of hostility. At the same time, they are able to play with other children (they do not cling to adults), giving the impression that they can enjoy both adults and children more than American children can. Another common observation (also reported from Italy) is that there seems to be no apparent sibling rivalry.

Studies comparing Mexican and North American college students show that the former have much greater respect for their parents and older relatives than do the latter. McGinn, Harburg, and Ginsburg (1963) compared the perceptions of the parents of students in Guadalajara and in Michigan. As might be expected, they found that the Mexican students saw their parents as stricter, more demanding of obedience, and more arbitrary, but also more affectionate and self-confident in their treatment of the child. This did not arouse resentment, but instead greater respect and admiration for

the parents. Consistent with this, Diaz-Guerrero (1965, p. 133) surveyed the attitudes of 472 male and female Mexican high school
students and found that the vast majority agreed with such statements as:

> To me the mother is the dearest person in existence.
> The place for women is in the home.
> Men should wear the pants in the family.
> A person should always obey his parents.
> A boy should always obey his parents.
> A father's word should never be questioned.
> A good wife never questions the behavior of her husband.

This respect of authority figures is touched with fear, however.
Maldonado-Sierra, Trent, and Fernandez-Marina (1958) found that
63 per cent of the male students and 67 per cent of the female students they surveyed agreed with the statement "Many boys are
afraid of their fathers," and 69 per cent of the boys and 76 per cent
of the girls agreed with the statement "Many girls are afraid of their
fathers." As we shall see below, Anderson et al. (1959, 1961) similarly noted a certain degree of fear in Mexican school children's
perceptions of their teachers.

While these latter studies have focused primarily on middle-class
subjects, the findings are so clear that they probably can be generalized to the lower classes without great danger of distortion, particularly since the lower classes are probably even more traditional
in outlook than the middle classes. However, it should be pointed
out that the lower-class city dweller is the Mexican about whom
there is the greatest dearth of anthropological and sociological data
(Edmonson, 1957).

Modal Personality Characteristics

Having surveyed some of the broad historical and familial patterns that help shape personality, we shall now examine some of the
modal personality characteristics of the lower-class Mexican city
dweller. Unfortunately, much less empirical data are available than
we had for the lower-class Anglo. Anthropologists have focused
more on Indians and *campesinos* in small villages than on city dwellers, and psychologists and sociologists have contributed more data
regarding the middle than the lower class. Many of the data are

descriptive and observational in nature, and there is a lack of large-scale quantitative studies, such as those of Maccoby or Davis and Havighurst.

AGGRESSION

Like the lower-class Anglo, the lower-class Mexican man is relatively uninhibited in his expression of aggression, for aggressiveness is an important part of *machismo* or masculinity. In this respect, lower- and middle-class men resemble each other more in Mexico than they do in the United States. Middle-class Mexicans are much readier to respond with aggression if their honor has been affronted than are their Anglo counterparts. This is not surprising if viewed in historical perspective. The Spanish and Aztec cultures, which were roots of modern Mexican culture, were hardly pacifist, and in the last two centuries Mexicans frequently have had to turn to the rifle or the machete to settle political differences within or to repel foreign intervention from without. The United States, on the other hand, has fought only one civil war since 1776, if we discount the Indian wars, and has never had to repel a large-scale invasion.

Unlike the men, Mexican women are much less aggressive than their Anglo counterparts. Aggression is masculine behavior, and the Mexican woman is expected to be passive and feminine. In lower-class Anglo culture, when Johnny does Frankie wrong, Frankie settles the matter with a revolver, but the Mexican wife whose husband neglects her or is unfaithful "is not apt to complain openly when he does show up, but will rather suffer in silence, meanwhile serving him, making much of him, treating him like visiting royalty, being especially careful to help maintain his authority with the children" (Maslow & Diaz-Guerrero, 1960).

SEX

Sex is an integral part of *machismo*, and infidelity of the man is an established part of Mexican mores. Diaz-Guerrero (1965, p. 133) found that 51 per cent of the men and 63 per cent of the women he sampled agreed with the statement "Most married men have lovers." Much of the discussion of the lower-class male peer group concerns sexual exploits and adventures.

While sex was important to the lower-class Anglo because it was one of the few pleasures he could afford, the Mexican gets additional

satisfaction from proving that he is superior to the female. The successful seduction of a previously unattainable girl brings great satisfaction, especially if it was necessary to outwit her through some
clever or devious strategy. Such a conquest brings much more pleasure than sleeping with an experienced girl, who might be able to
provide greater physical satisfaction. As in the case of aggression, it
is likely that the middle class shares this lower-class attitude regarding sexuality to a much greater extent than was the case among the
Anglos.

While there may be somewhat greater tolerance of male sexuality
in Mexico than in the United States, there is decidedly less tolerance
of female sexuality. The unchaste woman brings great disgrace to
her family's honor.

DRINKING

Just as he can demonstrate *machismo* by outfighting and outse-
ducing his peers, the Mexican male can also demonstrate it by out-
drinking them. The ability to drink vast quantities of alcohol without
showing the effects is highly prized. The invitation to a "friendly
beer" is often the challenge to a drinking contest; the hapless loser
can be sure that his fellows will not let him forget the foolish things
he did or the graceless way he slid beneath the table while his con-
queror continued drinking for hours without showing any trace of
drunkenness.

While women, including wives and children, are likely to be found
in a lower-class Anglo bar, the Mexican *pulquería* or *cantina* is a
place for men to gather. One does not see Mexican bars with signs
bearing the Spanish equivalent of "Tables for Ladies."

MASCULINITY: *Machismo*

In Spanish, the noun *macho* means "male"; it can also mean a "he-
mule" (Castillo & Bond, 1950). By keeping in mind a rather mulish
masculinity, we can closely approach the concept of *machismo*.

Next to family loyalty, *machismo* occupies the primary place in
the Mexican pantheon. It means being a man in all things: being
superior to women, taking no nonsense from anyone, deferring only
to one's father and one's God (in that order), and protecting one's
God-given holy honor. The Mexican male constantly seeks to demonstrate that he is *muy macho*, very much the man. He demonstrates

his superiority to all women by keeping them in their place and, whenever possible, by seducing them. He sires lots of male children and raises them to be men, second only to their father in manliness. He does not run from any challenge and does not break a deal. He attacks anyone who insults him or his family and is constantly alert for any covert insult, for to overlook a covert insult would be an affront not only to his honor but also to his intelligence.

Many Mexican women share in this idealization of *machismo*. A Mexican wife who learns her husband has been unfaithful might be upset, but she might also take pride in the fact that her man is so irresistible and virile that he can conquer countless women.

Machismo is thus a melange of the values of masculinity, toughness, and smartness that Miller (1958) described as being focal concerns of lower-class Anglo culture. It will be recalled that Miller suggested these values were the result of being raised in a female-dominated household without sufficient opportunity to establish an adequate masculine identity. In Mexico, too, there is a high incidence of broken or fatherless homes; the official 1950 census indicated that 10 per cent of the households in Nuevo León, in which our investigation was carried out, were headed by women, while in Mexico City and Jalisco the incidence was 17 per cent and 15 per cent, respectively. However, this is not sufficient to account for the importance of *machismo* in the Mexican personality.

Miller's central argument, however, was that excessive masculinity was a compensation for feelings of inadequacy. It has been suggested that this is true for the Mexican male as well; however, the source of these feelings has been attributed not to a matriarchal household but to broader historical and social forces (Ramos, 1962).

FEELINGS OF INFERIORITY

When certain behavior is strongly valued by an individual, psychologists often suspect that this is a camouflage for quite different feelings. Thus, the censor is suspected of latent voyeurism and the Don Juan of feelings of sexual inadequacy. Ramos (1962) has analyzed Mexican culture in a similar fashion and has interpreted many Mexican characteristics as being the result of a national inferiority complex.

Ramos suggested that Mexico adopted European culture in an uncritical fashion. Cathecting European values, Mexico was automatically placed in an inferior position, for she could never hope to compete with Europe on European terms. One result of this implicit disparagement of indigenous culture was a collective inferiority complex.

Mexico's foreign relations have done little to assuage any such feelings of inferiority. In the last four centuries her soil has been invaded by Spain, France, England, and the United States. In the United States War[7] she lost claim to half her territory, including the present states of California, Nevada, Utah, Arizona, and New Mexico, as well as part of Texas and Colorado. These foreign invasions, along with internal instability and civil strife, have not permitted the Mexican peasant any real feelings of economic or political stability.

This insecurity undoubtedly has contributed to feelings of helplessness among Mexican peasants. It is Ramos' (1962) contention that the excessively masculine behavior of the lower-class Mexican arises as a reaction against such feelings of inadequacy. This is most clearly manifested, according to Ramos (1962, pp. 58–61, 64–65), in the behavior of what he calls the *pelado*, a vulgar term for the lower-class city bum:

> The best model for study is the Mexican *pelado*, for he constitutes the most elemental and clearly defined expression of national character. . . . Our . . . interest here is his inner self and the elemental forces that determine his character . . . The *pelado* belongs to a most vile category of social fauna; he is a form of human rubbish from the great city. He is less than a proletarian in the economic hierarchy, and a primitive man in the intellectual one. Life from every quarter has been hostile to him and his reaction has been black resentment. He is an explosive being with whom relationship is dangerous, for the slightest friction causes him to blow up. . . . He is an animal whose ferocious pantomimes are designed to terrify others, making them believe that he is stronger than they and more determined. Such reactions are illusory retaliations against his real position in life, which is a nullity. . . . Any exterior circumstances that might aggravate his sense of inferiority will provoke a violent reprisal, the aim of which is to subdue his depression. The result is a constant irritability that incites him to fight with others on the most insignificant pretext. But his bellicose spirit does not derive from his sentiment of hostility toward all humanity. The *pelado* seeks out quarrels as a stimulus, to renew the vigor of his downtrodden ego. . . . He is like a shipwreck victim who,

[7] Called the Mexican War in the United States.

after flailing about in a sea of nothingness, suddenly discovers his drift-wood of salvation: virility. . . .

The most destitute of Mexican *pelados* consoles himself by shouting at everyone that "he's got balls" (*muchos huevos*) with reference to the testicles. . . . Since he is, in effect, a being without substance, he tries to fill his void with the only suggestive forces accessible to him: that of the male animal. . . . The *pelado* is neither a strong nor a brave man. The appearance he shows us is false. It is a camouflage by which he misleads himself and all those who come into contact with him. . . . However much the *pelado* deceives himself by this illusion, he can never be certain of his power, so long as his weakness is present and threatens to betray him. He lives in distrust of himself and in continuous fear of being discovered. So it is that his perception becomes abnormal; he imagines that the next man he encounters will be his enemy; he mistrusts all who approach him. (Pp. 58–61, *passim*)

The most striking aspect of Mexican character, at first sight, is distrust. . . . His distrust is not limited to the human race; it embraces all that exists and happens. . . . It is the Mexican's view that ideas make no sense and he scornfully calls them "theories." . . . In Mexico each man concerns himself only with immediate issues. He works for today and tomorrow but never for later on. The future is a preoccupation which he has banished from his conscience. . . . Obviously, a life without future can have no norms. (Pp. 64–65)

FATALISM

While resignation and fatalism were characteristics of the lower-class Anglo, they are even more important in the psychology of the Mexican, sometimes assuming religious overtones. A common saying is *Haga uno lo que haga, todo es lo que Dios quiere* (Do what you will, everything is as God wishes) (Madsen, 1964, p. 16).[8] This not only means that one should be resigned to one's lot, but also has the additional implication that anyone who strives to alter this fate is opposing God's will.

There is less fatalism among the *mestizos* and the city dwellers

[8] If we contrast this with these lines from Henley's *Invictus*, which many Anglo children are required to memorize, we can appreciate the difference in fatalism between Anglo and Mexican culture:

> It matters not how strait the gate,
> How charged with punishments the scroll,
> I am the master of my fate;
> I am the captain of my soul.

than among the *campesinos* and the Indians, whose lot is tied to the vagaries of rainfall and wind. Since the residents of Monterrey are urban *mestizos*, they would be more likely to attempt to alter their circumstances than would more fatalistic Mexicans.

RELIGION AND SUPERSTITION

Coming from cultures that stressed religious orthodoxy and, until the Constitution of 1917, close ties between Church and State, it is natural that Mexican life should be permeated by religion to a much greater extent than life in the United States. Modern Mexicans are usually Roman Catholic, but there is a strong infusion of pre-Hispanic paganism.

While the remote Indian villages are the strongholds of paganism, there are few lower-class *mestizos* who do not share in the folk beliefs to some extent. The most widespread manifestation is the belief in folk illnesses of mystical (or psychosomatic) origin. These include *mal ojo* (evil eye), a disease caused by witchcraft, and *susto* (fright), a disease caused by a surprise, such as seeing a ghost (Spicer, 1966). These diseases do not respond to orthodox medical treatment; instead, the sufferer must go to a curer or *curandero*, who treats the ailment by talking to the patient and praying with him for relief, who may prescribe herbal drinks or baths, or who may draw out the evil spirits by passing an egg over the victim's body (Madsen, 1964; Rubel, 1966). In addition to the beneficent *curanderos*, there are also evil *brujos*, or witches, who cast spells on people. A person who has had his honor affronted may seek a *brujo* to cast a spell on his enemy. Bad luck is often attributed to such evil spells.

Another important aspect of Mexican religious practice is the cult of the saints. Spicer (1966, pp. 92–93) has described this as follows:

The term cult probably does not do the institution justice. It is not uniform over the nation, it does not rest on formalized doctrine, it has a thousand varied expressions. The object of interest, for example, varies from a battered stone image newly uncovered by a plow in a Tarascan field to the Virgin of Guadalupe herself with the full official sanction of the Catholic Church. The saints, or "*santos*," are a strange variety, to the nonbeliever, of different objects or representations, but they have many essential features in common. The *santo* is a supernatural being which resides in a particular place and ministers to human beings only in that place. The *santo* has miraculous powers, especially for curing, but also for bringing various kinds of good fortune. The *santo* is on good terms with, if he is not actually one of, the Christian pantheon. The *santo* will respond to human actions and enjoys being honored by men. Every village in Mexico, whether Indian or *mestizo*, has its own saint, the patron, or patroness, of the community. The people of the village seem to think of the saint as theirs, or possibly it is a sentiment that they are the saint's. . . .

Often in the central part of Mexico a saint is the patron of a single *barrio*, a subdivision of a village or town, and his powers are not highly regarded outside that small area. Again the saint may have a reputation throughout a wide region for miraculous powers, such as San Esquipulas whose reputation extends from Guatemala as far north as Oaxaca. A regionally important saint becomes the object of pilgrimages and gives rise to local cults focused around images over the whole region where his powers are known . . . These local and regional systems of worship have a life of their own apart from the Catholic Church, and perhaps represent surviving cults of similar character in pre-Spanish days, but now very much re-interpreted in Christian terms and rituals. They are indeed in this respect bridges between Indian and *mestizo* cultures. . . . The greatest of all the saints in Mexico is, of course, the Virgin of Guadalupe, the dark-skinned Madonna of the ancient Aztec hill of Tepeyac and of the modern third largest basilica in the Catholic world. As patroness of the whole nation of Mexico, her cult, which is intensive among Indians and *mestizos* alike, is at present one of the strongest unifying powers in the country.

Strict adherence to religious precepts would interfere with the *machismo* of the Mexican male. Not only would it put a severe crimp in his sexual activities, but also it would mean acknowledging the authority of another man, the priest. As a result, most Mexican males are rather nominal Catholics and devotions are left to the women. Even if the father is not religious, however, he wants the mother to raise the children to be religious (as long as they don't make the mistake of placing the authority of God before that of the father). While this has not received much attention, it would appear likely that this attitude of "do as I say and not as I do" could cause conflicts and confusion on the part of an adolescent boy.

AUTHORITARIANISM

The child-rearing practices of the lower-class Mexican family are, as we have seen, quite authoritarian. It is made very clear to the Mexican child that he is to obey and respect his parents, older relatives, and godparents (*compadres*). Later it is made clear that, while he owes respect to some, he does not owe it to others, and to be subservient to peers or lessers is an affront to honor. Thus, the young Mexican learns a complex system of people to whom he does and does not owe respect.

The term "respect" is an important one in Mexican culture, and Peck and Diaz-Guerrero (1963) have empirically compared the connotations that the word "respect" has for Mexican and Texas students. They found:

Most of the Mexicans think that respect involves a positive duty to obey; and a third to a half of them, unlike most American students, feel that respect means you *have* to obey the respected person, whether you like it or not. Thus, in contrast to the American pattern, most of the Mexicans portray the respect relationship as an intricate web of reciprocal duties and dependencies, cast into a hierarchical mold, with strong feelings of emotional involvement to support it . . .

In another study, Diaz-Guerrero and Peck (1963) studied the objects of respect in the two nations and found that Mexican students are more likely than North American students to have high respect for older members of the family and female relatives; however, the Mexicans had less respect for equals.

Anderson, Anderson, Cohen, and Nutt (1959) and Anderson and Anderson (1961) used an incomplete story technique to determine the attitudes of adolescent students toward teachers in several countries that differed in authoritarianism. They found that the pattern for the Mexican children resembled that of the authoritarian German culture rather than the more egalitarian English or United States cultures. The Mexican children appeared to see the teacher as a more distrustful and punitive figure than did the North American children.

In discussing the authoritarianism of the lower-class Anglo, the relation between authoritarianism and racial prejudice was brought out. According to Spicer (1966), there is little if any biological racial prejudice in Mexico, so thorough has been the mixture of Spanish and Indian strains. However, there is cultural and regional prejudice.

Just as authoritarianism in the lower-class Anglo was a rather contradictory facet of his character, so, too, with the lower-class Mexican. While he proclaims his independence and his unwillingness to bow his head before anyone, save his father and his God, nonetheless, he is quite conscious of his position in the hierarchy and his responsibilities toward others, as well as others' responsibilities toward him. The Mexican is a strong parent to his children, but remains a dutiful child in his relationship to his own parents. He is respectful and dependent (whether he likes it or not) toward those to whom he owes obligations, but somewhat arrogant and independent toward those who are obliged to him. As might be expected, this can make for a certain tension and prickliness in interpersonal relations, particularly when any ambiguity is involved.

Surveying some of the modal characteristics of the lower-class Mexican, we have seen that he shares many traits with the lower-class Anglo. However, the Mexican often has them in greater degree. While the lower-class Anglo values masculinity, this is not as conscious a value as in Mexican culture. While the lower-class Anglo believes in luck and has superstitious magical rituals, they are not institutionalized in the form of *brujos* and *curanderos*. The lower-class Mexican shares his values, such as *machismo* and aggressiveness, to a greater extent with the middle-class Mexican than the lower-class Anglo shares his traits with the middle-class Anglo. Thus, there is greater consistency in Mexican culture, and the lower-class Mexican appears less likely to be viewed as an alien creature by his middle-class fellows.

Academic and Vocational Adjustment

While a great deal has been written about the adjustment of lower-class Anglos and Latins to North American schools, much less material describing the adjustment of lower-class Mexicans to Mexican schools is available. Therefore, this section is based primarily on inference and personal observation.[9]

In some respects, the lower-class Mexican is better prepared for school than is his Anglo peer. Coming from an authoritarian home, he probably finds it easier to adjust to the disciplined atmosphere of the school than does the relatively undisciplined lower-class Anglo. The Mexican school, like the Mexican home, is more authoritarian

---

[9] In April, 1966, one of the writers (E. I. M.) had the opportunity to sit in on classes at a number of secondary schools in Mexico City. The observations made at that time have strongly influenced this section. The writers are grateful to the authorities of the Department of Education and the principals, teachers, and students who made this possible.

than the Anglo. Students wear uniforms and rise when their teacher or a visiting adult enters the room, and there is much greater use of titles and formal courtesy. While lower-class schoolrooms are noisier and rowdier than those in middle-class districts, there still appears to be much more order and discipline than is found in comparable North American schoolrooms.

Since the goals of the Mexican school system are closer to the goals of lower-class Mexican parents, there is probably less culture conflict than in a lower-class Anglo school. Moreover, in the upper grades, it appears easier for a student to drop out and go to work if he wishes to do so. Consequently, there are probably fewer students who feel trapped, unwillingly serving their time until the law says they no longer must be forced to go to school. While one can debate the desirability of forcibly leading students to the trough of knowledge, there is little doubt that allowing unmotivated students to leave does result in a better classroom morale.

However, like his lower-class Anglo counterpart, the Mexican student also has problems. One of these is poverty. As is the case anywhere, having insufficient funds results in overcrowded classrooms, poorly paid teachers, insufficient textbooks, and inadequate equipment. The adequacy of the plant can be a function of personal influence and politics. One of the writers visited a school in a lower-class district of Mexico City that boasted facilities, including technical shops and laboratories, equalled by few high schools in the United States. The principal proudly stated that she had managed to get this support through her personal influence with the wife of a high official. In visits to other much more poorly equipped schools it was impossible not to wonder whether the poor facilities signified political disfavor.

Inadequate achievement motivation would appear to be an educational problem in Mexico as in the United States. Among tradition-steeped families that regard striving for success as improper self-aggrandizement, cultural attitudes probably hinder the child's school performance. Boys probably have less of a problem than girls, since school achievement can be regarded as a sign of virility. This same attitude can, however, throw a roadblock in the path of the girl who wishes to obtain an education. Too much education may hinder a woman in later getting married. More than her Anglo contemporary, the Mexican girl may have to regard marriage and a career as mutually exclusive goals.

Peer Relations of the Mexican Male

In Mexico, kinship ties are a major determinant of peer relations. As we have seen, the Mexican usually feels strong ties of obligation toward members of his own family. Within the family, his status is defined and he can relax somewhat. Outside the family, he must remain alert for possible slurs on his honor or attempts by others to prove that they are more virile or masculine.

The system of godparents (*compadrazgo*) helps prevent the community from fragmenting into mutually suspicious nuclear families. As in the case of many Mexican customs, *compadrazgo* has its roots in the Roman Catholic institution of godparents and in pre-Cortesian Indian practices of ceremonial sponsorship (Spicer, 1966). When some critical ritual is impending in the life of a child, his parents ask a man and woman to serve as godmother and godfather for the event. These events include not only baptism and confirmation, but also marriage, a major visit to the *curandero*, or entrance into some religious organization, as well as other rituals of local significance. The system has been most widely elaborated among the Yaquis in the north, who may have as many as 32 godparents (Spicer, 1966).

Once a person has served as a child's godparent, a lifelong bond of mutual obligation is established between godparent and godchild. Moreover, a tie is also established between the parents and the godparent, for the godparent serves as a coparent (*compadre*).[10] Gifts are exchanged between godparents and godchildren and between *compadres*, and *compadres* are obliged to help one another in times of economic crisis or illness.

The godparent system greatly extends family ties and allows meaningful peer relations to be established between adults. This formalized tie of mutual obligation helps to overcome some of the touchiness and suspicion that Mexicans are apt to feel in the presence of someone who is not otherwise a kinsman. It is also a useful

---

10 Technically, the term *compadre* is used to express the relation between the father and the godfather; it can be translated as comrade, crony, or pal, as well as cosponsor (Castillo & Bond, 1950).

way in which members of the lower class can form ties with wealthier people in the community.

Peer relations among children are also more circumscribed in Mexico than in the United States. As we have seen, the Mexican child spends more time with siblings and less with his age mates than does the typical Anglo child. Later, in adolescence, the boy joins a clique of male friends. As in the lower-class Anglo street-corner group, this male clique serves a definite function. It offers a refuge from the ties of respect and obligation, which can get quite stultifying at times. Here, within limits, a young man can be somewhat disrespectful. Verbal dueling takes place, with each boy trying to outsmart the other. The ultimate goal is to disguise one's insults so effectively that the unwary victim feels flattered. There are implicit, but nonetheless strong, guidelines within which such dueling can take place. It is understood that verbal insults are permitted within the clique that could not be allowed elsewhere. However, such banter must not go too far. Insults about one's family are never permitted. A remark that ordinarily would be allowed inside the group might become an insult if someone outside the clique is present to witness it.

With the members of the peer group, one can engage in masculine activities: bragging, drinking, admiring señoritas in the plaza, going to movies, and other diversions that take place outside the family. The members of one's peer group are not only companions, but also adversaries in contests, and an audience before whom one can demonstrate one's masculinity. In this respect, the male lower-class Mexican clique fulfills many of the same functions as the lower-class Anglo peer group. However, the Mexican adolescent's primary source of emotional support and his primary tie of loyalty are always to the family rather than the peer group, which is not always the case among Anglo boys.

The Mexican boy's relations with female peers are also more circumscribed than the Anglo boy's. The Anglo boy is, of course, greatly concerned with girls and he may try to idealize them or seduce them as assiduously as his Mexican counterpart. However, in Anglo culture, it is also possible for a boy to regard some girls simply as friends or as people with mutual interests, such as music or dramatics. Similar casual heterosexual friendships are less common in Mexico.

Our survey of the literature on lower-class Anglo peer relations showed that a major problem was rejection of the lower-class students by middle-class peers. While the writers have no adequate data to support this view, it is our subjective impression that while there undoubtedly is social-class prejudice in Mexico, it nevertheless is less of a problem in Mexican schools. There are several reasons for making this inference. In the first place, poverty is more widespread in Mexico, and the lower-class student is therefore less likely to be "different" or in the minority in a given school district. Secondly, the schools have attempted to reduce the external social-class differences through such devices as having all the children wear the same uniform. Thirdly, the lower and middle classes share the same values and the same religion to a greater extent in Mexico. A fourth factor, particularly prevalent in the upper grades, is a decrease in the heterogeneity of the school population as a result of the upper- and upper-middle-class parents' sending their children to private or parochial schools and the lower-class parents' allowing their sons to drop out to go to work. (We have already noted how many daughters of traditional families drop out in the sixth grade.) Because of these factors it would seem likely that there is less class rejection within the confines of the school in Mexico, although such prejudice may well be encountered in the community.

Summary of Lower-Class Mexican Culture

Modern Mexican culture is a result of the fusion and modification of Spanish and Indian customs and institutions that stressed strong family ties, religious orthodoxy and pageantry, fatalism, and authoritarianism. The Mexican family is founded on the authority of the father, the passive loyalty of the mother, and the respectful obedience of the children. As a result of widespread agreement regarding what is appropriate behavior for the male and the female child, an agreement that transcends class differences to a greater extent than is the case in the United States, the lower-class Mexican child is confronted with a more uniform set of expectations and limits than his North American counterpart, and there is less likely to be a sharp change in expectations when he leaves the family and enters the school. While many of the characteristics of the adult Mexican male are similar to those of the lower-class Anglo adult, including aggressiveness, sexuality, an emphasis on masculinity, and authoritarianism, these are shared more by the Mexican middle class than is the case in the United States. There is, however, a much greater cleavage between the behavior that is considered appropriate for the man and for the woman in Mexican culture; the lower-class Mexican wife is much more passive, self-sacrificing, and uncomplaining than her Anglo counterpart. The Mexican mother also appears to be more devoted to her children and concerned with raising them to conform to the traditional values than does the lower-lower-class Anglo mother.

Family relationships are dictated in large measure by culturally prescribed ties of mutual respect and responsibility. Nonfamilial peer relations for the Mexican male are colored by *machismo*, the need to prove oneself male by defending one's honor and outperforming other males at such masculine activities as fighting, drinking, and wenching. Outside the family, a certain degree of tension is likely to be involved when two males encounter one another, even if both belong to the same clique. *Machismo*, involving superiority of the man over the woman, also lessens the likelihood of friendships between men and women; male-female relations are almost exclusively romantic or sexual.

While there are little data on the subject, it appears that the Mexican child should have less trouble adjusting to school, because of his authoritarian upbringing and because the schools share the parents' values. However, the achievement-oriented girl is likely to have role conflicts.

III

MEXICAN-AMERICAN ("LATIN") CULTURE

The Mexican-American people of Texas, or "Latins," as we have chosen to call them, combine elements of lower-class Anglo and Mexican cultures. Unlike either Mexicans or Anglos, however, the Latin is a member of an alien minority group that has been subjected to considerable overt and covert discrimination. Over the years, this discrimination has played a significant role in shaping his personality.

Historical and Sociological Factors

Unlike the natives of Central Mexico, the original Indian inhabitants of Texas and the Southwestern United States had not developed elaborate urban civilizations by the time the Spanish arrived. The area was first explored by expeditionary forces searching for the fabled Seven Cities of Cibola. Later, scattered missions were established. In contrast to Central Mexico, the area remained sparsely populated, more primitive, and under looser governmental control.

In the 1820s, North Americans, attracted by the abundance of fertile land, obtained government grants to settle in Texas. Under the terms of the federal colonization law, grants were made to *empresarios*, who agreed to bring 100 immigrant families with them, all of whom would become Mexican citizens. The bulk of each grant was to be divided among these families. Several of the inducements given these *empresarios* were the rights to have private police forces, to set tariff barriers, and to introduce Negro slavery. The rapid colonization that resulted soon led to serious political and social conflicts between the Anglo colonists and Mexican residents. Eventually, the special privileges were revoked and the central government under Santa Anna sought to establish firm military control over Texas. This led to the Texas Revolution, which began in 1835 with the Battle of Gonzales, preceded by military incidents in 1826 and 1832, and, after the Battle of the Alamo, ended with the capture of Santa Anna at the Battle of San Jacinto in 1836. From this time on, the roles of Anglo and Latin were reversed. The Anglos controlled the government, and the Latins became a disenfranchised minority group.

Whereas the Spanish conquest of the Aztecs had been followed by a fusion of cultures, similar fusion did not take place in Texas. The Anglo culture did borrow to some extent from the Mexican, primarily in the adoption of corn-based dishes and the vocabulary and techniques of cattle-raising, but the gulf was too great for any true amalgamation to take place. Anglo Americans had always associated dark skin with inferiority, first in the Indian "savages" and later in the imported Negro slaves; it was not surprising that the slave-holding Texans regarded the Latin in similar fashion. Apart from skin color, there had been antipathy on the part of the English and, later, the Anglo Americans against the Spanish and their subjects for centuries, having its roots in the religious and economic conflicts that followed the Protestant Reformation and the discovery of the New World. While it would be ridiculous to attribute present-day ill feelings between Anglos and Latins to resentment over the Spanish Armada, Jenkin's Ear, or Morgan's raids on the Carribean,

nevertheless, if there had been less enmity between the English-
and Spanish-speaking peoples over the centuries it is likely that the
gulf between Latins and Anglos would be smaller today.

At present, the Latins are the third largest minority group in
the United States. Only a small percentage of the present Latin
population are descendants of the original settlers; most have immi-
grated from Mexico since 1900. Most Latins (85%) were born in
the United States, half of them to parents who were born in this
country. While Latins have historically been agricultural workers,
this pattern is changing and now 80 per cent live in urban areas
(Heller, 1966).

Like other minority groups, Latins have often been subjected to
shabby treatment by the Anglos. Until the Supreme Court handed
down the Delgado decision in 1948, Latins in Texas were required
to attend segregated schools, and *de facto* segregation is still not un-
common.[11] Throughout the Southwest, Latins have been and still are
economically exploited by Anglos, and have often been dealt with
harshly and repressively by police and Texas Rangers (Madsen,
1964; McWilliams, 1949; Rubel, 1966; Tuck, 1946). Like the Negroes, the Latins have suffered their share of lynchings; in the Los
Angeles "zoot-suit" riots in 1943 Latins were mobbed and beaten by
servicemen at the instigation of the press[12] and with the connivance
of the police. Similar incidents have taken place in other parts of
the country (McWilliams, 1949).

Most groups of recent immigrants start at the bottom of the socioeconomic ladder and with successive generations work themselves
up in prosperity and social acceptance. They also gradually move
away from the place where they entered the United States. The
Latins are unique among immigrant groups in that they have not
followed this pattern of social and geographic mobility. Despite the

[11] Segregation was also required in California until the Mendez decision in
1947. The rationale for segregation was that the presence of Spanish-speaking
students with poor English skills hindered the progress of the other students
(Heller, 1966). However, the fact that many restaurants, theatres, and pools
were also segregated suggests that the motives were not always purely educational (McWilliams, 1949).

[12] McWilliams (1949, p. 250) cites one newspaper editorial following the
Los Angeles violence as follows: "It is too bad the servicemen were called off
before they were able to complete the job. . . . Most of the citizens of the city
have been delighted by what is going on."

fact that they have been in the United States much longer than many other groups, they still occupy approximately the same low socio-economic position. In Texas, 14.4 per cent of the Anglo population is employed in professional or technical occupations, as compared with 3.9 per cent of the Latins; 17.3 per cent of the Anglos are managers or proprietors, but only 5.6 per cent of the Latins. On the other hand, 6.9 per cent of the Latins are farm laborers or foremen, compared with only 0.5 per cent of the Anglos, and 18.5 per cent of the Latins are laborers, compared with only 4.1 per cent of the Anglos (Heller, 1966, p. 13). Census data reveal that the median family income for Latins in Texas in 1960 was less than $3,000, and the median number of school years completed by Latin males was 6.2 years (Heller, 1966). While most minority groups show a trend for the second and third generations to be significantly better off than the more recent arrivals, this is not true of the Latins.

Latins have also shown little geographic mobility. The bulk of the Latin population of the United States lives in the Southwest in proximity to Mexico. Within the Southwest they live in separate parts of the towns. Heller states: "The residents refer to these enclaves as *colonia*, or *barrio* (neighborhood), but the dominant groups speak of them as 'Little Mexico,' 'Mextown,' or 'Spiktown.' About three fourths of all Mexican Americans in the United States live in the *colonias*" (1966, p. 21).

This pattern is not simply the result of Latin clannishness. Attempts to break out of the ghetto are resisted by the Anglos. A recent study of the 1960 census data showed Latins to be highly segregated from the Anglos in most of the 35 Southwestern cities examined, although the degree of segregation was less than for Negroes (Heller, 1966).

Most observers agree that the Latin population of the Southwest in general and Texas in particular is usually homogenous. Madsen (1964), however, has been able to discern some class differences among the Latins of South Texas. According to his analysis, the lower-lower class consists mostly of immigrants and first-generation Latins in urban areas, or all generations in rural Texas villages. Most are agricultural workers who are seasonally employed and earn about 50 cents per hour. This group is almost indistinguishable in its values from lower-class groups in Mexico. The lower-lower-class Latin values his membership in *la raza*, which sets him apart from the Anglos. He views agricultural work as a noble occupation in which he finds his place in nature caring for God's plants. Education is unimportant and children are encouraged to work in the fields; money is spent rather than saved.

The upper-lower class places a greater premium on upward mobility and education. The man in this class may work the year round in a factory or cannery. He feels it is good for his children to finish grade school and possibly even high school. While Spanish is spoken in the home, the children are not discouraged from learning English. He regards himself as a member of *la raza* and is unaware of the extent to which his values have been anglicized.

The Latin middle class started with the arrival of refugees from the Mexican Revolution who had sufficient capital to establish farms or small businesses; it has been augmented by returning servicemen who received a technical education in the service, followed, perhaps by additional training under the GI Bill. In the lower-middle class the man may have completed the equivalent of one or two years of high school and may work as a repairman, drive a truck, or run a store. He may own his home and a second-hand car. He wants his sons to complete high school but feels college would be not only useless but also presumptuous and likely to cause envy among the neighbors. The upper-middle-class Latins own small businesses or farms and may employ others. They respect education, and resentment of success is less common. Their sons want to do better than their fathers and may date Anglo girls.

Some Latins achieve upper-middle- or upper-class status by becoming physicians or lawyers. To do so, however, they often have to break their familial ties. While successful members of other groups, such as the Italians and Irish, often maintain their neighborhood ties and try to help others up, the upper-middle-class Latin is more likely to leave the *barrio*, renounce his Latin heritage, marry an Anglo girl, and not teach his children any Spanish.

Madsen's analysis suggests that increasing social status and increasing adoption of Anglo values go hand in hand. This is largely true, for, as we shall see in our analysis of achievement motivation, the traditional Mexican value system is a major hindrance to upward mobility in the United States. Madsen (1964) points out, however, that there is an extremely small, clannish, but nonetheless quite influential, upper class of wealthy Latins who look down on upper-class Anglos as being boorish and uncultured. Many are Hispanos, descendants of the original settlers. They cherish the culture of Europe and frequently send their children to European schools. This small group is an exception to the general rule that socioeconomic status and anglicization are correlated in the Latin community.

While the bulk of the Latin population in San Antonio is probably best classified as lower class, there are indications that this is changing. Military service removes many Latin boys from their families for two years or more and exposes them to Anglo ways in an unprecedented manner. When the boys return, they are more likely to be upwardly mobile, and veterans' programs have given them the means by which to act on these higher aspirations. The Latin community in Texas is at last becoming politically active through the formation of such groups as the League of United Latin American Citizens (LULAC) and through such direct action as the farm workers' attempt to form a union and strike for collective bargaining (La Huelga). These trends are signs that some of the traditions brought from Mexico and nourished through proximity to the Old Country may be gradually eroding. Nevertheless, the typical Latin's cultural roots still remain more strongly planted in the soil of Mexican than Anglo culture.

Family Relations

The nature of the Latin family relations varies somewhat as a function of the degree to which the family has been anglicized. In the Rio Grande Valley of Texas, adjacent to the Mexican border, family customs are quite similar to those in a rural Mexican village. The father is the *jefe de la casa* and is obeyed and respected (although perhaps resented) by the rest of the family. In an extended family, the patriarchal system is followed, with the eldest male having final authority.[13] Ties of familial obligation are strongly adhered to, and the people often believe that there would be divine retribution (*castigo de Dios*) if they should be disloyal to the family. When there is a conflict, ties of blood are those that are honored. For example, if a man's widowed mother is living with him and his wife, in case of any dispute he would naturally be obligated to side with the mother, for she bore him and suckled him. Of course, both women would respect his authority as final.

[13] Rubel (1966) writes of one man who was 47 before he dared to smoke in the presence of his father.

As in Mexico, the rural Latin wife is protected and shielded. She is expected to be passive, accepting, and totally devoted to her family. The children, as noted, are expected to be loyal and obedient, respecting and deferring to their parents. According to Madsen (1964, p. 17): "The most important role of the individual is his familial role and the family is the most valued situation in Mexican-American society. . . . The worst sin a Latin can conceive is to violate his obligations to his parents and siblings."

In urban areas, such as Los Angeles, these cultural traditions have weakened somewhat. With greater Anglicization, children are more independent of the parents. This is particularly true when it is necessary for the family to interact with the Anglo world. If the father does not speak English, the eldest son may have to act as an interpreter for the family and explain the situation to the family. When this occurs, the son has usurped one of the duties of the father and there is apt to be some bitterness on the father's part.

With greater Anglicization, the role of the woman is apt to change as well. If the family gets more eager for money and the possessions that money will buy, the wife may leave the home and go to work as a domestic or as a waitress. When she contributes to the family income, she is apt to express herself more strongly as to how it should be spent. Anglicization is also likely to make her less tolerant of her husband's philandering. Thus, contact with Anglo cultural institutions may erode the unquestioning deference to the husband's authority, which is the bedrock of the Mexican family. However, it is not likely to wash it away completely.

While a good deal of anthropological and sociological work has been done among the Latins of the small border town (Madsen, 1964; Rubel, 1966) and of Los Angeles (Heller, 1966; McWilliams, 1949), intermediate societies, such as that of San Antonio, have received less attention. It is likely that the San Antonio Latin family is less traditional than those of the Valley villages; however, it is probably considerably less Anglicized than the Los Angeles Latin family. For example, while *curanderos* are prevalent in San Antonio, Heller (1966) makes no mention of folk medicine in her description of Latin life in Los Angeles.

In the insulated predominantly Latin village, there is relatively little culture conflict. In the larger towns and cities, it is virtually impossible for the children not to have conflicting demands placed upon them. The typical focal point for such conflict is the school, for as we have noted, the school is the primary agent of acculturation. In Mexico the school shared the parents' values to a great extent, but the Latin has much less in common with the goals of the middle-class Anglo school system. For the child raised in a traditional family, there is a fundamental, uncompromising conflict between the demands of family loyalty and the demands of the school. As we shall see, this conflict has implications that influence the entire Latin life style and that lie at the root of the Latins' stalemated socioeconomic progress.

Modal Latin Personality Characteristics

HONOR: *Machismo*

Like his Mexican cousins, the Latin greatly values honor and manliness. In fact, it often appears as if he clings to these values all the more tenaciously because he lives among the Anglos. His membership in *la raza* and his honor seem to compensate in some degree for the exploitation he must endure at the hands of the Anglos. Loss of honor would mean loss of his highly valued identity as a Latin.

As in Mexico, *machismo* demands that a man be independent. As one Latin put it, "To us a man is a man because he acts like a man. And he is respected for this. It does not matter if he is short or tall, ugly or handsome, rich or poor. These things are unimportant. When he stands on his own two feet as he should, then he is looked up to" (Madsen, 1964, p. 18). This perceptive comment illustrates how the Latin, in spite of low socioeconomic status and prejudice, can achieve self-respect and the respect of his fellows through manliness.

In addition to showing manliness through aggression, virility, and drinking, the Latin shows it through his sense of honor. This fixation on honor has retarded the progress of the Latin community in numerous ways. A major part of manly honor is the independence of each individual male. The Latins say that each individual is a world unto himself (*a cada cabeza un mundo*). They are therefore reluctant to enter into entangling alliances or work together as a group, for to admit that one needs the help of others would reflect on masculinity. This reluctance to incur any obligation also makes the Latin unwilling to use the resources of social agencies. As a result, there are few Latin community action groups or social service agencies, and Latins have been reluctant to organize local labor unions. Above the community level, there are no national organizations comparable to the N.A.A.C.P. and the other Negro civil rights organizations.

Honor makes the Latin reluctant to take a firm stand on any principle or issue. There is no disgrace in remaining uncommitted. However, taking a stand leads to conflicts with those who hold different views and also makes it possible to suffer great loss of respect if one should compromise or alter one's position. Anglos reared in an environment that emphasizes taking a position and then making whatever compromises are necessary often find it difficult to appreciate the way the Latin feels on this point. To the Latin, commitment is like a bullfight. There is no disgrace in remaining in the stands and watching. However, once one enters the ring to fight the bull, there is no honorable way to retreat until the bull or the man is dead. The prudent man, therefore, remains uncommitted.

The Latin is also reluctant to do anything that might conceivably reflect on the honor of others lest he provoke retaliation. For example, he is unwilling to do anything that might arouse the envy of his fellows. If he buys a better car or a new suit this could be interpreted as an attempt on his part to make himself better than his peers. If he spends money on useless higher education for his children, his neighbors may regard this as an attempt on his part to imply that he and his children are somehow better than they are (Madsen, 1964). If the Latin does arouse the envy of his neighbors, they are likely to stop speaking to him and he may become the target of gossip and ridicule. There may even be direct attacks, such as vandalism of his property or the casting of evil spells by a *brujo*. As Madsen says, "While the Anglos try to keep up with the Joneses, the Latins try to keep the Garcias down to their own level" (1964, p. 22).

Foster (1967) has suggested that many Mexicans see the world as a closed system with inadequate amounts of love, manliness, honor, security, and happiness, as well as finite amounts of goods. Given this viewpoint, the happier or better off one's neighbor is, the unhappier and poorer one must be, since there is not enough to go around. Therefore, any positive gain arouses envy and resentments.

Thus, *machismo* manifests itself not only in drinking or sexuality, but also in subtle ways that undermine the unity of the Latin community, making it less assertive and less confident. While other minority groups have worked their way up through joint political and economic action, *machismo* and envy have divided the community to such an extent that progress has been seriously retarded. As one Latin said, "We are a people turned against ourselves. The greatness God intended for us will never be ours for we are too busy devouring each other" (Madsen, 1964, p. 23).

Juvenile Delinquency

Most of those people who write about Latin culture comment on the frequency with which Latin men and boys get into trouble with the law. There is little doubt that Latins are overrepresented in police ledgers. In Los Angeles, 34 per cent of the juvenile delinquents in 1956 were Latin, and the per capita rate for Latins was three times that for Anglos (Sutherland & Cressey, 1966). Of 718 delinquency petitions filed in Bexar County [San Antonio] Juvenile Court in 1959, 478 (67%) were for Latins.

To some extent this may be a result of police bias (McWilliams, 1949; Tuck, 1946). McWilliams (1949), an outspoken critic of police practices in relation to Latins, supports his contention that the police are biased with a quotation from an official report of the Los Angeles Sheriff's Department that suggests the Latin has certain innate tendencies that predispose him to crimes of violence. According to this report, while Anglos might occasionally resort to fisticuffs, "this Mexican element considers all that to be a sign of weakness, and all he knows and feels is a desire to use a knife or some lethal weapon. In other words, his desire is to kill, or at least let blood. . . . When there is added to *this inborn characteristic* that has come down through the ages, the use of liquor, then we certainly have crimes of violence" (McWilliams, 1949, p. 234).

In addition to incurring possible police bias, being a Latin means that one is likely to be a member of the lower class, have a low-status, poorly paying job, live in a rundown neighborhood, and be subjected to prejudice and discrimination—all factors associated with an increased delinquency rate (Heller, 1966; Tuck, 1946). Moreover, traditional behavior in itself renders Latins more vulnerable to arrest. If a Latin boy fails to go to school, drinks, or has sexual intercourse he has broken the law. When he hangs around with the members of his clique he is liable to be arrested for loitering. If he defends his honor or that of his family he is subject to arrest for assault. Thus, conformity with Latin cultural mores often necessitates deviation from the Anglo middle-class mores embodied in the juvenile and penal codes of the various states (Heller, 1966).

RELIGIOUS VALUES

Religion, both formal and informal, plays a more important role in the Latin community than it does in the Anglo. As might be expected, the religious values of the Latins are similar to those of the Mexicans, with some important differences.

Most Latins are members of the Roman Catholic Church; however, Protestantism is more prevalent than it is in Mexico. A study of the Latin community in San Jose, California, found that 70 per cent were Catholic, 26 per cent Protestant, and 4 per cent unaffiliated (Heller, 1966). Communities nearer the border would probably have fewer Protestants. Whether Catholic or Protestant, Latins tend to go to their own churches; few attend churches in which a large proportion of the congregation is Anglo (Heller, 1966).

At first glance the Latin Catholic may appear less religious than the Anglo Catholic. He is more likely to be anticlerical and to attend Mass infrequently, leaving the devotions to the women. While he scrupulously observes the sacrament of baptism, the sacrament of marriage is more apt to be overlooked (Heller, 1966). In this respect, the Latin's attitude toward the church resembles that found in many Mediterranean countries, while the Anglo Catholic's is closer to that found in Ireland.

However, religion probably pervades the Latin Catholic's life even more than it does the Anglo Catholic's. For the rural agricultural worker, particularly, God is always close by, determining everything that happens. One Latin said, "We see God in the beauty around us. He is in the water, the mountains, and the smallest of the plants. We live with God while the Anglos lock Him into Heaven" (Madsen, 1964, p. 17).

Among the lower classes, that feeling of divine determinism is quite fatalistic. According to Madsen (1964, p. 17):

Acceptance and appreciation of things as they are constitute primary values of *La Raza*. Because God, rather than man, is viewed as controlling events, the Latin lacks the future orientation of the Anglo and his passion for planning ahead. Many Mexican-Americans would consider it presumptive to try to plan for tomorrow because human beings are merely servants of God and it is He who plans the future.

Thus, the Latin feels that one must resign oneself and accept God's will. The only way one might possibly alter one's fate is through prayer. Like his Mexican cousin, the Latin may ask the saints to intercede for him, or he may try to bargain, promising the saint a candle in return for a favor. While Texas Latins used to punish the images of the saints in order to coerce them into granting favors, this custom is now dying out (Madsen, 1964).

The belief in divine determinism also leads to a belief in folk medicine and a reliance upon *curanderos*. It is obvious to many Latins that the *curandero* can do more than the physician, since the *curandero* works with God; the *curandero* can do even more than a priest, for while the priest's knowledge comes from books, the *curandero*'s power comes directly from God (Madsen, 1964). Such fatalism and reliance on folk medicine is most common among the members of the lower-lower class, who are closest to the land and who live nearest to Mexico. However, even in urban centers like San Antonio and Austin these practices continue, although the Anglo community remains largely unaware of them. With increasing Anglicization, of course, there is a decrease in this magical-religious practice.

PROJECTION AND DENIAL

Associated with beliefs in the importance of honor and in divine determinism, is a conspicuous tendency to use projection and denial. The Latin rarely blames himself as an individual for his misfortunes, although he may blame the sins of his people. If he gets drunk it is the fault of his host for serving too much wine. If he is found riding in a stolen car it is the fault of the man who provided temptation by leaving the car there to be stolen.[14] Since it is natural for men to be unable to resist temptation, it is the temptor who must be the guilty party (Madsen, 1964).

[14] For example, when Austin police asked one 15-year-old Latin boy where he had obtained the $6,000 sports car he was driving, he replied, "I found it." He then explained that he was searching for the owner in order to return his property lest someone succumb to the temptation to steal such a valuable automobile.

Feelings of Inferiority

In our discussion of Mexican culture, we noted Ramos' (1962) hypothesis that the Mexican is suffering from an unconscious inferiority complex, and that *machismo* is the result of an attempt to deny inferiority by proclaiming superiority. Latin culture differs from the Mexican somewhat in that there is a greater conscious awareness of feelings of inadequacy. While the Mexican is likely to believe that God has planned a great and glorious destiny for *la raza*, the Latin is more inclined to believe that although God once planned this, it will not come about, because the Latins have sinned. Similarly, the Latins share the Mexicans' reverence for the Virgin of Guadalupe, but feel that since she is in Mexico she has little time to worry about Texans (Madsen, 1964).

It is likely that discrimination by the Anglos has caused much of this pessimism, although the Latins rarely blame the Anglos for holding them back. Madsen reports they agree that Anglos exploit and take advantage of their weakness, but feel it is their own fault they are weak in the first place (1964). This attitude would appear to be a reversal of the tendency to project blame noted above. However, acceptance of collective guilt also implies that individual efforts are futile and that the individual is not responsible for his own misfortune.

Academic and Vocational Adjustment

The Latin shares many of the problems of the lower-class Anglo in coping with the middle-class Anglo school system. Like the lower-class Anglo, his family experiences have left him poorly prepared for school. His middle-class teacher is unlikely to understand his needs and is apt to be threatened by his impulsivity, aggressiveness, and sexuality. He lives in the present rather than the future, and he is not convinced of the value of an education.

In addition to these problems that he shares with the lower-class Anglo, the Latin has other handicaps as well. When he enters school he may find that his cultural heritage is in marked opposition to the demands of the school. His dark skin may subject him to prejudice. He is likely to suffer from a language handicap if Spanish has been the primary language at home. Later, the restricted range of vocational opportunities that are open to Latins may sap his motivation.

These obstacles, coupled with Latin fatalism and an unwillingness to attempt something in which there is a likelihood of failure, have retarded Latin educational and vocational progress.

ACADEMIC SKILLS OF THE LOWER-CLASS LATIN CHILD

The Latin child and the Anglo school are often basically incompatible. The longer he is in school, the more poorly the Latin child does, relative to the Anglo children. Even his IQ gets progressively lower, and he is much more likely to drop out than are his Anglo peers (Heller, 1966).

In part, this is the result of an initial language handicap. However, even if the Latin child is fluent in both English and Spanish, his vocabulary in either language is likely to be poorer than that of the child who knows only English. Test scores provide one yardstick of this handicap. Darcy (1946) administered the Stanford-Binet Intelligence Test and the Atkins Object-Fitting Test to 106 monolingual and 106 bilingual preschool children. She found that the bilingual sample had a mean IQ of 97.5 on the Atkins test, as compared with 89 for the monolingual children. Thus, on this nonlanguage test the bilingual children were superior. However, on the Stanford-Binet, a highly verbal test that predicts school performance quite well, the bilingual children had a mean IQ of only 90.7, as compared with the monolinguals' mean IQ of 98.7. This difference on the Binet shows how bilingualism is likely to impede the ability to succeed in the conventional Anglo school. The Anglo school rarely makes concessions to the Latin child's language difficulties. Classes are taught solely in English and there is rarely translation. Thus, inadequate English is likely to produce deficiencies not only in reading and spelling but also in other subjects like arithmetic.[15]

The lower IQ scores obtained by Latin children constitute a problem in their own right. As Heller (1966, p. 91) points out:

If the IQ scores of these children, as compared with those of Anglo Americans, were treated as indicators of initial disadvantages in terms of orientation and skills necessary for effective functioning in our society, then school programs probably could be designed to overcome these initial differences. But teachers tend to approach these scores as signs of fixed limits in innate ability.

[15] Legislation has recently been introduced which would permit some instruction in Spanish for Latin children in Texas schools.

This can result in less effort by the teacher because she feels that the child is incapable of learning. It has even resulted in the Latin child being placed in a class for the mentally retarded (Black, 1963).

In many ways, the Anglo school is as poorly equipped to meet the needs of the Latin child as the child is to meet the demands of the school. Bullock and Singleton (1966) have pointed out that Latin children are generally taught by middle-class WASP (white, Anglo-Saxon, Protestant) teachers who live outside the area and who have little understanding of their pupils. By and large, they tolerate less deviation in attire and behavior from their Latin pupils and thus demand greater conformity from the Latins than the Anglos. The textbooks they use are also biased toward Anglo use. Surveying some 116 texts authorized for use in California, Bullock and Singleton (1966) found that almost every illustration was of Anglos. In history books, little mention was made of the contributions of the Spanish and Latins in the exploration and development of the Southwest. Some school counselors routinely steer all Latins into vocational courses that teach obsolete skills.

Few Latin families object to the schools' attempts to teach English. However, many schools demand that the child speak English at home as well. Here the school places itself in direct opposition to the conservative family's desire for the child to cherish his cultural heritage. The child is placed in the difficult position of having to disobey either his teacher or his parents.

Occasionally, confronted with this sort of situation, a well-meaning teacher sallies forth to educate the family on why it is necessary for the child to stop speaking Spanish. In doing so she unwittingly breaks every Latin precept of good behavior. Uninvited, she trespasses on the family's property and demands that they let her intrude into the privacy of their home. Once there, she does not engage in polite conversation but instead insults the family by telling them how they should raise their son to be an Anglo. The fact that she, a woman, presumes to give advice to the father, a man, is all that is needed to complete the disaster. The *jefe de la casa* can only conclude from such behavior that she is stupid or rude; in either case, he is more likely than ever to oppose whatever she demanded, for one could not give in to a stupid, rude Anglo woman and be much of a man.

MOTIVATION OF THE LATIN CHILD

When the Anglo school teacher attempts to persuade the Latin family to alter its ways, the argument she usually advances is that this will help the student's educational progress. However, she fails to realize that the traditional Latin family is often not convinced of the value of an academic education. They feel that the education of the child to be manly or feminine, loyal to his family and his cultural heritage, and polite and respectful to his elders, is far more important than learning to read or do arithmetic (Madsen, 1964).

The usual reason advanced for educating the child is that it will help him get a better job. In the case of a girl, this may be an argument *against* education, for it implies she might become masculine and hence less marriageable. But even for a son, this argument may not be effective. In the first place, the father may not want his son to achieve more than he himself has (Heller, 1966). If the son does try to rise higher, he might be accused of trying to disgrace his father. Assuming, however, that the father does not mind his son's getting a better job, it may still be absurd to think that an education could aid in this. Job opportunities are limited for Latins, and parents cite numerous examples of Latins who have gotten a high school education and have not been able to advance vocationally (Heller, 1966; Tuck, 1946).

Honor also intrudes here. School is highly competitive, and to engage in this competition carries with it the twin dangers of arousing envy if one succeeds or of being disgraced if one fails. It is much safer not to try. Madsen (1964, p. 45) quoted a Latin graduate of The University of Texas to illustrate some of the conflicts that are engendered by high aspirations:

It's only a miracle that I went to a university. We had the money because my father has a good job with the county but I wanted to go to the University of Texas in Austin and that's a long way away from home. My mother and my sisters said they couldn't stand it without me for four years. My father was afraid I would disgrace myself. Moreover, I was frankly afraid to go off on my own but I did.

The fact that many Latins would prefer not to have an education to being disgraced is illustrated by Heller's (1966) finding that many Latins dropped out of high school just before graduation. She quoted one Latin boy as explaining, "When you graduate, the senior luncheon, the sweater, the prom and other things cost about 200 dollars. Many boys figure that there is no use going on with school if you are not able to afford these things" (Heller, 1966, pp. 55–56). The advantages of a high school diploma are insignificant compared with the disgrace of graduating without taking part in all the rituals.

This contrast between the value placed on education in Anglo and Latin culture is reflected in the significantly lower educational aspirations that Latin parents have for their children. A recent study by Shannon and Krass compared the educational aspirations of Latins, Anglos, and Negroes in Racine, Wisconsin. The results of that study (Heller, 1966, p. 40) showed the Latins to have the lowest educational aspirations for their children:

> The questionnaire responses of the recent Racine study seem to be consistent with the above observations based on qualitative data. Mexican American as well as Anglo American and Negro parents were asked how much schooling they would "like" their children to have. Only 25 percent of the Mexican Americans, in contrast to 50 percent of the Negroes and 67 percent of the Anglo Americans, mentioned college. When questioned whether they would be satisfied with various levels of education actually reached by their children, more Mexican Americans said that they would be content with a minimal amount than did either the Anglo Americans or the Negroes (37 percent of the Mexican Americans but only 6 percent of the Anglo Americans thought that they would be satisfied if their children received only a junior high school education). And finally, a substantially higher percentage of Mexican Americans than either Anglo Americans or Negroes felt that it would be "practically impossible," considering their financial condition, to keep their children in school beyond the ninth grade.

To be sure, not all Latin parents are opposed to education. Although they are in the minority, a substantial number of Latin parents have adopted Anglo values to the extent that they wish their children to succeed in school and possibly seek higher education. However, such *inglesado* students find themselves faced with problems similar to those confronting lower-class Anglo boys who are successful students. In order to achieve the good grades that his Anglicized family demands, the Latin boy must forsake the corner group in favor of his studies and engage in competitive behavior that may earn the enmity of his peers. At the same time, because he is a Latin he may not be able to find friends among the Anglo students who share his outlook. As a result, he can be rejected and isolated. As more parents and students become anglicized, this becomes less of a problem, for the *inglesado* students form their own subgroup (Madsen, 1964).

Such adoption of Anglo educational values is unusual, and while our own data show that Latin students are going farther in school than their parents did, nevertheless, as Heller (1966) so succinctly stated, a Latin youth's ambition to go to college represents a much greater deviation from Latin cultural values than does delinquency. Most Latin students are not interested in the goals set by the Anglo schools and would be unable to compete effectively for them if they were interested. "To summarize the situation as it exists now, Mexican American children are not prepared at home for the experiences which await them in school and the schools are not prepared or equipped to receive and hold these children" (Heller, 1966, p. 52).

VOCATIONAL ASPIRATIONS OF THE LATIN YOUTH

When the Latin youth enters the job market place he has several handicaps. As we have seen, his upbringing has often failed to instill in him the individualism, assertiveness, and devotion to the job that are prized by employers. He is likely to regard work as a necessary evil instead of a virtue. Trained to be dependent on the family, he has had little experience making independent decisions and is not likely to have learned the discipline and time management necessary for success in the Anglo business world (Heller, 1966, pp. 38–39).

Moreover, he is usually less likely than the Anglo to prize "success." While he respects the "big man" who achieves, to the Latin, the way in which success is achieved is more important than the achievement itself (Tuck, 1946). If success entails dishonor or breaking family ties, it is not valued (Madsen, 1964; Tuck, 1946).

For example, a high school teacher interviewed by Madsen (1964, p. 45) said:

> My sister had a beautiful voice and she had the chance to accept a fellowship to go to New York for study and training. But our father had to consult with his brothers and sisters, all ten of them, and the decision was that New York was too far away and too full of dangers for a young girl . . .

Simmons (1952, p. 261), who compared Anglos and Latins in South Texas, concluded that among the Latins there is "no motiva-

tion to mobility in the occupational structure since equivalent satis-
factions are obtained from sources within the Mexican-American
group."

The reluctance to arouse envy also handicaps the Latin employee.
Latins in South Texas are reluctant to achieve greater material success than their neighbors, and if they do get a raise or purchase a
new television, they try to conceal it from their friends. "Mexican-
Americans value inconspicuous consumption as highly as Anglos
value the conspicuous display of wealth" (Madsen, 1964, p. 22).
According to Madsen, Latins themselves realize that envy is destruc-
tive and privately admit that it has been one of the chief obstacles
in the material progress of their people (1964).

The Latin who does get an education and seeks a better job may
find that his parents were correct when they said an education is
useless, for being a Latin closes the doors of many potential employers, particularly in Texas. According to one educator cited by
Madsen (1964, p. 108):

> Unless the qualified Latin gets out of the valley, he doesn't have much
> chance. When a firm has its choice of a Latin or an Anglo with equal
> ability, the Anglo gets the job every time unless the firm is having financial
> difficulties. Then, the employers hire the Latin at an unfair salary and talk
> about how broadminded they are. I tell my young Latin friends who have
> ability or training to get out and go to Chicago or Los Angeles. But, being
> Latin, they don't want to leave their families so they stay here and grow
> bitter.

The Latins' sense of honor makes it difficult for them to overcome
such bias. If Latins feel they are not welcome, they withdraw; if
they feel they are not being treated fairly, they quit. Being proud
and sensitive, they are reluctant to force themselves into positions
in which they feel they are not wanted, nor will they complain to a
superior or an authority about perceived injustices. They have little
sympathy with the protests, sit-ins, and demonstrations of the Negro
civil rights movement. As a result, there has been greater harmony
between Anglos and Latins than between Anglos and Negroes in
recent years; however, the Negroes' assertiveness has succeeded in
opening up more opportunities for both Negroes and Latins than
has the Latins' passive acceptance (Heller, 1966).

While most writers have commented on the Latins' low level of vocational aspirations, Heller (1966) maintains that significant changes are taking place in the achievement motivation of young Latins. While there has been little progress for the past three or four generations, she thinks the present younger generation is much more achievement oriented, and, therefore, the next few decades are likely to witness socioeconomic progress similar to that of other immigrant groups.

Heller based these conclusions on her own studies of the aspirations of Latin high school seniors in Los Angeles. By using youthful subjects, Heller felt she obtained a truer picture of the current aspiration level than investigators who used older subjects. She found that, while 42 per cent of her teenage boys' fathers had unskilled or semi-skilled jobs, only 4 per cent of the boys expected that they too would have such low-level jobs. Only 2 per cent of the boys' fathers were in professional or semiprofessional occupations, but 35 per cent of the boys aspired to this level. While the absolute level of aspirations of the Latin students was still substantially below that of Anglo youths in general, these differences were slight when social class was controlled. It appears likely that if Heller had analyzed her data in terms of direction of mobility, as did Douvan and Adelson (1958), or in terms of relative aspiration level, as did Sherif and Sherif (1965), she might have found even greater similarity between the patterns for lower-class Latins and Anglos.

Heller found that these upwardly mobile vocational aspirations were matched by increased educational aspirations as well. Although only 5 per cent of the Latin boys' fathers had attended college, 44 per cent of the boys themselves intended to do so. Heller also found similar signs of Anglicization when 90 per cent of the Latin boys she queried indicated that they would not be satisfied to do merely well enough to stay in their chosen occupation but would have to do as well or better than the average person in that vocation. Indeed, one third indicated that they would never be successful enough to relax their efforts. Moreover, they also showed signs of the toughness, ability to defer gratification, and willingness to work hard and try new methods that characterize the achievement-oriented Anglo.

In order to evaluate these data properly, it must be pointed out that Heller's sample was not a random sample of Latin youth. In the first place, it is likely that it is the more achievement-oriented

Latins who migrate to Los Angles. A similar study of high school students in rural communities closer to the Mexican border would probably have revealed lower aspiration levels. Secondly, by using high school seniors, Heller confined her investigation to a relatively high-achievement group, for all those who had left school were automatically excluded.

Despite these limitations on the generality of Heller's findings, it is still noteworthy that a substantial group of Latin youths with such high ambitions does exist. These achievement-oriented young Latins will not only aid the socioeconomic progress of the Latin community directly, but will also help to create a climate of opinion in which achievement becomes more respectable. However, if these young Latins do not obtain jobs commensurate with their ability and ambitions, then instead of becoming success models for younger Latins they will become examples of the futility of hard work and lofty goals. As was the case with the lower-class Anglos, much depends on the job opportunities that society makes available to this generation of qualified Latins.

Peer Relations

As with familial and personality patterns, the nature of peer relations varies as a function of traditionalism. In the *barrios* of the rural villages near the Mexican border, patterns quite similar to those in Mexico may be observed. Here each family is an island unto itself. The home is a sacred private place for the protection of the wife and daughters. Neighborhood relations are tinged with suspicion and a visit is regarded as an intrusion. Feuds are frequent and there is considerable gossip about people in the community who may be using witchcraft against their neighbors. Only close family members are to be trusted, although, as mentioned before, this is alleviated somewhat through the godparent system (*compadrazgo*) (Rubel, 1966).

While the women remain at home, the male members of the family spend much of their free time in the company of other boys and men the same age. These male cliques are called *palomillas*[16] in

16 *Palomilla* literally means "moth." The term arose because the ever changing composition of the peer groups was similar to the fluttering of moths around a light.

Texas, and, like the male cliques in Mexico, they are the scene for such masculine activities as discussing sports, drinking, boasting, verbal dueling, and sexual adventures. While some *palomillas* may engage in delinquent activities, they are not delinquent gangs in the usual sense (Rubel, 1966). Indeed, the *palomilla* may serve to prevent delinquency (Sherif & Sherif, 1964). The *palomilla* is an extremely informal institution and the membership is quite fluid. This is partly because close friends can become enemies overnight as a result of some insult. Informality also serves to preserve the independence of the individual Latin male.

Membership in the *palomilla* is not supposed to interfere with one's family obligations, which should come before anything else. However, the Latin differs from the Anglo somewhat in his definition of his obligations to the family. If he spends the majority of his free time with the *palomilla* rather than at home, and if he may occasionally have some sex affairs, this is not construed as interfering with his obligations to his wife or children. If he failed to protect or support them or failed to tell his wife how to manage the home, this would be another matter. Indeed, Rubel (1966) tells of one man who was spending so much time with his wife and children that his parents and siblings urged him to spend more time with his *palomilla*, lest he be thought unmanly.

While the activities of the *palomilla* should not interfere with family obligations, observations indicate that this is not always the case. After observing one teenage *palomilla*, Sherif and Sherif (1964, p. 29) reported, "Of the numerous occasions when the boys had to make a decision between joining in a group activity and family obligation, or church duties . . . going with the group was by far the most frequent resolution."

As in Mexico, social relations in the *palomilla* are much more informal than those in the home. It is partly because of this that male members of the family tend to avoid one another outside the home. The father naturally has a different clique of cronies than his sons, but brothers, too, will tend to avoid each other and may even belong to different *palomillas*. This arrangement avoids awkwardness, for the banter that is a part of the *palomilla* could be regarded as an insult if another family member is present. For example, Rubel (1966) reports that while it was all right for one boy to tease another

about his laziness in the group, this became insulting when the
other boy's father was present, for it implied that the father had not
raised his son properly.

In less traditional communities, the folkways are more anglicized.
People are less likely to run to a *brujo* (witch) at the slightest insult, and there is apt to be less suspiciousness outside the family.
Still, the Anglo observer would find the atmosphere more formal
and the interpersonal relations more touchy than he is accustomed
to. He would also note that the roles of men and women were
defined more sharply than in the Anglo community.

As one moves away from the predominantly Latin village, there
is likely to be increasing integration of public facilities, schools, businesses, and neighborhoods, in about that order. However, even
when institutions like schools bring Latins into proximity to Anglos,
the Latins associate predominantly with one another. This is partly
because the Latins are reluctant to risk Anglo prejudice. It is also
because Anglos and Latins do not understand each others' rules for
social intercourse and may unwittingly insult each other by over-
familiarity on the one side or oversensitivity on the other. An even
more fundamental barrier is language. In Texas, a mixture of Spanish
and English called "Tex-Mex" is the principal language among
many Latins who may speak English only formally and with an
accent. According to Heller (1966, p. 30):

> This is a cause of considerable embarrassment and often results in their
> feeling self-conscious when in contact with Anglo-Americans. Frequently
> Mexican American youths are deficient in informal English: they do not
> know how to "kid" or use "small talk," so important in everyday en-
> counters.

It is in the peer contacts of adolescence that the strain of living
in two cultures is likely to become most acute. The Latin boy may
be faced with rejection by Anglo classmates or with problems in
finding a job. However, the *palomilla* gives him a culturally approved social outlet where he can find acceptance and respect even
in the face of Anglo disdain. Life is more difficult for the adolescent
Latin girl. The protected feminine role that is culturally prescribed
is in marked contrast to the freedom enjoyed by her Anglo classmates. If she is attractive, Anglo boys who have little to do with

Latin boys might become interested in her. Such questions as whether she may use make-up, whether she may wear short skirts, or whether she may go out alone with a boy and if so at what time she must return can become major sources of conflict between the Anglicized Latin girl and her traditional parents. One indication of this strain is the fact that of 634 girls referred to the Bexar County [San Antonio] Juvenile Court in 1959, 380 (60%) were Latin. Almost half of these Latin girls (185) had been referred for running away from home.

Summary of Latin Cultural Patterns

Despite the fact that Latins have lived in what is now the United States much longer than other groups of foreign extraction, they have achieved much less socioeconomic progress. Unlike other immigrant groups, there has not been a steady rise in power or income with successive generations.

The reasons for this lie in Mexican cultural values, which are continually nourished by close contact with the "Old Country." These include an emphasis on honor that makes Latins unwilling to partake in joint community action, resignation to the inability of the individual to alter that which God has planned for him, an emphasis on conformity and loyalty to the family, and envy of successful people coupled with attempts to hinder their progress. Pride in their cultural heritage causes Latins to resist the attempts of the Anglo community in general and the school in particular to alter their ways. The school and the family often engage in a power struggle for the child's loyalty. If the child follows the dictates of the school, he risks rejection by family and friends; if he conforms to the traditional cultural mores, he is likely to be poorly educated and unable or unwilling to compete in the vocational market place. Recent research indicates that in the large urban centers, such as Los Angeles, Latin parents and their children are becoming more achievement oriented. However, the ambitious Latin can be blocked by discrimination.

Since many Latin habit patterns are alien to those of the Anglo community, the Latin is likely to run afoul of the law. The male peer group, or *palomilla*, which lounges around the corner whistling at girls and drinking beer, is often regarded as a delinquent gang by the police. Latin sensitivity predisposes men to aggressive behavior that is not tolerated by the law. Thus, the Latin may find himself in trouble more frequently than do his Anglo or Mexican counterparts, who are not members of a minority group.

In the last two decades the solidarity of the Latin community has been broken by the conscription of Latin boys for military service and the integration of many formerly segregated schools and public facilities. One result of this has been increasing Anglicization. This may have the effect of increasing the Latin middle class and raising the socioeconomic level of the Latin community. At the same time, it is likely to cause more internal stress and conflict, for in order to achieve material success the Latin may have to sacrifice some of his devotion to his family and his culture.

CHAPTER 4

THE PROBLEM

The juvenile delinquent is a young person who has been labelled as antisocial by the local adult middle-class society, acting through its police and its courts. Perhaps the delinquent, in turn, has classified society as antijuvenile. In any case, a large body of research and theory has proliferated on the nature of the juvenile delinquent. Most of this research has focused on lower-class delinquents in the urban areas of the Northeastern United States. Some studies have compared delinquents with control groups of lower-class nondelinquents; others have used middle-class comparison groups; and still others have simply described the delinquent sample in a quasi-anthropological fashion. Some of the theories have been empirically based; others have been rationally derived.

Our description of the three cultures, in addition to setting the context for the present study, also served to focus our attention on two of the important issues to be confronted. First, it was apparent that many of the characteristics of the lower-class Anglo, as noted in Chapter 3, were quite similar to the description of the typical juvenile delinquent in Chapter 2. Indeed, Miller (1958) viewed delinquency as stemming directly from the focal concerns of the lower class. We must pose the question whether these "delinquent characteristics" are simply artifacts of failures to control adequately for lower-class status in some investigations, or do they differentiate the lower-class delinquent from the lower-class nondelinquent? This question has important practical implications. If there is little or no difference between the culture of delinquency and the culture

of poverty, then it would behoove us to devote our primary efforts
to attacking the problems of the poor, with a reasonable expectation
that this would also solve the problem of juvenile crime. If, on the
other hand, the problems of poverty and delinquency are separate
and distinct, then separate and distinct programs are required.

This leads us to the second basic issue. Research on the prevention or rehabilitation of delinquent behavior patterns has relied to a
great extent on demonstration projects. For example, the Boston
Juvenile Court has devoted much effort to the development of its
"citizenship training group" program and has reported considerable
success (Boston Juvenile Court, 1961). This program has been widely copied throughout the United States and in other nations, based
on the reasonable assumption that if a method works for delinquents
in Boston, it ought to work for delinquents elsewhere. Implicit in
this formulation is the further assumption that delinquency is a
relatively universal phenomenon: the punk in Boston is basically
the same as the *pachuco* in Phoenix, the Teddy Boy in London, the
Thunder Boy in Tokyo, the Halbstorken in Berlin, or the Stiryagi
in Moscow (Gottlieb, 1965). Scholars who attempt to derive general
principles about the nature or causes of delinquency from observations made upon delinquents within a single cultural group are
making the same implicit assumption.

This assumption, however, is largely untested. While there is
considerable agreement in the observations of delinquent behavior
and characteristics, as we saw in Chapter 2 most of the research has
been carried out on the same basic cultural group, lower-class Anglos
in the Northeastern United States. Before the results of this research
are uncritically applied to Anglo delinquents in other areas, not to
mention delinquents from other ethnic or cultural groups, the cross-
cultural generality of these patterns must be determined. This is the
task faced by the present investigation. If quite different patterns
should be found to characterize Anglo delinquents in the Southwestern United States, or Latin or Mexican delinquents, then considerable revision of our thinking and our programs will be required.
If the same basic patterns should be found despite these cultural
variations, then we will be able to pursue our present course with
greater confidence.

On the basis of our review of the literature and our description of
the three cultures, it is possible to define certain broad expectations.

Since our lower-class Anglo group is most similar to the groups that have been studied in the past, we expect that the patterns found in this sample will resemble those reported in the literature most closely. The Latin sample shares many of the Anglos' values as a result of acculturation. However, this sample also has strong roots in Mexican culture and, in addition, faces the stress associated with minority-group status. In this sample the effects of culture conflict, which Sellin (1938) suggested might be an important factor in delinquency, should be evident. The problems attendant upon going to a school with alien traditions should also be greatest for the Latins, as well as the frustrations caused by discrepancies between ambitions and the means to achieve them. Therefore, by studying this sample, we should have an opportunity to gauge the effects of the factors that Cohen (1955), Merton (1957), and Cloward and Ohlin (1960) have singled out. The Mexican sample, raised in a different nation with traditions, values, and family patterns that are quite different in many respects from those to be found in the United States, is least similar to the samples that have been investigated before. If differences in the patterns associated with delinquency are to be found, it is in the Mexican sample that we should be most likely to find them.

It was beyond the scope of the present investigation to test the generality of all the manifold observations that have been made of juvenile delinquency. For this reason, the study focused on the personality and health of the individual delinquent and on certain easily determined characteristics of his family. Within this general framework, it was possible to define broad expectations or hypotheses as to the differences that would be found between the delinquent and nondelinquent groups in the three samples on the basis of the findings reported in the literature.

Characteristics of the Individual Delinquent

ATTITUDES TOWARD PARENTS AND AUTHORITIES

On the basis of the review of the literature, it was hypothesized that the delinquents would be more antagonistic toward authority figures than the nondelinquents. It was expected that this rebelliousness would be most evident in the attitude of the delinquents toward their fathers. While the delinquents were also expected to be antagonistic toward other authority figures, such as police or school officials, it seemed likely that these latter attitudes might be shared by the nondelinquents and, hence, not differentiate the two groups.

It was also expected that the delinquents and nondelinquents would differ in their attitude toward their mothers. However, while it was definitely expected that the delinquents would be much more hostile toward the father than the nondelinquents, the nature of the maternal attitudes that could be expected was not clear from the literature.

WORLD VIEW

In conjunction with the hostility toward authority figures, it was expected that the delinquents would be characterized by a matrix of attitudes that, for want of a better term, we shall simply call a "negative world view." By this term we mean a mixture of cynicism, bitterness, pessimism, suspiciousness, and hostility—a perception of the world as a hostile threatening place populated by people who offer criticism and punishment but little support or encouragement.

VALUES

The theoretical literature also gave us reason to expect that the delinquents might have ethical values that differed from those of the nondelinquents; that is, there would be basic discrepancies about what is right and wrong.

ACHIEVEMENT

It was further hypothesized that the delinquents would be signifi- cantly lower in the general area of achievement. This general hy- pothesis included three subhypotheses. The first was that the actual level of accomplishment of the delinquents would be significantly lower; in school their grade level might be lower than that of the nondelinquents. Secondly, it was expected that the delinquents would have fewer of the abilities necessary for achievement. For example, they would have lower intelligence test scores and be less able to postpone immediate need gratification. Thirdly, it was hy- pothesized that the delinquents would have fewer of the attitudes required for achievement in our society. They might have less ambition or less faith in their chance for competing successfully in our economic system.

PHYSICAL CHARACTERISTICS

Our review of the literature demonstrated that many investigators have suggested that delinquents and nondelinquents differ in regard to physical fitness and other biological characteristics. This is a controversial area and the data were equivocal, to say the least. While the present investigators were inclined to doubt that any profound medical or physiological differences would be found between the delinquents and nondelinquents, nevertheless, a number of physical variables were studied.

Differences between the Families of Delinquents and Nondelinquents

A thorough study of the families of the delinquents and nondelinquents was beyond the scope or resources of the present investigation. While the focus of the study was on the individual delinquent, some data were collected that have an indirect bearing on the subjects' families as well. The review of the literature had also suggested areas in which the families of the delinquents and nondelinquents might be expected to differ.

FAMILY COHESIVENESS

The familial hypothesis in which we had the greatest confidence, and concerning which the investigation was likely to provide the most reliable data, was that the delinquents' families would be significantly less cohesive than the nondelinquents'. The term "cohesiveness" was adopted from the Gluecks and was used by the present investigators to connote close family ties based on mutual respect and affection. The cohesive family would be a warm one in which the members were considerate of each others' needs and well-being. A lack of cohesiveness could be indicated by the home being broken, but even the intact home could be lacking cohesiveness if there was an atmosphere of recrimination and distrust in which the various family members thought of themselves first and the other members of the family last, if at all.

PARENTAL ATTITUDES TOWARD CHILDREN

The attitudes of the parents toward the children are closely related to cohesiveness. It was expected that the delinquents' parents would be less concerned over their child's physical and emotional well-being. As parents they would be more aware of what the child owed them and less cognizant of their obligations to the child.

DISCIPLINE

Research has also shown that the parents of delinquents and non-delinquents are likely to differ in respect to the adequacy of the discipline and supervision they give the child. It was anticipated that the delinquents' parents would be less consistent in their discipline. In addition to being more erratic, it was felt they would be more punitive and less likely to use love-oriented or reasoning techniques.

SOCIALIZATION OF THE PARENTS

The review of the literature also indicated that there were higher delinquency rates among children whose parents engaged in criminal or deviant behavior. It was therefore hypothesized that the delinquents' parents would manifest more antisocial behavior or attitudes than the nondelinquents' parents.

ACHIEVEMENT LEVEL OF THE PARENTS

It has already been hypothesized that the individual delinquents would be less achievement oriented than the nondelinquents. It was expected that this would be true of their parents as well.

In the following chapters, the methodology and results of the investigation that tested these hypotheses will be described in detail. For maximum clarity, each procedure and its results will be described individually. However, a given psychological test may have implications for a number of these general expectations, while a given hypothesis may be tested by a number of different measures. This microscopic examination of the data may result in the reader's temporarily losing sight of some of the broader expectations. Therefore, in the final chapters we shall return to these expectations and discuss them in the light of the overall pattern of results.

PART II

The Empirical Study: Methodology and Results

CHAPTER 5

METHODOLOGY

Once it had been decided to do a cross-cultural study comparing delinquent and nondelinquent Anglos, Latins, and Mexicans, three methodological decisions had to be made. First, appropriate sites for the study had to be located; second, subjects had to be selected; and, third, procedures for data collection had to be chosen and standardized. This chapter describes the methodology in broad terms. In discussing the results of the study, additional details of the specific procedures used for individual measures will be added.

Selection of Sites

Several factors governed site selection. The primary requirements were that the sites be accessible to the investigators, that the cooperation of the local authorities could be secured, and that the United States site have a sizable Latin population. Large urban communities were preferred in order to ensure the availability of an adequate supply of delinquents and because the main body of delinquency research has been carried out in urban areas. These considerations led to the selection of San Antonio, county seat of Bexar County, Texas, as the site in the United States, and Monterrey, the capital of the state of Nuevo León, as the Mexican site (see map, p. 112). The two cities are both highly industrialized and located approximately the same distance from the border between Mexico and the United States; also, San Antonio has the largest Latin population of any city in the United States (Heller, 1966). In the pages that follow, the culture, history, and characteristics of the sites will be discussed in detail.

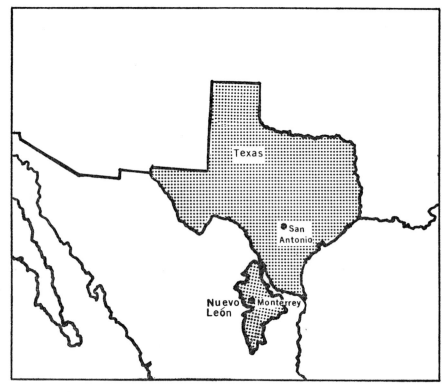

Area of Study

SAN ANTONIO

The city of San Antonio is located in south-central Texas about 150 miles west of the Gulf of Mexico and an equal distance north of the Rio Grande. It was originally settled in 1718, when a mission was established by the Spaniards. Not surprisingly, the isolated outpost was not attractive to colonists. To give impetus to settlement, the Spanish government induced 15 families of Canary Islanders to make their homes in San Antonio in 1731. For the next hundred years the town alternated between periods of meager prosperity and the ill fortunes of war, until at last peace was restored in the late 1830s. After that, colonists came in greater numbers—North Americans from the United States, Frenchmen, who settled Castroville, and Germans, some of whom formed new settlements north of San Antonio. Since that time, except for a cholera epidemic that took 500 lives in 1849, and a flood that killed 50 persons in 1921, the city has had no major disaster.

According to the United States census, it was the largest city in Texas in 1860, and in the years 1900, 1910, and 1920. The population was 587,718 in 1960, and is now (1967) estimated to be about 700,000. Like most large cities, San Antonio has a relatively youthful population (40.8% of the people are under 18) and a typically urban sex ratio[1] of about 92. It has rather large households (median size, 3.59 persons) and a high fertility ratio[2] (571). These latter characteristics are explained by the fact that about 40 per cent of the population is Latin and about 7 per cent is Negro.

The incomes of the people of San Antonio come from a variety of sources, chief among which are trade, industry, military payrolls, and tourism. The city is free from nearby competition of other large centers, giving it a monopoly in trade over a wide area. Industry is well developed and quite diverse. Meat packing, brewing, cement making, flour milling, fabrication of iron and steel products, clothing manufacture, and petroleum processing are among the important manufacturing activities. Servicing the personnel of the numerous military establishments located immediately adjacent to the city has for many years contributed steadily and generously to the city's income. In response to persistent advertising, tourists visit San Antonio in ever increasing numbers.

Despite these numerous sources of economic gain, the income of the people is not very high (median annual income of families in 1960 was about $4,700 per year). This may be due in part to lack of training on the part of the workers, since the population of San Antonio over 25 has completed an average of only 9.6 grades of school, as compared with 12.0 grades for the two larger cities in the state.

In the early 1850s, when the Anglo immigration was just beginning to get underway on a significant scale, the owners of the real property of San Antonio were Latins, though even then many were poor. Subsequently, these proprietors were gradually displaced by

[1] The number of males per 100 females.
[2] The number of children per 1,000 married females of child-bearing age.

the Anglo newcomers, who thenceforth "looked down" on the Latins as an inferior race. The former soon got for themselves most of the desirable jobs, leaving the low-paid, unskilled work for the latter. Until the coming of the railroads many Latins continued to be employed in the extensive freight-hauling business that brought supplies by wagon to San Antonio from the Gulf ports. The "cart war" of 1857 consisted of a series of attacks upon Latin freight haulers by the Anglo competitors, aided by Anglo settlers along the route. These incidents appear to have been part of a general, though unorganized, movement to drive out the Latin inhabitants of the city. The Latins were the object of complaint because of their alleged laziness and incompetence, their dedication to sports and amusements not approved by the Anglos, and their lack of cleanliness and sanitation. Some were the victims of vigilante activities, "justified" on the grounds that they were dangerous criminals and a menace to the community. The result was that San Antonio entered the twentieth century with a large Latin population that occupied a status in the social scale no higher than that of the Negro and that was devoid of significant influence or power in the community.

In the last two decades, however, important changes have occurred. Stimulated by the activities of World War II, the Latins of San Antonio have asserted themselves economically, politically, and socially to an amazing degree. At present they are recognized as customers well worth catering to, as a potent force in local elections, and as a people of dignity and respect. There is still poverty among them, but this is no longer the universal characteristic.

As far as the delinquency rate is concerned, the available figures suggest that as in most cities the Latins supply more than their share of youths who fall into the hands of the police, but, as noted in preceding chapters, there is no way of being certain that the statistics are not influenced by factors other than lawbreaking per se.

Today the city of San Antonio gives the impression of having two distinct cultures existing side by side. The Latin group has always been large enough to maintain its cultural autonomy and to keep the process of assimilation from moving too rapidly. Moreover, recruits from below the Rio Grande have helped to prevent the bonds with Mexico from weakening as rapidly as they otherwise might. It now appears that to be of Mexican origin is no longer a disgrace in San Antonio. The Spanish language seems more important and more dignified than formerly. One may readily conclude that the extent and influence of Mexican culture have expanded in recent years and that this is part of a continuing trend.

MONTERREY

The city of Monterrey, capital of the state of Nuevo León, is located about 500 miles northwest of Mexico City, and, like San Antonio, is also at a considerable distance from other large cities in the Republic of Mexico. Approximately 150 miles from the Mexico-Texas border and 290 miles from San Antonio, Monterrey has been, during a large part of its existence, in comparative isolation from the United States, as well as from the more densely populated areas of its own country.

The Indians who originally occupied the site gave way with little resistance to the intrusions of the Spaniards, and a settlement was formed in the early 1560s, earlier than any European settlement in the United States. Originally called León, the town was renamed Monterrey in 1596 by Diego de Montemayor. For the next two centuries Monterrey barely survived. It did not share in the mineral wealth found in other more favored localities in northern Mexico. The population in 1775 is estimated to have been 258.

With the coming of the revolutionary wars in Mexico, Monterrey endured the ups and downs of the country as a whole. It was the scene of a bloody battle in 1846, during the Mexican-American War. The town, however, remained a frontier outpost until the development of roads and the railroad. The roads broke through Monterrey's isolation and permitted the beginning of the continuously accelerating progress that has ever since characterized the city. It has become the leading highway and rail center of the northern part of the country, a circumstance that, both as cause and effect, has contributed to making Monterrey the chief manufacturer of iron and steel products in Mexico, and important in many other kinds of manufacturing as well. These include glassmaking, lead smelting, flour milling, textile production, and brewing. Commercial and financial businesses have flourished with the development of industry. The resulting increase in population has given a great stimulus to agriculture, which has responded with extensive production of grain, cattle, citrus fruits, and vegetables, a good deal of which is shipped out of the area. As the chief Mexican beneficiaries of the recently constructed Falcón Dam, the farmers in the vicinity of Monterrey have been able to expand their crop production notably.

Of the larger Mexican cities, Monterrey is closest to the United States and has come to have close ties with the North Americans. A majority of the 10,000 foreigners in the city come from north of the border. This fact, together with the long isolation of the city from the main centers of Mexico, has produced the unique culture of the Regiomontanos, which, though overwhelmingly Mexican, nevertheless differs enough from the culture of central Mexico to be clearly noticeable to the observant visitor.

Like most thriving modern cities, Monterrey shows astonishing recent growth. According to the 1960 census, the population was slightly over 600,000, an increase of 79 per cent over the population of 1950. The death rate is about 8.5, more than a third lower than the death rate for Mexico as a whole. The infant mortality rate is also significantly lower than that of the entire country. This suggests that Monterrey is one of the most modern of the cities of Mexico, further evidence of which comes from the fact that it has natural gas for heating and cooking and a pure water supply.

The rapid development of industry has not blinded the citizens of Monterrey to the advantages of culture in a narrower sense. The University of Nuevo León is in the process of moving to a greatly enlarged campus complete with new buildings just outside the city. In 1942 the Technological Institute of Monterrey was founded by a group of industrialists to provide the means of research and to increase the opportunities of youth for advanced technological and scientific training.

However, not all the residents of the city share these amenities, for there is a good deal of poverty in Monterrey. As in many other Western countries, there is a stratified society with a comparatively small number of rich people at the top and a large number of poor people at the bottom. Apparently, there is not as large a middle class in Monterrey as is found in comparable cities in the United States. Delinquency, at least that part of it that comes to official attention, is heavily concentrated in the low-income levels of the population. There appears to be a good deal of it, though considerably less than is noted in the United States. However, direct comparisons cannot be readily made owing to the differences in laws and practices between the two countries. It may be observed, however, that Monterrey has a modern juvenile court system, administered with reformation instead of punishment as an objective.

Selection of Subjects

Once San Antonio and Monterrey were chosen as sites, it was necessary to devise procedures for the location and selection of subjects. It was decided that 50 delinquent and 50 nondelinquent subjects should be selected from each of the three cultural groups: Anglos living in San Antonio, Latins living in San Antonio, and Mexicans living in Monterrey (see Table 2). Before sampling could take place, however, it was necessary to operationally define the three ethnic samples, as well as the difference between delinquents and nondelinquents. The first step was the operational definition of the ethnic groups to be studied.

OPERATIONAL DEFINITION OF THE ETHNIC GROUPS

Anglos

In the present study, the "Anglo" group consisted of adolescents who were neither Mexican-American nor Negro, as determined by surname and available juvenile court, police, or school records. In short, it corresponds to the "WMJ" or "White Male Juvenile" designation on police arrest reports.

Table 2

Paradigm

| Groups | CULTURAL SAMPLES | | | |
	North American (Anglo)	Mexican-American (Latin)	Mexican	Total
Delinquent	50	50	50	150
Nondelinquent	50	50	50	150
Total	100	100	100	300

Latins

The term "Latin" in the present study refers to subjects in San Antonio who are members of *la raza*, as defined in Chapter 3. The vast majority of these subjects are Mexican-American, although it is possible some may have come from other Latin American countries. The criterion for inclusion in this group was the indication of Mexican-American ancestry on official documents or the possession of a Spanish surname.

Mexicans

In the present study, "Mexican" refers to adolescents who are Mexican citizens in Monterrey. Although some Anglos live in Monterrey, none were included in the present study. The inclusion of such a group, assuming adjudicated delinquents could have been found in sufficient numbers, would have given a superficial touch of elegance to the study. However, such a group would have created more problems than it resolved, for the social and economic position of Anglos in Monterrey is in no way comparable to that of any of the other three groups.

OPERATIONAL DEFINITION OF DELINQUENTS

The problems of operationally defining the term "juvenile delinquent" have already been noted. Society, through its police and its courts, formally decides who is a juvenile delinquent. However, many other adolescents commit the same acts and perform the same behavior as those who are called delinquent, but their names, because of luck, shrewdness, or social position, never appear on police blotters (Short & Nye, 1958). If we define a delinquent as someone who engages in an illegal act, and a nondelinquent as someone who does not, then we can never separate the delinquent from the nondelinquent with any degree of certainty. On the other hand, if we use the social definition and define as delinquent only those whom society has judged delinquent, we can avoid the methodological difficulties associated with a behavioral definition while remaining closer to the meaning of the term "delinquent" in everyday parlance. Thus, for the purpose of this study, a delinquent was operationally defined as a person who had been judged delinquent by the local juvenile court.

In the state of Texas, a delinquent is defined in the Juvenile Court Act (Article 2338, Sec. 3) as follows:

The term "delinquent child" means any female person over the age of ten (10) years and under the age of eighteen (18) years and any male person over the age of ten (10) years and under the age of seventeen (17) years:

(a) who violates any penal code of this State of the grade of felony;

(b) or who violates any penal law of this State of the grade of misdemeanor where the punishment prescribed for such offense may be by confinement in jail;

(c) or who habitually violates any penal law of this State of the grade of misdemeanor where the punishment prescribed for such offense is by pecuniary fine only;

(d) or who habitually violates any penal ordinance of a political subdivision of this State;

(e) or who habitually violates a compulsory school attendance law of this State;

(f) or who habitually so deports himself as to injure or endanger the morals or health of himself or others;

(g) or who habitually associates with vicious and immoral persons.

(Anderson & Gurley, 1966, p. 95)

If a child engages in behavior that would be included under one of the provisions of this Act, and this behavior comes to the attention of the authorities, several things may happen. The authority in question, such as a policeman or a school official, may deal with the matter directly or in conjunction with the boy's parents. If so, nothing more comes of it and the child is not officially a "delinquent." On the other hand, the case may be referred to the local Juvenile Court. Once again several things may then occur. The child may be reprimanded and released. A caseworker may be assigned to supervise the boy on an informal basis. If the situation is deemed serious enough, official action may be taken for the benefit of the boy or the community. In this instance, the Juvenile Court officer files a legal petition alleging that the boy is a delinquent child. In this event, which typically occurs only after other courses of action have failed, the case is heard by a Juvenile Court Judge, who then determines whether or not the child is a delinquent child, as alleged, and who dictates a course of action designed to best meet the needs of the boy and protect the community.

All the Anglo and Latin delinquents in the present study had been judged delinquent by the Juvenile Court of Bexar County. For most, this came after a series of offenses that had been handled informally by the police or by probation department caseworkers. The use of adjudicated delinquents meant that only the more serious delinquents would be sampled, in terms of the frequency and/or the severity of their crimes. Since only 586 of the 2,068 Anglo and Negro boys referred to the Bexar County Juvenile Court in 1959 had petitions filed so that their cases were placed on the court docket, it can be seen that only serious cases were sampled and casual offenders were not included. As the Anglo and Latin samples both resided in the same community and came under the jurisdiction of the same Juvenile Court and Probation Department, it is probably safe to regard the operational definition of delinquency as being roughly equivalent in these two groups.

It should be noted, however, that there are scholars who might disagree. Tuck (1946) has stated that one explanation for the over-representation of Latins in the Los Angeles Juvenile Court statistics is the extra vigilance that police devote to Mexican-American youth. "It is certain . . . that the prejudices, conscious or unconscious, of law enforcement officers provide further impetus to frequent arrest" (Tuck, 1946, p. 212).

There is no doubt that Latins are overrepresented in Bexar County Juvenile Court statistics as well. In 1959, Latins accounted for 65 per cent of the 2,907 cases referred to the Juvenile Court, and for 67 per cent of the 718 cases appearing on the court docket. At that time Latins constituted 40 per cent of the population of San Antonio. Anglos, who constituted 56 per cent of the population, accounted for only 27 per cent of the referrals and 29 per cent of the court cases. It is, therefore, possible that San Antonio authorities may have been more likely to arrest or file petitions on Latins than Anglos. If so, the Anglos in the present study could have been more seriously delinquent than the Latins. On the other hand, it is also possible that the Latins were overrepresented simply because they engaged in more delinquent behavior, a more parsimonious explanation. In regard to the issue of possible bias, it should be pointed out that in Bexar County, as in most Texas counties, it is the juvenile probation officer who usually decides whether to file a petition alleging that a boy is a delinquent child, and in Bexar

County, as is generally the case throughout Texas, Latin boys are assigned to Latin caseworkers.

Since most of the analyses to be reported will involve the comparison of delinquents with nondelinquent subjects *within* each ethnic group, the possibility of a slightly different standard being applied to the Anglo and Latin groups is not a matter of great concern. The basic question to be answered still remains: "What are the differences between boys that society has declared delinquent and boys who have not been declared delinquent in each ethnic group?" The effect of any systematic bias that might influence law enforcement officers to be more prone to arrest and file on Latins would be to lessen the difference somewhat between the Latin delinquent and control groups.

In Monterrey, juvenile delinquents are defined as, "People younger than eighteen years of age who infringe the penal laws."[3] A special juvenile tribunal situated in Monterrey with jurisdiction over the entire state of Nuevo León determines whether or not a young person has in fact violated the *Código Penal* and, if so, what should be done with him. The juvenile tribunal consists of three appointive members: a lawyer, a physician, and an educator. Officers designated by this juvenile court investigate the facts of the alleged violations as well as the youngster's educational records, physical and mental condition, and family situations. If the tribunal decides that the youngster has indeed violated the penal laws, the court can then prescribe whatever kind of treatment it deems appropriate. On the basis of the seriousness of the offense and the individual child's circumstances the court may place him in his home, in a school, in an "honest home, foundation, or similar institution," in a medical institution, in a special technical educational institution, or in a correctional educational institution. Children under 12 years of age who are found to be "morally abandoned, perverted, or in danger of becoming so" are placed in educational institutions or with a trustworthy family where the child can be educated and supervised by a court officer. Those under 12 who are not morally abandoned or perverted or in danger of becoming so, or who do not require

[3] The authors wish to thank Edward A. Jameson, Consul General of the United States of America in Monterrey, for providing us with the relevant passages of the *Código Penal* and Angel Velez-Diaz, for translating it for us.

special medical treatment are admonished or reprimanded and their parents are advised and counseled as to appropriate action.

Youngsters between the ages of 12 and 18 who are found to be morally abandoned, perverted, or in danger of becoming so are confined in correctional homes or turned over to trustworthy families. Their education is to be supervised and, while they are confined, the delinquent children are obligated to work in accordance with their ability.

Any children coming before the court who require special treatment because of mental illness, blindness, epilepsy, alcoholism, drug addiction, retardation, or deafness, are to have the appropriate medical treatment.

The juvenile tribunal may request a suspended sentence and probation for the child if it chooses. When the child successfully completes probation his record is expunged. If he violates the conditions of probation, then he is to be confined.

It can be seen that in Monterrey as in San Antonio there is considerable latitude and discretionary power available to the court. The Nuevo León Code differs from Texas' in that it allows younger children to come before the court and also permits court intervention on more offenses without the necessity of demonstrating that such misbehavior is habitual. Despite these differences, in both states whether or not a person is declared a delinquent and, if he is so declared, the treatment he receives depends in large measure upon his family circumstances as well as upon the details of his specific offense. Therefore, in both Texas and Nuevo León the youngsters were living under similar legal systems in so far as how the local court chose to exercise its discretionary powers. Unfortunately, there is no way this could be evaluated in the present study.

Thus, in all three ethnic groups, those members of the group who had been defined as delinquent by society, acting through its normal judicial processes, constituted the overall delinquent populations from which samples would be drawn. However, before drawing the samples, further restrictions were placed on the subjects who could be selected. It was decided to exclude the following delinquents:

1. *Females.* As Cavan (1962, p. 101) has stated, "The delinquency of girls is of a different kind than the delinquency of boys." While a cross-cultural study of female delinquents would be valuable and

interesting, it was beyond the projected scope of the present investigation.

2. *Male delinquents under 13 years of age.* This decision was based on the results of a pilot study of 60 subjects in San Antonio. This preliminary study, in which many of the test materials were pretested, indicated that a large percentage of the delinquents under 13 did not have sufficient reading ability to respond to the materials. By excluding those under 13, about 7 per cent of the potential subjects were eliminated.

3. *Those obviously mentally retarded or severely emotionally disturbed.* This decision was based on two considerations. In the first place, it was desired to study boys whose primary problem was the social problem of delinquency and not those whose delinquency was merely a minor symptom of a major personality disturbance. Secondly, it was not desirable to include subjects who were so severely disturbed or so limited in intellect that they would be unable to respond meaningfully to the test materials.

4. *Male delinquents over 13, not severely retarded, or disturbed, who were no longer under the jurisdiction of the court.* This decision was based solely on economics and convenience. Given unlimited time and resources, the investigators might have preferred to use some sort of survey technique of various census areas, or a method whereby delinquents who were no longer under court jurisdiction were located and induced to take part in the study. Indeed, in the pilot study, an attempt was made to use paid volunteers randomly selected from census tracts as subjects. The difficulties encountered indicated that this was not practical, even if sufficient funds could have been obtained.

The use of subjects under the court's jurisdiction eliminated the difficulties associated with locating the subjects and also resulted in a high degree of cooperation. The probation officers and institutional officers told the boys they had been selected for study and would be examined. If a boy asked whether he had to take part, he was told that he did not. However, the boys were approached in such a routine, matter-of-fact fashion that the idea of refusing to participate rarely arose.

The procedures for selecting the delinquent samples differed in the two countries. If the study had been designed to determine whether there were significant differences between Anglo, Latin, and Mexican delinquents, these systematic differences would have fatally confounded it. (Indeed, such a study would have been confounded in a number of ways. The inevitable differences between English and Spanish test materials or the differences in the examiners who tested the different samples would also have resulted in systematic differences between the different ethnic groups.) However, as we have noted, the investigation was designed as three roughly parallel studies, each of which compared delinquents and nondelinquents within a single ethnic group. Therefore, the fact that local conditions necessitated different sampling procedures was inconvenient, but was not a serious problem for the analyses that were planned.

The procedure in the United States was the same for both the Anglo and Latin delinquent samples. For each ethnic group, the 100 most recent cases of adjudicated delinquents were selected from the files of the Bexar County Juvenile Court. Those who did not fit the criteria for age, intelligence, and the like were eliminated and from the remaining cases the 50 boys that the Juvenile Court authorities could most readily make available were used in the study. At the time of the examination, about 40 per cent of the Anglo and 60 per cent of the Latin delinquents were in institutions and the balance were on probation or parole.

This procedure naturally demanded extensive liaison work, since it was necessary to secure the cooperation of authorities at several different institutions as well as the extensive assistance of the Bexar County caseworkers. As it was necessary to adopt a simpler procedure in Monterrey, delinquents were selected from a single training school, the Escuela Prevocacional. In December, 1960, all the boys in the school who met the requirements for age, psychological adjustment, and intelligence were examined. Since less than 50 subjects were obtained, new admissions who met the criteria were selected until 50 had been examined. Thus, the Mexican sample, being limited to institutionalized delinquents, was less representative of the delinquent population as a whole than were the samples tested in San Antonio.

The mean ages of the Anglo, Latin, and Mexican delinquent samples were 15–7, 15–6, and 16–0, respectively (see Table 3). The offenses of the three delinquent groups were recorded and are tabulated in Table 4. In order to provide a rough indication of the

Table 3

Ages of the Subjects in Years and Months

Age	Anglo		Latin		Mexican	
	C*	D*	C	D	C	D
Mean	15-8	15-7	15-8	15-6	16-1	16-0
Standard deviation	1-3	1-2	1-1	1-0	1-3	1-4
Range	12-8–17-7	12-8–17-2	13-3–17-7	13-3–17-2	13-3–17-7	12-8–17-7

* C, comparison group; D, delinquent group.

Table 4

Comparison of Present Offenses for Anglo and Latin Samples
with Overall Statistics for Bexar County Juvenile Court in 1959

| Offense | Anglo Delinquents | | | | Latin Delinquents | | | | Mexican Delinquents | |
| | 1959 Bexar County | | Present Sample | | 1959 Bexar County | | Present Sample | | Present Sample | |
	N	%	N	%	N	%	N	%	N	%
Theft (not otherwise specified)	112	19.75	4	8	210	13.99	6	12	34	68
Burglary	112	19.75	21	42	332	22.11	16	32	0	0
Robbery	2	0.35	0	0	44	2.93	4	8	0	0
Auto theft	33	5.82	7	14	89	5.92	3	6	0	0
Incorrigibility	41	7.23	1	2	42	2.79	5	10	0	0
Armed robbery	0	0	2	4	0	0	2	4	0	0
Malicious mischief	55	9.70	8	16	168	11.19	2	4	1	2
Runaway	86	15.16	1	2	96	6.39	3	6	0	0
Murder	1	0.17	1	2	0	0	1	2	0	0
Truancy	22	3.88	0	0	56	3.73	1	2	0	0
Liquor law violation	21	3.70	2	4	95	6.32	3	6	3	6
Rape	10	1.76	2	4	30	2.00	1	2	0	0
Carrying a gun	0	0	0	0	0	0	2	4	0	0
Armed assault	15	2.64	1	2	61	4.06	1	2	4	8
Bad companions	0	0	0	0	0	0	0	0	1	2
Forgery	0	0	0	0	0	0	0	0	1	2
Sanitation law violation	0	0	0	0	0	0	0	0	1	2
Breach of trust	0	0	0	0	0	0	0	0	1	2
Simple assault	4	0.70	0	0	48	3.19	0	0	0	0
Other	53	10.05	0	0	230	15.32	0	0	0	0
No information	0	0	0	0	0	0	0	0	4	8
Total	567		50		1501		50		50	

correspondence between this sample and the overall population from which it was drawn, the data for the Anglo and Latin samples have been contrasted with the offenses committed by the overall population of Anglo and Latin delinquents in Bexar County in 1959. Since these latter statistics included cases that were handled informally as well as those that were adjudicated, it would be expected that the present samples would show a higher frequency of more serious offenses. It will be noted that our sample of Anglos includes more property offenders and fewer runaways than were found in the overall county statistics, while in the Latin sample, burglars and incorrigibles are overrepresented and malicious mischief cases underrepresented. Unfortunately, no similar comparison data are available for Monterrey. The data suggest some differences in the offenses of the Mexican delinquents as compared with the Latin and Anglo samples. This may have been a result of the fact that all the Mexicans were institutionalized; however, it is also likely that much of this is the result of the differences in classifying and reporting crimes in Nuevo León and in Texas.

SELECTION OF SUBJECTS FOR NONDELINQUENT COMPARISON GROUPS

The selection of comparison-group subjects involved walking a methodological tightrope. Insufficient controls would make the results meaningless. If all the delinquents came from a run-down section of town and the nondelinquents from an expensive suburban area, it would be impossible to decide whether obtained differences were associated with differences in ecology or delinquency. On the other hand, if the delinquent and nondelinquent groups were matched on every possible difference except delinquency, then the matching might well obscure the very things we wished to determine. For example, if the samples were matched on family background, it would be impossible to determine if there was a higher divorce rate among the delinquents' parents.

The procedure adopted struck a compromise between these extremes. The comparison samples were first of all subjected to the same restrictions as the delinquent samples. All subjects had to be 13 years of age or older, male, not obviously emotionally disturbed or mentally deficient, and available for examination. Whereas availability in the case of the delinquents meant they were under the jurisdiction of the juvenile authorities, in the case of the controls it meant they were enrolled in a public school. (Efforts to include parochial school children were unsuccessful.) In Monterrey parental consent was also required, but no parents refused to allow their sons to be examined.

The criterion of school enrollment had both favorable and unfavorable aspects. The most positive aspect, from the point of view of the investigators, was that of convenience. It was inestimably easier to use a relatively captive school population than to locate children in the community, approach them or their parents, secure their cooperation, and arrange a mutually satisfactory time and place for the examination. (The latter would have been especially difficult in view of the fact that a thorough physical examination by a medical doctor was a part of the procedure.)

A school population had other advantages as well as the obvious one of practicality. It will be recalled that the delinquents were first approached by probation officers or training school personnel and told that they had been selected to take part in the study. Since they had the right to refuse, they were not coerced in the strict sense of the word. Still they were hardly volunteers. In the school setting a similar procedure could be followed, with the boys' being told by school authorities that they had been chosen to take part in the study. Because of this similarity it is likely that their initial attitude toward the testing was much closer to that of the delinquents than if volunteers had been solicited.

The primary disadvantage of this procedure was that the school dropouts or boys whose attendance was extremely irregular were excluded. It could be argued that insofar as habitual truants are in violation of the compulsory school attendance laws, at least in Texas, it would be inappropriate to include them in a comparison group even if they had not been formally declared delinquent. However, the logical extension of this argument would be to exclude anyone who had ever violated the law, whether apprehended or not. The statistics on the number of unreported offenders in high schools suggest that this would not be practical.

Similarly, it might be argued that the population of boys enrolled in school is not representative of the nondelinquent population as a whole. This argument is probably not too valid in San Antonio, where, under the Texas Compulsory School Attendance Law, more than 95 per cent of the boys aged 13 to 17 were listed as attending school. In Monterrey, however, the use of public school students probably did result in a biased sample, since only a minority of the boys in this age group attend the public schools; the balance either attend private schools or are gainfully employed.

Having decided to use public school students as the comparison group, the next step was to select the schools. Insofar as possible in both sites, schools were selected that were located in the same neighborhoods in which the majority of the delinquents lived. In many cases they were the same schools that members of the delinquent sample attended or had attended; in other cases they were schools located in similar areas. To some extent this imposed a rough control for socioeconomic status (SES) and tended to minimize its importance as a differentiating variable. However, there are still social-class and occupational differences within neighborhoods, so it was possible for SES to vary, although not to the extent that it might have if control subjects had been drawn from each city as a whole.[4]

Once the schools were selected, individual subjects were chosen from the school files. Starting at an arbitrary, randomly selected point in the files, consecutive cases that fell within the criteria for the study and that matched the delinquent samples on ethnic group, age, and neighborhood were selected until there were 50 students in each of the three control samples, Anglo, Latin, and Mexican. The mean ages of the three groups were 15–8, 15–8, and 16–1, respectively (see Table 3).

Procedures

GENERAL METHODOLOGICAL PROBLEMS

Once all the subjects were selected, it was necessary to collect data on them. Experience during the pilot study indicated that the best sources of data were the boy himself and information available in the records kept by juvenile courts, correctional institutions, and schools. The latter were supplemented in Monterrey by visits to the home by social workers who gathered salient information on the family background. During the pilot study, attempts had been made to secure systematic data from teachers, probation officers, and other people who were personally acquainted with the boy.

[4] Socioeconomic differences are discussed in Chapter 6.

However, these sources of data proved to be quite variable in the extent and accuracy of their knowledge about the boy. Moreover, in the case of the delinquents, these people were very difficult to locate. Therefore, this procedure was abandoned.

The pilot study had also served to identify methodological problem areas. Among the more critical were the following:

1. *Language problems.* In working with three cultures, we were dealing with two major languages, English and Spanish, as well as "Tex-Mex," an idiomatic mixture of the two, which is common in San Antonio. Therefore, Spanish and English versions of all verbal materials had to be prepared.

It is difficult to overestimate the problems that are involved in coping with several languages. As any translator knows, it is not too difficult to translate the formal meaning of a word or phrase; however, it is almost impossible to ensure that both Spanish and English versions have the same cultural connotations. This problem is compounded when it is necessary to use idiomatic rather than formal language. However, lower-class boys respond much better to idiomatic language bordering on slang than they do to pedantic formal statements.

To contend with the language problem, extensive pretesting of verbal materials was undertaken. Statements were kept as simple as possible and nonverbal materials were used as much as possible.

2. *Lack of verbal facility.* The problem of dealing with several languages was compounded by the generally low level of verbal facility that was often found. Among the Latins, this was partly a result of bilingualism, but it also stemmed from intellectual retardation and lack of educational achievement common to all three samples. This low verbal facility was another reason why clear, simple test materials had to be used, and in the pilot study questions or statements that were too complex or difficult were either simplified or eliminated.

3. *Attention span.* The pilot study also indicated that many boys in the populations to be sampled had an extremely short attention span. It was therefore necessary to use materials and procedures that would be likely to sustain their interest and attention. Rather than having the boys fill out a true-false questionnaire, for example, they were asked to sort cards bearing various statements into "true" and "false" piles. Pictorial material was also useful, for not only did

it short-cut many of the language problems noted above, but also it sustained interest. Whenever possible, the testing program was divided into three sessions rather than one long session.

4. *Interviews and interviewers.* The pilot study also made it apparent that extensive interviews like those conducted by Bandura and Walters (1959) would not be feasible in the present study. It was soon found that little valid or useful information was to be gained from inquiring directly about delinquent behavior, and a good deal of defensiveness was also encountered in response to direct questions about family life, parent-child relations, and the like. It became clear that such interviews could be fruitful only if considerable time were spent building rapport and if highly trained, skilled interviewers were used. Moreover, the interviewers should be members of the same ethnic group as the subject. Standardized interview schedules also would have to be constructed, and, to ensure accurate records of the interviews, mechanical recording equipment would have to be used and stenographers employed to transcribe the protocols. The 100 Spanish protocols would then have to be translated out and retyped in English. It soon became obvious that the magnitude of this undertaking was far beyond the scope and budget of the project. The interview as a device was therefore abandoned.

In place of the interview, a series of psychological tests was devised. These tests had several advantages. In the first place, they served to establish a distinction between the examiner and the law enforcement officials in the minds of the delinquents. Delinquent boys associate lengthy interrogations with police and probation personnel, and they apparently had responded to the pilot interviews with similar defensiveness. However, being asked to sort cards or tell stories about pictures was a relatively novel experience and therefore less threatening. The pilot studies indicated that while a boy might say "I don't know" or remain silent if asked whether his parents love each other, he would take a card with the printed statement "My father and mother seem to love each other very much" and unhesitatingly classify it as "true" or "false."

The tests also required less training for the examiners, since their function was only to introduce the subject to each task and then let him carry it out at his own pace. Moreover, the procedures involved in responding to some of the tests automatically yielded objective, readily quantifiable sets of data, although the responses to more open-ended tests, such as the Cartoon Test and the Symonds, still required the examiner to record the responses, which later had to be translated and classified into various scoring categories.

TYPES OF DATA COLLECTED

Sociological Data

Most of the sociological data came from the records kept by the schools, juvenile courts, and institutions for delinquent boys. As is usually the case with file research, the completeness of the data available in these records varied tremendously. In some cases voluminous data were to be found; for others very little was noted. At times internal inconsistencies would be found. In Monterrey all the file data were supplemented by home visits by social workers.

On the basis of the records and home visits, the following demographic and sociological data were collected about each boy and his family:

1. Boy's age
2. Data regarding parents' marriage
   a. Parents' marital status
   b. Incidence of divorce for mothers
   c. Date(s) of mother's divorce(s)
   d. Date of current marriage for mother
   e. Incidence of divorce for fathers
   f. Date(s) of father's divorce(s)
   g. Date of current marriage for father
3. Composition of the boy's home (i.e., both natural parents, single parent, or other)
4. Sibling patterns
   a. Number of older brothers
   b. Number of younger brothers
   c. Number of older sisters
   d. Number of younger sisters
   e. Total number of siblings
5. Socioeconomic status
   a. Socioeconomic rating of father's occupation
   b. Father's weekly income
   c. Presence or absence of telephone in home

6. Education of boy and his parents
   a. Boy's current grade placement
   b. Highest grade completed by father
   c. Highest grade completed by mother
7. Data regarding religion
   a. Church attendance of boy
   b. Church attendance of father
   c. Church attendance of mother
   d. Religious affiliation of boy
   e. Religious affilation of father
   f. Religious affiliation of mother

Psychological Data

GENERAL PROCEDURES

The psychological data were collected directly from the boy himself in the form of answers to questions or responses to various psychological tests. Data collection in San Antonio was carried out under the supervision of the senior author with the assistance of Professor and Mrs. James Forester of St. Mary's University. Because the sampling procedure demanded that the nondelinquent subjects be selected from the same neighborhoods in which the delinquent boys resided, it was necessary to examine the nondelinquents after the testing of the delinquents had been substantially completed. Examinations of the Anglo delinquents commenced in July, 1959, and were completed in December, 1960. The nondelinquent Anglos were tested from December, 1960, through May, 1961. The Latin sample was tested over the same time span, examinations of the delinquent Latins starting in May, 1959, and ending in January, 1961, with testing of the nondelinquent Latins starting in March, 1961, and ending in May, 1961. Testing the delinquents before the nondelinquents could possibly have introduced some systematic bias, since the latter group was thus examined by more experienced personnel. However, it is impossible that this made much difference, for the examiners were thoroughly trained prior to testing any subjects and the nature of the materials was such that relatively little examiner-subject interaction took place. Moreover, personnel changes during the course of the project also diminished the likelihood of ordinal effects.

A number of examiners, both male and female, participated in data collection in San Antonio. All were Anglo, although several spoke excellent Spanish. Their educational backgrounds ranged from the B.A. degree to the Ph.D. All the examiners who administered the Wechsler Intelligence Scale for Children (WISC) or the Wechsler Adult Intelligence Scale (WAIS) had degrees in psychology; however, a few who administered the other procedures had their academic training in other disciplines.

As a general rule, each subject in San Antonio was seen on three separate occasions. During the first session the WISC or the WAIS was administered, depending on the age of the subject. About an hour was required for this test. During the next session, which generally took one and one half hours, the remaining psychological tests were given. The final session was always devoted to the physical examination. On a few occasions, both the intelligence test and the other verbal tests were administered in a single session. Sometimes the same examiner saw a boy for both of the first two sessions and sometimes the sessions were conducted by different examiners. Testing conditions varied from adequate to fair. The examinations were always carried out at the school, with the exception of the institutionalized delinquents, who were tested at the institutions. Tests at the institutions and at some of the schools were conducted in private rooms; however, in other schools any available space had to be utilized so that some testing was done in such unlikely locations as a corner of the school cafeteria.

In Monterrey, the collection of data was carried out under the direction of Dr. Luis Lara-Tapia. The situation in Monterrey differed in certain aspects from that in San Antonio.

Data collection in Monterrey took place during two periods. The first was from December, 1960, to January, 1961. During this period all but four of the delinquents were examined in the Escuela Prevocacional. The testing was done by Dr. Lara-Tapia and two assistants, both of whom had master's degrees in psychology. The conditions for testing were quite poor. Not only were the surroundings far from attractive, but also the winter cold penetrating the broken windows of the examination rooms made them extremely uncomfortable. Usually, the entire test-and-question battery, as well as the physical examination, was performed in a single session, although in some cases the physical was given at a later time.

The second period of data collection was during December, 1961, and January, 1962. At this time all the nondelinquents and the four remaining delinquents were examined. Once again, Dr. Lara-Tapia directed and participated in the examinations, but with different assistants. One had an M.A. degree in psychology and the other was an undergraduate who had had training in test administration and interviewing at a psychiatric hospital. These two interviewers were somewhat less able than those who had assisted Dr. Lara-Tapia the year before.

Once again, the testing conditions at the Escuela Prevocacional were poor. The testing conditions for the comparison sample, however, were excellent. Rather than being evaluated at their respective schools, the members of the comparison group were picked up by car and transported to a central institute where the testing was carried out. Conditions here were excellent in every respect. Because of the transportation problems, the entire battery of tests, as well as the physical examination, was administered on the same day.

In order to insure the maximum possible uniformity of procedures, the examiners in both countries were provided with detailed written instructions about how to proceed and the order in which the tests were to be administered.

The general instructions to the examiners were as follows:

Study these instructions so that you will not have to consult them continuously during the testing.

Make all arrangements for the time and place of testing beforehand. Be sure you have the consent of the appropriate authorities for the work you are going to do, and that the authorities thoroughly understand the nature of that work. This means that the head of the school, institution, or court where you expect to do the testing should be given as much information as he will accept, that you have, if not too inconvenient, his written permission to proceed, and that his subordinates have been told about their part in the proceedings.

Come as near as you can to securing a conveniently located, small, private room, well lighted, reasonably quiet, with a door that will close. See that it is furnished with two straight-backed chairs and a table. It needs no other furniture; books, pictures, and other paraphernalia are merely distracting.

Check to make sure you have all your testing materials; paper, pencils, forms, stop watch, and the like. Have them accessible so that you can produce them promptly when and as needed.

Arrive on the scene at least fifteen minutes before the designated time
for beginning your work.

Receive the first subject (never more than one) at the door of the testing room. Introduce yourself to him in a chatty, friendly manner. Shake
hands with him and ask him his name, his age, and some general facts
about his family, so that he will realize the testing may involve something
about his family relationships. Do not insist on complete or comprehensive
answers. Change the subject immediately if you sense that he is reluctant
to reply to any particular question. Carry on the conversation for as long
as may be necessary to put him at ease. When you feel that you have
gained his confidence or at least that he seems disposed to cooperate, explain to him that you have nothing to do with the school (or institution, or
court) and that what he tells you will be held in strictest confidence. He
may not necessarily believe you, but he will at any rate feel less certain
that you are trying to catch him off guard.

Tell the subject you are carrying on a study of the personality development of boys and that you will appreciate his cooperation. Say nothing
whatever about delinquency. Tell him you have some things you would
like to have him do, things that are not difficult and that you think he will
find interesting. Explain to him that the quality of his performance will
have no effect upon his school record. If he is on probation or in an institution, tell him that his performance will not affect his relations with the
guards, probation officers, or the court.

PSYCHOLOGICAL TEST BATTERY

1. *The Wechsler Intelligence Scale.* A general intelligence test was
the first test to be administered. Depending on the subject's age,
either the Wechsler Intelligence Scale for Children (WISC), which
was standardized on children up through the age of 15-11, or the
Wechsler Adult Intelligence Scale (WAIS), for persons 16 and over,
was administered. All the examiners had had prior experience administering the Wechsler scales.

In San Antonio the standard WISC or WAIS was administered in
English, while in Monterrey a Spanish version of the WISC (Wechsler, 1951), which was standardized in Puerto Rico, was used on all
subjects, regardless of age. It was felt that the use of the standardized Spanish WISC was more appropriate for the older boys than an
unstandardized translation of the WAIS into Spanish would be.

The examiners recorded the answers verbatim. The protocols were
all scored at least twice by Mrs. Carl Rosenquist, M.A., a psycholo-

gist who had participated in the national standardization of the WISC.

2. *The Card Sort Test.* The Card Sort Test was generally administered at the start of the second session. However, as noted above, in Monterrey the Card Sort Test immediately followed the Wechsler.

The Card Sort Test consisted of 140 statements printed on 3 x 5 inch cards (see Table 43 for a complete list of the Card Sort statements). The 140 cards were presented to each subject in a standard order along with two cigar boxes, labeled "True" and "False" (*Verdad* and *Falso* in Monterrey), respectively.

The examiners were given the following instructions on the administration of the Card Sort Test:

When you feel that the subject is ready to proceed, that he is not frightened, that he will in fact cooperate, show him the packet of cards for the Card Sort Test and the two boxes marked "True" and "False." Make a statement approximately as follows: "Here is a packet of cards, each one of which has on it a typewritten statement that has something to do with your life. Look at the first one. It says: *I was happier when I was a small child than I am now.* Can you read it and understand it all right?"

If the subject seems hesitant or reluctant, pursue the question of his ability to read until you know whether he can read well enough to understand the sentences on the cards. (If his ability is not satisfactory, skip the directions from here to *Procedure for Poor Readers.*) Otherwise, go on as follows: "Now I am going to ask you to read these cards, one by one, carefully, decide whether they are true or false, and drop each one into the box where it belongs."

Open the boxes and place them before the subject on the table, with the labels plainly showing and with the "True" box on the subject's right.

"Try to think of yourself and your family and friends as you read the sentences on the cards. This will make it easier for you to understand what the card says. If you meet any word or something you do not understand, ask me and I shall be glad to explain. Here are the cards. Now go ahead. Don't hurry. Be sure you understand each sentence before you decide where to put the card."

Remain nearby while the subject is working, but do not obviously watch him. Pretend to read or otherwise keep busy at something, so that the subject will not feel that he is being watched, without appearing so absorbed in what you are doing that the subject will be reluctant to ask for help if he needs help or if he is tired. If he wishes to rest, let him do so. Do not make him hurry.

Do not say anything about the statements that may suggest how they should be answered. If the subject tells you he cannot answer a particular statement, encourage him to try, but if he still cannot make up his mind tell him to lay the card aside unanswered. Questions are likely to arise in connection with statements relating to the members of the subject's family. He may say, for example, "My father is dead," or "I always lived with my grandmother." In such cases tell the subject it is proper to regard the statement as applicable to the person who occupies the relationships indicated. Thus, a statement about the father could be considered as applying to a stepfather, grandfather, or even an uncle, if the individual involved occupied a paternal relationship to the subject.

After he has finished, ask him to look again at the cards about which he is uncertain and see if he cannot place all or some of them satisfactorily. Do not attempt to force him to make a decision.

Procedure for Poor Readers

Take up the Reading Cards (8 in number),[5] present them to the subject and ask him to look at them. Say nothing about this being a reading test. Tell him, if an explanation seems necessary, that he might like to practice before starting in with the Card Sort Test and that these cards are to practice with. Ask him to read them one at a time and drop them in the right box. When he has finished take the cards out of the boxes and reassemble them, noting his score. If he has them all right or only one wrong, proceed with the Card Sort Test. If he has two or three wrong, ask him to look at these two or three again and place them where they belong. Do not tell him they were wrongly placed. If he asks for an explanation tell him, "I just want to see what you will do with these cards a second time." If he gets them right on the second trial, start with the Card Sorting. If still he has one or more wrong, or if on the original trial he had four or more wrong, take the first 44 cards from the Card Sort packet and say to the subject, "I am going to read aloud what it says on these cards. When I hand the card to you, you will put it in the box where it belongs. If you think what the card says is true, put it in the box marked "True." If you think what the card says is not true, put it in the box marked "False." If it seems that he does not understand, explain again, using whatever means necessary, including explanations in Spanish or in translation. If, as you go along, he does not understand all the words, explain them to him until he does understand.

If the subject asks you why you are not letting him read, tell him you are doing the reading to save time. Do not under any circumstances tell

[5] See Appendix 2 for a list of the Reading Cards.

him he has failed the test or that he does not read well enough. And do not suggest the answers.

Be sure to identify the subject's performance by writing his name on the record.

As noted above, the Card Sort procedure was adopted when direct interviews proved to be unfruitful during the three months of pretesting. Some thought was given to substituting the Minnesota Multiphasic Personality Inventory (MMPI) (Hathaway & McKinley, 1943) for the interview. However, the wording and the sentence structure of the MMPI proved to be too complex for many of the boys in the pilot study. Moreover, the 566-item MMPI consumed an excessive amount of time, particularly in view of the limited attention span of the subjects.

As a result, it was decided to select only those MMPI items most relevant to the study on the basis of their manifest content, excluding statements that were so personal or so directly related to delinquency that they might arouse an inordinate amount of defensiveness, simplifying the wording and sentence structure of other items, and constructing new statements more directly relevant to the needs of the study when necessary. Consequently, the finished version of the "Card Sort Test," as it came to be termed, bore only a vague family resemblance to the MMPI that had been its inspiration.

3. *The Picture-Story Test.* A number of psychological tests have been developed in which the subject is shown a picture and asked to tell a story about it. Sharing the same basic assumptions and procedures, they differ primarily in the scenes and figures depicted in the pictures (Megargee, 1966b, p. 406). Despite the fact that a number of problems are associated with the interpretation of such apperception tests, they have been used widely in cross-cultural research because the telling of stories is a natural activity in many cultures, and pictures often aid in overcoming language barriers.[6]

During the pilot study, subjects were asked to tell stories about pictures clipped from magazines. The responses were sufficiently good to convince the investigators that the inclusion of an apperceptive device would be worthwhile in the main investigation. Of

[6] For an excellent discussion of the use of apperception tests in cross-cultural research, see Lindzey (1961).

the various apperception tests available, including some homemade ones designed for the study, the Symonds Picture-Story Test (Symonds, 1948, 1954) was finally selected as the most appropriate. It is a basic assumption of apperceptive-test users that responsiveness is enhanced when the central figures in a story resemble the subject. One of the advantages of the Symonds Picture-Story Test is that it was specifically designed for use with adolescents and the central characters are all young men or women.

In a cross-cultural study it is essential that the stimuli should be appropriate to each culture or nation tested. The Symonds cards met this criterion, for the features and clothing of the figures, as well as the furniture, buildings, landscapes, and other background details, were such that they could be found in either Mexico or the United States.

A third feature that made the Symonds cards attractive for use in the present study was that, unlike some apperceptive and projective tests, they were not primarily designed to elicit diagnostic signs of mental disturbance or psychiatric illness. Symonds instead indicated that the purpose is to aid (1948, p. 2):

> . . . in making a personality study of an adolescent boy or girl and especially in securing the personal history. As contrasted with a series of interviews it serves as a rapid method for studying the psychodynamics (drives, frustrations, anxieties, conflicts, and methods of dealing with these processes) of an individual and the relationships of an individual with others close to him, particularly members of his family. This method may also be used for studying attitudes and sentiments.

The Symonds Picture-Story Test includes a total of 20 pictures. Symonds recommends that the examiner administer 10 cards on one day and the remaining 10 the following day. He estimated that approximately an hour is required to administer each set of 10 cards. In the present study, there was not enough time to administer the complete test, or even half of it. Therefore, only the four pictures that appeared to be the most useful for the present investigation, A–4, A–7, B–1, and B–6, were administered.

One difficulty with projective tests like the Symonds is that the responses can be influenced not only by the individual's cultural milieu and personality, but also by the setting in which the test is given, the specific instructions used, the personality of the examiner, and so forth (Lindzey, 1961). This was particularly likely to be a problem in the present study, in which 11 different examiners collected data during the course of the project. Moreover, geographical and linguistic problems made it impossible to control for possible examiner differences by having each examiner see the same number of subjects from each of the six groups. In fact, it was not even possible to ensure that the same examiner always saw the same number of delinquents and nondelinquents within each ethnic group.

Given these practical difficulties, it was necessary to standardize the administration of the Symonds (as well as the other tests) as much as possible to minimize the influence of possible interexaminer differences. Research with other projective tests has indicated that when administration procedures are made quite simple and explicit adequate interexaminer reliability can be achieved, even on such sensitive projective devices as inkblot tests (Holtzman, Thorpe, Swartz, & Herron, 1961; Megargee, Lockwood, Cato, & Jones, 1966).

Since the test followed the Wechsler and the Card Sort, Symonds' suggestion that administration be delayed until the examiner and the subject had had time to establish a working relationship and develop rapport was heeded. However, his recommended administration procedure was amended somewhat. The instructions read to the subject were simplified to eliminate such difficult terms as "creative imagination," "illustration," "character," "stenographer," and "conventional." In Symonds' standard administration there is an "association period" in which the examiner reads the stories back to the subject and inquires about them. This was also eliminated because individual differences between examiners are most likely to be manifested in inquiry periods like these. Because these modifications departed so much from the standard Symonds procedure, this measure will be referred to as the "Picture-Story Test" rather than the "Symonds Test" so that any negative findings will not be misinterpreted as reflecting on the standard Symonds procedure.

The final instructions to the examiners on the administration of the four Symonds Cards were as follows:

Take up the Symonds Cards and say to the subject, "Here are some pictures. I should like to have you look at them and make up a story about each one. Tell me what is going on in the picture, what the persons in the picture are saying, and how they feel about it. Tell me what has happened that led up to the present situation and how it is going to turn out. Here is the first picture." Modify or repeat the directions until you are sure the subject understands.

The subject will often produce only a brief description of the scene presented by the picture. In such cases it is appropriate to say "And what next?" or some other encouraging words to urge him on. However, do not force him beyond his inclinations. Write down verbatim what he says. Ask him to wait or talk more slowly if you cannot keep up with him.

Be sure to identify the subject's performance by writing his name on the record.

The examiners devoted considerable effort to inducing reluctant subjects to tell some story in response to the pictures. So successful were they that only five of the 300 subjects failed to respond. No restrictions were imposed on the length of the stories, with the result that they varied from one story that consisted of a single six-word descriptive sentence to another that went on for more than 500 words.

4. *The Cartoon Test*. On the Card Sort Test the subjects were restricted to one of two responses, "True" or "False." The Symonds, on the other hand, allowed a great deal of freedom in responding. This freedom, which is one of the advantages of a relatively unstructured technique like the Symonds, also poses problems for the researcher, for the responses may range so widely that there are too few in any given category to allow meaningful group comparisons to be made. For example, Cards A–4 and A–7, in which an adolescent boy is depicted interacting with an adult man and an adult woman, were selected in the hope that attitudes toward the parents might be revealed by the stories they elicited. However, each boy was free to interpret the figures in any way that he desired, so that there was no guarantee his story would have any relation to family interactions. For this reason, a specially designed test called "The Cartoon Test" was added to the battery. It was hoped this test would retain some of the freedom of the Symonds while focusing the boys' attention specifically on parental attitudes and behavior, particularly concerning moral or ethical dilemmas.

In the Cartoon Test each boy was presented with a series of line drawings of two figures. One was easily recognized as a teen-age boy and the other figure was of an adult man or woman who was identified by the examiner as the boy's father or mother. A statement by the boy was shown in a balloon over his head. A similar balloon

over the head of the parent was left blank, and the boy was asked
to indicate what the mother's or father's response would be. Williams' (1958) PALS Test was the immediate inspiration for this
technique, although the procedure is also closely related to Rosenzweig's (1945) Picture-Frustration Study procedure.

A number of cartoons were prepared and tried out on delinquent
and nondelinquent Anglos and Latins in Austin, Texas. Almost all
the boys responded freely, seemed to enjoy the task, and gave answers that indicated they understood the situations well and were
readily able to place themselves in the position of the cartoon characters. On the basis of this pretesting, four situations were selected
for use in the main investigation.

The four situations that were depicted were:

a. "The Car": In this cartoon the teen-age boy appears before his
father or mother and states, "I want a car."

b. "The Cigarette": The boy is represented as standing before his
father or mother holding a smoking object behind his back that
should be recognized as a cigarette. The boy is saying, "A boy
gave it to me."

c. "The Police": The boy is shown just inside a door that is
slightly ajar. He is facing his father or mother and saying, "There
is a policeman at the door."

d. "The Wallet": The boy is depicted extending his hand holding
a wallet or pocket book toward his father or mother, who is seated.
The boy says, "I just found this wallet with 500 dollars [pesos] in
it."

For each situation, two cartoons were prepared, one indicating
the boy interacting with his mother and the other the boy interacting
with his father. The cartoons were reproduced by mimeographing
the line drawings on 8½x11 inch sheets of paper. The cartoons are
illustrated in Chapter 11.

The instructions for the examiners administering the Cartoon Test
read as follows:

Take up the first cartoon, turn it face up and say, "Here is the first of
some pictures of a boy and one of his parents. As you can see, the boy says
something and the question is what does the father or the mother say.
What does the father say in this one?" If the subject cannot read, tell him
what the boy in the cartoon is saying, translating into Spanish if necessary.

When you have written down the answer, hand the subject the second picture of the series and say, "Here is the next picture. Look at it carefully. What do you think the mother says?" Repeat for each of the eight pictures. If the subject demurs at any point, urge him to give a reply of some sort. If his reply is clearly irrelevant or seems to be based upon misunderstanding, ask him to look at the picture again and to change his answer if he cares to.

Be sure to identify the subject's performance by writing his name on the record.

5. *The "Choices Test."* In reviewing the literature, we found that a number of scholars have commented on the inability of delinquents to make realistic long-range plans, on their impulsivity and hedonism, and on the importance of discrepancies between their aspirations and their means for achieving them. It was in an effort to explore these areas that a series of questions was devised, which, loosely collected together, was dubbed the "Choices Test."

The first series of questions focused on what the subject would do with various sums of money. The examiner told the subject that he was going to ask him about his choices of things he might like to have if he had various sums of money to spend. He then asked the following four questions and wrote the boy's answers down in full:

a. "If you had 25 cents [20 centavos in Monterrey], what would you do with it?"
b. "If you had two dollars [pesos], what would you do with it?"
c. "If you had 20 dollars [pesos], what would you do with it?"
d. "If you had 200 dollars, what would you do with it?"

The next question was designed to focus on recreational activities. The examiner asked each boy, "If you could go somewhere tonight, where would you go?"

The final question was, "What kind of work would you like to do when you are grown up?"

If the boy hesitated in his response to this or any of the other questions, the interviewer encouraged him to reply without worrying too much about what to say. No comments were made by the interviewer and the answers were written down verbatim as soon as they were given before the next question was asked.

6. *The "Offenses Test."* The review of the literature also indicated that many scholars have attributed juvenile crime to deviant value

systems. According to this argument, delinquents and nondelinquents disagree about what is considered right and wrong and about the relative seriousness of various acts. Some theorists have suggested that certain subcultures' value systems differ from those of the larger society and that this conflict of values could result in delinquency (see Chapter 2). Therefore, an examination of values and moral judgments seemed relevant for a cross-cultural study of delinquency.

The "Offenses Test" was devised to provide a relatively gross measure of the gravity with which the samples regarded 10 different offenses. Each infraction was typed on an individual card and the packet of 10 cards, arranged in alphabetical order in English, was presented to the subject by the examiner, with the instructions to arrange the cards in the order of their badness—the worst one at the bottom of the pile, the next worse following, and so on, ending with the least bad at the top of the pile.

The 10 offenses were:

a. Accidentally breaking a window while playing ball
b. Being rude to grandparents
c. Breaking into a house and stealing something
d. Carrying a knife or gun
e. Failing to stop at a red light
f. Murder
g. Rape
h. Shooting a BB gun in the park
i. Staying away from school
j. Stealing a car

The same order of presentation, no longer alphabetical, was used in the Spanish version.

Physical Examination

The review of the literature in Chapter 2 indicated that for decades scholars have sought reliable constitutional or physiological differences between criminals and noncriminals. The most valuable feature of the physiological approach to criminology was that it initiated a vigorous empirical tradition in which theories and speculations were tested by the examination of data rather than by argument or appeals to authority. However, despite the great masses of data that have been collected, there has been a good deal of disagreement about the adequacy of the controls and sampling procedures used in the various studies and in the interpretation of the differences that have been found. In a broadly based cross-cultural investigation such as this it seemed mandatory to collect data on the physical condition of the subjects.

Unfortunately practical limitations and economy measures limited the range of physical data that could be collected and also made questionable the validity of some of the data that were collected. The physical examination took place as the last part of the evaluation in all cases. (This ensured that the psychological test measures would not be influenced by the physical examination.) All subjects were examined by a medical doctor who was provided with a form on which to record his observations. This form was designed with the aid and advice of a physician and included items that could be observed quickly with only the simplest equipment (watch, ruler, scales, and stethoscope) and that seemed most likely to be related to social adjustment.

It was expected that the physicians would be able to follow the form without the need for the specialized training that had been provided for the psychological examiners. This proved to be an erroneous assumption. For the strictly medical items there was little difficulty, but when it came to such variables as "handsomeness," the physicians had problems making the required judgments. Unfortunately, these difficulties did not become apparent until after the data had been collected, since, to economize on the expensive services of physicians, the physical examination had not been included in the pilot studies. The problems resulting from ambiguity in the examination form were compounded by the fact that four different physicians were used, each of whom interpreted the form in a slightly different fashion. Since the physicians and subjects were not assigned on a purely random basis, systematic intergroup errors could have resulted.

Another problem that arose was the tendency for some physicians occasionally to leave a category, such as "adenoids," blank. This could mean that the physician examined the adenoids, found nothing remarkable about them, and hence recorded nothing. On the other hand, it could mean that he failed to examine them, or that they had been removed. By the time these omissions were discovered, there was no way of determining what they meant, so they were simply recorded as "no information."

These difficulties limited the usefulness of some of the physical data that were obtained. It was unfortunate that these preventable errors occurred; nevertheless, a great many reliable and useful data were obtained from the physical examinations.

Analysis of the Data

The first step in the digestion of the many data that were collected was the translation of the Spanish protocols into English. Next, the data for each group were scored. For some data, such as the Wechsler, the scoring process was simple and obvious. For other measures, scoring categories had to be derived before the data could be classified. Data analysis had proceeded to the point where all the data had undergone this initial classification when the project suffered a major blow. During the senior investigator's move from Texas to California the individual protocols were lost. The summaries of the classified group data were all that remained. This naturally limited the statistical comparisons that could be undertaken. By and large, the data analysis was restricted to nonparametric analyses of the relative frequency of various response classes. In most instances this would have been the method of choice in any case, but in others parametric statistical analyses would have been preferable. Loss of the individual data also meant that it was impossible to reclassify any data to test further hypotheses that occurred as data analysis progressed.

The sociological, psychological, and physical examination data were treated by comparing the results for the delinquents and the nondelinquents within each ethnic group. Thus, the design was essentially that of a single study repeated in three different ethnic groups. While similarities and differences in the factors that differentiate the delinquents and nondelinquents in the various cultures will be discussed in the following pages, in the strict sense of the word, no *cross-cultural* analyses were undertaken. For example, the IQs of the Anglo, Latin, and Mexican samples were not compared to determine which ethnic group was the "most intelligent." Such analyses would not have been valid, because language problems made it impossible to present each group with stimuli that had identical cultural connotations and because of the unavoidable differences in sampling procedures in the three ethnic samples, which have already been discussed.

Since the study was essentially a correlational one to determine which variables are reliably associated with delinquency in the different samples, no unequivocal causal conclusions can be made. If a variable is found to be reliably associated with delinquency, the investigators may hypothesize that it might have causal significance. However, like any hypothesis, such speculations must be validated by future research. No retrospective or correlational study of people who are already delinquent can conclusively establish that a given variable caused the delinquency, for it can always be argued just as logically, if not as plausibly, that this difference might have been a *result* of delinquency, or that delinquency and the variable were *both* caused by some unknown third variable. For example, it might be found that the delinquents in all samples come from homes broken by divorce or discord significantly more often than do the members of the nondelinquent comparison groups. If such an association is found, we will naturally suggest that marital discord could have been a cause of delinquency. However, such data could not *prove* this, for it is possible that it was the child's delinquent tendencies that drove the father from the home or that some other factor, such as poverty, caused both the broken home and the delinquency.

As is usually the case, negative findings can be interpreted more definitely. If a variable that some theorist has postulated as a basic cause of delinquency is not found more often among the delinquents, it will be possible to conclude that this variable, although it may be a cause of delinquent behavior for some groups in some areas, is not a necessary or sufficient explanation for delinquency in all cultures.

Discussing this in the abstract, it is easy to agree that "correlation does not prove cause." Indeed, the reader might well be annoyed and feel that we are apparently underestimating his intelligence by dwelling on this obvious principle. However, studies like this have an insidious effect and it is all too easy to treat some finding as if it did have causal significance, once concrete data are being discussed, especially when it agrees with one's own theoretical expectations. On the other hand, alternative hypotheses or explanations are easy to find when the data do not agree with one's predilections. We have noted this tendency too often in ourselves to doubt that it exists in others. When bitten with this "causal bug," we have found it a good remedy to look again at some unexpected finding that did not fit our biases for which we were able to find other *ad hoc* explanations, and then to reflect that the logical basis for our pet findings was no sounder than that of some others we would have preferred to forget. Such reflections never completely cured the incorrigible desire to assign causal significance to correlational data, but they did aid in reducing the more extreme symptoms.

Summary

One hundred and fifty boys age 13 or older, who were not obviously grossly disturbed or retarded, who had been judged delinquent by the Juvenile Courts of San Antonio, Texas, or Monterrey, Nuevo León, Mexico, and who were still under the courts' jurisdiction were selected for study. Of the delinquents, 50 were "Anglos," Americans in San Antonio who were not Negro and not of Mexican descent, 50 were "Latins," Americans of Mexican descent living in San Antonio, and 50 were Mexican nationals.

In the United States the delinquent subjects were chosen by starting with the 100 most recently adjudicated Latin and Anglo cases and selecting the 50 most readily available subjects who met the criteria. In Mexico inmates of the Escuela Prevocacional, a training school for delinquents, were used.

Another 150 boys, 50 Anglos, Latins, and Mexicans, respectively, who were not delinquent and who were attending public schools in the same neighborhoods in which the delinquent subjects lived, were also selected by choosing consecutive cases from a randomly chosen point in the schools' files. They were matched with the delinquent samples on age, and, as with the delinquents, none who were under 13 or who were obviously retarded or disturbed were included.

Sociological data were collected on all subjects from school, court, and institutional files. These data were supplemented for almost all the Mexican boys by interviews with the parents, conducted by social workers who called at the homes. The data collected included the marital histories of both parents, the number of older and younger siblings, the socioeconomic status of the family, the educational level attained by the parents and the son, and the religious affiliation and church attendance of the parents and the son.

The boys were also seen for psychological examinations. Pilot studies were carried out to devise techniques and to standardize procedures, since a number of examiners would be seeing the different boys. Test materials and instructions had to be designed to minimize the problems engendered by the limited verbal facility of many subjects, their limited attention span, and the fact that equivalent English and Spanish materials had to be devised. Each subject was given a Wechsler Intelligence Scale, either WISC or WAIS, depending on age, save for the Mexican samples, all of whom were given the WISC in Spanish, regardless of age.

The Card Sort Test, a set of 140 specially adapted items that the subjects were to divide into "True" and "False" categories was also administered, as were four cards of the Symonds Picture-Story Test. These were followed by the Cartoon Test, a series of eight cartoons depicting a boy interacting with either his mother or his father in each of four tense social situations in which the subject had to indicate what the parent would say. The examination was concluded by a set of questions about how the boys would spend various sums of money, how they would choose to spend leisure time, and their occupational ambitions (the Choices Test), followed by a task in which they were to rank 10 different offenses in order of gravity (the Offenses Test).

Finally, each subject was examined by a physician. He noted the general health in various areas, sensory or physiological defects, as well as his opinion about the boy's nutrition, complexion, appearance, and so forth. A lack of standardized instructions or pretraining of the physicians unfortunately limited the usefulness of some of the physical examination data.

The data were treated by comparing delinquents and nondelinquents in each of the three samples to determine what factors, if any, were reliably associated with delinquency. The dangers of assigning causal significance to correlational data were discussed.

CHAPTER 6

RESULTS OF THE SOCIOLOGICAL INVESTIGATION

The review of the literature indicated a number of sociological variables that have been found to be associated with juvenile delinquency. One, neighborhood, has been controlled for in the present study; most of the others have been left free to vary. Of these, four general areas were investigated: the marital pattern of the parents, sibling patterns, religious behavior, and socioeconomic and educational level.

Marital Patterns of the Parents

Since the family is the major agent of socialization in Western society, it is natural that investigators should regard disturbed family patterns as a possible cause of numerous behavior disorders, juvenile delinquency included. One of the primary variables that has been investigated is the stability of the family constellation as reflected in the incidence of broken homes.

Peterson and Becker (1965) reviewed a number of studies of broken homes and delinquency and concluded, "The gross relationship is well established—the families of delinquents have been disrupted by death, desertion, divorce, separation, or prolonged parental absence much more frequently than the families of nondelinquents." Some investigators have assigned causal significance to this association. Other scholars have held that both broken homes and delinquency may be the results of other variables, such as unstable economic conditions, lower-class culture, and antisocial fathers.

Peterson and Becker's survey of the literature showed that it is important to consider not only the fact that a home is broken, but also the cause of the break. The majority of the studies they reviewed indicated that when the home was broken through marital discord (divorce, separation, or desertion) it was more likely to be associated with delinquency than if the home was broken by some external factor, such as death, in which there was no parental disharmony involved. Monahan (1957, p. 321) described the differences in the psychological effects of a home broken by death as opposed to one broken through disharmony, as follows:

At the death of a parent no cultural opposition is imposed upon the situation. Rather, social and economic assistance, both public and private, is readily forthcoming. Furthermore, the acquisition of a step-parent through remarriage of the remaining parent may even re-establish something of a family norm for the bereaved child.[1]

But, in cases of desertion and divorce (and illegitimacy) we have an entirely different set of circumstances. Here we frequently find the child exposed to a highly emotionalized atmosphere of discontent and discord. The child most often remains with the mother only, financial support may be withheld by the father, or the parents may fight over the child's custody. In cases of desertion no new father may legally become part of the child's home. And the subtle challenge of public disapproval of the family situation and the psychological impact of a seeming rejection by one's parents may becloud the child's outlook.

The majority of the studies reviewed by Peterson and Becker used designs similar to the present investigation in which matched groups of delinquents and nondelinquents were compared on various factors. A study by Gregory (1965) used anterospective data on children who had lost parents during childhood, and found that delinquency was much more frequent than average among boys who had lost a parent by divorce or separation. The delinquency rate for boys who had lost a parent by death or who had experienced other varieties of parental loss was also somewhat above average, but was less than that found in those who had lost parents by divorce or separation. This procedure thus obtained results similar to those found using the more common retrospective matching method.

In the present study, several indices of marital stability were used. These included the present marital status of the parents and parent

[1] Moore and Holtzman's (1965) study, cited below, would tend to contraindicate the value of remarriage in stabilizing the home for some family patterns.

surrogates, the composition of the parental home, the incidence of divorce among the parents and parent surrogates, the dates of the parents' divorces, and the date of the present marriage.

PRESENT MARITAL STATUS OF THE PARENTS

In the present study, information was obtained on the present marital status of all but 13 of the parents of the 300 subjects. These data are presented in Table 5. This table reports only the *present* marital status of the parents. A parent who had been divorced and remarried would be classified as "married, together." Each family was fitted into the most appropriate category and none was included in more than one such classification. In the case of families in which the natural parents may have been divorced and one partner remarried and the other not, a decision had to be made as to which partner constituted the boy's reference family. This presented relatively little difficulty. The family with which the boy lived (or had

Table 5

Present Marital Status of Parents and Parent Surrogates

Marital Status	Anglo C*	D*	Latin C	D	Mexican C	D	Overall C	D
Married, together	37	40	33	29	38	22	108	91
Married, separated	2	7	3	11	2	6	7	24
Divorced or deserted	5	1	7	4	1	1	13	6
Unmarried	2	0	0	0	1	9	3	9
Father dead	2	0	5	0	3	3	10	3
Mother dead	0	0	2	0	4	2	6	2
Both parents dead	0	0	0	0	0	3	0	3
Other	0	2	0	0	0	0	0	2
No information	2	0	0	6	1	4	3	10
Total	50	50	50	50	50	50	150	150

* C, comparison group; D, delinquent group.

been living most recently) and that had legal custody was considered the reference family. As might be expected, the natural mother was usually, if not always, the reference family, and it is safe to assume that it is almost always her present marital status that is depicted in Table 5.

In order to determine if significant differences existed between the present marital status of the parents of the delinquent and nondelinquent boys in the three ethnic groups, the data in Table 5 were combined into the following three broad categories: (a) married, living together; (b) unmarried, separated, divorced, or deserted; and (c) one or both parents dead. On the basis of the literature reviewed above, it was hypothesized that the comparison group subjects would be more likely than the delinquents to come from homes in which the parents were married and living together or in which a break, if it had occurred, was the result of parental death rather than parental discord. These hypotheses were tested by chi-square (χ^2) analyses; the results are presented in Table 6.

Table 6 shows that in the Latin and Mexican samples there was

Table 6

Chi-Square Analyses of Present Marital Status
of Parents and Parent Surrogates

Marital Status	Anglo		Latin		Mexican		Overall	
	C*	D*	C	D	C	D	C	D
Married, living together	37	40	33	29	38	22	108	91
Unmarried, separated, divorced, or deserted	9	8	10	15	4	16	23	39
One or both parents dead	2	0	7	0	7	8	16	8
Total	48	48	50	44	49	46	147	138
χ^2	2.18		7.92		11.48		7.98	
p (two tail)	N.S.		$<.02$		$<.005$		$<.02$	

* C, comparison group; D, delinquent group.

a significant difference between the present marital status of the delinquent and comparison group subjects' parents. The differences in the Latin sample were in the predicted direction ($\chi^2 = 7.92$, $p < .02$). In the Mexican sample the significant differences ($\chi^2 = 11.48$, $p < .005$) were as predicted, in that the nondelinquents exceeded the delinquents in the number of parents married and living together, while the delinquents exceeded the nondelinquents in the incidence of homes broken by divorce, separation, and so on. However, the number of homes broken by death was slightly higher for the delinquents (8) than for the comparison subjects (7); nevertheless, death accounted for only 33 per cent of the broken homes among the Mexican delinquents, while for the Mexican nondelinquents it accounted for 64 per cent. Thus, for the Latin and Mexican samples, the nondelinquents were less likely to come from broken homes, and, when the home was broken, there was a greater likelihood of its having been broken by death than was the case in the delinquent samples. This finding thus lends some cross-cultural validity to the pattern that has been observed in many studies of Anglo samples, and supports Monahan's (1962) notion that breaking of the home by death is somewhat less traumatic than separation through parental discord.

In the Anglo sample no significant differences in the present marital status of the parents of the delinquents and nondelinquents were observed. This unexpected finding will be discussed in greater detail below. The overall pattern of the data suggests that this was the result of a greater tendency on the part of the Anglos who had unhappy marriages to obtain legal divorces and remarry. Data supporting this *ad hoc* hypothesis will be found in the tables showing the composition of the parental home (Tables 7 and 8) and the incidence of divorce in the various groups (Table 10).

The data for the three samples were then combined and an overall analysis was made. In the overall analysis the combined comparison groups were found to be more likely to have parents who were married and living together or who were deceased, while the delinquents' parents were more likely to be unmarried, separated, divorced, or deserted. This difference was statistically significant ($\chi^2 = 7.98$, $p < .02$). The overall data thus supported the generality of the patterns observed in other studies.

It is interesting to compare these data with those obtained by

Sheldon and Eleanor Glueck (1950) in their classic study, in which 500 Anglo delinquents in Massachusetts were compared with 500 Anglo nondelinquents. They found that, while 73.4 per cent of the parents of the nondelinquents were alive and living together, only 54.3 per cent of the parents of the delinquents were. The Gluecks did not include stepparents among those classified as "married, living together" in their study. About 21 per cent of the Gluecks' delinquent sample had parents who were divorced or separated, in contrast to 11 per cent of their comparison group. This pattern found by the Gluecks is similar to that obtained for the Mexican sample in the present study and, to a lesser degree, the Latin. Lower incidence of remarriages among the predominantly Catholic Latin and Mexican samples may be the reason why the data from these samples resemble the Gluecks' more closely than those from our predominantly Protestant Anglo sample.

COMPOSITION OF THE BOYS' HOMES

The adults who compose a boy's home play a major role in his socialization. Kvaraceus (1964), for example, has pointed out the problems that beset an adolescent boy in a home without a father figure. As a reaction against feminine identification he may test and prove his masculinity through delinquent behavior with street corner peers. Moore and Holtzman (1965), in a study of 13,000 Texas high school students, found that adolescents' adjustment was significantly associated with whether they lived with both natural parents, a single natural parent, or a natural parent and a stepparent.

Therefore, in the present investigations, the exact composition of each boy's home was determined. These data, presented in Table 7, while most interesting, were not amenable to statistical tests, because of the large number of situations for which very few cases were found. Therefore, the data were combined and classified into four broad categories: (a) both natural parents, (b) a single natural parent (mother only or father only), (c) a single natural parent and a stepparent (mother and stepfather or father and stepmother), and (d) outside the parental home (grandparents, adoptive parents, other relatives, independent, and foster home). This resulted in Table 8, which had cell entries large enough to permit meaningful chi-square analyses.[2]

[2] Some statisticians, inspecting Table 8 and some of the other tables in this book, may object that even after combining conceptually similar categories, some

Table 7

Composition of Boys' Present Homes

Home Situation	Anglo C*	Anglo D*	Latin C	Latin D	Mexican C	Mexican D	Overall C	Overall D
Both natural parents	38	27	32	25	37	20	107	72
Mother only	4	8	11	13	5	7	20	28
Father only	1	0	2	1	4	2	7	3
Mother and stepfather	4	11	2	4	0	5	6	20
Father and stepmother	0	2	1	1	0	4	1	7
Grandparents	0	0	1	5	0	2	1	7
Adoptive parents	1	1	1	0	0	0	2	1
Other relatives	0	0	0	0	3	4	3	4
Independent	0	0	0	0	0	2	0	2
Foster home	0	1	0	1	0	0	0	2
No information	2	0	0	0	1	4	3	4
Total	50	50	50	50	50	50	150	150

* C, comparison group; D, delinquent group.

The data for the composition of the Anglo homes indicated that a higher proportion of the nondelinquents came from homes with both natural parents living together, while the delinquents more

cells still have expected cell frequencies less than five. This violates a condition for chi-square that is invoked by many authorities (e.g., Siegel, 1956). However, Knetz (1963) recently tested this precept empirically by computing large numbers of chi-squares from random data with up to 50 per cent of the cells having expected values of zero. He demonstrated that even under these conditions only about 5 per cent of the chi-squares computed were "significant" at the .05 level and only about 1 per cent at the .01. This indicated that, even with small cell entries, the chi-square analysis is valid. The investigators are most grateful to Quinn McNemar for bringing this study to their attention.

Table 8

Chi-Square Analyses of Composition of Homes

Home Situation	Anglo C*	D*	Latin C	D	Mexican C	D	Overall C	D
Both natural parents	38	27	32	25	37	20	107	72
Single natural parent	5	8	13	14	9	9	27	31
Natural parent and stepparent	4	13	3	5	0	9	7	27
Outside parental home	1	2	2	6	3	8	6	16
Total	48	50	50	50	49	46	147	146
χ^2	7.63		3.40		16.25		23.43	
p (two tail)	<.06		N.S.		<.005		<.001	

* C, comparison group; D, delinquent group.

often lived with a single natural parent, with a natural parent and a stepparent, or outside the parental home. This tendency approached statistical significance (p [two tail] <.06). The same tendency was observed in the Latin sample, but it failed to approach statistical significance. In the Mexican sample, once again, the nondelinquents more often came from homes with both natural parents living together, while the delinquents were more likely to live with stepparents or outside the parental home; however, there was no difference between the two groups in the number of subjects living with a single natural parent. The differences between the living arrangements of the nondelinquents and delinquents in the Mexican sample attained statistical significance ($\chi^2=16.25$, $p<.005$). When the data from the three ethnic groups were combined the comparison subjects were most likely to have both natural parents living together and the delinquents to have some other arrangement. The difference was highly significant ($\chi^2=23.43$, $p<.001$).

In examining Table 8, it will be noted that 17 of the 98 Anglo subjects for whom data were available lived with a natural parent and a stepparent. However, only eight of the 100 Latin subjects and nine of the 95 Mexican subjects had this arrangement. It thus appeared that remarriage of a divorced or widowed parent was about twice as frequent in the Anglo sample. It will be recalled that a natural parent-stepparent union was classified as "married, together" in the analysis of the present marital status of the parents (Tables 5 and 6). It would seem likely that the greater tendency for divorced or widowed Anglo parents to remarry might have been a factor minimizing the differences between the number of parents of Anglo delinquents and nondelinquents classified as "living together."

As with the data on marital status, it is interesting to compare the results in Table 8 with those obtained by the Gluecks (1950) in their investigation. The Gluecks also found significant differences between the living arrangements of their delinquent and nondelinquent groups, with more of the nondelinquents living with both natural parents (71.2%) than the delinquents (50.2%), while the delinquents were higher than the nondelinquents in the number living with one natural parent (34.6% vs. 19.8%), with a parent and a stepparent (8.0% vs. 4.4%), or in some other arrangement (7.2% vs. 4.6%). The present data are quite close to the Gluecks' in regard to the proportion of delinquents and nondelinquents living with both natural parents, not only in the Anglo sample, but also in the Latin and Mexican. The situation differs in regard to those living with a single parent. Only 13 per cent of the total Anglo sample had this arrangement, about half the incidence found in the Gluecks' sample. Remarriage, as evidenced by a stepparent in the home, was, however, more common in the present Anglo sample, accounting for about 17 per cent of the cases, while for the Gluecks only about 6 per cent of the cases fell into this category. This probably reflects the fact that two thirds of the Gluecks' Anglo subjects were Roman Catholics and thus prohibited from remarriage after divorce, while only 15 per cent of the Anglos in the present study were Catholic. In the predominantly Catholic Latin and Mexican samples, the number of boys living with a single parent exceeded those with a stepparent—a pattern that more closely approximated the Gluecks'.

In stressing the cultural attitudes toward divorce, it would be an error to lose sight of the fact that the Anglos in the present sample are also more likely to be able to afford the expense of a divorce than are the Latins or Mexicans. This would not, of course, account for its lower incidence in the Gluecks' Massachusetts Anglo sample.

Thus, while the greater propensity for delinquents to be found living in some arrangement other than the home of their two natural parents appears to have cross-cultural generality, the exact nature of the alternative arrangements will vary, with cultural attitudes toward divorce and remarriage playing a major determining role.

Relative Frequencies of Single-Parent and Stepparent Homes

One of the most interesting findings to emerge from Moore and Holtzman's (1965) study of a representative sample of 13,000 Texas high school students was the fact that a home containing a natural parent and a stepparent, particularly a stepfather, appeared to have more family tension than did a home with a single natural parent or a home with both natural parents, especially in better educated families. This indicated that the addition of a stepparent to a broken home does not necessarily improve the situation for the children, and, in fact, may make it more difficult. This finding contrasts with Monahan's (1957) apparent optimism regarding the beneficial effect on the child of the single parent's remarriage, although it is consistent with Rubel's (1966) observation that the lot of the orphaned Mexican-American child is hardly improved by the parent's remarriage.

If the broken home containing a stepparent is more traumatic, it might be expected that a higher proportion of delinquents would come from such homes than from broken homes with a single natural parent. The incidence of delinquency in homes with a single natural parent and in homes with a natural parent and a stepparent was therefore compared in the various samples, and the results are presented in Table 9. In all the samples the data tended to be in the direction one would expect on the basis of Moore and Holtzman's observations, with delinquency associated more with a broken home consisting of a natural parent and a stepparent than a single natural parent. The differences were not significant in the Anglo or Latin samples, but did attain significance ($\chi^2 = 4.68$, $p < .05$) in the Mexican sample and for the three samples combined ($\chi^2 = 6.49$, $p < .02$).

The Gluecks' data (1950, p. 88) allow a similar analysis to be made. In their sample there were no differences found. Of the boys who lived with either a single parent or with a parent and stepparent, exactly the same proportions came from the delinquent and nondelinquent groups.

Table 9

Comparison of the Relative Incidence of Single-
Parent and Single-Parent-Plus Stepparent Homes

Home Situation	Anglo C*	Anglo D*	Latin C	Latin D	Mexican C	Mexican D	Overall C	Overall D
Single parent	5	8	13	14	9	9	27	31
Single parent plus stepparent	4	13	3	5	0	9	7	27
Total	9	21	16	19	9	18	34	58
χ^2 (corrected)	1.24		0.02		4.68		6.49	
p (two tail)	N.S.		N.S.		<.05		<.02	

* C, comparison group; D, delinquent group.

Thus, the observations that were originally based on attitude
scales administered to a stratified survey sample in Texas appear
somewhat generalizable to a quite different index of maladjustment
—delinquency—in samples living in San Antonio and Monterrey, but
not to samples in Massachusetts.

*Relative Frequencies of Father-Absent
and Mother-Absent Homes*

Miller (1958) and Kvaraceus (1964) have argued that the matriarchal home in which the father or a suitable male identification
figure is not present on any dependable basis can lead to delinquent
behavior. According to Miller (1958, p. 9):

> . . . the intense concern over "toughness" in lower class culture is prob-
> ably related to the fact that a significant proportion of lower class males
> are reared in a predominantly female household, and lack a consistently
> present male figure with whom to identify and from whom to learn the
> essential components of a "male" role. Since women serve as a primary
> object of identification during pre-adolescent years, the almost obsessive
> lower class concern with "masculinity" probably resembles a type of com-
> pulsive reaction-formation.

This concern with masculinity and toughness leads to the formation of male peer group gangs and may well lead to delinquent behavior, according to Miller's analysis.

Cross-cultural data that have been collected show that some boys reared in societies in which the father is absent during infancy and in which there are no adequate male identification figures react with overly masculine behavior in a pattern consistent with Miller's hypothesis (Burton & Whiting, 1961).

It is difficult to test this hypothesis because father-absence is usually confounded with a number of other variables, such as lower-class status, reduced income, the effects of a broken home per se, and ethnic and racial group membership. One analysis that would help determine whether the matriarchal, father-absent household is particularly conducive to delinquency would be to compare the incidence of delinquency in father-absent and mother-absent homes in which ethnic group membership, socioeconomic status, and neighborhood were roughly controlled. If the absence of a male identification figure is a crucial factor over and above the effects of living in a broken home, then a higher incidence of delinquency might be expected in the matriarchal or mother-only home than in the patriarchal or father-only home.

The relative scarcity of father-only homes makes such an analysis difficult. However, as there were some such homes in the present investigation, a comparison of the incidence of delinquency in the two types of households was undertaken. The results of this analysis are presented in Table 10. In the total sample, there were 58 single parent homes; 48 were mother-only homes and 10 were father-only homes. There was a slight tendency for the delinquency rate to be higher in the mother-only homes than in the father-only homes, as would be expected on the basis of Miller's hypothesis. However, this tendency failed to approach acceptable levels of statistical significance. While Miller's hypothesis remains unproven, the data indicate that further analyses of this sort using larger samples might be useful.

INCIDENCE OF DIVORCE

The marital histories of the parents were investigated to determine the incidence of divorce in the various groups. It has been generally found, as noted above, that the incidence of homes broken by marital

Table 10

Relative Incidence of Mother-Only
Homes and Father-Only Homes

Home Situation	Anglo		Latin		Mexican		Overall	
	C*	D*	C	D	C	D	C	D
Mother only	4	8	11	13	5	7	20	28
Father only	1	0	2	1	4	2	7	3
Number of one- parent homes	5	8	13	14	9	9	27	31
p^a		N.S.		N.S.		N.S.		N.S.

* *C*, comparison group; *D*, delinquent group.
a Determined by Fisher Exact Probability Test.

disharmony is higher among delinquents; therefore, it was expected that a higher divorce rate would be noted among the parents of the delinquent boys in the present samples. Because of deficiencies in the available records, as well as reticence on the part of parents, reasonably reliable data were obtainable for only two thirds of the parents. Data were more readily available for the nondelinquents' parents in the Anglo and Mexican groups and for the delinquents' parents in the Latin group. There is, of course, no way of determining the degree or nature of the bias introduced by the lack of data on a third of the cases.

The available data are presented in Table 11. The incidence of divorces was substantially higher among the mothers of the Anglo delinquents (60.7%) than among the mothers of the Anglo nondelinquents (21.1%) ($\chi^2 = 10.78$, $p < .001$) and there was a similar noteworthy trend for the Anglos' fathers ($\chi^2 = 2.78$, p [two tail] $< .10$).[3] In the Latin and Mexican samples, there were no significant

[3] The reader who compares Table 11 with Table 5 might notice some apparent discrepancies. For example, Table 11 lists 47 maternal divorces in the six groups, while Table 5 shows only 19. The reason for this difference is that in Table 5, showing the *present* marital status, mothers who had remarried were not listed as divorced, but according to their current status.

Table 11

Incidence of Divorced Parents

	MOTHERS							
	Anglo		Latin		Mexican		Overall	
Status	C*	D*	C	D	C	D	C	D
Divorced	8	17	5	10	3	4	16	31
Never divorced	30	11	22	26	42	21	94	58
Total number with known histories	38	28	27	36	45	25	110	89
χ^2	10.78		0.73		1.56		11.22	
p (two tail)	<.001		N.S.		N.S.		<.001	

	FATHERS							
	Anglo		Latin		Mexican		Overall	
Status	C	D	C	D	C	D	C	D
Divorced	6	8	3	8	2	2	11	18
Never divorced	30	14	19	19	44	18	93	51
Total number with known histories	36	22	22	27	46	20	104	69
χ^2	2.89		1.78		0.80		7.15	
p (two tail)	<.10		N.S.		N.S.		<.01	

* C, comparison group; D, delinquent group.

differences between the delinquents and nondelinquents in the incidence of parental divorces. In the Mexican samples, divorce was
quite infrequent, no doubt as a result of the disapproval of divorce
in Mexican culture, religious prohibitions, and economic factors. The
divorce rate for the Latins was about midway between that of the
Anglos and Mexicans.

TIME OF PARENTS' DIVORCE

It would be reasonable to suppose that the age of the child at the time his parents obtained a divorce could be a major factor influencing the divorce's psychological effects. If the divorce occurred when the child was an infant, it is likely that he was exposed to less actual marital strife than if it occurred when he was older. Since children typically remain with their mothers following a divorce, the later the divorce occurs the more chance the boy has had to identify with his father, which ordinarily would be beneficial. On the other hand, the older child is apt to feel more keenly the divided loyalties and rejection that a divorce often involves. It thus seemed that the timing of a divorce might be of importance, although the investigators were unwilling to speculate in advance as to the relative merits of early or late divorces.

For those parents who were known to have been divorced, the year in which the divorce occurred was determined. Since the boys in the samples were matched for age, the earlier the date of divorce, the younger the child was at the time. (In fact, those divorces prior to 1940 occurred before the birth of any of the present subjects.) The years in which divorces occurred are tabulated in Table 12. It can be seen from this table that there was no relation between the time of the divorce of either parent and delinquency in any of the samples. It cannot be determined whether this indicates that the time at which a divorce is obtained is unimportant, or, more likely, if it is too complex and varied in its effects to be reflected in such a crude measure as incidence of delinquency.

TIME OF PRESENT MARRIAGE

The final index of marital stability was the duration of the parents' present marriage. This was reflected by the date at which the marriage occurred. It was felt that the marriages of the delinquents' parents might be of shorter duration and hence have occurred more recently. The dates of the parents' present marriages were tabulated by years and the results are presented in Table 13. Inspection of this table reveals no significant association between the date of the present marriage and the incidence of delinquency in any of the samples.

Table 12

Years of Parents' Divorces

Year of Divorce	FATHERS								MOTHERS							
	Anglo		Latin		Mexican		Overall		Anglo		Latin		Mexican		Overall	
	C*	D*	C	D	C	D	C	D	C	D	C	D	C	D	C	D
1920–1924	1	0	0	0	0	0	1	0	0	0	0	0	0	0	0	0
1925–1929	0	0	0	0	0	0	0	0	0	0	0	0	0	0	0	0
1930–1934	0	0	0	0	0	0	0	0	0	0	0	1	0	0	0	1
1935–1939	2	0	0	1	0	1	2	2	1	1	0	1	0	1	1	3
1940–1944	0	1	0	0	0	0	0	1	0	2	0	2	1	0	1	4
1945–1949	1	3	1	5	1	0	3	8	4	7	2	3	0	1	6	11
1950–1954	1	1	1	0	0	1	2	2	1	3	2	1	1	2	4	6
1955–1959	0	3	1	2	0	0	1	5	1	4	1	2	0	0	2	6
1960–1964	1	0	0	0	1	0	2	0	1	0	0	0	1	0	2	0
Never divorced	30	14	19	19	44	18	93	51	30	11	22	26	42	21	94	58
No information	14	28	28	23	4	30	46	81	12	22	23	14	5	25	40	61

* C, comparison group; D, delinquent group.

Table 13

Years of Parents' Present Marriage

	FATHERS								MOTHERS							
	Anglo		Latin		Mexican		Overall		Anglo		Latin		Mexican		Overall	
Year of Marriage	C*	D*	C	D	C	D	C	D	C	D	C	D	C	D	C	D
1900–1904	0	0	0	0	0	0	0	0	0	0	2	0	0	0	2	0
1905–1909	0	0	0	0	0	0	0	0	0	0	0	0	0	0	0	0
1910–1914	0	0	0	0	0	0	0	0	0	0	0	0	0	0	0	0
1915–1919	0	0	0	1	0	0	0	1	0	0	0	1	0	0	0	1
1920–1924	0	0	0	1	1	0	1	1	0	0	0	0	2	1	2	1
1925–1929	0	1	2	2	7	3	9	6	0	1	0	2	8	3	8	6
1930–1934	3	3	3	2	6	2	12	7	3	3	3	3	6	3	12	9
1935–1939	5	8	9	8	8	6	22	22	5	9	8	10	6	6	19	25
1940–1944	17	14	9	12	14	8	40	34	17	12	9	14	14	7	40	33
1945–1949	3	3	4	3	3	1	10	7	2	3	4	4	3	1	9	8
1950–1954	3	1	2	2	2	0	7	3	4	0	1	2	1	2	6	4
1955–1959	2	4	0	0	0	1	2	5	2	4	1	0	0	1	3	5
1960–1964	1	1	1	0	0	1	2	2	1	1	0	0	0	1	1	2
Never married	2	0	2	0	2	2	6	2	2	1	3	0	2	3	7	4
No information	14	15	18	19	7	26	39	60	14	16	19	14	8	22	41	52

* C, comparison group; D, delinquent group.

SUMMARY OF THE DATA RELATING
TO MARITAL PATTERNS OF THE PARENTS

The data indicated that there were significant associations between delinquency and family disorganization, as reflected in the parents' marital status, the living arrangements for the boys, and the incidence of divorce. The index of family disorganization that was related to delinquency varied from sample to sample, probably in part because of the cultural attitudes and religious sanction against divorce and remarriage in the Latin and Mexican samples. Whenever significant differences were found, however, it was always the delinquent samples that had the higher rate of disorganization.

In the Anglo samples, family disorganization was reflected primarily in the significantly higher divorce rate noted in the mothers of the delinquents. There were also noteworthy trends for the delinquents' fathers or father surrogates to have higher divorce rates, and for the delinquents to live more often with a single parent, a parent and a stepparent, or outside the parental home. The nondelinquents, on the other hand, were more likely to live with both natural parents. There was, however, no significant difference in the present marital status of the Anglos' parents. This was attributed to a greater propensity on the part of the Anglo mothers to remarry after obtaining a divorce.

In the Latin sample, there was a significant difference in the parents' present marital status; this was the only index of family disorganization on which significant differences were obtained between the Latin delinquents and the Latin comparison group.

The Mexican delinquents and nondelinquents also showed significant differences in the present marital status of the parents, and, in addition, highly significant differences were obtained between the groups on the composition of the parental home. As in the Latin sample, the Mexicans had no significant differences in the incidence of divorce.

When the data from all three ethnic samples were combined and overall tests of the differences between the delinquents and nondelinquents were conducted, significant differences in the expected direction were found on all the indices of family disorganization. In none of the individual samples, nor in the overall combined data, were any noteworthy associations found between delinquency and the dates of the parents' divorces or marriages.

In addition to supporting the general finding that adjudicated delinquency is related to family disorganization, the data also tended to support the notion that the death of a parent is less likely to be associated with delinquency than is the dissolution of the home as a result of family disharmony. In the total sample, 24 boys had one or both parents dead, and of these 24, 16 were from nondelinquent samples and eight from delinquent samples.

Moore and Holtzman's (1965) observation that greater problems of adjustment are likely to be found in the broken home in which a stepparent is present than in the one in which a single natural parent is present also received some support. All samples showed a relatively greater incidence of stepparent homes than single-parent homes among the delinquent samples, with the differences in the Mexican sample and in the combined overall data attaining significance.

Comparisons of the data regarding some of the indices with those reported by the Gluecks (1950) illustrated the importance of cultural and religious factors in influencing these sociological patterns. In several instances the data for the Mexican sample, and to a somewhat lesser degree the Latin sample, were closer to those reported by the Gluecks, both in the patterns observed and in the absolute values of the percentages reported, than were those for the present Anglo sample. However, Massachusetts in the late 1940s was probably closer to present-day Monterrey than to the San Antonio Anglo community, not only in religion, but also in cultural attitudes toward divorce and remarriage.

It is tempting, of course, to assign family disorganization a causal role in the formation of delinquent attitudes or behavior. A number of plausible *ad hoc* links between the experiences and learning patterns in a broken home and the development of delinquent behavior can easily be formulated. Once again, it must be emphasized that correlational data do not necessarily imply causation. The same data conceivably could be regarded as consistent with the Lombrosian theory that delinquents are atavistic reversals to a more primitive type, or with the notion that delinquency has a genetic basis. For example, if delinquent behavior is inherited, then the parents of the delinquents would probably be more antisocial than those of the nondelinquents, and this could easily be reflected in greater family disunity. Or, if an atavistic reversion is involved, the presence of a primitive person in the household could well drive between the hapless parents an irreparable wedge that might destroy the marriage. (Those who question this would be well advised to examine the incidence of marital instability among parents of children with serious birth defects.)

Our own biases are quite frankly on the environmentalist side of such disputes about delinquency causation. We feel that it is both more plausible and more parsimonious to hypothesize that parental discord is a direct cause of delinquency. However, from a strictly logical viewpoint, there is nothing in the present associational data to support the environmentalist view, which we favor, more than the constitutional explanation presented above.

There is another problem that must be confronted by those who would infer causality from these data. This problem, which confronts everyone who would explain any form of pathological behavior, is that no one factor, such as family discord, can be demonstrated as being either necessary or sufficient as an explanation of delinquency. The present data gave ample evidence that while marital discord was more frequent among the parents of the delinquents, there were many nondelinquents whose families had also displayed such discord, just as there were delinquents whose families apparently had been harmonious, at least on the measures selected for study.

Data collected by Robins (1966) add another dimension to this problem. In her study, Robins traced the subsequent adult careers of children seen as patients in a child guidance clinic and attempted to determine which factors differentiated those who, as adults, were diagnosed sociopathic from those who were not so diagnosed. She found no significant differences in the percentage of adults diagnosed sociopathic who were from broken homes (23%) and those from intact homes (19%). When the homes were classified as harmonious or discordant, again a higher percentage of sociopaths were found to come from the discordant homes (24%) than the harmonious (16%), but still the difference was not statistically significant. Robins was finally able to obtain a significant difference in sociopathy rate by adding together the number of patients diagnosed sociopathic from homes broken by discord and from intact discordant homes and contrasting this proportion (26%) with the rate in intact harmonious homes (16%) ($p<.05$).

Robins' data show that causal factors, as illustrated in a longitudinal study, are highly complex and interrelated. That even these longitudinal data are open to varying interpretations is illustrated by the fact that after Robins had managed to demonstrate a significant association between marital discord and sociopathy, she herself did not feel that this discord had caused the sociopathy. Instead, she was more inclined to regard *both* the discord *and* the subsequent sociopathy as resulting in large part from antisocial behavior on the part of the father. This possibility that any observed association between two variables, such as discord and delinquency, is the result of covariation with some third factor can never be disregarded, and is yet another reason why causal inferences from correlational data are hazardous.

Sibling Patterns

No one can deny the importance of parents in a child's life. However, families are not composed only of parents and individual delinquent (or nondelinquent) children. Typically, there are other children in the family, and the relationships that the individual child has with these siblings may also be important determinants of his character and personality. The Gluecks (1950, p. 128), for example, found that their nondelinquent sample was regarded with significantly more warmth and less hostility by their brothers and sisters than the delinquents were. The models provided by siblings may also be of importance. The Gluecks (1950, p. 102) found a significantly greater incidence of criminality, drunkenness, and emotional disturbance among the siblings of their delinquents than of the comparison group. Moreover, significantly more of their delinquents had siblings with serious physical ailments or mental retardation, problems that could add considerable stress within the family milieu. Thus, sibling relations and patterns may have an important influence on the individual child's personality.

In the present study, three aspects of the sibling patterns within the family were studied: the number of siblings, the sex of siblings, and the birth order, indicating the proportions of older and younger siblings of each sex.

NUMBER OF SIBLINGS (FAMILY SIZE)

The number of siblings is important not only as an index of the peer relationships that may be found, but also as a measure of family size. Family size and number of siblings have been studied by other investigators, who have noted that larger families tend to be associated with higher delinquency rates. Tappan (1949) cited several early studies that found such a pattern. More recently, the Gluecks (1950, p. 119) found that the subjects in their delinquent sample came from significantly larger families than did the subjects in their control sample. The Gluecks pointed out that the increased crowding of the home, which probably was associated with the larger families, "meant increased competition on the part of the children for parental attention, more likelihood of emotional strain, tension, friction, and loss of privacy, with resulting sexual and other emotional trauma . . ." (1950, p. 120).

This analysis of the effects of living in large families was strengthened by the findings of Moore and Holtzman (1965). They found that high school students from large families (6 to 9 children) were the most negativistic, pessimistic, and authoritarian, and most distrustful of relations with others. Family tension was high in such households and was accompanied by marked resentment of the family life style. Moore and Holtzman pointed out that in large families there is a strain on both the economic and personal resources of the parents, with parental attention diluted and surrogate parenthood by the older siblings the rule rather than the exception.

In addition to engendering family tensions, large families also can hinder the individual's chances for achievement. Heller (1966), in her research on the achievement motivation of Latin high school students in Los Angeles, found that, while 43 per cent of the students with only one sibling were pursuing an academic course, only 14 per cent of those with four or more did so. When she compared Latin students who had three siblings or less with those who had four or more, she found that three times as many of the students from the smaller families anticipated finishing college or graduate school. Since blocks in the path of upward mobility have been suggested as a factor contributing to delinquency, these findings would also suggest that delinquents might be found to come from larger families than do nondelinquents.

In order to test this hypothesis, the mean number of siblings in each group was determined and the difference tested by analysis of variance. The results are presented in Table 14. It can be seen that the hypothesis was confirmed only in the Anglo sample, in which the members of the delinquent group had about twice as many siblings as the comparison group. It would thus appear that the observation that delinquency is associated with family size (Tappan, 1949; Glueck & Glueck, 1950) cannot be generalized beyond the Anglo group.

Some studies of family size and delinquency among Anglo groups can be criticized in that the size of the delinquents' families is compared with the average family size in the general area rather than the immediate area and in that religious or ethnic differences are not taken into account. Since these variables were controlled in the present sample, this indicates that, among Anglos, the larger family size noted for delinquents is probably not an artifact of these other variables.

The present data also show larger families among the Latin and Mexican samples, who would be less likely to practice birth control, than among the Anglos. While the sampling differences in the present study make cross-ethnic comparisons quite tenuous, it is likely that this is a reliable difference, for the 1960 census data also indicate a substantially higher proportion of large families among Mexican-American families than among Anglo families in the Southwestern states (Heller, 1966, p. 66).

Table 14

Analysis of Family Size

Size	Anglo C*	Anglo D*	Latin C	Latin D	Mexican C	Mexican D
Mean number of siblings per group	1.68	3.22	4.37	4.90	5.04	4.48
Standard deviation	1.00	6.72	5.11	5.97	6.21	6.05
F	15.41		1.26		1.29	
p	.001		N.S.		N.S.	

* C, comparison group; D, delinquent group.

SEX OF SIBLINGS

A major determinant of the nature of the sibling relationships within the family is the sex of the siblings. Few studies have focused on the association, if any, between sex of siblings and the occurrence of delinquency. Sletto (1934), in a study of the sibling patterns among delinquent boys and girls, noted that the highest delinquency rates were found among boys who had both older and younger brothers but no sisters. Similarly, girls who had brothers but no sisters had a relatively high delinquency rate. These findings could suggest a predominance of brothers could be conducive to delinquency, although Sletto did not advance this as a hypothesis. If this did prove to be the case among Anglos, however, one wonders whether a similar pattern would be found in Latin or Mexican families, in which the older brothers are expected to assume responsibility for the discipline of younger siblings.

In order to test some of these speculations, the numbers of brothers and sisters in the families of the delinquent and comparison subjects were compared. These comparisons are presented in Table 15. The relative proportion of brothers and sisters was almost identical in the delinquent and comparison groups of each ethnic sample. Therefore, whether a boy had sisters or brothers did not appear to be related to the likelihood that he would engage in delinquent behavior.

Table 15

Number of Brothers and Sisters in the Families
of the Delinquents and Comparison Subjects

Siblings	Anglo C*	D*	Latin C	D	Mexican C	D	Overall C	D
Sisters	42	69	107	123	125	109	274	301
Brothers	40	91	104	122	120	102	264	315
Total	82	160	211	245	245	211	538	616
χ^2	<1.0		<1.0		<1.0		<1.0	
p (two tail)	N.S.		N.S.		N.S.		N.S.	

* C, comparison group; D, delinquent group.

BIRTH ORDER

In recent years there has been a great deal of research on the association between birth order in the family and many aspects of behavior. However, investigations of the relation between birth order and delinquency preceded this current surge of research by several decades. One of the first problems to be attacked was whether the eldest child was more likely to become delinquent. Unfortunately, early research on this question was crippled by problems in selecting appropriate controls and in analyzing the data. Levy (1931) used data from the Institute of Juvenile Research on the ordinal position of 431 problem children; he compared these data with the frequency of children reported at each ordinal level in a sample of 35,256 nonproblem children in Chicago. He found that 37.1 per cent of the problem children were first borns, while only 30.9 per cent of the nonproblem children in Chicago were first borns. He next looked at similar data for 187 problem children and 1,530 nonproblem children in a wealthy community and found no such relationship.

Rosenow and Whyte (1931) obtained data indicating an excessive number of problem children among first borns in two-child families and first borns in three-child families. However, they pointed to statistical problems, which they felt indicated that the validity of this finding could not be regarded as established.

Goodenough and Leahy (1927) performed a study that is erroneously interpreted in the criminological literature as supporting the notion that first borns are more likely to be delinquent. Actually, they found the first-born children in their sample of kindergarten pupils to be less aggressive, low in self confidence, suggestible, and introverted—hardly delinquent characteristics. Goodenough and Leahy (1927, p. 46) did cite a study by Breckinridge and Abbott (1912) in which a large number of delinquents were found to be first born, but they pointed out that this cannot be evaluated without knowing the ordinal positions to be found in a random control sample.

Recent research on birth order has shown that first borns tend to have relatively greater achievement, have higher intelligence test scores, be more cooperative, and have greater conscience development than later borns (Altus, 1966). On the basis of these data, one would expect first borns to be less likely to be delinquent rather than more likely, as the early investigators had suggested. Consistent with this, Nye (1958) found that oldest children and only children show less delinquent behavior than intermediate or youngest children, and Tappan has concluded (1949, p. 140), ". . . the high incidence of delinquency in the oldest child, pointed to in earlier researches, was artificial."

Research has also focused on the related question of whether or not only children show a disproportionate amount of delinquency. Sutherland and Cressey (1966, p. 231) reviewed a number of studies on this question. Some studies reported an unusually high rate of delinquency among only children, others found no imbalance, while still others reported less delinquency among only children. Thus, the literature does not indicate any clear relationship between only-child status and delinquency.

Rather than focusing on oldest children or only children, some scholars have looked at the full range of sibling positions and have attempted to determine which patterns, if any, are most associated with the occurrence of delinquent behavior. The results of some of these studies have suggested that sibling position could be significantly related to delinquency. Sletto (1934) compared 1,145 pairs of delinquents and nondelinquents, matched for age, sex, and sibling position. He found that delinquency rates were higher in certain sibling combinations than in others. For example, boys with older and younger brothers but no sisters had the highest delinquency rate, while those with both older brothers and sisters but no younger siblings had the lowest delinquency rate. The results of the Gluecks' (1950) study also suggested that ordinal relations could be important. They classified the 500 delinquents and nondelinquents in their sample into four categories—only child, first born, middle, and youngest—and found a significant difference in the numbers of delinquents and nondelinquents falling into the various categories, with the delinquents tending to be more frequent in the "middle" category and the nondelinquents in the other three.

Sutherland and Cressey (1966) have reviewed studies of birth order and delinquency conducted in England and Norway and among various ethnic groups in the United States. There was a tendency in these studies for youngest children to be somewhat less likely to become delinquent than those in other sibling positions. However, Sutherland and Cressey concluded (1966, p. 230), "In general, there are variations of such sizes and types that a conclusion on the significance of ordinal position seems unjustified."

To the authors' knowledge, no studies have investigated the relations between sibling position and delinquency in Mexican or Latin families. It would appear on an a priori basis that there might be a greater relation between ordinal position and delinquency rate in such families because the roles of the older and younger siblings are so clearly defined, with the older siblings, especially the brothers, expected to assume quasi-parental responsibilities toward the younger siblings, who in turn are expected to give them respect and deference second only to that reserved for the parents.

Because of the unfortunate loss of the individual data, it was impossible to determine the exact birth order of each individual subject. However, group data that were available indicated the number of individuals in each group who had 0, 1, 2, . . . n, older brothers, younger brothers, older sisters, and younger sisters. These data are presented in Table 16. From these data it was possible to test several relevant hypotheses.

The first aspect of these data to be studied was the frequency of eldest sons in the various groups, that is, the number of boys who had no older brothers. It was the investigators' expectation, based on the recent research on the personality patterns of first borns (Altus, 1966), that there would be more eldest sons found among the nondelinquents than the delinquents. However, as noted above, other investigators have advanced the opposite hypothesis. Therefore, a two-tail test was performed despite the fact that a directional prediction had been made.

The incidence of eldest sons in the three ethnic groups and overall is presented in Table 17, along with chi-square analyses. These analyses were based on the null hypothesis that the number of first-born sons in an ethnic group should be equally distributed between the delinquent and nondelinquent groups (i.e., $P=Q=.50$) so that the expected value for each group would be N/2.

In the Anglo samples, there was a noteworthy trend ($p<.10$) for the eldest sons to be more likely to come from the nondelinquent group. The differences in the Mexican and Latin samples were not noteworthy. The Anglo data were thus consistent with the recent studies on the characteristics of first-born Anglos (Altus, 1966), but

Table 16

Sibling Patterns of Subjects

No.	NUMBER OF OLDER BROTHERS								NUMBER OF YOUNGER BROTHERS							
	Anglo		Latin		Mexican		Overall		Anglo		Latin		Mexican		Overall	
	C*	D*	C	D	C	D	C	D	C	D	C	D	C	D	C	D
None	37	23	26	19	17	25	80	67	29	22	22	18	26	18	77	58
One	11	14	15	21	10	11	36	46	17	14	9	10	11	10	37	34
Two	2	4	3	7	5	6	10	17	3	9	8	7	8	13	19	29
Three	0	2	3	2	10	4	13	8	1	2	6	11	3	5	10	18
Four	0	4	0	1	5	2	5	7	0	1	3	2	1	2	4	5
Five	0	0	1	0	2	0	3	0	0	1	0	0	0	0	0	1
Six	0	0	0	0	0	0	0	0	0	0	0	2	0	0	0	2
Seven	0	0	1	0	0	0	1	0	0	0	1	0	0	0	1	0
No information	0	3	1	0	1	2	2	5	0	1	1	0	1	1	2	2

NUMBER OF OLDER SISTERS

No.	Anglo C	Anglo D	Latin C	Latin D	Mexican C	Mexican D	Overall C	Overall D
None	35	27	24	27	20	24	79	78
One	11	12	15	12	9	14	35	38
Two	4	7	5	7	13	8	22	22
Three	0	2	0	3	3	2	3	7
Four	0	0	3	1	1	0	4	1
Five	0	0	2	0	2	0	4	0
Six	0	0	0	0	1	0	1	0
Seven	0	0	0	0	0	0	0	0
No information	0	2	1	0	1	2	2	4

NUMBER OF YOUNGER SISTERS

No.	Anglo C	Anglo D	Latin C	Latin D	Mexican C	Mexican D	Overall C	Overall D
None	28	23	19	13	22	16	69	52
One	20	13	13	11	10	9	43	33
Two	2	10	9	11	7	12	18	33
Three	0	2	4	5	4	5	8	12
Four	0	0	3	9	2	1	5	10
Five	0	0	1	0	1	3	2	3
Six	0	0	0	0	2	1	2	1
Seven	0	0	0	0	0	0	0	0
No information	0	2	1	1	2	3	3	6

* C, comparison group; D, delinquent group.

Table 17

Incidence of Eldest Sons

| | Anglo | | Latin | | Mexican | | Overall | |
---	C*	D*	C	D	C	D	C	D
Number of eldest sons	37	23	26	19	17	25	80	67
χ^2	3.27		1.11		1.52		1.15	
p (two tail)	<.10		N.S.		N.S.		N.S.	

* C, comparison group; D, delinquent group.

suggest that the findings from these studies may not be generalizable to other cultures with different family patterns. There was no evidence in this analysis that the greater responsibilities placed on the first-born sons in traditional Mexican households either facilitated or inhibited the incidence of delinquency among them.

The next set of analyses focused on birth order in a more general way. It was designed to determine if there was any association between delinquency and the ratio of older to younger siblings. Separate analyses were conducted for sisters, brothers, and siblings in general. In each analysis the number of older and younger siblings of the members of the delinquent and comparison groups was contrasted and chi-square analyses were performed. These data are presented in Table 18.

The results were quite clear cut and showed major ethnic differences. In the Anglo sample, there was no difference in the relative proportions of older and younger sisters, brothers, or total siblings. In the Mexican sample the differences were highly significant. The Mexican comparison group had a significantly higher proportion of older brothers ($\chi^2=13.41$, $p<.001$), of older sisters ($\chi^2=8.49$, $p<.005$), and older siblings in general ($\chi^2=28.24$, $p<.001$) than did the Mexican delinquents. The results for the Latin sample were between those of the Anglo and Mexican. There was no significant difference between Latin delinquents and nondelinquents in the proportion of older and younger brothers. However, the tendency for the nondelinquent Latins to have a greater predominance of

Table 18

Relative Proportion of Older and Younger Siblings

| | BROTHERS | | | | | |
| | Anglo | | Latin | | Mexican | |
Siblings	C*	D*	C	D	C	D
Older	14	44	42	45	80	43
Younger	26	47	62	77	40	59
Total	40	91	104	122	120	102
χ^2	2.01		0.29		13.41	
p (two tail)	N.S.		N.S.		<.001	

| | SISTERS | | | | | |
| | Anglo | | Latin | | Mexican | |
Siblings	C	D	C	D	C	D
Older	18	32	47	39	64	36
Younger	24	37	60	84	61	73
Total	42	69	107	123	125	109
χ^2	0.12		3.66		8.49	
p (two tail)	N.S.		<.06		<.005	

| | ALL SIBLINGS | | | | | |
| | Anglo | | Latin | | Mexican | |
Siblings	C	D	C	D	C	D
Older	32	76	89	84	144	79
Younger	50	84	122	161	101	132
Total	82	160	211	245	245	211
χ^2	1.58		3.00		28.24	
p (two tail)	N.S.		<.10		<.001	

* C, comparison group; D, delinquent group.

older sisters came quite close to significance with $\chi^2 = 3.66$ ($p < .06$). The tendency for the Latin nondelinquents to have a greater proportion of older siblings in general also approached significance ($\chi^2 = 3.00$, $p < .10$).

It thus appeared that the presence of older siblings in the home could have had something of an inhibiting effect on the occurrence of delinquency in the Mexican sample. Considering the authority vested in the older siblings to look out for the younger ones, this would not be surprising. The boy with many older brothers and sisters would get more attention and supervision, which could easily decrease the likelihood of his becoming delinquent.

This was less true in the Latin sample, possibly because of a breakdown in Old Country patterns among San Antonio Latins. If such a breakdown is occurring, it is likely that the role of the Latin male would change more rapidly than that of the Latin female, since the male is more likely to be in contact with the culture outside the home. In this regard, it is noteworthy that the presence of older sisters had a strong tendency to be associated with less delinquency in the Latin sample, but the presence of older brothers did not. Once again, however, it must be emphasized that while it is permissible to engage in causal speculations on the basis of correlational data, these ruminations have no more scientific standing than any other ex post facto rationalizations.

Among the Anglos, sibling order had no association with the occurrence of delinquency. This further illustrates how the behavioral effects of sibling order are tied to cultural role prescriptions. It would appear from these data that it would be useful to attempt to replicate much of the phenomena that have been found to be associated with birth order in samples of Anglo college sophomores among other cultural groups.

Summary of Sibling Data

The literature on the relation of number and order of siblings to delinquency and other personality variables that could relate to delinquency was reviewed. Three sorts of sibling data were selected for study. The first was the number of siblings, which is an index to family size. It was expected on the basis of the literature that the delinquents would come from larger families than the comparison subjects. This hypothesis was verified for the Anglos but not for the Latin and Mexican samples.

Second, the relative proportion of brothers and sisters in the boys' families was compared. No tendency was found for any differences in the ratio of brothers to sisters between any of the delinquent and comparison groups.

Third, the number of eldest sons in the different samples was compared. While the present investigators hypothesized that there would be more eldest sons found in the comparison groups, other scholars have held the opposite position. A noteworthy tendency ($p<.10$) appeared in the Anglo sample for there to be more eldest sons among the comparison group. This finding was consistent with other recent studies of the personalities of eldest sons in Anglo college students. No such differences or noteworthy trends were found in the other ethnic groups. It was suggested that since cultural role prescriptions for children vary, cross-cultural research on the effects of birth order would be most useful.

Finally, the proportions of older and younger brothers, sisters, and total siblings in the delinquent and nondelinquent groups of each ethnic sample were compared. No differences were noted among the Anglos, but in the Mexican sample a highly significant pattern emerged in which the nondelinquents were consistently found to have a higher proportion of older siblings. It was suggested that this might be related to the responsibility of the older siblings in Mexican culture to aid in supervising and looking after the younger ones. In the Latin sample, there was no tendency for the nondelinquent Latins to have a higher proportion of older brothers, but there was a strong trend, which fell just short of significance, for them to have a higher proportion of older sisters. It was suggested that possibly the older daughters were acting more in accord with the traditional cultural patterns than were the boys in the Latin households.

Religion and Delinquency

Because few people are neutral on the subject of religion or on the subject of delinquency, it is natural that opinions on the relationship of the two should be polarized. On the one hand, there are many who believe that a weakening of religious faith is the primary cause of juvenile crime. On the other hand, as Tappan

(1949, p. 516) has pointed out, "It has been popular among some criminologists to assume the irrelevance of religion to crime, or even its harmful effects, using the common observation of high offense rates among Roman Catholics as 'proof'."

The argument that there is a strong relation between irreligious behavior and delinquency is in part a circular one based on semantics. Since most religions defined what was moral or ethical behavior and since these definitions were embodied in the legal codes, most delinquent behavior is, by definition, irreligious. Empirical research has therefore defined religion independently of ethical behavior. Generally, it has focused on two aspects of religion, church attendance and church affiliation. The study of both, however, has been hampered by a number of methodological difficulties.

CHURCH ATTENDANCE AND DELINQUENCY

To study the effects of religious behavior on delinquency, we should ideally use a longitudinal design in which the degree of religious indoctrination, the amount of religious conviction, and the nature of the individual's beliefs were determined at an early age, using a variety of measures including not only church attendance but also interviews with parents and children as well as reliable, external observations of the amount of Sunday School attendance and other factors. The use of external observations as well as self-report data is necessary because of the well-known tendency of individuals to give "socially desirable" responses that might exaggerate the intensity of their religious fervor (cf., Edwards, 1957). Continuing observations would chart the changes in religious attitudes, the degree to which the subjects engaged in various types of delinquent acts, and whether or not they were apprehended or brought before a court for them.[4] This mythical study would, of course, have a large enough sample to allow stratified sampling of all denominations so

---

[4] This point is particularly important in determining the effect of different religious affiliations on delinquency, for many religions operate social agencies that deal with delinquent behavior. A boy who belongs to such a church may be turned over to the church agency without ever being referred to the juvenile court, while a boy who does not have this resource available might be referred to the court and legally declared a delinquent for the same offense (Tappan, 1949; Robison, 1960).

that different denominations could be compared with environment, SES, nativity, and so forth, all controlled.

Of course, actual studies of the relation of religion and crime have never approached this ideal. Typically, they have studied delinquents after they have been apprehended and brought before a court. Any selectivity on the part of police or probation officials has thus already had its effect, and such factors as race, nationality, ethnic background, and SES, all of which are known to covary with religion, are left uncontrolled. Indeed, it is rare for any sort of nondelinquent comparison group to be used.

The delinquents are typically asked about their church attendance and religious preference. No external validation of the individual's self-report is made. Since it is usually to the delinquent's advantage to impress the officials with his holiness, it is likely that an exaggerated account of his church attendance will be obtained. Indeed, Sutherland and Cressey (1966, p. 249) cited one study of adult offenders that indicated a much higher degree of religious conviction among the inmates of a penal institution than was to be found in the general population of the United States at that time. Moreover, even if the reports were accurate, most clergymen would agree that the mere fact of church attendance is probably one of the poorest gauges of a person's faith.[5]

One of the few studies of church attendance to use a control group was that of the Gluecks (1950), who found significantly poorer church attendance on the part of the delinquent group ($\chi^2 = 77.00$, $p < .001$). The data they obtained regarding the church attendance of their delinquent group shows somewhat poorer attendance than that noted by Kvaraceus (1944) in Passaic and Wattenberg (1950) in Detroit (see Table 19). Of course, as Sutherland and Cressey have pointed out (1966, p. 249), "These studies . . . do not indicate the percentage of regular church attendants who commit delinquencies, and this percentage is a necessary prerequisite to a de-

---

[5] In the spring when their parishioners must file income tax returns reporting to the government the extent to which they have financially supported their churches, clergymen have particular cause to ponder on the extent to which religion permeates the total pattern of their congregation's lives as they reflect on the discrepancy between the amount reported given and that actually received by the church.

Table 19

Relation of Church Attendance to Delinquency
as Reported in the Literature

| Investigators | Locale | Group | Church Attendance % | | | |
			Regular	Occasional	Seldom	Never*
Kvaraceus (1944)	Passaic	437 delinquent males	53	22	0	26
Wattenberg (1950)	Detroit	2,137 delinquent males	44	26	16	14
Glueck & Glueck (1950)	Boston	500 delinquent males	39	54	0	7
		500 control males	67	29	0	4

* "Never" defined as seldom or never in church.

tailed analysis of the relationship between church attendance and delinquency."

Robison (1960) has reported on the research of Hartshorne and May, which bears on the issue of the relationship between Sunday School attendance and the propensity to cheat in various situations; these studies showed no relation between attendance at Sunday School and noncheating. The sampling procedures and experimental controls in this research were closer to the ideal described above and to the approach advocated by Sutherland and Cressey. Another study summarized by Robison also went beyond the mere inquiry into frequency of church attendance. This study, by Dominick, was carried out at a Catholic institution for delinquent girls. In the study 162 delinquent girls, of whom 25 per cent were Catholic, were interviewed individually and as a group, given projective tests, and asked to write individual essays. Robison (1960, p. 165) summarized the results as follows:

. . . only 2 per cent of the total group . . . attended church regularly. Religious values had apparently not been integrated in their home life. The girls evidenced no positive feelings of love, reverence, or adoration for God; only a few said they believed in Him. Some who said that as children they had been forced to attend church were not hostile or indifferent to religion. In the group sessions, these girls revealed feelings of being unloved and rejected by their families. Many girls who had dominating mothers were emotionally confused. These findings actually suggest the interdependence of many factors in delinquent behavior.

Dominick's study thus suggested that a lack of religious feeling was part of a general matrix of alienation from family and society. As in so many other areas, the relation between religion and delinquency is complex. The Gluecks' finding that some boys who were not particularly religious were also not delinquent shows that a lack of religion does not necessarily result in delinquent behavior, just as the Hartshorne and May research indicated that church attendance does not automatically result in honesty.

Church Attendance of the Boys

Information was not available on the frequency of church attendance of all the boys in the sample. For those for whom these data were available, the church attendance was classified as "regular," "occasional," or "never."

The data regarding the church attendance of the boys in the various delinquent and comparison groups are presented in Table 20. In each ethnic group and in the overall comparison the data indicated significantly more frequent church attendance on the part of the nondelinquents.

Church Attendance of the Boys' Parents

Did the poorer church attendance of the delinquent boys stem from social learning in a less religious home environment? Or was it simply part and parcel of a general rebellion against parentally and socially approved values? To answer this question, an attempt was made to determine the parents' patterns of church attendance. The data for the church attendance of the mothers and fathers of the subjects, when obtainable, were classified in the same manner as those for the boys, and are presented in Table 20. In every comparison less frequent church attendance was reported for the parents of the delinquents than for the parents of the nondelinquents. The statistical tests indicated that these differences were highly significant. The fact that the same pattern was found among the parents as was observed among the children suggested that the significantly

Table 20

Reported Church Attendance of Boys and Their Parents

| | BOYS | | | | | | | |
| | Anglo | | Latin | | Mexican | | Overall | |
Frequency	C*	D*	C	D	C	D	C	D
Regular	22	11	27	12	49	24	98	47
Occasional	14	3	18	0	0	5	32	8
Never	2	29	0	31	0	3	2	63
Total	38	43	45	43	49	32	132	118
χ^2	34.10		54.75		13.54		89.08	
p (two tail)	<.001		<.001		<.01		<.001	

| | FATHERS | | | | | | | |
| | Anglo | | Latin | | Mexican | | Overall | |
Frequency	C	D	C	D	C	D	C	D
Regular	19	7	17	15	47	26	83	48
Occasional	17	4	23	1	0	10	40	15
Never	9	22	3	9	0	1	12	32
Total	45	33	43	25	47	37	135	95
χ^2	17.58		19.93		16.09		23.58	
p (two tail)	<.001		<.001		<.001		<.001	

| | MOTHERS | | | | | | | |
| | Anglo | | Latin | | Mexican | | Overall | |
Frequency	C	D	C	D	C	D	C	D
Regular	28	7	26	20	47	30	101	57
Occasional	17	4	20	1	0	10	37	15
Never	0	26	2	12	0	2	2	40
Total	45	37	48	33	47	42	140	112
χ^2	46.32		23.15		15.54		53.48	
p (two tail)	<.001		<.001		<.001		<.001	

* C, comparison group; D, delinquent group.

less frequent church attendance of the delinquents stemmed from the patterns learned in the home and was not the result of a rebellion against parental values. These data must be interpreted cautiously, however, since they were based on the reports of the boys and their parents rather than on direct impartial observations. The perfect church attendance invariably reported for the nondelinquent Mexican boys, their mothers, and, particularly, their fathers is especially suspect in light of the fact that Mexican males are inclined to leave such matters as church attendance to their wives.

The present data thus confirmed other studies that reported the church attendance of delinquents was significantly poorer than that of appropriate comparison groups. They further suggested that this was not an artifact of systematic ethnic differences, and that this finding has generalizability beyond the Anglo culture to Latin and Mexican cultures as well. Moreover, they indicated that the reported religious behavior of the parents is similar to that of their sons. If the data are reasonably accurate indices of the actual church attendance and were not too distorted by bias or halo effects, they would support the notion that the family is one of the primary transmitters of religious as well as delinquent values and that understanding the behavior of the parents is one of the most potent keys to understanding the behavior of their sons.

RELIGIOUS AFFILIATION

Another variable studied by sociologists of crime and delinquency is the relation between delinquency and denominational preferences. It is well established that in the United States, Roman Catholics and Baptists are overrepresented in prisons, while Jews are underrepresented (Caldwell, 1965; Robison, 1960; Sutherland & Cressey, 1966). However, there are artifacts shallowly buried in these statistics. For one thing, Roman Catholics and Baptists are more likely to come from the lower class (Sutherland & Cressey, 1966). Secondly, recent immigrants are likely to be Catholic while Negroes are apt to be Baptists, and both immigrants and Negroes are subject to special criminogenic influences (Caldwell, 1965). Finally, the greater prevalence of Jewish social agencies makes it more likely that a Jewish boy who acts out will be dealt with unofficially (Robison, 1960). Studies that have adequately controlled these extraneous elements are relatively rare.

The Gluecks (1950) did not examine religion as a dependent variable. Nevertheless, the fact that their samples of delinquents and nondelinquents were unusually well matched for socioeconomic status and ethnic background makes the religious affiliations of their subjects and their subjects' parents of more interest than those reported in many less well-controlled studies that focused on religion. In a note to Chapter 4, the Gluecks (1950, p. 40) described the religious orientation of their subjects as follows:

> Since religion is very largely related to ethnic origins, our findings concerning the religion of the boys and their parents are presented here as a matter of interest. Among the parents, 67.6% of the parents of the delinquents and 65.4% of those of the non-delinquents were both Roman Catholic; 12.3% and 20.3%, respectively, were both Protestant; 1.2% and 2.2% were both Hebrew; 1.9% and 2.6% were both Greek Catholic; among 15% and 8.5%, respectively, one parent was Catholic and one was Protestant; and 2% and 1% belonged to other mixed religions. As for the boys themselves, 81.2% of the delinquents and 71.6% of the non-delinquents were Roman Catholic; 15.8% and 23.6%, respectively, were Protestant; 2% of each group were Hebrew; and 1% and 2.8%, respectively, were of other faiths.

Two noteworthy factors emerge from the Gluecks' data. First, despite the close ethnic matching, the Catholics were overrepresented in the delinquent sample. Secondly, delinquents appeared more likely to come from homes in which one parent was Protestant and one Catholic. Since the children in such mixed marriages were usually supposed to be reared as Catholics according to a prenuptial agreement signed by the non-Catholic partner, this could account, at least in part, for the overrepresentation of Catholic boys in the delinquent sample.

Religious Affiliation of the Boys and Their Parents

The religious preferences of the boys and their parents or parent surrogates were classified as Roman Catholic, Protestant, Jewish, none, or no information. The results of this classification are presented in Table 21. It can be seen from an inspection of Table 21 that no significant differences or noteworthy trends emerged in the patterns of denominational affiliation between the delinquent and the comparison groups in the various samples. As would be expected,

Table 21

Religious Affiliations of Boys and Their Parents

	BOYS							
	Anglo		Latin		Mexican		Overall	
Affiliation	C*	D*	C	D	C	D	C	D
Roman Catholic	8	9	42	44	48	43	98	96
Jewish	1	0	0	0	0	0	1	0
Protestant	30	37	4	2	1	0	35	39
None	1	1	0	1	0	0	1	2
No information	10	3	4	3	1	7	15	13

	FATHERS							
	Anglo		Latin		Mexican		Overall	
Affiliation	C	D	C	D	C	D	C	D
Roman Catholic	5	6	42	33	47	38	94	77
Jewish	1	0	0	0	0	0	1	0
Protestant	39	32	4	2	0	2	43	36
None	2	0	0	0	0	0	2	0
No information	3	12	4	15	3	10	10	37

	MOTHERS							
	Anglo		Latin		Mexican		Overall	
Affiliation	C	D	C	D	C	D	C	D
Roman Catholic	7	8	45	40	47	42	99	90
Jewish	1	0	0	0	0	0	1	0
Protestant	37	32	4	2	0	2	41	36
None	0	0	0	0	0	0	0	0
No information	5	10	1	8	3	6	9	24

* C, comparison group; D, delinquent group.

the Latin and Mexican samples had a higher percentage of Roman Catholic subjects than did the Anglo.

SUMMARY OF THE DATA REGARDING RELIGION

Two gross measures of religious behavior—reported church attendance and religious affiliation—were investigated. It was found that the reported church attendance of the boys in all three comparison groups was significantly better than that of those boys in the delinquent groups. Thus, the observation that the reported church attendance of delinquent boys is poorer than that of their peers was found to have cross-cultural generality. The additional finding that this pattern applied to the church attendance of the parents as well indicated that this reflected familial patterns that in all likelihood preceded the occurrence of delinquency, and that the decreased church attendance of the boys was not part of a general rebellion of the boy against his parents' values. Limitations concerning the data in the present and other studies, such as the lack of objective verification of the reported church attendance and the inadequacy of church attendance as an index of religious devotion, were discussed. It was pointed out that an adequate study of the relation of religion and delinquency should use large stratified samples studied over a period of time.

The relation of church affiliation and delinquency was also explored. In the present study, in which ethnic and ecological factors were controlled, no relation between church denomination and delinquency was noted. Possible artifacts in other studies were discussed.

Socioeconomic Status of the Family

One of the most basic observations about crime rates is that they tend to be higher in the lower classes. The review of the literature indicated that there are a number of theories why this is the case. As we have already noted, there can be little doubt that the higher rate of official delinquency in the lower class is in part an artifact. If an upper-class boy and a lower-class boy both commit a given offense, such as being drunk, the lower-class boy is more likely to come to the attention of the police. Once he comes to their attention, he is more likely to be taken into custody instead of being escorted home. Once in custody, it is more likely that the case will be referred to the juvenile court authorities instead of being handled by notifying the parents. Once the juvenile authorities are involved, they are more likely to attempt to supervise the case or file a petition. If a petition is filed, the upper-class boy, who is able to afford counsel, may have a better chance of not being declared delinquent or, if he is so declared, of not being sent to a training school.

This should not be interpreted as an accusation of bias being leveled at police or court authorities. In many situations the upper-class boy will have a family and environment more conducive to aiding his adjustment than does the lower-class boy. A fundamental principle of juvenile court practice is minimal official involvement consistent with the protection of society and the rehabilitation of the boy. The bias is on the part of communities that are reluctant to make available to all on a low- or no-cost basis resources equivalent to those that the upper-class boy's parents may be able to secure for him privately.

Despite these artifacts, it is still probable that more delinquent behavior takes place among lower-class boys. As we have seen, various theoretical explanations have been offered to account for this preponderance of delinquency in the lower class. Shaw and McKay (1942) looked at the area, Miller (1958) examined the focal concerns of the lower class, Cloward and Ohlin (1960) discussed the discrepancy between aspirations and the legitimate means to achieve them, while Cohen focused on the rebellion against the imposition of middle-class norms in the school situation.

In the present study milieu was controlled by drawing the delinquent and comparison samples from the same neighborhoods. The ethnic backgrounds were also controlled, unlike some studies in which socioeconomic status and minority group membership have been confounded. These data thus permit us to investigate whether socioeconomic status still varies when neighborhood and ethnic background are controlled, and whether similar differences will be found in the different cultural groups.

Three indices of socioeconomic status were available. The first and most reliable was the occupation of the father, the second was the family's weekly income, and the third was the presence of a telephone in the home.

OCCUPATIONAL STATUS OF THE FATHERS

The fathers' chief occupations were rated on the Revised Minnesota Occupational Rating Scales (MORS) (Paterson, Ggerken, & Han, 1953). The MORS assigns to each of more than 400 occupations a numerical value determined by the minimal requirements of each occupation with respect to seven abilities placed according to their relative importance in descending order as follows: (a) academic ability, (b) mechanical ability, (c) social intelligence, (d) clerical ability, (e) musical talent, (f) artistic ability, and (g) physical ability. With the possible exception of the last, these abilities are not, except in the broadest sense, inborn. Thus, academic ability is not limited to the individual's capacity for learning academic subjects; it includes also the skills he possesses by virtue of already having learned those subjects.

The levels of achievement required in each of the seven abilities by the various kinds of jobs are divided on a four-point, equal-interval scale, designated from the highest to the lowest as A, B, C, or D. In accordance with this arrangement, the rank of an occupation can be determined by noting the letters and the order in which they appear in the pattern representing the occupation. For our purpose, it was possible to ignore the technical details and utilize the numbers assigned by the MORS in the table entitled, "Ability Patterns Listed in the Order of Decreasing Difficulty and Complexity of the Human Abilities Required in the Various Occupations" (Paterson et al., 1953, pp. 66–74). In this table the larger the number, the lower the rank of occupation concerned. By a process of simplification a set of numbers from 1 to 25 was derived by which the occupations of the subjects' fathers were rated. Some difficulty was encountered in the tabulation when a man was reported as "employed by the Acme Distributing Company" or as a "civil service worker" or as "retired." When there was no additional information permitting a logical inference as to the actual occupation, such an occupation had to be listed under "no information."

The distribution of occupational ratings in each group, along with the means, standard deviations, and the results of t tests are presented in Table 22. It can be seen from this table that the occupations of the fathers in all groups clustered at the lower end of the scale.

Table 22

Socioeconomic Level of Father's Chief Occupation

SES Level	Anglo C*	Anglo D*	Latin C	Latin D	Mexican C	Mexican D
1	0	0	0	0	1	0
2	2	0	0	0	0	0
3	1	1	0	0	0	0
4	0	0	0	0	0	0
5	2	1	0	0	0	0
6	5	2	1	0	1	0
7	2	0	0	0	0	1
8	0	0	0	0	0	0
9	0	2	0	0	2	3
10	1	0	0	0	0	0
11	1	0	0	0	1	1
12	0	0	0	0	0	0
13	2	5	0	1	0	1
14	0	1	1	3	0	5
15	9	9	4	3	6	5
16	1	0	0	0	3	0
17	13	8	5	5	0	1
18	1	4	2	2	5	4
19	0	2	4	2	5	3
20	6	3	13	9	15	12
21	3	6	13	17	8	6
No information	1	6	7	8	3	8
Mean	13.90	16.29	18.84	16.57	17.60	16.40
σ*	5.64	4.52	2.86	2.51	4.27	3.92
t	2.27		3.89		1.38	
p (two tail)	<.05		<.001		N.S.	

* C, comparison group; D, delinquent group; σ, standard deviation.

In the Anglo sample, the fathers of the nondelinquent subjects had occupations significantly higher in status than did the fathers of delinquents ($t=2.27$, $p<.05$). However, for the fathers of the Latins a surprising reversal was found. The fathers of the delinquents had significantly higher status jobs than did the fathers of the comparison subjects ($t=3.89$, $p<.001$). There was a nonsignificant tendency for the delinquent fathers to have higher status jobs in the Mexican sample as well.

In examining the means for the various groups, it is quite evident that ratings for the fathers of the delinquents were quite stable, the means for the Anglo, Latin, and Mexican samples being 16.29, 16.57, and 16.40 respectively. However, the data for the comparison groups varied considerably from sample to sample. The nondelinquent Anglos' fathers had relatively high-status jobs (13.90), while the Latin and Mexican nondelinquents' fathers had relatively low-status jobs (18.84 and 17.60). This was in spite of the fact that, as will be seen below, the fathers of the Mexican nondelinquents were significantly better educated than the fathers of the Mexican delinquents and that there was a similar trend for the Latin nondelinquents' fathers.

This unexpected reversal may have theoretical significance. If it had been found that the fathers of the *delinquents* were better educated but had poorer jobs, then it would be possible to infer bitterness at an unfair rejection by the social system. Such bitterness could be transmitted to the son and perhaps cause his antisocial attitudes and poorer school performance. This would fit neatly with the differential-opportunity theory. However, the reverse finding is inconsistent with what one would expect on the basis of this theory. Defenders of differential-opportunity theory will be quick to point out, and quite rightly, that here we are discussing relative achievement levels. While the fathers of the Latin delinquents may be relatively better off than the fathers of the nondelinquents, they are not necessarily aware of this and probably would not be greatly reassured if they were. Their position on the status hierarchy is still low. Nevertheless, the fact remains that on the basis of differential opportunity theory one would infer greater dissatisfaction and frustration on the part of the fathers of the nondelinquent Latins, yet their sons have not become delinquent. Therefore, economic frustration is obviously not a sufficient explanation for delinquency, at least in Latin or Mexican culture.

ECONOMIC INDICES: WEEKLY INCOME AND TELEPHONES IN THE HOME

The remaining two indices of socioeconomic status are quite crude. The first is the weekly income of the father in local currency. The use of this index without relating it to the source of the income (salary, gambling, burglary, welfare) is, of course, questionable. However, the data, presented in Table 23, are noteworthy for the close agreement between the weekly income of the fathers of the delinquents and nondelinquents, particularly in the Anglo and Latin groups. In the Mexican sample, there was a trend for the fathers of the nondelinquents to earn more pesos per week than the parents of the delinquents.

The close similarity between the income of the delinquents' and nondelinquents' families in the three cultures disagrees with the findings obtained by the Gluecks. Despite the fact that their samples were matched for residence in underprivileged areas, the Gluecks found the delinquents' families to have a significantly lower mean weekly income (Glueck & Glueck, 1950, p. 86). They also obtained data regarding the source of family income and found that the delinquents' families were less likely to be supported by legitimate earnings and more likely to be supported by welfare or relief agencies, income from boarders, loans from relatives, or unemployment or accident insurance. The Gluecks felt these differences were (1950,

Table 23

Indices of Economic Status

Index	Anglo		Latin		Mexican	
	C*	D*	C	D	C	D
Mean weekly income of father in local currency	$108	$105	$79	$80	$255	$215
Number of homes with telephones	40	40	21	21	3	0

* C, comparison group; D, delinquent group.

p. 280) "attributable, at least in part, to the far poorer work habits of the fathers, and in part also to less planful management of the family income."

The second index, the number of homes with telephones, is even cruder, although the editors of the late *Literary Digest* can testify to its potential ability to differentiate families with different political attitudes. This index is particularly crude in Mexico, since it can be quite difficult for even upper-middle-class families to obtain telephone service, even after a long waiting period, in many Mexican cities. In any case, as with the weekly income, the data show an extraordinary degree of concordance between the families of the delinquent and comparison subjects in the various samples.

On both economic indices, it will be noted that the Latins were considerably lower than the Anglos. Since minority groups are typically in poorer economic straits than the majority group, this offers some validation of the measures used. Valid comparisons between the United States and Mexican samples, however, cannot be made. While the dollar value of the Mexicans' salaries can be computed ($20.40 for the nondelinquents and $17.20 for the delinquents), the differences in purchasing power preclude direct comparisons.

SUMMARY OF SOCIOECONOMIC DATA

The socioeconomic status of the parents of the delinquent and comparison groups in the three samples was compared using three indices: ratings of the status of the father's occupation, the father's weekly income, and the presence of telephones in the home. On the first and most sensitive index of status, father's occupation, the fathers of the nondelinquent Anglos had significantly higher-status jobs than the fathers of the Anglo delinquents, a not too surprising finding. However, it was found that, contrary to expectation, the fathers of the nondelinquent Latins had significantly lower-status jobs than did the fathers of the delinquent Latins. This was interpreted as being inconsistent with theories of delinquency that emphasize economic frustration as the major cause of delinquency. No noteworthy differences were found in the various groups on the two economic indices, weekly income of the fathers and the presence of phones in the homes.

Educational Level of the Boy and His Parents

The final sociological variable to be considered is the educational attainment of the boys and their parents. Since educational level is another factor determining status, both directly and through the increased income it may yield, this variable is closely related to the preceding discussion of socioeconomic status. However, it is useful to keep the two distinct. No one is guaranteed a basic weekly wage, a job consistent with one's abilities, or a telephone, in either the United States or the Republic of Mexico. However, in both countries children are provided with a basic education at public expense. To be sure, economic factors may prevent a person from making full use of this privilege, since some may have to leave school to go to work, while others may have their educational ability crippled by cultural deprivation. However, both countries come closer to providing education for all who can and will make use of it than they do to providing opportunities in almost any other sphere.

The importance of education as a factor influencing delinquency can scarcely be overestimated. As we have seen, Cohen (1955) placed central importance on the lower-class child's reaction to the school system as a cause of delinquency. Other theories, such as Cloward and Ohlin's (1960) differential-opportunity theory, also highlighted the importance of education, for with an adequate education it may be possible for the lower-class child to attain his goals by legitimate rather than illegitimate means.

Schools emphasize not only learning but also conformity to certain prescribed rules of conduct. It has been debated whether this is good or bad, but it is an inescapable fact of life. Whether or not conformity stifles creativity and spontaneity, no teacher can teach a class of thirty or forty children who are all freely expressing themselves and exercising unbridled individualism and retain her sanity, much less impart any information. While the school's emphasis on conformity can be debated when it extends to prescribing the style of clothes or haircuts that will be permitted, there are few who will disagree with the idea that the individual child's right to swing his arm ends where his fellow pupil's nose begins. Thus, schools must be agents of socialization as well as institutions for the transmission of knowledge. Since delinquents by definition are less socialized than nondelinquents, it is natural that they would be at odds with the school system.

As we saw in Chapter 3, the lower-class child, whether delinquent or nondelinquent, faces special problems in the school setting. McCandless (1967) has written eloquently of the conflict in values between the lower-class child and his middle-class teacher. He has pointed out how the lower-class child knows from experience that violence is often necessary, that the person who saves for tomorrow may lose what he has today, and that the person who decorously restrains his emotions often loses out in the struggle to get a fair share of the family food ration. The conflict of values is particularly severe for the Latin child, who comes from a culture in which individual ambition and achievement is often regarded as unseemly and in which striving to surpass the level reached by one's father may be regarded as a sign of disrespect.

In addition to the conflict of values that the lower-class child may face, there is also the sheer difficulty encountered with school work itself. It has been well established that cultural deprivation can lead to intellectual deprivation. The child who comes from a home in which verbal interaction is encouraged, in which resources such as books, atlases, and encyclopedias are provided, in which academic achievement is encouraged, and in which a place to study is made available, will do better in school than the child without these advantages. Once again, the Latin child is likely to have special problems because of his bilingualism.

Thus, for the lower-class or minority-group child, school can be a very frustrating experience. The relation between frustration and anger or aggression has been well documented (Berkowitz, 1962). The more stressful the school situation, the greater the likelihood of disturbed behavior, including antisocial acting out. In a vicious cycle this can, in turn, lead to greater difficulties in school, more stress added to the system, and more disturbance. The end result can be dropping out of school, which can lead to further frustrations in the competition for jobs and to children being reared by parents who are embittered against society and have negative attitudes toward school, which can start the next generation down the same path in the so-called poverty cycle.

It is therefore natural, all things considered, that delinquency should be associated with poorer scholastic performance. Given the broader view of the transmission of attitudes from generation to generation, it is reasonable to suppose not only that poorer scholastic achievement would be found in delinquent boys themselves, but also that their parents would not have done as well in school as the parents of nondelinquent boys.

The literature on school dropouts and delinquency is quite consistent with this expectation. Studies on the relation of social class and dropping out of school clearly show an increased rate in dropouts the farther down the socioeconomic scale one goes (Cavan, 1962).

Studies of prison and correctional school populations almost always indicate substandard educational attainment. The Gluecks (1950) found that their delinquent sample was significantly lower in grade placement than their controls. Sutherland and Cressey report (1966, p. 251), "Of 4,000 inmates over age 17 admitted to the Texas prison system, 5 per cent had not completed the first grade, 44 per cent had not completed the eighth grade, 89 per cent had not completed high school, and 99 per cent had not completed college." While many studies are poorly controlled and the data are undoubtedly influenced by the fact that the more ignorant offenders are more likely to be apprehended, convicted, and sentenced to prison, there appears to be little doubt that the educational level of adult and juvenile offenders is below average, even for their own ethnic and economic reference groups.

It was therefore hypothesized that in the present study the delinquents in all three groups would be significantly lower than the nondelinquents in their educational attainment. It was further hypothesized that the educational level of their parents would be below average. To the authors' knowledge the educational level of the parents of delinquents and nondelinquents has not been systematically contrasted in prior studies.

EDUCATIONAL ATTAINMENT OF THE SUBJECTS

The grade level of most of the boys in the sample was determined, and the grade placement of the delinquent and nondelinquent subjects in the various samples was contrasted by means of *t* tests. The grade-level distributions, means, standard deviations, and results of the *t* tests are presented in Table 24. In each of the three ethnic groups, the nondelinquents had achieved a significantly higher

Table 24

Highest Grade Completed by Boys and Their Parents

Grade	BOYS Anglo		BOYS Latin		BOYS Mexican		FATHERS Anglo		FATHERS Latin		FATHERS Mexican		MOTHERS Anglo		MOTHERS Latin		MOTHERS Mexican	
	C*	D*	C	D	C	D	C	D	C	D	C	D	C	D	C	D	C	D
No schooling	0	0	0	0	0	0	0	0	7	4	4	3	0	0	5	6	9	13
1	0	0	0	0	0	1	0	0	0	0	3	2	0	0	1	1	0	3
2	0	0	0	0	0	1	0	0	0	0	5	8	0	0	0	1	4	2
3	0	0	0	0	0	6	0	0	1	3	5	9	0	0	2	3	8	8
4	0	0	0	2	1	5	0	1	1	4	7	5	0	1	4	1	3	6
5	0	2	0	3	4	8	0	1	3	2	2	0	1	1	5	7	5	3
6	1	5	2	11	15	9	0	3	4	4	15	4	1	2	3	2	11	5
7	3	6	9	17	3	7	1	2	4	6	0	0	1	2	3	3	0	0
8	4	9	11	8	11	2	7	1	4	0	1	0	2	8	6	0	4	0

9	12	10	14	3	15	2
10	11	14	6	5	0	1
11	8	2	2	0	0	0
12	2	0	0	0	0	1
13	0	0	0	0	0	0
14	0	0	0	0	0	0
15	0	0	0	0	0	0
16	0	0	0	0	0	0
17	0	0	0	0	0	0
No information	9	2	6	1	1	7
Mean	9.49	8.46	8.43	7.12	7.31	5.58
σ*	1.38	1.58	1.23	1.48	1.49	2.18
t	3.25		4.94		4.33	
p (2 tail)	<.005		<.001		<.001	

9	2	2	6	0	6	19
10	8	2	2	2	0	0
11	2	0	2	0	0	0
12	16	7	4	1	1	0
13	1	2	0	0	0	0
14	4	4	1	0	0	0
15	0	1	0	0	1	0
16	3	1	0	0	0	0
17	1	1	0	0	0	0
No information	5	22	11	24	6	19
Mean	11.31	10.50	6.77	5.12	4.34	2.87
σ*	2.42	3.53	4.00	3.12	2.95	1.67
t	1.06		1.87		2.73	
p (2 tail)	N.S.		<.07		<.01	

9	2	3	4	3	1	0
10	2	3	0	2	0	0
11	2	5	9	1	0	0
12	21	4	0	1	0	0
13	3	0	0	0	0	0
14	3	1	0	0	0	0
15	0	0	0	0	0	0
16	5	0	0	0	0	0
17	0	0	0	0	0	0
No information	7	18	7	19	5	10
Mean	11.53	9.6	6.7	5.0	3.90	2.5
σ*	2.50	2.69	3.88	3.58	2.64	2.17
t	1.13		1.95		2.69	
p (2 tail)	<.005		<.06		<.01	

* C, comparison group; D, delinquent group; σ, standard deviation.

grade level than the delinquents. As might be expected from the handicaps mentioned above, the grade level achieved by the Latin groups was less than that of the Anglos, although, because of differences in sampling procedure, no statistical tests were carried out. The fact that the Mexicans were lower than the Latins cannot, of course, be accounted for by hypotheses regarding minority group status.

EDUCATIONAL ATTAINMENT OF THE BOYS' PARENTS

Earlier in this chapter, we examined the question of whether the poorer church attendance of the delinquents was part of a general familial pattern by comparing the church attendance of the parents of the subjects in the delinquent and comparison groups. The same question can be raised about the poorer school achievement of the delinquent boys. Kraus (1964) has established that the educational aspirations of lower-class boys are directly related to the educational achievement of the parents. We might expect from this that non-delinquents' parents would be better educated than the delinquents' parents.

Accordingly, the highest grade completed by the parents of each subject was determined whenever possible. Because of the prevalence of broken homes, however, there were considerable missing data regarding the education of the parents, particularly the parents of the delinquent boys. How these missing data might have biased the results could not, of course, be determined. However, it seems reasonable that it was the more poorly educated parents who could not be located; if so, the effect of the incompleteness of the data would be to make the comparison more conservative.

In all three groups, there was a tendency for the fathers of the nondelinquents to have attained a higher grade level than the fathers of the delinquents. The trend was not significant in the Anglo sample. It approached significance in the Latin sample ($p < .07$) and attained significance in the Mexican sample ($p < .01$).[6]

It will be recalled that in spite of their superior education the fathers of the nondelinquent Latins had significantly lower-status occupations than the fathers of the delinquent Latins, and there was

---

[6] The p levels reported are two tail, although the directional nature of the hypothesis would have justified a one-tail test. If a one-tail test had been used, the reported p values would, of course, have been halved.

a tendency in this direction in the Mexican sample as well. Nevertheless, despite the fact that their increased education did not pay off in the job market place, the fathers of the nondelinquents, who had apparently valued education more highly as youths, managed either to transmit this to their sons or to at least create an atmosphere in which their sons could achieve more scholastically than did the delinquent boys. One way they achieved this was by marrying women who had gone farther in school than had the mothers of the delinquents.

The differences between mothers of the delinquents and nondelinquents were significant in the Anglo and Mexican samples ($p<.005$ and $p<.01$, respectively) and closely approached significance in the Latin sample ($p<.06$).

In general, then, the results for the parents resembled those for the sons, as the parents of the nondelinquents were better educated than the parents of the delinquents. Once again, this points up the long-term transmission of values and attitudes from one generation to another.

Examination of the means indicates that the Anglos' parents were better educated than the Latins' who in turn were better educated than the Mexicans'. It is encouraging to note, however, that the magnitude of these ethnic differences was much less for the younger generation than for their parents, and that the mean grade level of the Latin and Mexican boys already surpasses that of their parents, although few of the 300 boys had completed their education at the time the study was conducted.

In each subgroup (i.e., Anglo comparison group) the correspondence between the mean education level of the fathers and the mothers was noteworthy. In no group was there any systematic tendency for the women to receive a poorer education than the men.

SUMMARY OF EDUCATIONAL DATA

The problems encountered by the lower-class boy, particularly when he is a member of a minority group, in the school system were reviewed. It became apparent that for many such boys, particularly those with delinquent tendencies, school could be a very stressful experience.

It was hypothesized that, as in other studies, the educational attainment of the delinquent boys in each ethnic sample would be significantly lower than that of the comparison groups. This was confirmed.

It was further hypothesized that the educational attainment of the fathers and mothers of the delinquent boys would be lower than that of the comparison groups' parents. In each of the six comparisons made, the data were in the predicted direction, with three of the comparisons attaining significance and two others approaching significance (p [two tail] $<.07$).

The data showed that the mean educational level of the Anglo boys and their parents was higher than that of the Latins, who, in turn, were higher than the Mexicans. However, in the latter groups the mean educational attainment of the sons has already surpassed that of their parents. There was little difference between the educational attainment of the fathers and mothers within each of the six subgroups.

Summary of Sociological Findings

By and large, the sociological data that were obtained were consistent with findings already reported in the literature and tended to lend cross-cultural generality to them. A number of indices of marital instability were examined, including the present marital status of the parents, the divorce records of the mothers and fathers, and the composition of the parental home. No one index was significant in all three ethnic groups, yet, surveying the data as a whole, it can be safely concluded that the delinquents in all three groups came from more unstable and broken homes than did the comparison group subjects.

Family size and birth order were also examined. It was found that the delinquent Anglos came from significantly larger homes than did the nondelinquent Anglos, but no differences were found in the Latin or Mexican families. There was a slight tendency for delinquency to be less common in the eldest sons in the Anglo sample, but not in the other samples. In the Mexican sample it was found that the nondelinquents had a significantly higher proportion of older brothers and sisters, while the nondelinquent Latins had a significantly higher proportion of older sisters. This was interpreted as being consistent with the quasi-parental responsibilities assumed by older children in traditional Mexican households, assuming that increased attention and care inhibit delinquency.

In all three samples it was found that the reported church attendance of the nondelinquents and their parents was significantly more regular than that of the delinquents and their parents. There was no association, however, between religious denomination and incidence of delinquency.

The only major deviation from expectation came in the area of socioeconomic status. On indices of economic well-being there was little if any difference between the delinquent and comparison samples, which was not surprising, since neighborhood was controlled. The fathers of the nondelinquent Anglos had significantly higher-status jobs than did the fathers of the Anglo delinquents, but the reverse was found in the Latin sample and there was a similar insignificant trend in the Mexican sample. This was despite the fact that the fathers of the nondelinquent Mexicans and Latins were significantly better educated than the fathers of the delinquents in these samples. This finding seemed inconsistent with theories that emphasize economic frustration as a major cause of delinquency. While economic frustration could have been a factor in the Anglo group, it did not appear to fit with the data from the Latin and Mexican samples.

As just noted, the fathers of the nondelinquents, and their mothers as well, had gone farther in school, with the differences often attaining statistical significance. The boys in the comparison groups, as expected, had significantly higher grade placements than did the delinquents in all three ethnic groups. These differences in both generations further emphasized the intergenerational transmission of values in all three cultures.

CHAPTER 7

THE WECHSLER INTELLIGENCE SCALES

Our present judicial system is founded on the assumption that man is a rational creature. In modern Western jurisprudence, for example, it is necessary to prove not only that a person committed an act but also *mens rea*, that is, he did so voluntarily and willingly. In a case where a person does not have sufficient reasoning ability to form a criminal intent, as with very young children or offenders who are legally insane or incompetent, the person is regarded as not guilty of a criminal act.

The roots of the assumption of man's rationality go deep in Western culture, stemming in no small measure from the early Church and the writings of such scholars as St. Augustine and St. Thomas Aquinas, as well as from the influence of the "social contract" philosophers, such as Hobbes, Locke, Rousseau, and Voltaire. They saw man as an individual making an implicit contract with society in which he receives protection and the other benefits of membership in society in return for his agreement not to violate society's rules of behavior. Man then rationally decides whether to follow the path of good or the path of evil. This freedom of choice, with full knowledge of the consequences, is exemplified by the Garden of Eden allegory. If man willingly and knowingly violates the terms of his social contract, then society has the right to take steps to ensure that further violations do not occur. In Medieval Europe violation of the social contract frequently led to the death penalty or banishment, which, though harsh, were effective in preventing recidivism.

Cesare Bonesana, Marchesa de Beccaria (1735–1795), the first of the so-called Classical School of Criminologists, adopted this rationalistic point of view in his writings, which were to serve as the cornerstone of the French Code of 1791, and which, with modifications, underlie many of our present-day penal codes (Vold, 1958). Beccaria held that a primary purpose of a penal code is to deter crime and that a scale of punishments should be devised so that each involved just enough pain to outweigh the pleasure involved in a given criminal act. Thus, today we have different penalties assessed for different crimes. The most typical punishment involves segregation from society in a penitentiary where the offender can do penance and reflect on his crimes. This experience should be sufficient to convince a rational man to mend his ways.

Assuming that man is rational and that crime is irrational behavior, the question naturally arose as to how one could account for the fact that men nevertheless did commit crimes. One could resort to the old notion of possession by a devil, but, as Vold (1958) has pointed out, the rationalistic *Zeitgeist* also encouraged a search for explanation in natural rather than supernatural events.

With the nineteenth century and the work of Darwin on biological evolution, the research of Galton and Dugdale on the role of heredity in eminence and degeneracy, and Freud's early work laying the groundwork for psychoanalysis, man's biological nature was increasingly emphasized. It was natural that in attempting to account for criminality various biological theories would come to the fore. One that received great attention in Italy around the turn of the century was the theory of Lombroso and the Positivist School that the criminal was an atavistic throwback to a more primitive life form. Another, which received more attention in the United States, was that perhaps the criminal was unable to make an intelligent choice between right and wrong because of inherently inferior reasoning ability. Interest in this theory coincided with the development of the first instruments for measuring defective reasoning or intelligence by Binet and Simon in 1905. It was thus natural that these newly developed tests should be pressed into immediate service in order to test the hypothesis that criminals were of defective intelligence. Unfortunately, this effort was made before the early scales had been developed and standardized to the point where they were equal to the task. The result was that the early work gave a totally misleading picture of the intelligence of the criminal as compared with that of the noncriminal.

One of the first to investigate the intelligence of criminals was H. H. Goddard. Using his own literal translations of Binet's early scales, Goddard started testing the mental age of inmates of correctional institutions around 1912 (Caplan, 1965). In his research with mental retardates at the New Jersey State Training School for the Feeble Minded at Vineland, New Jersey, Goddard had found that none of the retardates had a mental age over 13. He therefore made the obvious inference that an adult who has a mental age of 12 or less can be classified as feebleminded (Vold, 1958). A number of studies of incarcerated criminals were carried out using this criterion. In 1914, Goddard summarized these studies and reported that the percentage of feebleminded persons among the criminal groups sampled ranged from a low of 28 per cent to a high of 89 per cent, with a median of 70 per cent (Vold, 1958).

Sutherland and Cressey (1966, p. 162) report that Goddard held that "feeblemindedness of a delinquent *fully* explained the delinquency" (italics in original). They quote Goddard as follows (Goddard, 1920, as cited in Sutherland & Cressey, 1966, p. 162):

> Every investigation of the mentality of criminals, misdemeanants, delinquents, and other antisocial groups has proven beyond the possibility of contradiction that nearly all persons in these classes, and in some cases, all, are of low mentality. . . . It is no longer to be denied that the greatest single cause of delinquency and crime is lowgrade mentality, much of it within the limits of feeble-mindedness.

With the entry of the United States into World War I, large numbers of normal young adult draftees were examined with the Army Alpha and other new intelligence tests that had been used primarily with abnormal populations, such as retardates and prisoners. For the first time adequate sets of adult norms became available with which the mental ages of the criminal groups could be compared. It was found that over 30 per cent of the young men in the draft army had mental ages of 12 or below and would, according to Goddard's original criterion, be classified as feebleminded. Since, as Goddard pointed out in 1921, no one felt that more than 1 per cent of the general population was feebleminded, it was obvious that the original criterion and, therefore, the reported incidence of mental deficiency in criminal samples were erroneous (Vold, 1958). Goddard himself recognized this and admitted his error (Goddard, 1927, as cited in Vold, 1958, p. 83):

The war led to the measurement of intelligence of the drafted army with the result that such an enormous proportion was found to have an intelligence of 12 years and less that to call them all feeble minded was an absurdity of the highest degree. . . . We have already said that we thought 12 was the limit, but we now know that most of the twelve, and even of the ten and nine, are not defective.

Investigations of the intelligence of criminals continued to be carried out. Terman devised the IQ, the ratio of mental age to chronological age multiplied by 100. Kuhlman studied the intelligence of prisoners in Minnesota institutions and found that a high percentage had IQs below 75. Vold reanalyzed Kuhlman's data, however, and found that while the IQs were indeed low, the median mental ages from which the IQs were calculated were quite similar to those obtained for the World War I draft army in one institution and somewhat higher at the other. Vold attributed the apparent lowness of the prisoners' IQs to "the inaccuracy of the arbitrary base age chosen (16) for converting mental age into IQ scores" (Vold, 1958, p. 85).[1]

[1] As noted above, the original Binet intelligence scales were scored in terms of the Mental Age (MA) of each testee by comparing his performance with the average performance of children at various ages. Thus, if a person's performance was equivalent to that of the average 10 year old, his MA was 10. If his chronological age was less than 10 his performance was above average; if he was 10 his performance was average; if he was older than 10 his performance was below par. The process rested on the assumption of intellectual ability increasing regularly with chronological age (CA).

In order to communicate such test data better, Terman devised the intelligence quotient (IQ), which had the advantage of immediately communicating whether the person was higher or lower than his reference group. However, this system broke down when calculating adult IQs, since the development of mental ability does not continue to increase in adults in the same manner that it increases in children, although chronological age does of course increase. Therefore, an arbitrary age had to be chosen as the CA at which mental development ceased, and this CA was then used in calculating the IQs of all adults whether their actual CAs were 20, 40, or 80. If too high an arbitrary CA were chosen, the result would be an excessive number of low IQs, just as the choice of too low a CA would result in too many high IQs. Vold is therefore arguing that Kuhlman chose too high a CA with which to divide the obtained MAs, and it was this

In his review of the early literature, Vold reported that other studies using control groups did not find the criminals to be mentally defective. Murchison compared the Army Alpha scores of prisoners from five states with the draftee population in 1926, and Adler and Worthington contrasted the Alpha performance of Illinois prisoners with the draftees in 1925. In both cases, according to Vold, the prisoners ranked higher than the soldiers. In 1939, Tuchin controlled for regional differences by comparing Illinois prisoners with Illinois draftees and found no significant differences (Vold, 1958). As a result of these and similar investigations, mental deficiency has disappeared as a necessary or sufficient explanation for crime or delinquency.

It would be a mistake, however, to infer that there is no association between tested intelligence and delinquency. While mental deficiency alone cannot account for crime, nevertheless, groups of offenders tend to score consistently lower than the normative groups on modern intelligence tests. Caplan (1965), reviewing recent work on the intellectual functioning of delinquents, cited one study of 500 delinquents using the 1937 revision of the Stanford-Binet that obtained a mean IQ of 92.5, another study of 500 male delinquents using the Wechsler-Bellevue that obtained a mean of 92.4, and a third of 8,003 court cases using the Otis that obtained a mean IQ of 91.4. Caplan concluded (1965, p. 104), "Therefore, it appears that the most recent evidence, based on a variety of intelligence tests, consistently reveals a difference of about 8 points between the mean IQs of delinquent and general population samples." He went on to explain: "This 8-point difference does not, however, mean that delinquents are significantly inferior in intelligence to nondelinquents. It simply means that the delinquent samples under investigation tested lower than the random samples used in standardizing the test norms."

It may seem paradoxical, after citing three major investigations in which the intelligence of delinquents was compared with that of nondelinquents and found to be significantly lower, that Caplan should then assert this does not mean that delinquents are significantly inferior in intelligence. The problem centers on the meaning of the word "intelligence." If we accept Boring's (1923) dictum,

---

error that led to the apparently low IQs among the criminals. Comparison of these IQs with a control group, such as the draftees, would have shown just as many low IQs in both groups.

"Intelligence is what the tests test," then Caplan's position is untenable. However, most psychologists now agree that intelligence, as tested by intelligence tests, is a combination of native ability and present functioning level. Hebb (1949, p. 294) has stated:

> From this point of view it appears that the word "intelligence" has *two* valuable meanings. One is (*A*) an *innate potential*, the capacity for development, a fully innate property that amounts to the possession of a good brain and a good neural metabolism. The second is (*B*) the functioning of a brain in which development has gone on, determining an *average level of performance or comprehension* by the partly grown or mature person.

Thus, Caplan's point is that because the current functioning level of the delinquent samples is lower than that of the standardization samples (Intelligence *B*) we should not necessarily infer that the delinquents are innately inferior (Intelligence *A*). It may be that they are innately inferior, but it also may be cultural deprivation, resistance and negativism to tests, specific reading disabilities, or a host of other factors that influence functioning level but not innate ability that cause the differences. Caplan therefore called for research using appropriate controls that take into account differences in class and locale. The present study was designed to do this and to investigate ethnic background as well.

Procedures

The first step in investigating intelligence is choosing an intelligence test. There seemed to be little doubt that in studying the intelligence of lower-class delinquents an individual intelligence test was to be preferred over a group test. In the first place, individual administration allows material to be presented verbally so that the score is not directly influenced by poorly developed reading ability. Secondly, the short attention span of many delinquents can be coped with by a skilled examiner who can encourage the subject, allow for brief rest periods, or vary the presentation of material in such a way as to maintain the individual's interest.

Given the selection of an individual test, a number of considerations led to the choice of the Wechsler Intelligence Scales. First and foremost, the Wechsler Intelligence Scale for Children (WISC) and the Wechsler Adult Intelligence Scale (WAIS) are, along with the Stanford-Binet, the standard individual intelligence tests that serve as criterion measures for other tests. The Wechsler scales have the advantage of providing separate estimates of verbal and performance ability based on the responses to a number of different subtests in addition to an overall IQ. Since performance scores are less likely to be influenced by cultural deprivation or by language difficulties, it seemed preferable to use the Wechsler. To be sure, a completely "culture-free" test, if such a thing exists, might have been preferable as a measure of Intelligence A, but since school is not a culture-free situation it seemed better to use an instrument more closely related to functioning level that, as we have seen, is a combination of both innate potential and past learning.

The final factor that influenced the decision was the availability of a Spanish translation of the WISC that had been recently standardized in Puerto Rico. Since the present data were collected, subsequent research has indicated that the Puerto Rican standardization of the WISC is not as well suited to Mexico as we had hoped it would be. One difficulty with the Puerto Rican WISC was the fact that time and distance have produced significant differences in the Spanish language as spoken in Puerto Rico and Mexico. Another problem was that of cultural bias. Puerto Rico, as part of the United States, shares in the United States culture to a much greater extent than does Mexico. The North American bias in questions asking the distance from New York to Chicago or the height of the average (North) American man is obvious. However, cultural factors influence many other items as well, as recent attempts to adapt the WISC to Mexican culture have demonstrated (Lagunes, 1965; Rodriguez, 1965; Rodriguez & Diaz-Guerrero, 1964). Lagunes (1965), for example, found that the question "What would you do if you were sent to buy a loaf of bread and the grocer said he did not have any more?" is considerably more difficult for Mexican children than it is for United States children. One reason for this may be that, because loaves of bread are so rare in Mexico, where tortillas are the staple, the intelligent thing to do is go home if the grocer has none. More important is the fact that to obtain a high score on this item the respondent has to exercise individual initiative in going to another store without consulting the parent. In the authoritarian Mexican culture this would be very disrespectful. The child is expected to do as he is told and, if that does not work, to report home for further instructions. The cultural bias of the Puerto Rican version of the WISC when used in Mexico is not of any great concern for our purpose of comparing the scores of the Mexican delinquents and nondelinquents. However, it does make it impossible to contrast meaningfully the scores of the Mexicans with those of the Anglos or Latins.

Table 25 shows the form of the Wechsler administered to the various groups of subjects. The Puerto Rican standardization of the WISC was used on all the Mexican subjects, regardless of age, and the regular English WISC or WAIS was used on all the United States samples. Five Verbal subtests (Information, Comprehension, Arithmetic, Similarities, and Vocabulary) and five Performance subtests (Picture Completion, Picture Arrangement, Block Design, Object Assembly, and Coding) were used.

All tests were administered by examiners trained in Wechsler administration who recorded the answers verbatim. To insure reliability, each protocol was scored at least twice by Mrs. Carl Rosenquist, M.A., a psychologist who had participated in the standardization of the WISC.

Results

Group means and standard deviations were computed for the Verbal, Performance, and Full Scale IQs, as well as for each Wechsler subscale. Differences between the delinquent and comparison groups within each sample were tested with t tests. The results are presented in Table 26.

Table 25

Form of Intelligence Test Given

Test	Anglo		Latin		Mexican	
	C[*]	D[*]	C	D	C	D
WISC	29	45	31	45	0	0
WAIS	21	5	19	5	0	0
SPANISH WISC	0	0	0	0	50	50

[*] C, comparison group; D, delinquent group.

Table 26

Results of the Wechsler Intelligence Scales

		Anglo			Latin			Mexican		
		C*	D*	t	C	D	t	C	D	t
Information	$\bar{x}$*	11.2	9.6	2.90	8.4	5.4	5.66	6.4	6.6	0.39
	σ*	2.7	2.8	$p<.005$	2.8	2.5	$p<.001$	2.2	2.9	N.S.
Comprehension	$\bar{x}$	11.4	9.7	2.78	8.9	6.1	0.54	13.4	9.4	3.73
	σ	3.3	2.8	$p<.01$	2.8	2.4	N.S.	5.6	5.1	$p<.001$
Arithmetic	$\bar{x}$	11.3	10.7	0.09	8.3	6.1	4.40	6.4	9.0	4.73
	σ	3.0	3.5	N.S.	2.5	2.5	$p<.001$	1.7	3.5	$p<.001$
Similarities	$\bar{x}$	12.0	10.9	1.95	9.5	7.3	4.00	8.2	10.7	3.32
	σ	2.5	3.1	$p<.06$	2.7	2.8	$p<.001$	4.1	3.4	$p<.005$
Vocabulary	$\bar{x}$	10.2	9.1	1.83	7.1	4.3	5.71	8.8	6.9	3.11
	σ	2.8	3.2	N.S.	2.5	2.4	$p<.001$	2.9	3.2	$p<.005$
Verbal IQ	$\bar{x}$	108.0	100.0	2.90	93.0	76.0	6.79	88.0	91.0	0.997
	σ	14.0	14.0	$p<.005$	12.0	13.0	$p<.001$	13.0	17.0	N.S.
Picture	$\bar{x}$	11.8	13.2	2.09	10.1	9.5	0.85	7.0	11.0	6.67
Completion	σ	3.3	3.4	$p<.05$	3.1	3.9	N.S.	2.9	3.1	$p<.001$
Picture	$\bar{x}$	12.3	10.6	2.82	9.8	8.3	2.49	5.8	10.1	6.35
Arrangement	σ	2.8	3.2	$p<.01$	2.8	3.2	$p<.02$	2.3	4.2	$p<.001$
Block Design	$\bar{x}$	12.1	11.3	1.66	10.2	8.5	2.98	7.7	8.5	1.39
	σ	2.3	2.5	N.S.	2.9	2.8	$p<.005$	3.2	2.5	N.S.
Object	$\bar{x}$	11.7	11.6	0.15	9.6	9.3	0.44	6.8	9.6	4.58
Assembly	σ	3.3	3.4	N.S.	3.3	3.5	N.S.	2.9	3.2	$p<.001$
Coding	$\bar{x}$	10.5	9.7	1.45	9.2	8.0	2.39	6.3	5.1	1.90
	σ	2.9	2.6	N.S.	2.3	2.7	$p<.02$	3.1	3.2	N.S.
Performance	$\bar{x}$	112.0	109.0	1.03	99.0	91.0	2.91	76.0	94.0	6.67
IQ	σ	15.0	14.0	N.S.	11.0	16.0	$p<.005$	13.0	14.0	$p<.001$
Full Scale IQ	$\bar{x}$	111.0	105.0	2.14	95.0	82.0	5.16	81.0	92.0	3.89
	σ	14.0	14.0	$p<.05$	11.0	14.0	$p<.001$	12.0	16.0	$p<.001$

* C, comparison group; D, delinquent group; $\bar{x}$, mean; σ, standard deviation.

ANGLOS

In the Anglo sample the nondelinquents had significantly higher Verbal and Full Scale IQs than the delinquents. On the Verbal subtests the nondelinquents were significantly higher on the Information subtest, which depends on the number of facts a person has learned and is closely related to formal education, and on the Comprehension subtest, in which socially appropriate solutions to common problems are required. There was a nearly significant difference ($p<.06$) in favor of the nondelinquents on the Similarities subtest, which measures abstract verbal ability. The lower scores on these tests are consistent with Wechsler's (1958) observations regarding the typical pattern for delinquents. However, the fact that no difference was observed on the Arithmetic subtest, which is also related to formal education, was not consistent with his findings. The Gluecks (1950), who had first matched their delinquent and nondelinquent subjects on Full Scale Wechsler IQ, also found the delinquents to be significantly lower than the nondelinquents on Information and Comprehension. As in the present study, the Gluecks found no significant differences in Arithmetic, and the trend for a lower score on Similarities fell short of significance. Unlike the present study, the Guecks found their delinquent sample to be significantly lower on Vocabulary.

On the Performance subtests, the Anglo delinquents were significantly higher than the nondelinquents on the Picture Completion subtest. This high performance on Picture Completion was surprising, since the Gluecks found no significant differences on Picture Completion in their matched samples, and Wechsler (1958) maintained that delinquents should do better on Picture Arrangement and Object Assembly than on Block Design or Picture Completion.

The nondelinquent Anglos did significantly better than the delinquents on Picture Arrangement. This is somewhat contrary to Wechsler's hypothesis noted above that Picture Arrangement is a test on which delinquents do well relative to other subtests. However, it is consistent with some theorists' interpretation of Picture Arrangement as a sign of "social intelligence" or ability to correctly assess social situations and respond appropriately.

The Anglo delinquents had Performance IQs that were higher than their Verbal IQs ($p<.005$), as shown in Table 27. This is a typical

Table 27

Comparison of Verbal and Performance IQs within Each Group

	Anglo		Latin			Mexican	
Higher IQ	C* Performance	D* Performance	C Performance	D Performance		C Verbal	D Performance
t	1.58	3.21	2.61	5.14		4.61	0.96
p (two tail)	N.S.	<.005	<.02	<.001		<.001	N.S.

* C, comparison group; D, delinquent group.

finding in delinquent samples. A similar but insignificant trend was found for the comparison group as well, suggesting that this pattern could be in part an artifact of the lower-class background of most delinquents. This is supported by the fact that Cropley (1964), in a study in which he contrasted the WISC scores of high- and low-SES boys, found the low-SES boys to have a Performance IQ higher than the Verbal, while the reverse was found for the high-SES boys.

Despite the lower-class background of most of the Anglo boys, they obtained relatively high IQs. The Anglo comparison group obtained scores in the high-average to bright-normal range, while those of the delinquents were average or high average (see Figure 1).

LATINS

Like the Anglos, the nondelinquent Latin subjects had Verbal, Performance, and Full Scale IQs that were significantly higher than those obtained by the delinquents. As is typical in delinquent samples, the Latin delinquents' Performance IQs were significantly higher than their Verbal IQs ($p<.001$), as shown in Table 27. This was also true of the comparison group ($p<.02$), which is not surprising, since this is the usual pattern in bilingual samples.

The nondelinquent Latin subjects were significantly higher than the delinquents on all of the Verbal subtests except Comprehension, and on all of the Performance subtests except Picture Completion and Object Assembly. The pattern of the Verbal subtests was thus not like that of the Anglos nor like that described by Wechsler. The fact that the Latin delinquents did their best work on the Picture Completion and Object Assembly subtests, however, was similar to the pattern of the Anglo delinquents. As noted above, Wechsler and a number of other investigators reviewed by Caplan (1965) have observed that Object Assembly and Picture Arrangement are the Performance subtests on which delinquents do relatively well, while they tend to fall down on Block Design and Picture Completion, presumably because of impulsivity. In the Latin sample, however, the delinquents did relatively poorly on Picture Arrangement, as had the Anglo delinquents. While both the Anglo and Latin delinquents did relatively well on Object Assembly, their best performance was on Picture Completion.

Thus, the Wechsler data for both the Anglo and Latin delinquent and comparison groups were by and large consistent with what has

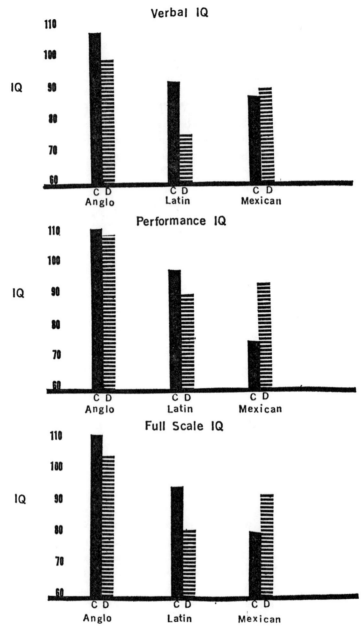

Figure 1. Comparison of the Verbal, Performance, and Full Scale IQs of the groups.

been found by other investigators of the intelligence test performance of delinquent and lower-class youth (Caplan, 1965; Cropley,
1964; Wechsler, 1958). In both the Anglo and Latin samples, the delinquents scored lower than the nondelinquents, the disparity between the delinquent and comparison groups was greater on the
Verbal, school-type, tests than on the Performance tests, and the
Performance IQ was higher than the Verbal IQ for all four groups.
The subtest patterns were also generally consistent with the patterns
reported by Wechsler, with the exception of the fact that the delinquents did relatively better than expected on Picture Completion and
poorer than expected on Picture Arrangement. Finally, as expected,
the bilingual Latins did poorer than the Anglos, but, somewhat contrary to expectation, the Anglo delinquents did not have below-
average IQs. The net effect of these data, then, was to add generality
to many of the patterns that have been observed in other parts of
the country on youths drawn from different delinquent and lower-
class populations.

MEXICANS

This generality broke down when the Puerto Rican standardization
of the translated WISC was given to Mexican youths in Monterrey.
It cannot be determined whether this was because of sampling problems, because a different instrument was used, or because Mexican
delinquents and nondelinquents simply have different patterns of
intellectual functioning, but it was clear that the results were different from those obtained in the other two samples.

The most noteworthy difference was the fact that the delinquents
obtained significantly higher scores than the nondelinquents on five
of the 10 subtests, and on the Performance and Full Scale IQs. While
some of these subtests were ones on which one would expect delinquents to do fairly well, such as Picture Completion, Picture Arrangement, and Object Assembly (thus adding some generality to
the patterns observed among the Anglos and Latins and that described by Wechsler), the delinquents were also higher on the
school-related Arithmetic subtest and on the Similarities subtest.
This was particularly noteworthy in view of the fact that in the
Latin sample significant differences in the opposite direction were
found on these very subtests. Only on Vocabulary and Comprehen-

sion did the nondelinquent Mexicans obtain significantly higher scores.

Despite the deficiencies of the Puerto Rican standardization of the WISC, the Mexican delinquents obtained Full Scale, Verbal, and Performance IQs in the average range; indeed, the IQs obtained by the Mexican delinquents were higher than those of the Latin delinquents. (If there had been no cultural bias this would not be surprising, since the Mexican delinquents took the test in their native language and were not hindered by bilingualism. The effect of language problems was demonstrated by the fact that the Mexican delinquents were only three points higher than the Latins on the mean Performance IQ but fifteen points higher on the mean Verbal IQ).

The pattern for the nondelinquent Mexicans differed from the pattern found for the Anglo and Latin comparison groups in that the Verbal IQ was significantly higher than the Performance IQ ($p<.001$). This was particularly surprising in view of the fact that the cultural bias of the Puerto Rican version of the WISC would be expected to influence the verbal material more than the performance tasks. The Mexican delinquents' Performance scores exceeded their Verbal IQs in the typical delinquent pattern, although, unlike the results of the Anglo and Latin delinquent groups, the difference was not statistically significant.

The poorer performance of the nondelinquent Mexican cannot be attributed to the fact that a test standardized on another population was used. Nor can differences in testing conditions explain the discrepancy, because, while testing conditions did differ systematically, it was the delinquents rather than the nondelinquents who were tested under poor conditions that would, if anything, have hindered their performance. (This is in one sense a reassuring finding, for later, when systematic differences between the Mexican delinquents and comparison subjects are found on the personality tests, it can be regarded as unlikely that these are transitory reactions induced by the poorer surroundings in which the delinquents were tested.)

Next, it was hypothesized that, since many of the delinquents and comparison subjects were tested by different examiners, perhaps the results reflected some systematic examiner bias. The results for the different examiners were studied and no evidence to support the hypothesis of an examiner bias was found.

While it is not possible to determine with any certainty the reason for the rather surprising reversal in the scoring pattern for the Mexican delinquents and nondelinquents, it appears likely that it was a function of the sampling. While it is possible, as one cynic who viewed these data remarked, that in Mexico the more intelligent lower-class boys become delinquent, the investigators are more inclined to lean toward the hypothesis that in Mexico the more intelligent lower-class boys do not go to the public schools. The public schools of Monterrey, unlike those of San Antonio, do not enroll an overwhelming majority of the school-age boys. Many boys in Monterrey who would have been in the public schools in San Antonio are gainfully employed or attending private schools. Possibly, it is the less intelligent boys who remain in the public school and who were sampled.

Another possibility is that the delinquents at the Escuela Prevocacional are more intelligent than the overall delinquent population. While we have no knowledge of whether or not this is the case, it is possible that some sort of screening took place, either formally or informally, so that only the more intelligent delinquents, who were able to benefit from vocational training, were sent to this institution, while some other disposition was made of the less able delinquents.

In any case, while some of the subtest patterns for the Mexican sample were similar to those found in other groups, for some unknown reason the delinquents, contrary to expectation, obtained higher scores than the nondelinquents. While it is possible to speculate at length about explanations for this, the only thing that can be said with certainty on the basis of these data was that in the Mexican sample there was no support for the notion that nondelinquents score higher on intelligence tests than delinquents with similar backgrounds. Judging from the present study, this observation cannot be regarded as having cross-national validity.

Summary

The Wechsler Intelligence Scales were chosen for administration to the 300 boys in the various groups. The data for the Anglo and Latin samples were quite similar to those obtained in other studies in the literature as the delinquents scored lower than the nondelinquents and the bilingual Latin boys scored lower than the Anglos. The subtest patterns, with certain exceptions, were also similar to observations that have been made in the literature.

For the Mexican samples, the Puerto Rican standardization of the WISC was chosen. While subsequent research on the use of this test in Mexico has highlighted its cultural bias, this appeared to be the best choice among those tests available at the time the data were collected. In the Mexican sample some of the subtest patterns were similar to those obtained in the other samples. However, unlike the other samples, the delinquents scored significantly higher than the nondelinquents on the Full Scale and Performance IQs, as well as on five of the 10 subtests. The Mexican comparison group was also the only one that obtained a Verbal IQ significantly higher than the Performance IQ. While various *ad hoc* speculations about the possible reasons for this reversal were entertained, nothing conclusive could be established beyond the fact that the data offered no support for the cross-national validity of the common observation that delinquents usually do significantly poorer than nondelinquents on intelligence tests.

CHAPTER 8

THE CHOICES TEST

The purpose of the Choices Test was to learn something about each subject's aspirations and attitudes. This was done by asking a series of simple questions. The first set of questions inquired how the subject would spend various sums of money, the second how he would spend leisure time, and the third about his occupational choice. While this was a simple and direct procedure, it was hoped that the data would not be without theoretical significance. As we have noted, various scholars have commented on the apparent impulsivity and lack of foresight that characterize delinquents; others have discussed the discrepancy between their ambitions and what they can realistically hope to achieve. It therefore seemed important to gather data relating to these characteristics and attitudes in order to determine if they are peculiar to delinquents or if they are common to all lower-class youth, as well as to ascertain if they apply to other cultures.

Choice of How To Spend Various Sums of Money

RATIONALE

As noted above, the Choices Test consisted of a series of questions that the examiner asked the boy. The examiners wrote down the boys' answers without making any comments. The first question asked, "If you had 25 cents, what would you do with it?" This was repeated for $2.00, $20.00, and, for the United States samples,

$200.00.[1] The questions were phrased in terms of dollars and cents for the Anglos and Latins and pesos and centavos for the Mexicans.

It was felt that the answers to these questions could be a good index of short-range hedonism and the willingness to delay gratification. Various scholars have commented on the delinquent's apparent inability to postpone gratification. "The delinquent is, then, an individual in whom instinctive drives are strong, conscience is weak, and the ego is bent upon immediate pleasure without respect to the generally accepted norms of behavior (Cole & Hall, 1966, p. 440).

Other scholars have commented on the fact that the delinquent appears to have a different time orientation than the nondelinquent. He appears to be a creature of the present, unable or unwilling to think in terms of the long-range consequences of his acts. Not only does he demand gratification, but he also demands it immediately.

Quay, reviewing studies comparing the time orientation of delinquents and nondelinquents, concluded (Quay, 1965b, p. 141):

> Taken together, these studies certainly suggest that the delinquent is more present-oriented than the normal when both groups are predominantly from the lower and lower middle classes. If one can extrapolate from the concept of future time orientation to the concept of an attenuated gradient of reinforcement, then these findings suggest a mechanism by which the self-defeating behavior of the delinquent may be understood; the delinquent behaves so as to maximize immediate reward, failing to be influenced by the possibility of later punishment. . . . The results of these studies are also relevant to a theory of delinquency which ascribes the problem to the nature of lower class values per se (Miller, 1959). One of the cardinal assumptions of this theory is that lower class culture places more emphasis on immediate gratification than on the anticipation of longer range rewards. While it may be that lower class children are more present-oriented than those of the middle class . . . it also appears that this orientation exists in even greater magnitude in those guilty of delinquency. Thus the notion that a direct transmission of this particular orientation in equal strength to all lower class children is a primary causative notion in delinquency is certainly questionable: individual differences must be considered.

If the delinquent is more hedonistic and less able to delay gratification than his peers, we would expect him to have different ideas

---

[1] The question, "If you had $200.00, what would you do with it?" was inadvertently omitted in the examination of the Mexican subjects.

about what to do with various sums of money. He would probably be more likely to spend it immediately for some short-term pleasure and with little thought for the future, while nondelinquents would probably be more willing to save money and to postpone gratification.

However, the absence of foresight that has been observed may be associated more with membership in the lower class than with delinquency per se. McCandless (1967, p. 587) has commented that the lower-class child is less likely to be thrifty than the middle-class child, for:

> . . . the lower-class group has nothing to be thrifty about. One must *have* money to save money. A certain faith in the dependability of the future is essential if one is to plan for it. For the typical lower-class child, faith in the future has received little support—he has learned instead that he had better grab while the grabbing is good because if he doesn't, one of his brothers and sisters, or his parents or his peers, will grab instead; and the supply is limited. . . . He simply doesn't comprehend the principle of saving.

It was hoped that the results of the first four questions on the Choices Test would shed some light on whether immediate-need gratification is more common in delinquents than in other lower-class boys.

RESULTS AND DISCUSSION

If You Had 25 Cents (20 Centavos), What Would You Do With It?

The boys in the various groups indicated a number of ways in which they would dispose of 25 cents or 20 centavos.[2] The most frequent response categories were determined by an overall inspection of the data, and then the frequency of the most common replies was tabulated. Table 28 presents these choices in order of their overall frequency. It can be seen from this table that the most common choice was to spend the money on food, followed by saving it. The least common choice was to spend it on oil or gas. Idiosyn-

---

[2] The Mexican boys were asked what they would do with 20 centavos rather than 25 centavos because 20 centavos represents a single coin just as 25 cents does in United States money.

Table 28

Disposition of 25 Cents or 20 Centavos

Choice	Anglo		Latin		Mexican	
	C*	D*	C	D	C	D
Food	7	7	19	6	5	12
Save it	14	6	10	4	12	0
Candy	3	2	0	5	12	19
Soft drinks	10	11	4	4	0	2
School supplies	7	2	8	0	9	1
Cigarettes	0	9	0	13	0	2
Spend it	0	2	0	7	5	0
Movies	1	2	0	3	0	0
Gum	1	0	1	0	2	2
Oil, gas	2	2	2	0	0	0
Other	5	7	6	8	5	12

*C, comparison group; D, delinquent group.

cratic choices, which were endorsed by less than six of the 300 subjects, were lumped together in the "other" category.

Next, the specific choices were grouped into three broad categories: (a) saving, (b) spending on school supplies, and (c) immediate pleasurable consumption (i.e., spending the money for food, candy, soft drinks, cigarettes, movies, gum, fuel or simply spending it). It is possible that a re-examination of the replies in the "other" category might have revealed some that would have been included in these broader categories. Unfortunately, this phase of the data analysis took place after the individual data had been lost, so it was impossible to reinspect or reclassify these data. This was also true of the other items in the Choices Test, and it is impossible to determine to what extent this might have biased the results.

It was hypothesized that if nondelinquent subjects had a greater ability to defer immediate gratification and to think in terms of the future than the delinquents, they would choose to save the money or invest it in school supplies significantly more often than the delinquents. On the other hand, the delinquents would be more likely to spend it on immediate pleasurable consumption. The results of this grouping and the tests of this hypothesis are presented in Table 29.

In all three ethnic groups and in the overall analysis, the hypothesis was confirmed. Chi squares ranged from 7.98 ($p<.02$) to 37.69 ($p<.001$). These highly significant differences showed that, despite the fact ethnic background and class were controlled, the nondelinquent subjects were much more likely to display thrift and an orientation toward the future. It was particularly noteworthy that 36 of the 150 nondelinquent boys (24%) chose to save such a small amount, in view of McCandless' remarks about how alien thrift is to people from such a poverty-stricken background as the boys in

Table 29

Chi-Square Analyses of the Disposition of 25 Cents or 20 Centavos

Choice	Anglo		Latin		Mexican		Overall	
	C*	D*	C	D	C	D	C	D
Saving	14	6	10	4	12	0	36	10
School supplies	7	2	8	0	9	1	24	3
Immediate pleasurable consumption	24	35	26	38	24	37	75	110
Total	45	43	44	42	45	38	134	123
χ^2	7.98		12.80		20.73		37.69	
p (two tail)	<.02		<.005		<.001		<.001	

*C, comparison group; D, delinquent group.

this sample. The fact that these differences were found in all three groups adds greatly to the generality of the observation that delinquents are less likely to defer gratification until the future than are nondelinquents of the same social status. Moreover, the data contradicted the stereotyped picture of Latins and Mexicans as being more pleasure- and present-oriented than Anglos, for the Latin and Mexican comparison subjects were no less willing than the Anglos to forego immediate pleasurable consumption.

If You Had Two Dollars (Pesos), What Would You Do With It?

The most common response to the question of what to do with $2.00[3] are presented in order of frequency in Table 30. Spending it on clothes was chosen most frequently and saving it next most often. The least frequent category ("spend it") was endorsed by only two of the 300 delinquents. In the case of disposing of $2.00 there were 76 unique choices endorsed by only one subject; these were placed in the "other" category.

As in the case of spending 25 cents, the responses were next grouped into broader categories. The first of these was "saving or spending on school supplies." The number indicating they would buy school supplies was too small to justify placing this response into a separate category, as had been done in the previous analysis. Therefore, it was combined with saving, since it was felt that both responses represented deferred gratification and a future-time orientation.

The second category was "spending the money on clothes." Spending money on clothes could not be considered delayed gratification in the sense that savings or school supplies would, for there is much more pleasure involved in buying clothes. As objects of adornment they are certainly more exciting and glamorous purchases than pencils or erasers. On the other hand, it would be a mistake to put clothes in the same category as cigarettes or candy, since they serve a more useful function and represent a more mature expenditure by a teenager. Therefore, it was felt best to put clothes into a special category.

The third classification was "immediate pleasurable consumption,"

---

[3] The symbol "$" indicates both dollars and pesos.

Table 30

Disposition of 2 Dollars or 2 Pesos

Choice	Anglo		Latin		Mexican	
	C*	D*	C	D	C	D
Clothes	2	5	4	8	16	37
Save it	17	9	15	7	8	1
Movies	3	10	7	10	1	4
Food	2	7	4	4	0	3
Cigarettes	4	4	0	3	0	0
Gasoline	4	3	3	0	0	0
Date	1	4	0	2	1	1
School supplies	2	1	3	0	2	0
Spend it	0	1	0	0	1	0
Other	15	6	14	16	21	4

*C, comparison group; D, delinquent group.

which included spending the $2.00 on movies, food, cigarettes, gasoline, or a date, or simply spending it.

It was hypothesized that, as in the case of 25 cents, the nondelinquents would be more likely to either save the $2.00 or spend it on school supplies, while the delinquents would be more apt to spend it pleasurably. Because of the ambiguity of the meaning of spending the money on clothes, no specific prediction was made about this category.

The results of the statistical analyses are presented in Table 31. The differences were in the predicted direction and were significant in all four analyses, with chi squares ranging from 8.38 ($p<.02$) to 28.80 ($p<.001$). The delinquents were more likely to spend the money, both on immediate pleasurable consumption and on clothes, than were the nondelinquents, who in turn were more likely to save the money or spend it on school supplies. These data thus served to confirm the pattern noted for 25 cents and indicated that it could also be found when somewhat larger sums were involved. However, it should be pointed out that the nondelinquents had considerably more responses in the "other" category. If these unique responses had involved using the money for immediate pleasurable spending, the result would have been quite different.

If You Had 20 Dollars (Pesos) What Would You Do with It?

When the amount reached $20.00 the difference between the currency of the two countries was likely to become a major factor influencing what might be done with the money. According to the official rate of exchange, 20 United States dollars are equivalent to 250 Mexican pesos, while 20 Mexican pesos are equivalent to $1.80 in United States currency. However, the official exchange rates are of little help in equating the psychological value of the various sums

Table 31

Chi-Square Analyses of the Disposition of Two Dollars or Two Pesos

Choice	Anglo		Latin		Mexican		Overall	
	C*	D*	C	D	C	D	C	D
Save and school supplies	19	10	18	7	10	1	47	18
Clothes	2	5	4	8	16	37	22	50
Immediate pleasurable consumption	14	29	14	19	3	8	31	56
Total	35	44	36	34	29	46	100	124
χ^2	8.83		6.88		14.90		28.80	
p (two tail)	<.02		<.05		<.001		<.001	

*C, comparison group; D, delinquent group.

of money. For some items, notably food, handmade objects, and services, a given sum of money will purchase far more in Monterrey than in San Antonio. For other items, there is little difference in purchasing power.

Moreover, the psychological value placed on a sum of money is a function not only of what it will purchase, but also of the relation of that sum to one's usual income. It will be recalled from Chapter 6 that the fathers' weekly incomes were about $106.00, $80.00, and $235.00 (pesos) for the Anglos, Latins, and Mexicans, respectively. Therefore, 20 United States dollars would be about 20 per cent of the fathers' weekly wage for the Anglos and 25 per cent of the Latins' fathers' wage, while 250 pesos would be 106 per cent of the Mexican fathers' average weekly income. Obviously, simply presenting the question in terms of 20 United States dollars or 250 Mexican pesos would not equate the question for the various samples. It was therefore felt that it was best simply to leave the question as asking for the disposition of 20 dollars for the Anglos and Latins and 20 pesos for the Mexicans, and to take the differences in currency into account in the interpretation. Thus, the Mexican subjects were asked how they would dispose of a sum equal to about 10 per cent of their fathers' weekly income.

The most frequent responses are listed in Table 32. With the jump from $2.00 to $20.00 in local currency, the number of choices was reduced. While clothes and saving were still the most frequent responses, gifts and expenditures on a vehicle made their appearance for the first time. As with the case of $2.00, about 76 of the 300 choices fell into the "other" category.

For the Anglos and Latins, the specific responses were divided into four broad categories: (a) saving, (b) clothes, (c) gift to mother, and (d) spending on a vehicle (bicycle, car, scooter). As only one of the Mexican subjects used the vehicle category, the analysis was confined to the first three categories for the Mexican subjects. (It is likely that the differences in purchasing power between dollars and pesos were responsible for infrequent use of the vehicle category in Mexico.)

As in the previous analyses, it was anticipated that the nondelinquents would be more likely to save their money. It also seemed likely that the nondelinquents would be more likely to demonstrate filial loyalty by giving the money to their mothers or spending it

Table 32

Disposition of 20 Dollars or 20 Pesos

Choice	Anglo C*	D*	Latin C	D	Mexican C	D
Clothes	11	13	18	25	17	39
Save it	17	13	8	14	13	3
Give it to mother	1	3	4	3	3	1
Bicycle	0	3	3	1	0	1
Specific item for mother	0	1	2	1	2	1
Repair car or scooter	5	2	0	0	0	0
Other	16	15	15	6	15	5

*C, comparison group; D, delinquent group.

on them. The remaining, more hedonistic expenditures (vehicle or clothing) were expected to be more frequent among the delinquents.

There were no significant differences in the patterns of expenditures between the delinquents and nondelinquents in the Anglo and Latin samples, as shown in Table 33. In the Mexican sample the differences were highly significant ($\chi^2 = 15.31$, $p < .001$) and in the predicted direction. The chief factor responsible for the significant difference in the Mexican sample was the fact that four times as many nondelinquents indicated they would save the money. Little difference was noted in the frequency of delinquents' and nondelinquents' using the money for a gift for mother. However, the delinquents were much more likely to spend it on clothes.

The data thus indicated that, for the Anglos and Latins, there were significant differences in the use to which they would put relatively small sums of money, such as 25 cents or two dollars, particularly in the incidence of those who would save it, but that there was little difference in what they would do with larger sums of money like 20 dollars. It is impossible to say whether the significant difference noted for the Mexicans in regard to the expenditure of 20 pesos was the result of the fact that 20 pesos will purchase less than 20 dollars, or because the differences between the spending patterns of delinquents and nondelinquents in Mexico are more fundamental in some fashion than in the United States. One way of testing this would have been to determine how the Mexicans would have spent a larger sum of money, but, unfortunately, these data were not obtained.

If You Had 200 Dollars, What Would You Do with It?

The question concerning 200 dollars was asked only of the San Antonio samples and inadvertently was not included in the schedule of questions used in Monterrey. This proved to be an unfortunate omission, for it would have been desirable to determine if the significant differences noted for the Mexicans continued when larger sums were involved.

The trend to use fewer choices with the expenditure of larger sums of money continued in the responses of the Anglos and Latins. Of course, as the amounts increased to a level of $200.00, the choices

Table 33

Chi-Square Analyses of the Disposition of 20 Dollars or 20 Pesos

Choice	Anglo		Latin		Mexican		Overall	
	C*	D*	C	D	C	D	C	D
Saving	17	13	8	14	13	3	38	30
Clothes	11	13	18	25	17	39	46	77
Gift for mother	1	4	6	4	5	2	12	10
Vehicle	5	5	3	1	0	0	8	7
Total	34	35	35	44	35	44	104	124
χ^2	2.48		3.20		15.31		7.32	
p (two tail)	N.S.		N.S.		$<.001$		$<.10$	

*C, comparison group; D, delinquent group.

involved moved more and more out of the realm of reality and into the realm of fantasy, particularly for the Latins.

Inspection of the data in Table 34 indicated that the same four categories used in the preceding analysis would be sufficient to account for most of the replies. However, when the data for the Anglos were cast into these four categories—(a) saving, (b) clothes, (c) gift to parent(s), and (d) vehicle—it was found that only four subjects had made use of Categories b or c. Therefore, the table was collapsed and the number of delinquents and nondelinquents who saved their money or gave it to their parents (Categories a and c) was contrasted with those who spent their money on clothes or a vehicle (Categories b and d). It was predicted that the nondelinquents would be more likely to be in the former category and the delinquents in the latter. This hypothesis was not confirmed (chi square=2.37, N.S.), as is shown in Table 35.

The hypothesis tested was, in effect, based on two premises:

Table 34

Disposition of 200 Dollars Made by Subjects in San Antonio

Choice	Anglo		Latin	
	C*	D*	C	D
Save it	21	13	13	15
Car	13	18	15	12
Give it to mother	0	2	5	7
Clothes	0	1	3	4
Repair car	3	3	0	1
Give it to parents	0	1	1	3
Scooter, motorcycle	1	4	3	2
Other	12	8	10	6

*C, comparison group; D, delinquent group.

Table 35

Chi-Square Analyses of the Disposition of 200 Dollars

		ANGLO				
Analysis 1				Analysis 2		
Choice	C*	D*	Choice		C	D
Saving or gift	21	16	Saving		21	13
Clothing or vehicle	17	26	Clothing or vehicle		17	26
Total	38	42	Total		38	39
χ^2		2.37	χ^2			3.75
p (two tail)		N.S.	p (two tail)			<.055

	LATIN	
Choice	C	D
Saving	13	15
Clothes	3	14
Gift	6	10
Vehicle	18	15
Total	40	44
χ^2	1.37	
p (two tail)	N.S.	

*C, comparison group; D, delinquent group.

(1) that the nondelinquents would be more likely to save their money and (2) that they would be more likely to show family loyalty by giving it to their parents. Upon inspection of the data, it was apparent that it was the latter premise that was false. Only three Anglo subjects elected to give the money to their parents and all were delinquents. In order to determine if there were differences in the tendency to save as opposed to spend $200.00, the number of delinquent and nondelinquent Anglos saying they would save the money (Category *a*) was contrasted with those who would spend it

on a vehicle or on clothing (Categories *b* and *d*). This analysis fell just short of significance ($\chi^2 = 3.75$, $p < .055$), using a two-tail test. Since the directional prediction would have justified the use of a one-tail test, it seems safe to conclude that there was a very noteworthy tendency for the nondelinquent Anglos to be more likely than the delinquents to say they would save the $200.00.

In the Latin sample, there were enough subjects to use all four categories. No significant differences or noteworthy trends were found between the delinquent and comparison groups. It is noteworthy, however, that while only three Anglo boys indicated they would give the money to their parents, 16 Latin boys said they would do so, demonstrating the stronger family ties and obligations that would be expected in Latin culture.

SUMMARY OF DATA ON SPENDING VARIOUS SUMS OF MONEY

The subjects in the three samples were asked what they would do with various sums of money, to determine if the delinquents were more likely to be hedonistic and present-oriented, and the nondelinquents more likely to delay immediate-need gratification and display a future orientation.

For the smaller sums of money, the differences between the delinquents and nondelinquents were quite significant. The nondelinquents were much more likely to save their money or spend it on school supplies than the delinquents, who were more likely to spend it immediately on various pleasurable items. This confirmed the observation that delinquents are more likely to be hedonistic and less concerned with the future than nondelinquents, even when both groups are from low income populations. Moreover, the data indicated that this observation applied not only to Anglos but also to Latins and Mexicans. The incidence of thrift and foresightedness in spending small sums was approximately the same in all three ethnic groups and there was no tendency for the Anglos to be more oriented toward deferred gratification than the Latins or Mexicans.

With larger sums of money, the differences between the delinquents and nondelinquents broke down. While among the Anglos and Latins there had been highly significant differences in how the delinquents and nondelinquents would dispose of 25 cents or two dollars, there was no significant difference as the amount shifted to

20 or 200 dollars. One possible reason for this was that, while the questions dealing with 25 cents or two dollars were realistic, the disposition of 20 or 200 dollars approached the fantasy level, so that all the subjects tended to start responding in terms of stereotypes that might have been quite different from what they would actually do. While the number of nondelinquents who indicated they would save the money was relatively constant, the number of delinquents who indicated they would do so increased steadily as the sum involved got larger. Still, there was a noteworthy tendency for the Anglo comparison group to be more inclined to save 200 dollars.

There was less change of pattern with increasing amounts of money in the Mexican sample. However, this could easily have been an artifact of the fact that (*a*) the Mexicans were not asked what they would do with with 200 pesos and (*b*) pesos are worth considerably less than dollars so that the disposition of 20 pesos was a more realistic task for the Monterrey adolescent than the disposition of 20 dollars was for the San Antonian, even when differences in income level are taken into consideration.

As already noted, the data contraindicated the stereotyped picture of the Latin or Mexican as being less concerned with the future than the Anglo. Another stereotype is that all delinquents are completely self-centered hedonists, concerned only with the present and having no regard for the future. While the data showed greater hedonism in regard to smaller sums of money, the lack of difference in regard to the larger amounts indicated that it is erroneous to think of the delinquent as being guided only by the pleasure principle. The data indicated that there are boundaries within which the delinquent is guided more by hedonism than his peers but outside of which he is not. In regard to spending 200 dollars, it is noteworthy that 16 of the Anglo and 15 of the Latin delinquents indicated they would overcome the strong temptation to buy a car and would save the money or turn it over to their parents. While this may not be what they would do in practice, nevertheless, it showed they were sufficiently cognizant of social mores to be willing to guide at least their verbal behavior by them.

Thus, the first part of the Choices Test showed that in all three ethnic groups the delinquents displayed less concern for the future and greater emphasis on immediate pleasures when asked how they would spend relatively small sums, but that their behavior conformed fairly closely with the comparison groups' when larger sums were involved.

Choices of Places To Go

The next question on the Choices Test was, "If you could go wherever you like tonight, where would you go?" It was felt that the answers to this question could be relevant to such questions as whether delinquents have a greater tendency than nondelinquents to seek solitary, asocial activities than to join a group, or if delinquents manifest greater discontent with their environment by choosing distant places, or if nondelinquents exhibit greater family cohesiveness by choosing to remain home or visit relatives.

It was found that all but 50 choices fell into the following categories: movies, distant places, home, a girl friend's house or a date, visiting friends, going to the plaza or park, visiting relatives, and

Table 36

Choices of Places To Go

Choice	Anglo		Latin		Mexican	
	C*	D*	C	D	C	D
Movie	11	7	16	7	22	30
Distant place	10	11	0	17	5	1
Home	2	8	5	9	0	7
Girl's house or date	12	11	1	3	0	1
Visit friends	4	3	4	2	6	1
Plaza or park	1	1	4	2	5	2
Visit relatives	0	0	5	1	2	2
Dance	1	0	5	1	0	1
Other	9	9	10	8	10	5

*C, comparison group; D, delinquent group.

going to a dance. The frequency of these responses for the various groups is presented in Table 36.

For the chi-square analyses, the two least frequent categories were combined with other similar categories. Going to a dance was combined with going to a girl's house or on a date, and visiting relatives was combined with visiting friends. This resulted in six categories, plus the category "other." The numbers of delinquents and nondelinquents in each of the six categories (the "other" category being excluded) in each of the three ethnic samples were compared using chi-square. No significant differences were found in the Anglo group ($\chi^2 = 4.82$, N.S.). The delinquents did differ significantly from the nondelinquents, however, in the Latin ($\chi^2 = 25.69$, $p < .001$) and Mexican ($\chi^2 = 16.20$, $p < .01$) groups.

The percentage of subjects in the different categories is presented graphically in Figure 2. An inspection of these histograms shows that the pattern of responses, as well as the nature of the differences between the delinquent and comparison groups, varied markedly from one cultural group to another.

In the Anglo sample, there were few marked differences between the delinquents and nondelinquents, as would be expected on the basis of the insignificant chi-square. The nondelinquents tended to prefer going to a movie, while the delinquents endorsed "home" more often.

In the Latin sample major differences were found between the delinquent and comparison groups. The nondelinquents preferred going to a movie, visiting friends or relatives, dating, and going to the park more than the delinquents. All of these activities, with the exception of going to the park, were ones that the nondelinquent Anglos had also preferred. On the other hand, 34 per cent of the Latin delinquents chose going to a distant place, while none of the Latin comparison group did so. Since no discrepancy of this sort occurred in either the Anglo or the Mexican samples, perhaps this indicates some dissatisfaction with San Antonio, possibly related to minority group treatment, which was felt more keenly by the Latin delinquents. The Latin delinquents, like the Anglo and Mexican delinquents, also endorsed "home" significantly more often than the comparison group did. It is almost certain that this response was in large part due to the fact that a large proportion of the delinquents were incarcerated at the time of the examination.

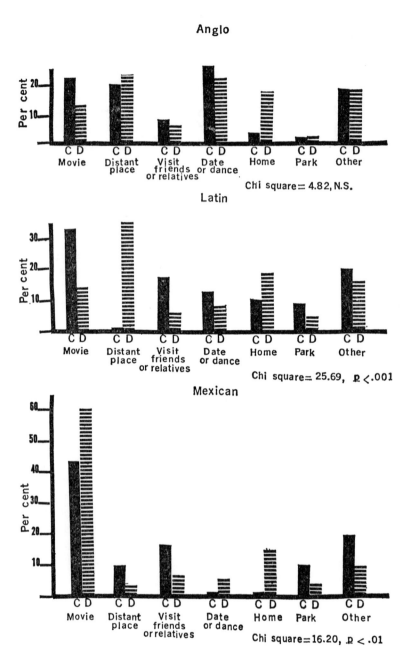

Figure 2. Choice of places to go.

The Mexican sample also showed marked differences between the delinquent and comparison groups. However, the patterns differed from those observed in either the Latin or Anglo samples. Whereas in the United States samples the nondelinquents had endorsed going to the movies more than the delinquents had, the opposite pattern was obtained in the Mexican sample.[4] (The overall popularity of movies in the Mexican sample was especially noteworthy. While movies had been one of the favorite places for the Anglos and Latins to go, they did not receive the overwhelming vote that they did in the Mexican sample. Perhaps in 1960 the movies still occupied a role in Mexico similar to the role they occupied in the United States before the advent of television.) The Mexican sample also differed from the others in that the delinquents preferred dating more than the nondelinquents, possibly representing some rebellion against traditional folkways, and the nondelinquents favored going to a distant place more than the delinquents did.

Despite these differences, there were some uniformities evident throughout the various samples. Visiting friends and relatives was preferred by the nondelinquents more than the delinquents in every sample, possibly indicating greater social or family interests. Going home received more votes from the delinquents, probably because of the above-noted effects of confinement.

The pattern of results is not easy to fit into any simple theory. It cannot be said that the delinquents were always more or less engaged in peer group activities or solitary activities than the nondelinquents, or that they were uniformly discontended with their milieu and wished to go far away. Nor can it be said that the nondelinquents always displayed more family ties and loyalties than the delinquents. In short, the findings from the question "If you could go wherever you like tonight, where would you go?" were that, in two of the three cultures studied, the delinquents and nondelinquents displayed highly significant differences in response to it and that the pattern of places mentioned and the delinquent-comparison group differences were strongly dependent on the cultural membership of the respondents.

---

[4] In a study of New Haven delinquents and their nondelinquent siblings, Healy and Bronner (1936) found "excessive movie attendance" in 31 per cent of the delinquents, as compared with 10 per cent of the nondelinquents.

Choices of Occupation

The final question on the Choices Test was, "What kind of work would you like to do when you are grown up?" This question was included because so much has been written about the aspirations of juvenile delinquents and about the role that a discrepancy between these aspirations and the means to follow them might play in causing delinquency.

Unfortunately, this final item of the Choices Test was one of the

Table 37

Choices of Occupation

Choice	Anglo C*	Anglo D*	Latin C	Latin D	Mexican C	Mexican D
Armed service	7	16	6	5	0	0
Mechanic	4	4	1	5	3	5
Lawyer	2	1	1	1	11	2
Don't know	3	2	6	3	1	0
Engineer	5	1	3	1	1	2
Doctor	1	1	2	1	3	0
Carpenter	0	1	0	4	0	3
Professional baseball	3	1	1	2	0	0
Electrician	1	2	0	1	0	3
Policeman	2	1	2	0	1	0
Factory worker	0	0	0	0	1	5
Other	22	20	28	27	29	30

*C, comparison group; D, delinquent group.

measures that was most severely affected by the loss of the individual data. The subjects chose a wide variety of individual occupations. At the time the individual data were lost, the frequency tabulations for the most common specific occupations had been completed. The number of subjects selecting each of these occupations is presented in Table 37. However, 156 subjects selected occupations that were so infrequent they had been lumped together in the "other" category.

Later, in analyzing the data, it seemed best to group the occupations in Table 37 into the following broad categories: (*a*) professional (doctor, lawyer, engineer), (*b*) skilled trades (electrician, carpenter, mechanic, factory worker), (*c*) military or police, and (*d*) don't know.[5] It is likely that many of the infrequent occupations listed in the "other" category could have been included in these broader categories had the individual data been available for reclassification. It is of course impossible to determine how the results might have been influenced by the large amount of data in the "other" category; however, it is somewhat reassuring to note that the numbers of delinquents and nondelinquents whose responses were lost were almost identical. Table 38 shows the grouped data and presents the results of the statistical tests.

The overall differences between the occupational choices of the Anglo delinquent and comparison groups were not statistically significant ($\chi^2=5.02$, $p<.20$). The differences in the Latin sample did attain statistical significance, however ($\chi^2=10.06$, $p<.02$). In the Mexican sample, only one subject chose the military or police category and only one said he did not know. Because of these low cell entries, the table was collapsed, and the number choosing professional careers was contrasted with all those selecting skilled trades or the military or police, or indicating they did not know (Category *a* vs. *b*, *c*, and *d*). The resulting test was significant ($\chi^2=8.97$, $p<.005$). For the combined data it was possible to use all four categories, of course, and the resulting test showed highly significant differences between the delinquents and nondelinquents ($\chi^2=23.57$, $p<.001$).

In all three samples more nondelinquents than delinquents indi-

---

[5] The occupation of professional baseball player did not fit readily into this framework and was therefore added to the "other" category.

Table 38

Chi-Square Analyses of Occupational Choices

Choice	Anglo C*	Anglo D*	Latin C	Latin D	Mexican C	Mexican D	Overall C	Overall D
Professional	8	3	6	3	15	4	29	10
Skilled trade	5	7	1	10	4	16	10	33
Military or police	9	17	8	5	1	0	18	22
Don't know	3	2	6	3	1	0	10	5
Total	25	29	21	21	21	20	67	70
χ^2	5.02		10.06		8.97[a]		23.57	
p (two tail)	N.S.		$<.02$		$<.005$		$<.001$	

* C, comparison group; D, delinquent group.
a Chi-square computed from collapsed 2×2 table comparing number choosing "professional" category with number selecting "skilled trades," "military or police," or "don't know."

cated they would like professional jobs (see Figure 3). This suggested higher aspirations on the part of the nondelinquents, a finding similar to those of Gold's Flint, Michigan, study. The proportion of delinquents choosing skilled trades slightly exceeded the nondelinquents in the Anglo sample and greatly exceeded the nondelinquents in the other two samples. Military or police careers attracted more nondelinquents than delinquents among the Latins and Mexicans, but the reverse pattern was found among the Anglos. (Possibly because of the draft, many subjects in the United States indicated an interest in the military but none did in Mexico.)

In all six groups only a minority of the boys aspired to the highest status jobs: 30 per cent of the Mexican comparison group had professional aspirations, 16 per cent of the Anglo, and 12 per cent of the Latin. The proportion of delinquent groups selecting the professions ranged from 4 to 6 per cent. These data are consistent with those reported by Hollingshead in *Elmtown's Youth* (1949), in which he reported that only a minority of the lower class in New

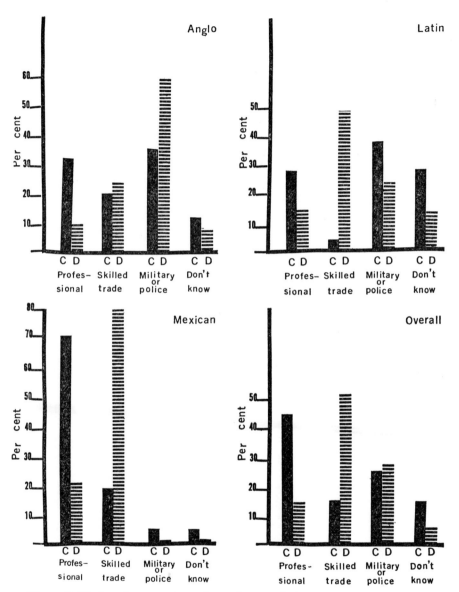

Figure 3. Choice of occupations. Those choosing "other" occupations deleted.

Haven were upwardly mobile, and that this was generally limited
to one step upward rather than a great leap from the lower to the
middle class. This finding has been replicated in other studies
(Cavan, 1962).

In one respect, however, the findings are discrepant with those
generally reported. Cavan, reviewing the literature on aspiration
level, reported: ". . . in all social class levels, the brighter boys are
more likely to aspire to an occupational position above that of their
fathers than are the boys of average ability" (1962, p. 88). However,
in the present study it will be recalled that the Mexican comparison
group, which had the lowest mean Full Scale IQ of all the groups,
had by far the largest number of boys aspiring, probably unrealistically, to professional status. Despite this discrepancy, it is likely
that as a general rule the nondelinquent boys would have better
chances for upward mobility. Not only had they already achieved
more in school, but they also had the advantages of a more stable
family situation and no police record.

These data on occupational choice also have theoretical relevance.
Some theories attribute crime and delinquency to a desire for wealth
on the part of lower-class individuals that cannot be legally satisfied.
If the milieu provides delinquent or criminal role models and illegal
opportunities to achieve goals that are unattainable through legitimate endeavor, a criminal career may result (Cloward & Ohlin,
1960).

An important test of this theory, according to Rubenfeld (1965),
is the relative aspiration level of lower-class individuals. Status
discontent should be greatest in those lower-class individuals who
have the highest aspirations. He asks:

> Do lower-class individuals aspire toward jobs and income levels *beyond*
> those usually attained by their class? How frequently, for instance, are
> lower-class youths' absolute aspirations directed toward semi-skilled and
> skilled jobs which are usual for their class? . . . In other words, since lack
> of legitimate opportunities is more meaningful to those aspiring to higher
> levels, the lower a person's aspirations, the less liable should he be to ex-
> perience his economic prospects as disadvantageous. (Rubenfeld, 1965,
> p. 131)

Rubenfeld's analysis receives some support from Rhodes' (1964)
study of the relation between aspiration level and anomie in high

school students. He found anomie was directly related to the *dis-crepancy* between aspirations and the means to achieve them. Among subjects with few chances for success, it was those who had the highest aspirations who had the highest anomie scores. Since many theorists have related anomie to delinquency, these data are consistent with Rubenfeld's argument.

Thus, the present data could be used to argue against Cloward and Ohlin's theory. Certainly, there is no evidence that the delin-quents in the present sample had a greater discrepancy between their aspirations and opportunities than did the nondelinquents. If anything, the *nondelinquents* had a greater discrepancy, for despite their significantly better school performance, it would still be diffi-cult for them to make the jump from the lower class to the profes-sional class in a single generation, particularly if they were Latin or Mexican.

However, while the present data did not support differential-opportunity theory, it would nevertheless be presumptuous to cite them as "disproving" this theory, for *ad hoc* explanations consistent with this theory can be found to account for the present data. For example, it could be pointed out that Cloward and Ohlin have defined four basic types of adjustments that the lower-class person can make. He can cathect both middle-class status and wealth and strive to achieve them through legitimate ends, such as education. (This is the "college boy" pattern, to use Whyte's terminology.) A second adjustment is to cathect the middle-class status but not necessarily the wealth. This can be satisfied through low-paying white-collar civil service jobs, teaching, nursing, and the like. Boys making either of these two adaptations would not be candidates for delinquency unless their strivings were thwarted, in which case reaction formation may take place as in Cohen's (1955) theory. A third adjustment is for the lower-class person to remain as he is and not strive for either middle-class status or wealth. It is only in the case of the fourth adjustment, when a person wishes to attain mid-dle-class wealth but cares little about the means or his reputation, that we have a potential delinquent.

Given this framework, it could be argued that the nondelinquents who choose professional jobs belong to the first type and are striving to achieve their goals legitimately. On the other hand, the delin-quents have made the fourth adjustment and have already abandoned legitimate means for achieving wealth. Therefore, it is not likely that they would endorse a high-status job. Those who wish to uphold Cloward and Ohlin's theory could therefore argue that the present data regarding occupational choices reflect differences in *means* rather than differences in *ends*, and the fact that the nondelinquents chose legitimate means does not necessarily indicate any basic differences in final goals for wealth or power.[6] In this fashion differential-opportunity theorists could account for the present data, although not in a very parsimonious or elegant fashion.

To summarize, the data indicated that the nondelinquents had higher occupational aspirations than the delinquents. By and large this is a finding that is not consistent with differential-opportunity theory. However, the theory is sufficiently flexible so that, while it might not have predicted this result, an unparsimonious ex post facto explanation can be found for it.

Summary of the Choices Test Results

The Choices Test consisted of six questions that the examiners asked the subjects. The first four questions asked what the boys would do with various sums of money ranging from 25 cents to $200.00 in local currency. For the lower sums, 25 cents and $2.00, the data indicated that the nondelinquents in all three ethnic samples were significantly more likely than the delinquents to defer immediate hedonistic gratification by saving the money or spending it on school supplies as opposed to using the money for immediate enjoyment. This finding indicated that the tendency some scholars have noted for delinquents to be more impulsive and pleasure-oriented and less concerned with the future was not simply associated with the fact that delinquents often come from the lower class, but instead distinguished delinquents from nondelinquents within the lower class. Moreover, it applied to Latin and Mexican groups as much as it did to Anglo.

For larger sums of money ($20.00 or $200.00), the differences in the value of local currency became an important factor to be

---

[6] Of course, none of the delinquents specifically stated they would like to be in charge of the numbers racket or some other illegitimate goal, but that could be attributed to defensiveness. The high proportion of delinquents indicating they would like to pursue a skilled trade would be somewhat more difficult to explain.

reckoned with. While there were no significant differences in how the Anglos or Latins would dispose of 20 dollars, there were highly significant differences in how the Mexicans would dispose of 20 pesos, with the comparison group once again showing a greater propensity for saving or using the money for their family, while the delinquents were more likely to spend it on clothes. The Mexicans were not asked how they would dispose of 200 pesos, but when the Anglos and Latins were asked about spending 200 dollars, there were no significant differences. However, there was a strong tendency (which would have been significant with a one-tail test) for the nondelinquent Anglos to indicate they would save the money more often than did the delinquent Anglos. These data for the larger sums of money thus indicated that the impulsive hedonism of the delinquents that was manifested for smaller sums of money was no longer as evident for larger sums; instead, the delinquents conformed more to the cultural norms. The data indicated that this was more a result of changes in the response patterns of the delinquents than of the nondelinquents. Instead of the nondelinquents exhibiting more impulsivity as greater (and more fantastic) sums were reached, the delinquents displayed greater conservatism with an increasing amount, indicating they would save the money or turn it over to their parents. Thus, while the monetary questions confirmed the validity of some common observations about delinquents, they also indicated that there are certain bounds within which these characteristics apply. In less important situations, where relatively small sums were involved, the delinquents responded more hedonistically with less sense of the future, but for more important (and less realistic) situations involving larger sums, their responses did not deviate significantly from those of their peers.

The second topic on the Choices Test was concerned with where the boys would like to go. Significant differences were found between the responses of the delinquents and nondelinquents in the Latin and Mexican samples but not in the Anglo. The patterns varied greatly from one ethnic group to another, making broad generalizations untenable. As with the questions on how they would dispose of money, the answers indicated that, while many differences could be found between delinquents and nondelinquents, they were complex and did not lend themselves to all-inclusive "pat" explanations.

The final question asked each boy what sort of work he would like to do when he grew up. When the replies were grouped into broad response categories, it was found that in all three groups more nondelinquents aspired to the professions, while more delinquents selected skilled trades. In the Anglo sample more delinquents wished to join the armed forces or the police, but the reverse was true in the Latin and Mexican samples. These differences were significant in the Latin and Mexican but not in the Anglo sample. Thus, the data generally indicated a higher aspiration level for the nondelinquents. However, missing data diminished the meaningfulness of this finding.

The significance of these data for theories that ascribe delinquency to position discontent, that is, to a discrepancy between the lower-class boy's aspirations and what he realistically can hope to achieve, was discussed. While at first glance the nondelinquents would appear to have greater position discontent because of their higher aspirations, this was not necessarily the case, because they also had a better chance of achieving their aspirations because of their better school records, stabler family backgrounds, and lack of police records. While close scrutiny of the data thus did not necessarily indicate that the comparison groups had *more* status discontent, nevertheless it also did not indicate that the *delinquents* had more discontent, as these theories would suggest. Possible ex post facto explanations, by means of which adherents of these theories would explain away these data, were discussed. It was concluded that, while the results were not particularly favorable to status discontent theories, there are ways in which these theories could account for them. Although these results could lessen one's confidence in status discontent as a necessary or sufficient explanation of delinquency, they cannot be regarded as having "disproved" this position.

CHAPTER 9

THE OFFENSES TEST

Juvenile delinquency is behavior that deviates from the norms and values prescribed by society. How are such deviant habits learned and maintained in the face of all the efforts of society to transmit approved values through the schools and churches and to stamp out deviance through the police and courts? Some deviance can be attributed to stupidity or psychological aberrations, but much delinquent behavior occurs in apparently normal young people who seem to have values different from those held by most members of society. To account for the development and transmission of such deviant mores, sociologists have postulated the existence of criminal subcultures whose values and norms conflict with those of the overall society; they have disagreed, however, on the nature of the forces that shape and create such delinquent subcultures.

Surveying the field of delinquency, it is possible to discriminate two types of deviant subcultures, those we might call "exogenous" and those we can term "indigenous." The exogenous subculture comes when, as a result of immigration between nations or regions within a nation, people who have been raised with one set of values find themselves in a society with a different set of values. Some years ago such exogenous subcultures were seen as a major cause of crime. Research has indicated, however, that most immigrant groups have a lower crime rate than the native United States population. For example, Sutherland and Cressey (1966, p. 152) report that the arrest and imprisonment rate for native-born white Americans is about twice the rate for foreign-born whites. While the foreign born may have lower crime rates, this is not always true of later generations. In 1956 the delinquency rate among Latin boys in Los Angeles was 170.5 per 10,000 juveniles, three times the Anglo rate of 54.4 per 10,000 (Heller, 1966). Some have attributed this higher rate among Latins to factors other than culture conflict. For example, it may be that Latins, being more "visible," are picked up more often by the police, that minority-group membership in itself causes delinquency, or that discrimination engenders frustrations that culminate in delinquency. However, the Nisei in Los Angeles, who are an equally visible and frustrated minority group, have a much lower rate of juvenile crime than the Anglos, so these are not sufficient explanations (Heller, 1966).

It is more likely that the subcultural values of the Latin group, which emphasize manliness, group activities by the young men away from the home, revenge for an insult, and so on, contribute to the delinquency rate. Trouble with the law appears to be a normal part of the Latin subculture. Heller (1966, p. 63) states: ". . . Mexican American boys in general perceive 'getting in trouble with the police' as a natural state of affairs and 'staying out of trouble' as a stroke of fortune."

Thus, potentially delinquent subcultures may form around immigrant groups who are raised in the traditions of another culture whose values differ from those of the dominant culture. However, it is likely that exogenous culture conflict causes more delinquency indirectly through anomie than directly by condoning illegal acts. The term "anomie," originally coined by Durkheim, is used to describe a state of normlessness or confusion about values or appropriate standards of behavior. In the case of the young Latin, anomie can arise from a conflict between the values of traditional Mexican culture and the demands of Anglo culture. As we noted in Chapter 3, the school may insist that he speak English at home instead of Spanish and encourage him to compete with his fellows and to achieve personal success. If he fails to do so he may be rejected by his teachers and regarded as alien or un-American. His family and friends, on the other hand, may encourage him to speak Spanish and to respect others' honor by not attempting to outdo them. If, instead, he obeys the school's dictates he may be rejected by his family and peers and regarded as a traitor to his culture and un-

Mexican. Such conflicting demands can lead to anomie and to rebellious acting out that would be approved of by neither culture.

Sociological theorists have focused more attention on indigenous than exogenous deviant subcultures. The theories of Merton (1957), Cloward and Ohlin (1960), and Cohen (1955) suggested how cultural conflicts can produce subgroups with values quite different from those of the larger middle-class society, and Sutherland (1939) described how these deviant mores can be transmitted and maintained (see Chapter 2).

The common core of all these theories is the notion that, through either exogenous or indigenous causes, there exist delinquent subcultures, which fail to share the values of the dominant middle-class culture and in which there are some fundamental disagreements about what constitutes appropriate behavior.

Method

The Offenses Test was designed to test the notion that delinquents' values differ from those of nondelinquents. Brief descriptions of 10 different transgressions were typed on separate cards, which the subjects were asked to arrange in order of badness. The 10 offenses were:

 a. Accidentally breaking a window while playing ball
 b. Being rude to grandparents
 c. Breaking into a house and stealing something
 d. Carrying a knife or gun
 e. Failing to stop at a red light
 f. Murder
 g. Rape
 h. Shooting a BB gun in the park
 i. Staying away from school
 j. Stealing a car

The investigators realized that merely asking the boys to place these 10 offenses in rank order was a crude device and certainly not a definitive exploration of all the manifold possible differences in values that might exist between delinquents and nondelinquents in three cultures. A thorough cross-cultural investigation of the values of delinquents and nondelinquents as assessed by the rating of criminal offenses could easily comprise a book in itself.[1] Nevertheless, despite these limitations, which were necessary because of the subjects' short attention span and the brief amount of time available, it was hoped that the results would have some value in indicating the amount of agreement or lack thereof among the delinquents and nondelinquents in the three samples.

Results

For each offense, the mean and standard deviation of the rankings assigned by each group were determined.[2] From these data, the rank order of seriousness for the 10 offenses was determined, as judged by each group and by the combined groups. These data are presented in Table 39.

Murder was regarded as the most serious offense by all the groups, although not by all the individual subjects. Rape was regarded as the second most serious offense by all but the Mexican delinquents, who preferred for this rank "breaking into a house and stealing something." There was less agreement on the third most serious offense. "Stealing a car" was third ranked for the Anglo delinquents and the Anglo and Latin comparison groups; the Mexican nondelinquents chose "breaking into a house and stealing something," the Latin delinquents chose "carrying a knife or gun," and the Mexican delinquents selected "rape."

The fourth most serious offenses were "breaking into a house and stealing something," selected by the Anglo and Latin nondelinquents and the Anglo delinquents, and "stealing a car," selected by the Latin delinquents and both the delinquent and nondelinquent Mexicans.

"Carrying a knife or gun" was rated as fifth most serious by all but the Latin delinquents, who placed "failing to stop at a red light" in this position.

Wide disagreement was evident in the choices for sixth place. "Staying away from school" was selected by the Anglo delinquents

[1] In fact, since the present data were collected, Sellin and Wolfgang (1964) have ably proved this point by publishing a 400-page book reporting how three groups of normals in a single culture rate various offenses.

[2] The frequency distributions for each group on each offense may be found in Appendix 3.

and nondelinquents and the Latin comparison group. "Breaking into a house and stealing something" was preferred by the Latin delinquents. "Shooting a BB gun in the park" was chosen by the nondelinquent Mexicans, and "being rude to grandparents" by the Mexican delinquents.

The last-named offense, "being rude to grandparents," was given seventh place by the Anglo delinquents and the Latin and Mexican nondelinquents. The nondelinquent Anglos and the delinquent Latins and Mexicans gave seventh place to "shooting a BB gun in the park."

"Failing to stop at a red light" got the vote for eighth place by all but one of the groups, the Latin delinquents, who preferred "being rude to grandparents" for this position.

Ninth place was shared by three items: "shooting a BB gun in the park" was the choice of the Anglo delinquent and the Latin comparison groups; "staying away from school" was the choice of the Mexican comparison group and the Latin and Mexican delinquent groups; and "being rude to grandparents" was the choice of the Anglo delinquents.

The tenth and last place brought the groups into unanimity again. All selected "accidentally breaking a window while playing ball" as the least serious of the 10 offenses.

Despite the inconsistencies from group to group, particularly for the middle items on the list, the data in Table 39 show that there were broad areas of agreement among the delinquent and comparison groups regarding the relative seriousness of various offenses. Discrepancies appeared to be related more to differences between cultures than to differences between delinquents and nondelinquents. For example, both Anglo delinquents and nondelinquents placed "staying away from school" in sixth place, while the Mexican groups both placed it in ninth place.

In order to determine the amount of agreement between the delinquent and comparison groups in each of the three samples, Spearman Rank Order correlation coefficients (*Rhos*) were computed. The correlations were all positive and significant. The correlation between the mean ranking of the 10 offenses for the Anglo delinquent and comparison groups was +.95, the correlation between the rankings of the Latin groups was +.81, and the correlation

Table 39

Results of the Offenses Test

Offense	OVERALL Mean Rank	ANGLO C; N=48 Mean Rank	σ	Group Rank	ANGLO D; N=44 Mean Rank	σ	Group Rank	LATIN C; N=49 Mean Rank	σ	Group Rank	LATIN D; N=42 Mean Rank	σ	Group Rank	MEXICAN C; N=50 Mean Rank	σ	Group Rank	MEXICAN D; N=49 Mean Rank	σ	Group Rank
Murder	1.50	1.37	0.48	1	1.23	0.42	1	1.51	0.54	1	1.79	1.34	1	1.42	0.75	1	1.71	1.23	1
Rape	2.55	1.67	0.55	2	1.86	0.66	2	1.82	1.22	2	3.17	1.76	2	3.12	2.16	2	3.65	2.14	3
Stealing a car	4.02	3.31	0.65	3	3.52	0.72	3	3.49	0.84	3	5.31	2.02	4	4.18	1.55	4	4.29	1.64	4
Breaking into a house and stealing something	4.18	4.02	0.80	4	3.70	0.66	4	4.06	0.82	4	6.05	2.72	6	3.96	1.77	3	3.29	1.34	2
Carrying a knife or gun	4.97	5.48	1.15	5	5.07	1.07	5	5.10	1.57	5	3.93	1.35	3	5.46	2.21	5	4.80	1.74	5

Offense	OVERALL Mean Rank	ANGLO C; N=48 Mean Rank	σ	Group Rank	ANGLO D; N=44 Mean Rank	σ	Group Rank	LATIN C; N=49 Mean Rank	σ	Group Rank	LATIN D; N=42 Mean Rank	σ	Group Rank	MEXICAN C; N=50 Mean Rank	σ	Group Rank	MEXICAN D; N=49 Mean Rank	σ	Group Rank
Being rude to grandparents	6.82	7.19	1.72	9	8.02	1.52	7	7.37	2.14	7	6.50	2.25	8	6.72	2.37	7	5.11	2.31	6
Shooting a BB gun in the park	7.10	7.87	1.42	7	7.27	1.19	9	7.90	1.22	9	6.24	2.31	7	6.24	1.84	6	7.06	2.08	7
Failing to stop at a red light	7.36	7.85	1.26	8	7.89	1.60	8	7.67	1.42	8	5.93	3.18	5	7.34	1.45	8	7.47	1.92	8
Staying away from school	7.37	6.71	1.41	6	7.18	1.17	6	7.18	1.67	6	7.62	2.07	9	7.82	1.90	9	7.71	2.05	9
Accidentally breaking a window while playing ball	9.03	9.52	0.82	10	9.25	1.11	10	8.90	1.39	10	8.48	1.56	10	8.74	2.12	10	9.31	0.94	10
		$Rho_{C-D} = .95^*$						$Rho_{C-D} = .81^*$						$Rho_{C-D} = .98^*$					

Coefficient of Concordance (W) = $.90^{**}$

$^*p$ (two tail) $< .025$

$^{**}p$ (two tail) $< .001$

between the Mexican delinquent and nondelinquent groups was a near-perfect $+.98$. All these correlations were statistically significant $(p<.025)$.

It is particularly noteworthy that, while significant positive correlations were obtained within all three ethnic groups, there was substantially less agreement between the delinquents and nondelinquents in the Latin sample than in the other two samples. Since the Latins were the only group experiencing exogenous culture conflict between Mexican and Anglo value systems, it would be expected that they would experience the most anomie, which might be reflected in less agreement about values. This point will be examined further below.

In order to determine the overall agreement among the rankings of all six groups, the Kendall Coefficient of Concordance (W) was computed (Siegel, 1956). This, too, showed highly significant agreement, with $W = +.90$ ($p<.001$).

Thus, the data on the mean group rankings showed a high rate of agreement between the mean judgments of the delinquent and nondelinquent groups in each ethnic sample, and even among all six groups overall. The question can be raised, however, as to whether this agreement indicates that all six groups shared in a common lower-class subculture, which may have deviated markedly from the dominant culture, or if it indicates instead that all the groups were in fairly close agreement with the basic values of the larger society. Since only lower-class subjects were examined, the data from the present study alone did not allow for an answer to this question. However, a recent study by Sellin and Wolfgang (1964) on the measurement of juvenile delinquency did obtain data relevant to this issue. The basic purpose of their study was to determine if it was possible to measure the severity of various offenses through psychophysical techniques. In the course of this study various groups of normal subjects in Philadelphia made category and magnitude estimates of the severity of 141 different offenses. In their book, *The Measurement of Delinquency*, Sellin and Wolfgang published the category scale ratings of these offenses, as judged by samples of police line officers and Pennsylvania State University students enrolled in an introductory sociology class. By selecting offenses similar to those used in the present study and comparing the rank order of the ratings, it was possible to obtain a rough approximation of the amount of agreement between the judgments of our lower-class samples and Wolfgang and Sellin's middle-class policemen and students.

The first step was to survey the list of 141 offenses used by Sellin and Wolfgang and select those that most nearly approximated the ones used in the present study. No offenses were found that were similar to "being rude to grandparents," "failing to stop at a red light," or "accidentally breaking a window while playing ball." Sellin and Wolfgang did obtain ratings for "the offender throws rocks through windows," but because of the difference in the amount of damage and in the intentionality of the act, it was felt that this was too dissimilar from "accidentally breaking a window while playing ball" to be used.

For the remaining seven offenses rough approximations were found. The list of offenses and their approximations in the Sellin and Wolfgang study are presented in Table 40, along with the rank order of seriousness as determined from the category scale ratings reported by those investigators.

The rank order of the ratings of the seven offenses made by the police officers and the students were then correlated with the mean rank orders made by each of the six groups in the present study. The resulting Spearman Rank Order correlation coefficients ranged from +.75 to +1.00, with a median value of +.86 (see Table 41). All were significant.[3] Given the differences in testing situation and possible language differences, as well as the differences in the wording of the items, it is impressive that this much agreement was obtained between samples of lower-class, teen-age Anglos and Latins in San Antonio and Mexicans in Monterrey, half of whom were delinquent, and adult policemen and college students in Philadelphia, an unknown percentage of whom were delinquent. To be sure, the heterogeneity of the items contributed greatly to the size of the obtained coefficients; nevertheless, the similarity was sufficiently great to allow us to conclude that, as a group, the subjects sampled in the present investigation had values not too dissimilar from those of middle-class Anglos, insofar as they can be determined by the ranking of criminal offenses.

[3] Because the hypothesis tested was clearly directional, one-tail tests were used.

Table 40

Matching of Offenses Test Items with
Items Used by Sellin and Wolfgang (1964)

Offenses Test Items	Similar Sellin and Wolfgang Items	Rank Order By: Police Officers	Students
Murder	The offender stabs a person to death.	1	1
Rape	The offender forces a female to submit to sexual intercourse. No physical injury is inflicted.	2	2
Stealing a car	The offender steals an unlocked car and abandons but does not damage it.	4	4
Breaking into a house and stealing something	The offender breaks into a residence and steals $5.	3	5
Carrying a knife or gun	The offender, while being searched by the police, is found in illegal possession of a gun.	5	3
Shooting a BB gun in the park	The offender is found firing a rifle for which he has no permit.	6	6
Staying away from school	A juvenile plays hookey from school and thereby becomes an offender.	7	7

Does this mean that there is no validity to the idea that the lower class in general and delinquents in particular experience more anomie or confusion about values? Not only would it be premature to come to such a conclusion on the basis of a single instrument as crude as the Offenses Test, but also a closer examination of the data does not support such a conclusion. Thus far we have been examining the amount of *consensus* between groups as expressed by the

Table 41

Rank-Order Correlations of the Rankings of Offenses Test Items
with Those Made of Similar Offenses by Philadelphia
Students and Policemen (Sellin and Wolfgang, 1964)

Middle-class group	Anglo		Latin		Mexican	
	C†	D†	C	D	C	D
Police officers	.93**	.93**	.93**	.86*	1.00**	.96**
Pennsylvania State students	.86*	.86*	.86*	1.00**	.86*	.75*

* p (one tail) $<.05$
** p (one tail) $<.01$
† C, comparison group; D, delinquent group.

degree of agreement in their rankings. However, anomie is better
estimated by looking at the amount of *disagreement* to be found
within the various samples, as indicated by the variance. For example, in each of two groups a certain offense may have a mean
rank of 5.5. This indicates overall consensus about the severity of the
offense. If, however, the mean score of 5.5 was achieved in the first
group by 50 per cent of the subjects assigning a rank of 5 and 50
per cent a rank of 6, while in the second group it was achieved by
10 per cent of the subjects assigning it each rank from 1 to 10, then
obviously the second group would have manifested much less agreement and much more confusion about values than the first. This
confusion would not be reflected in the mean, which would be the
same for both groups, but in measures of variability, such as the
range, variance, or standard deviation.

Therefore, the variability of rankings in the delinquent and comparison groups in each sample were compared using two-tail F tests,
and the overall variability of the six groups was compared using
Hartley's F_{max} test, as described by Walker and Lev (1953).[4] It
was anticipated that these analyses would indicate that, by and
large, the delinquents' ratings had significantly more variance than
those of the nondelinquents, and that this would be especially true

[4] The authors would like to thank Quinn McNemar, whose suggestions were
most helpful in making these analyses.

in the Latin sample, in which cultural conflict would presumably have resulted in the greatest amount of confusion regarding values. The results of these tests are presented in Table 42. In the Anglo

Table 42

Tests of Heterogeneity of Variance of Offenses Test Ratings

Offense	Anglo (A) F^a	Group with Greater Variance	Latin (L) F^b	Group with Greater Variance	Mexican (M) F^c	Group with Greater Variance	F^d_{max}	Overall Group with Greater Variance
Murder	1.33	C†	6.15**	D†	2.68**	D	10.16**	L-D
Rape	1.42	D	2.06*	D	1.02	C	8.44**	M-C
Stealing a car	1.24	D	5.84**	D	1.13	D	9.65**	L-D
Breaking into a house and stealing something	1.48	C	11.03**	D	1.73*	C	7.15**	L-D
Carrying a knife or gun	1.16	C	1.35	C	1.61	C	4.55**	M-C
Being rude to grandparents	0.78	C	1.11	D	1.05	C	2.44**	M-C
Shooting a BB gun in the park	1.41	C	3.60**	D	1.28	D	3.73**	L-D
Failing to stop at a red light	1.62	D	5.00**	D	1.75*	D	6.39**	L-D
Staying away from school	1.03	C	1.53	D	1.16	D	3.12**	L-D
Accidentally breaking a window while playing ball	1.85*	D	1.26	D	5.09**	C	6.72**	M-C

^{a} $F_{.05}=1.78$ $F_{.01}=2.19$
^{b} $F_{.05}=1.81$ $F_{.01}=2.19$
^{c} $F_{.05}=1.71$ $F_{.01}=2.10$
^{d} $F_{.05}=2.38$ $F_{.01}=2.80$
* p (two tail) $<.05$
** p (two tail) $<.01$
† C, comparison group; D, delinquent group.

sample, there was no noteworthy tendency for the delinquents to be more variable in their rating of offenses than the comparison group. On four of the 10 offenses the delinquents had the higher variance and on six the controls did. Of the 10 offenses, the only one that had a significant difference in variance was in the predicted direction, with the delinquent being higher.

As anticipated, the results for the Latin sample showed many significant differences. Of the 10 offenses, the delinquents had the higher variance on nine (a difference which is in itself significant at the .01 level) and the variances were significantly different on six of these. Significantly greater variability for the delinquents was obtained not only on offenses like "failing to stop at a red light," on which substantial disagreement might be expected, but also for such offenses as "murder" and "rape."

In the Mexican sample the nondelinquents were higher in variance on five of the offenses and the delinquents on the remaining five. Four of the offenses had significant differences in the variance of the ratings, two of which indicated significantly higher variance for the delinquents and two higher variance for the comparison group.

Overall, the F_{max} tests showed that the six groups differed significantly in the variability of their ratings on all 10 offenses. On six of the 10 offenses it was the Latin delinquents who had the highest variance. The comparisons of the variance of the delinquent and comparison groups within samples indicated that 11 of the 30 comparisons were significant; nine of the 11 indicated significantly more variance for the delinquents. Six of the nine significant differences in favor of the delinquents were obtained in the Latin sample. These data thus indicated that while there was an overall group consensus on values, as reflected in the mean rankings of criminal offenses, the Latin delinquent group was characterized by much more confusion or disagreement about values than the nondelinquent Latins or, indeed, any of the other five groups. The Anglo and Mexican samples showed no tendency for the delinquents to have greater variance than the nondelinquents. The data were thus consistent with the expectation that anomie resulting from exogenous culture conflict would be associated with delinquency among the Latins.

Some might object that there is an alternative explanation for the results that does not involve anomie or culture conflict. It could be that because of bilingualism the Latins experienced the most diffi-culty comprehending the directions and understanding the de-scriptions of the offense. Moreover, it is possible that the Latin delinquents may have experienced significantly more confusion regarding the directions than did the Latin nondelinquents, for the data in Chapter 7 showed that the mean Verbal IQ of the Latin delinquents (76) was significantly lower than that of the Latin comparison group (93). Thus, the greater variance for the Latins could be attributed to language problems rather than anomie.

While linguistic problems may have contributed to the variance to some degree, the present investigators are inclined to feel that disagreement over values is a more parsimonious explanation for the obtained results. It will be recalled that pretesting of the items in the Offenses Test indicated that they could be comprehended even by those whose reading skills were below average. While the Latin delinquents were significantly lower than the nondelinquents in Verbal IQ and in achieved grade level, nevertheless, their mean grade level was 7.15 and only five had not completed the sixth grade. Fifth- or sixth-grade reading skills should have been sufficient to understand the items in the test. Moreover, it is clear from the data that none of the subjects completely misunderstood the instruc-tions. If they had, they would have arranged the cards in reverse order. Yet none of the Latin delinquents gave "murder" a rating lower than 4, which almost certainly would have happened if any sets of cards had been arranged in reverse order. Therefore, while the possibility that reading difficulties associated with bilingualism were responsible for the results cannot be completely ruled out, it appears to the present investigators that the data primarily reflect differences in anomie rather than differences in reading skills.

Summary of Offenses Test

Most scholars agree that many delinquents are quite normal ex-cept for the fact that they break the law. To account for such behavior, some theorists have postulated the existence of "delinquent subcultures" with values that deviate from those of the overall society. A person raised in such a subculture would learn, as normal behavior, habits that might be regarded as delinquent by the mem-bers of the larger society and their agents, the police.

Such delinquent subcultures may be "exogenous" or "indigenous";

that is, they may grow out of the conflict in values engendered when people raised in the traditions of one culture, such as Mexico, attempt to live in a society controlled by the traditions of another culture, such as the United States, or they may grow out of conflicts in values and opportunities within the culture itself. In either case they can result in a state of confusion of values, normlessness, or "anomie," which in turn may result in delinquent behavior.

In order to test some of these notions, the values of the members of the various samples were tested in a rough fashion by asking them to rank various transgressions from the most evil to the least evil. The mean rankings of the various groups showed a good degree of consensus, with the rank-order correlations between the three sets of delinquent and comparison groups all being high and significant. Moreover, high overall agreement was demonstrated by a high (.90) Coefficient of Concordance. As might be expected, the Latins, who by virtue of being the only minority group would be expected to experience the most cultural conflict or anomie, had the lowest correlation between the ranking of the delinquents and nondelinquents.

Next, the agreement of these six lower-class teenage samples with representatives of North American middle-class adult society was investigated by identifying seven offenses in the present study that were approximated in Sellin and Wolfgang's (1964) study of the estimation of the severity of 141 offenses by Philadelphia police officers and Pennsylvania State University students. Despite differences in the wording of the items, as well as the many differences between the methodology and subject samples employed in the present study and that of Sellin and Wolfgang, significant positive correlations were again obtained. This indicated a fair degree of group consensus, not only within the present groups but also between the present samples and samples that could be considered representative of middle-class values.

These data analyses indicated that the delinquents and nondelinquents within the various ethnic groups, and across ethnic groups as well, probably had more values in common with one another and with representatives of the middle class than they had values that differed. By emphasizing the differences between groups, it is likely that many shared values are overlooked.

It was pointed out that studying only the agreement between

mean ratings tended to minimize differences. Anomie and normlessness were more likely to be reflected in measures of within-group variability than in the measures of central tendency. It was predicted that the delinquent subjects in general and the Latins in particular would display greater variability in their rankings than the nondelinquents. When this was tested, no tendency for the delinquents to have significantly more variability than the nondelinquents was noted in the Anglo or Mexican samples. However, such a pattern was found in the Latin sample in which the delinquents' variance was significantly higher than that of the comparison group on six offenses. This was interpreted as indicating greater anomie for the Latin delinquents than the Latin comparison group, probably as a result of exogenous culture conflict.

The overall analysis of differences in variability over all six samples indicated significant differences for all 10 offenses. On six of the 10 offenses the Latin delinquents had the highest variance. The data for the Offenses Test thus indicated that, while there is a large area of consensus in value judgments, nevertheless, significant individual differences exist. The pattern of these differences was consistent with the notion that significant disagreement as to values is associated with the occurrence of delinquency among minority groups experiencing culture conflict. Further study of value differences between various groups of delinquents and nondelinquents using more refined instruments and procedures, such as those developed by Sellin and Wolfgang would be valuable.

CHAPTER 10

THE CARD SORT TEST

The Card Sort Test consisted of 140 statements, most concerning attitudes toward family figures, which the boys were to sort into "true" and "false" categories. This test, and the Cartoon Test, which is discussed in the following chapter, shifted the focus of the investigation away from the characteristics of the boys themselves toward their subjective perceptions of, and reactions to, the characteristics of others.

In order for these data to be properly evaluated, it is necessary to place them in context. A number of studies have examined the characteristics of the families of delinquents, as perceived by the delinquents themselves as well as by external observers. Before the results of the present investigation are discussed, a representative survey of some of the major studies of the psychological characteristics of the family backgrounds of delinquents will be presented.

Research on the Families of Delinquents

Studies of the psychological characteristics of delinquents' family backgrounds have focused on such factors as the amount and the nature of affection shown by the parents, the consistency and severity of the discipline, the attitudes of the members of the family toward one another, and the identification of the delinquent boys with their fathers. Because of the subtlety of these variables, a variety of research designs have been adopted. In most studies a sample of delinquents and nondelinquents, matched on certain variables that investigators feel should be controlled, have been contrasted.

In some the delinquents' attitudes were assessed directly without reference to a contrast group. In others the parents were interviewed about their feelings toward the boy and toward their spouses. Still others employed ratings made by external observers. When significant differences were obtained, it was very rare for them to be cross-validated on a new sample. However, enough studies employing similar methods have been carried out so that the generality of the reported findings can be determined with reasonable certainty.

One of the earliest and best known comparisons of a matched group of delinquents and nondelinquents was the classic study by Glueck and Glueck (1950) in which a number of familial factors were studied through interviews with the boys and their parents, as well as by investigation of the records of various social service agencies. The Gluecks found that the delinquents' parents were more uncongenial and that their families were considerably less cohesive than those of the nondelinquents. The delinquent boy was more apt to be rejected by both parents, to feel his parents were indifferent to his welfare, and to be hostile to his father, mother, and siblings.[1] The father was more likely to provide an unsuitable model for the delinquent boy to identify with. More than half the delinquent boys had inadequate supervision, combined with lax discipline on the part of the mother and harsh or erratic discipline by the father. The Gluecks summarized their findings regarding familial patterns as follows:

> In interpersonal family relationships, however, we found an exceedingly marked difference between the two groups under comparison. A much higher proportion of the families of the delinquents were disorganized (not cohesive). . . .
> Apart from the lesser cohesiveness of the families in which the delinquents grew up, many more of their fathers, mothers, brothers, and sisters have been indifferent or frankly hostile to the boys. A far *lower* proportion of the delinquents than of the non-delinquents have been affectionately attached to their parents; and considerably more of them have felt that their parents have not been concerned about their welfare. Final-

---

[1] In all these comparisons, it should be pointed out that only a minority of the delinquent boys had these feelings and attitudes; nevertheless, they were still significantly more characteristic of the delinquents than the nondelinquents. This will be true in other studies, including the present one.

ly, twice as many of the delinquents do not look upon their fathers as acceptable symbols for emulation. . . .

The greater inadequacy of the parents of the delinquents is also reflected in the extremes of laxity and harshness with which they attempted to meet the disciplinary problems of their children and in the greater carelessness of their supervision of the children, amounting often to outright neglect. (Glueck and Glueck, 1950, p. 280)

Another husband-and-wife team of investigators, Joan and William McCord (1958), used data from the Cambridge-Somerville Youth Project to further explore family patterns and delinquency. This study used a longitudinal approach. The independent variables, assessed when the child was young, were the deviance (criminality, alcoholism, or promiscuity) of the parents, the degree of affection shown by the parents toward the child, and the disciplinary methods the parents employed. The dependent variable was the child's subsequent criminal career, as determined at age 27.

The McCords found that parental deviance was clearly related to the criminality of the sons, but that it interacted with the warmth shown toward the sons and the techniques of discipline. Affection and consistent discipline from either parent could largely offset the effects of a deviant parent, while passivity or rejection could exacerbate it. Lack of affection from both parents was associated with a high level of criminality, regardless of the parental role model.

Thus, the McCords' data were quite consistent with those of the Gluecks in underlining the importance of affection and consistent discipline in determining whether or not the child becomes a juvenile or adult criminal; however, the McCords' investigation placed somewhat greater emphasis on the example provided by the parents.

Becker, Peterson, Hellmer, Shoemaker, and Quay (1959) studied the familial differences between a group of 25 families whose children were in no need of clinical services and another group of 32 families who were seeking help for their children. Both groups consisted of white children, six to 12 years of age, whose parents were living together. The data derived from interviews and psychological tests indicated that the families of those children referred to the clinic because of aggressive or uncontrollable behavior showed a syndrome indicating "that in families with conduct problem children, both parents are maladjusted, give vent to unbridled emo-

272

tions, and tend to be arbitrary with the child. In addition the mother tended to be active (tense), dictatorial, thwarting, and suggesting, whereas the father tended not to enforce regulations" (Becker et al., 1959, p. 117). This study thus added emotionality and aggressiveness on the part of the parents to the list of traits associated with aggressiveness and delinquency on the part of the child.

In a broad study, Bandura and Walters (1959) interviewed 26 aggressive delinquents, 26 normal control subjects, and their respective families. The two sets of families were matched for size, the boy's age and IQ, and the socioeconomic status of the fathers' occupations. Bandura and Walters found that the fathers of the aggressive delinquent boys were colder and more rejecting than those of the controls. It was apparent that even in early childhood, before any delinquent behavior had developed, there had been little affectionate interaction between fathers and sons. Consequently, the delinquent boys' identification with their fathers had probably been disrupted. While the delinquent boys' mothers were warmer than their husbands, Bandura and Walters found them also to be somewhat rejecting and punitive when their sons behaved in a dependent fashion. Not too surprisingly, the aggressive boys were found to feel more hostility toward their fathers than did the control boys, but there was no significant difference in the feelings of hostility toward the mother.

Summarizing their results, Bandura and Walters stated that, in contrast to the controls, the aggressive delinquents were:

. . . more openly antagonistic to authority and less positive in their feelings toward their peers. They felt somewhat rejected by both parents, but retained a good deal of affection and respect for their mothers. In contrast they were critical and resentful of their fathers, with whom they showed only limited identification. They were markedly distrustful; they feared and avoided situations in which they might have become emotionally dependent on others. . . . Their behavior, moreover, was apparently self-defeating, because it alienated them from the affection of which they already felt deprived and brought them under the more direct control of the authority figures whom they distrusted and resented. (Bandura and Walters, 1959, pp. 312–313)

While the studies thus far reviewed relied primarily on interviews with individual delinquents and their parents, Peterson,

Quay, and Cameron (1959) adopted a procedure similar to that used in the present investigation. These investigators administered the items from two previously developed delinquency scales to groups of white delinquents and nondelinquents matched for age and place of residence. The resulting true and false responses to these items, which had previously been found to discriminate delinquent from nondelinquent adolescents, were then factor analyzed. One interpretable factor that emerged consisted primarily of antisocial and amoral attitudes and was labeled "psychopathy." Another, which had many items containing expressions of guilt or remorse, was called "neuroticism." Two others were labeled "inadequacy" and "scholastic maladjustment."

The factor most relevant to family adjustment was one that Peterson et al. labeled "family dissension." Items with high positive loadings on this factor indicated unpleasant home conditions and family strife: for example, "My mother and father argue a lot," "My stepfather (or stepmother) treats me badly," "I was often punished unfairly as a child," "My folks yell at us kids a lot," "My mother and father have never really been friends of mine," "My home life as a child was less peaceful than those of most other people," or "I have run away from home because my folks treated me bad." Items that had substantial *negative* loadings were ones indicating family warmth or "cohesiveness," to use the Gluecks' term: for example, "My home life was always very pleasant," "The members of my family were always very close to each other," or "My home life was always very happy." These data thus indicated that the delinquents' subjective perceptions of their family life, as revealed by the questionnaire data, were in substantial agreement with those of outside observers reported in other investigations.

The role of parental affection in delinquency was further studied by Andry (1962) in samples of 80 delinquents and 80 nondelinquent controls, aged 12 to 15, from working-class homes in a high-delinquency area of London. A questionnaire designed to test the boys' perceptions of their parents' attitudes was administered and a number of specific hypotheses tested. The results of the study overwhelmingly indicated that the delinquent boys felt much more deprived of affection, particularly from their fathers, than did the nondelinquent boys. Seventy-eight per cent of the nondelinquent boys indicated that both their parents were "very satisfactory" in the amount of love they gave, but only 11 per cent of the delinquents felt this way. On the other hand, 75 per cent of the delinquents indicated that one or both parents were "very bad" in this regard, in contrast to only 11 per cent of the controls.

Andry found also that only 15 per cent of the delinquents felt both parents loved them equally, while 69 per cent believed their fathers loved them less than their mothers; by contrast, 56 per cent of the nondelinquents felt their parents loved them equally and only 14 per cent of the controls felt the father loved them less. This negative perception of the father by the delinquents was further indicated by the fact that 54 per cent of the delinquent boys felt their fathers should love them more, while only 7 per cent of the nondelinquents felt this way.

Bandura and Walters' (1959) observations regarding dependency and the expression of affection were also borne out in Andry's research. He found that 52 per cent of the delinquents' mothers, 65 per cent of their fathers, and 56 per cent of the boys themselves were embarrassed about showing affection, compared with 12 per cent of the controls' mothers, 23 per cent of their fathers, and 14 per cent of the boys themselves. This indicated mutual estrangement similar to the lack of cohesiveness noted by the Gluecks.

Finally, in regard to discipline and authority problems, Andry's English delinquents, like their American counterparts, seemed to feel that they were treated with undue harshness. While only 10 per cent of the controls felt that either of their parents "nagged" them, 58 per cent of the delinquents felt "nagged" by one parent or the other; similarly only 5 per cent of the controls felt "picked on" by their parents, in contrast to 37 per cent of the delinquents.

Thus, a number of studies have compared the family dynamics of delinquents and nondelinquents, as seen by the boys themselves, by neutral observers, and by the boys' parents. Despite the diversity of investigative procedures, a striking degree of uniformity has been found in the data. Most studies revealed that the parents of the delinquent boys were seen as giving less affection, and, as might be expected, that their families were less cohesive, with fewer ties of mutual respect, affection, or enjoyment of each other's company. Extremes of parental discipline were also found to characterize the delinquents' homes, with either laxness or harshness, or an alternation between the two, being more common than in the nondelinquents' homes, in which a more consistent, moderate approach was used. As might be expected, the example provided by the parents was also important, with antisocial parents tending to have more antisocial children unless the effects of a poor model were offset by good discipline and affection. Poor relations with the father were frequently found, with indications that the delinquent boys had great difficulty identifying with and respecting their fathers.

Other studies employing somewhat different designs have obtained data consistent with these observations. Healy and Bronner (1936) compared 105 delinquents with their nondelinquent siblings who were closest in age, thus controlling for overall family atmosphere. They found that in 46 cases the delinquent siblings keenly felt "either *rejected, deprived, insecure, not understood* in affectional relationships, unloved, or that love has been withdrawn" (Healy & Bronner, 1936, p. 581, italics in original). Moreover, in 34 cases Healy and Bronner noted "intense feelings of *discomfort about family disharmonies*, parental misconduct, the conditions of family life, or parental errors in management and discipline," and, in 31 cases, "bitter feelings of *jealousy* toward one or more siblings, or feelings of being markedly discriminated against because another in the family circle was more favored . . ." (Healy & Bronner, 1936, p. 582, italics in original).

Most studies, including the present one and all the studies reviewed thus far in this chapter, have used delinquent subjects who have been through some sort of formal adjudication process or at least have been arrested by police. Nye (1958, p. 10) has pointed out that one drawback of such studies is:

. . . that the *institutionalization process* of numerous arrests by police, temporary confinement, parole, and institutionalization itself usually involves a series of traumatic experiences for the adolescent as well as the parent which are very likely to reorient the feelings of each toward the other and may transform the entire family structure and attitudes. A study of family relationships in this context would reveal spurious differences between the family relationships of delinquents and nondelinquents.[2]

[2] In fact, as Nye could have gone on to point out, the basic goal of the entire judicial process is to alter significantly the attitudes and feelings of the delinquents and their families.

The only way to rule out the possibility that the differences observed between delinquent and nondelinquent samples may be the result of the judicial process is to study "delinquents" who have never been through a formal judicial procedure. Obviously, this involves changing the operational definition of delinquent. Nye did this in his study of family relationships and juvenile delinquency. Instead of relying on a social definition, he used a self-definition. High school students were administered a questionnaire listing various law violations and were asked to indicate anonymously the frequency with which they had, if ever, engaged in each of the acts. The questionnaire also included a number of items dealing with family relationships. Nye was thus able to use the students' self-reports of illegal behavior as the criteria for selecting groups of "more delinquent" and "less delinquent" boys and girls, whose responses to the items on family relationships could be compared.

The results obtained with this method were quite similar to those reported for adjudicated delinquents. "More delinquent" boys were found to perceive their parents as being significantly more rejecting of them than did the "less delinquent" boys; the more delinquent subjects were also much more likely to reject the parents in return. Regarding discipline, it was found that the more delinquent boys regarded their fathers' administration of punishment as unfair and significantly more felt that the father showed partiality in meting out punishment than did the less delinquent boys. The less delinquent boys reported their fathers to be significantly more likely to explain the reason for punishment. The amount of strictness shown by either parent was not related to the boys' delinquency, however.

Nye also obtained data regarding the students' perceptions of their parents' character and disposition. The more delinquent students had significantly more unfavorable attitudes toward both parents and indicated that their parents were significantly less cheerful and more easily upset and that their fathers were harder to please. The parents of the more delinquent boys were also regarded by their sons as less truthful, less honest, less considerate of their neighbors, and more inclined to find scapegoats than were the parents of the less delinquent boys. Moreover, the data indicated that the parents of the more delinquent students were less likely to agree on values.

It can be seen that Nye's research using nonadjudicated "delin-

quents" yielded results that were consistent with those obtained using institutionalized delinquents. Some differences did appear, however. The correlation between parental rejection and delinquency, while significant, appeared to be of lower magnitude than would be expected from the literature, suggesting the possibility that additional rejection by the parents might result from the boys' delinquent behavior and subsequent judicial procedures. The overall findings, similar to those of other studies, indicate an association between delinquent behavior and perceived rejection by the parents, particularly the father, perceived injustice in the father's administration of discipline, and negative opinions about the personality and character of the parents.

A somewhat different approach has been taken by Walter Reckless and his associates at The Ohio State University. It will be recalled from our discussion in Chapter 2 that Reckless has focused on the interaction of personal and social factors, pointing out how a good self-concept learned in a favorable family atmosphere can insulate the individual from the criminogenic forces operating in a high-delinquency area; by the same token a poor self-concept can make the adolescent more susceptible to the pernicious effects of a high-delinquency neighborhood.

In an effort to explore these hypotheses, Reckless, Dinitz, and Murray (1955) studied a sample of 125 white boys in the sixth grades of schools located in the highest delinquency areas of Columbus, Ohio, who were not known to the police and who had been nominated by their teachers as being unlikely to ever experience any contact with the police or the courts. In a follow-up study, Scarpitti (1959) located 103 of the 125 boys four years later when they were about 16 years of age. Only four of the 103 "good boys" living in high-delinquency areas had had contact with the police, one for malicious mischief, one for truancy, one for drinking and violating curfew, and one for borrowing a neighbor's car to deliver papers. Obviously, the boys in this sample were considerably less delinquent than most of their peers in these neighborhoods.

Reckless and his associates studied the boys, as well as the parents of these 125 "good" boys, at the age of 12 and Scarpitti studied them further in his follow-up study four years later, using attitude scales, including some devised and used by Nye (1958) in his research, as well as the more traditional demographic sociological indices. The data were compared with those obtained on a sample of 101 "bad boys" who had been nominated by their sixth-grade teachers as heading for trouble with the law, 24 of whom already had police contacts by age 12 (Reckless, Dinitz, & Kay, 1957). As a cross check, the California Psychological Inventory Socialization scale (Gough, 1957) was administered and the "good boys" were found to have scores equivalent to the scores typically obtained by good citizens, while the "bad boys" scored in the same range as court-martialed military prisoners, truants, and reformatory inmates.

The differences that Reckless and his associates found between the "good" and "bad" boys were consistent with those reported by other investigators. The families of the "good boys" were more stable and cohesive. Not only was there a lower incidence of broken homes, but also there was more family solidarity and loyalty. The parents were intensely interested in their children and determined that they should grow up to be good citizens. The boys and their parents indicated there was a lot of mutual affection and relatively little conflict and bickering in the home. Unlike those of the "bad boys," the families of the "good boys" were more likely to engage in recreation together and the parents were more likely to know and to approve of their son's friends. Both the parents and sons indicated that there was closer supervision and less laxity or harshness in disciplinary practices. Nye's scales showed less rejection of the parent by the boy and of the boy by the parent than is found in delinquent samples.

One discrepancy that was noted was the fact that most of the mothers of the "good boys" indicated that their sons did not get enough attention and warmth from their rather aloof fathers. The boys' ratings, however, did not indicate they perceived that much difference in the warmth displayed by their mothers and fathers (Reckless, Dinitz, & Murray, 1957).

A major factor that differentiated the "good" from the "bad" boys in Reckless' studies, and which has been overlooked in other studies, was a positive determination on the part of the "good boys" to avoid trouble at all costs. They rarely engaged in the petty theft and minor offenses common in their milieus and few had friends who had been in trouble with the law. They regarded themselves as obedient sons and avoided behavior that their parents would disapprove of (Reckless, Dinitz, & Kay, 1957). Thus, there was not merely an absence of delinquent behavior, but instead a positive effort to do the right thing and to resist the temptations offered by the high-delinquency neighborhoods in which they resided.

A study by Bacon, Child, and Barry (1963) added further generality to some of the patterns observed in research comparing delinquents and nondelinquents. Bacon et al. set out to determine the importance of certain family patterns as possible causes of crime by using cross-cultural data collected on 48 preliterate societies on which sufficient ethnological data had been collected to allow the investigators to determine the incidence of crimes against the person and crimes against property. They reasoned that if certain familial and social conditions are indeed causes of criminal behavior, then those societies in which such conditions were present should have a higher incidence of crime than those in which such conditions were absent. Bacon et al. found a correlation of $-.41$ $(p<.01)$ between the incidence of theft and the amount of childhood indulgence in a society. They interpreted this as indicating that theft is in part motivated by feelings of deprivation of love.

Another variable that Bacon et al. investigated was the amount of contact between a child and his father. The living arrangements found in different societies permit different degrees of contact between fathers and sons; the nuclear monogamous household provides the most, and polygamous mother-child households, in which each wife sleeps in a separate hut with her children, the least.[3] Bacon et al. found that the amount of contact with the father, as reflected in the living arrangements in the different societies, correlated $-.58$ with the amount of theft and $-.44$ with the frequency of personal crime. Both correlations were significant, supporting the hypothesis that the more opportunity children in a society have to identify with their fathers, the lower the crime rate will be.

These studies thus indicated that the familial factors found associated with juvenile delinquency are not artifacts of the adjudication process and that they have cross-cultural generality. Turning to the data from the Card Sort Test presented in this chapter and the Cartoon Test in the next chapter, the present investigators, therefore, expected to find similar differences between the delinquent and

---

[3] The latter arrangement is, of course, similar to what Miller (1958) called the "female based household" in lower-class United States culture.

comparison groups in the Anglo, Latin, and Mexican samples. It was hypothesized that the delinquents would perceive their homes as being less cohesive, that they would feel rejected by their parents, and that they would reject them, particularly their fathers, in return. It was expected that the discipline in the delinquents' homes would be reported to be more erratic, extreme, and unfair. It was also expected that the delinquents would be more likely to perceive their parents as having antisocial attitudes.

Procedures

The Card Sort Test consisted of 140 statements individually typed on 3 x 5 inch cards that the subjects were asked to sort into "true" and "false" groups. No limitations were placed on the sorting so that a boy could, if he wished, indicate that all were true or all were false. A complete list of the 140 statements is presented in Table 43.

Table 43

Statements Comprising the Card Sort Test

1. I was happier when I was a small child than I am now.
2. Sometimes I wish I was only five years old.
3. I have many good friends.
4. I wish I could be like my mother.
5. My mother scolds me no matter what I do.
6. No one but me remembers my birthday.
7. My father worries about losing his job.
8. If you go to church you will not get into trouble.
9. My parents quarrel and fight much of the time.
10. I always tell the truth.
11. My mother is always kissing and hugging me.
12. When I am in trouble, I call on my father for help.
13. Dad is the boss at our house.
14. I will be glad when I am old enough to join the armed forces.
15. I liked the first teacher I ever had.
16. My mother says never let anybody get the best of you.
17. My mother treats me like a baby.
18. My mother thinks she has to work too hard.
19. My father and mother often talk and laugh together.
20. I like to be with my mother.

21. Our house is very crowded.
22. I like one of my parents much better than I like the other.
23. I sleep very well.
24. Almost all my friends smoke.
25. I have had lots of fights with my brothers and sisters.
26. When I grow up I want to be like my father.
27. Mother is the real boss in our family.
28. My parents often go to parties or to the movies together.
29. My father always makes me be at home by ten o'clock at night.
30. I get mad sometimes.
31. I smoked my first cigarette before I was ten years old.
32. I like everyone I know.
33. My father always says to go ask mother—she's the boss.
34. My father spends most of his nights at home.
35. I like movies.
36. My father acts like he is mad all the time.
37. Children under sixteen are too young to drive cars.
38. Sometimes I think of things too bad to talk about.
39. I am popular with girls.
40. I go to school only because I have to.
41. Everyone in my family seems to be against me.
42. My mother and father seem to love each other very much.
43. I am afraid of some things.
44. My mother stands up for me when I am in trouble.
45. Sometimes I have been homesick.
46. Birthday parties are for sissies.
47. My mother doesn't care what I do.
48. My father always gives his pay check to mother.
49. My grandmother is always telling my father or my mother what to do.
50. Once in a while I put off until tomorrow what I ought to do today.
51. My parents do not seem to have much fun.
52. My folks treat me fair.
53. I can play a musical instrument.
54. Sometimes I think I am an adopted son.
55. Most girls only want you to spend money on them.
56. My father gets mad easily.
57. My father thinks anything you can get by with is all right.
58. My mother often asks my friends to visit me in my home.
59. My father likes other people.
60. I can never save any money.
61. Many of the boys I know would like to run away from home.

62. My grandparents have always liked me.
63. I often feel tired.
64. I like to read comic books.
65. My father goes off by himself when he does not like something.
66. I hardly ever play games with my parents.
67. Some day I expect to have an expensive car.
68. My father says a policeman is a boy's best friend.
69. My father would never cheat anybody.
70. Sometimes when I am not feeling well I am cross.
71. I usually talk over things that are worrying me with my mother.
72. My parents treat me as if I did not know right from wrong.
73. Old people are very wise because they have lived a long time.
74. My mother does not like the way I act.
75. My parents hardly ever go to church.
76. My father thinks only of himself.
77. When my father hears of something bad I have done he laughs and says boys will be boys.
78. My father likes the other children in the family better than he likes me.
79. Girls are just as smart as boys.
80. Someone in my family has been in a car accident.
81. Everyone in my family has a regular seat at the table where they sit at meals.
82. The boys I know usually do what their parents tell them.
83. I always keep my troubles to myself.
84. My spending money was always given to me by my mother.
85. Some of the boys I know get more spending money than I do.
86. My father has always given me all the money I needed for spending.
87. My father thinks you should obey the law even when there is not a policeman around.
88. My mother says children should fight for their rights.
89. Grownups are usually too hard on children.
90. If I could go into a movie without paying and be sure I was not seen, I would probably do it.
91. At Christmas time we always have a big celebration.
92. I have to take care of the younger children in our family.
93. I do not like my name.
94. A son expects to have a better job than his father.
95. My mother says I do bad things just to make her feel bad.
96. My father gets mad when I break something, even if I don't mean to.

97. My father often tells about the trouble he got into when he was a boy.
98. My mother parks in the wrong place if she thinks she can get by with it.
99. Most boys will grow up to make more money than their fathers did.
100. I have always been my mother's favorite child.
101. I am ashamed sometimes of the way my parents behave.
102. My father thinks my mother spends too much money.
103. I like western movies best.
104. My mother does my homework for me when I can't do it.
105. My mother brags a lot.
106. The boys I know often ask their fathers what to do.
107. Young people are better drivers than older people.
108. My father thinks everyone should have a pistol to protect himself.
109. My father gives up easily when things are hard to do.
110. Every once in a while I get mad at my parents.
111. I always receive lots of presents for Christmas.
112. When I get home I always tell my parents where I was and what I did.
113. I have gone to the movies about once a week or more ever since I was about eight years old.
114. My mother is always nagging me to help around the house.
115. Most teachers understand boys.
116. My father is usually too busy to play around with me.
117. Grownups understand me very well.
118. My mother hates policemen.
119. My father has a hard time making up his mind.
120. The Boy Scouts are a bunch of sissies.
121. My mother gets mad if I try to explain why I did something.
122. Sometimes I think my father is not very smart.
123. Sometimes I stay away from home overnight by myself.
124. My mother tells my father on me when I do something.
125. A good education will help you get ahead in the world.
126. Most parents give their sons spending money every week.
127. My father wants me to make up my own mind about what to do.
128. My father thinks it is not so bad to break the law once in a while if you do not get caught.
129. My father thinks every one is against him.
130. My mother thinks my father does not make enough money.
131. My mother usually knows where I am when I am not at home.
132. Most parents like to play with their children.
133. I like baseball.

134. My grandfather and grandmother are too old to know much.
135. Some people in our neighborhood are always making trouble.
136. The boys I know usually try to keep grownups from finding out what they do.
137. I read comic books about crime whenever I can.
138. My mother knows many of my friends.
139. Our family always seems to owe money.
140. I always talk over what I am going to do with my parents.

An inspection of this list indicates that many of the statements concerned family attitudes and relations, including the amount of affection displayed by members of the family toward one another, the relative authority of the mother and the father, the boy's identification pattern, the amount of communication between parents and children, and the boy's perceptions of his parents' attitudes toward authorities and regulations. Other items related to mild deviance, such as smoking, running away or disobedience, attitudes toward police and other authorities, peer relations, and economic conditions and opportunities. Most items were phrased simply and positively so that they could be easily comprehended.

Since the Card Sort items were devised, much research has focused on the problem of the influence of acquiescent response set on true-false questionnaires. It has been argued that some people have a set to respond "true," no matter what the content of the item. If there were systematic differences between delinquents and non-delinquents with respect to this response set, they could bias the results of the Card Sort Test, since one group would use the "true" category more than the other regardless of the content of the item. It would have been more elegant from this standpoint to have each item accompanied by its logical opposite so that the presence of such a set could be determined. It is, however, difficult to manufacture adequate opposites for most items. If the reader reflects on how he would go about creating an item exactly opposite in meaning to the first Card Sort item, "I was happier when I was a small child than I am now," the difficulties will become apparent. "I was not happier as a small child than I am now" focuses too much on changes in happiness. "I am happier now than when I was a small child" or "I am just as happy now as when I was a small child" and other logical alternatives never precisely reverse the connotations of the original item. Moreover, they have the disadvantages of doubling the length of the test and, through the frequent addition of double negatives, making it much more difficult to understand. These disadvantages would probably offset the increased sophistication of having both positively and negatively phrased statements of each point to control for possible response bias.

Therefore, in interpreting these results, the reader should be aware of the possibility that response sets as well as manifest content may have influenced the response pattern. It is the present investigators' opinion, based on recent research that tends to minimize the importance of acquiescent response set as an important determinant of responses to unambiguous items such as these (Block, 1965; Megargee, 1966b, Chap. 6), that the response set of acquiescence probably did not play a major role in determining the Card Sort responses.

For each of the 140 statements, the number of boys in each group responding "true" and the number responding "false" was determined.[4] The significance of the differences between the number of delinquents and nondelinquents responding true and false to each item in each ethnic sample was then determined by chi-square.[5]

Results

The items that significantly differentiated between the delinquents and nondelinquents in each sample are presented in Tables 44, 45, and 46. In each of these tables, the items that the delinquents answered true significantly more often than the nondelinquents are presented first, and the items that the nondelinquents endorsed more often are presented next. Within each category, the items are arranged in order of significance, with the item having the lowest p value first and the one with the highest p value last. No items with two-tail p values $>.05$ are included in these tables.

[4] The number of boys in each group responding "true" to each item is presented in Appendix 4. The number responding "false" is equal to 50 minus the number responding "true."

[5] The investigators wish to thank The University of Texas Computation Center for providing computer time for these analyses, and Dr. Earl Jennings for his generous assistance in developing a program to analyze these data.

Table 44

Card Sort Statements on Which Significant Differences
between Anglo Delinquents and Nondelinquents Were Obtained

Statements answered "true" significantly more often by the delinquents:

No.	Content	p	% True C*	D*
	<.005			
31.	I smoked my first cigarette before I was ten years old.	.004	22	52
74.	My mother does not like the way I act.	.004	20	50
24.	Almost all my friends smoke.	.005	34	64
36.	My father acts like he is mad all the time.	.005	6	30
	<.01			
9.	My parents quarrel and fight much of the time.	.01	8	30
	<.05			
51.	My parents do not seem to have much fun.	.02	22	46
14.	I will be glad when I am old enough to join the armed forces.	.03	54	76
89.	Grownups are usually too hard on children.	.03	14	34
136.	The boys I know usually try to keep grownups from finding out what they do.	.04	40	62
83.	I always keep my troubles to myself.	.04	28	50
123.	Sometimes I stay away from home overnight by myself.	.04	30	52
21.	Our house is very crowded.	.05	4	18
54.	Sometimes I think I am an adopted son.	.05	8	24
61.	Many of the boys I know would like to run away from home.	.05	20	40

Statements answered "true" significantly more often by the comparison group:

No.	Content	p	% True C*	D*
	<.05			
48.	My father always gives his pay check to mother.	.02	48	24
3.	I have many good friends.	.03	98	84
140.	I always talk over what I am going to do with my parents.	.04	60	38
131.	My mother usually knows where I am when I am not at home.	.05	88	70
82.	The boys I know usually do what their parents tell them.	.05	88	70

* C, comparison group; D, delinquent group.

Table 45

Card Sort Statements on Which Significant Differences
between Latin Delinquents and Nondelinquents Were Obtained

Statements answered "true" significantly more often by the delinquents:

No.	Content	p	% True C*	D*
	<.001			
55.	Most girls only want you to spend money on them.	.0003	36	76
40.	I go to school only because I have to.	.0003	12	50
123.	Sometimes I stay away from home overnight by myself.	.0006	6	38
37.	Children under sixteen are too young to drive cars.	.0009	42	78
1.	I was happier when I was a small child than I am now.	.001	32	68
	<.005			
24.	Almost all my friends smoke.	.002	36	70
7.	My father worries about losing his job.	.002	20	52
33.	My father always says to go ask mother—she's the boss.	.002	14	44
31.	I smoked my first cigarette before I was ten years old.	.002	8	36
5.	My mother scolds me no matter what I do.	.002	6	34
	<.01			
29.	My father makes me be at home by ten o'clock at night.	.009	36	64
101.	I am ashamed sometimes of the way my parents behave.	.01	10	32
	<.05			
36.	My father acts like he is mad all the time.	.02	6	24
4.	I wish I could be like my mother.	.03	38	62
6.	No one but me remembers my birthday.	.03	8	26
61.	Many of the boys I know would like to run away from home.	.03	8	26
89.	Grownups are usually too hard on children.	.04	18	38
134.	My grandfather and grandmother are too old to know much.	.05	4	18
104.	My mother does my homework for me when I can't do it.	.05	4	18
122.	Sometimes I think my father is not very smart.	.05	12	30

(Continued on next page)

Statements answered "true" significantly more often by the comparison group:

No.	Content	p	% True C*	D*
	<.001			
50.	Once in a while I put off until tomorrow what I ought to do today.	.0001	88	46
47.	My mother doesn't care what I do.	.0001	84	42
67.	Some day I expect to have an expensive car.	.0006	94	62
94.	A son expects to have a better job than his father.	.001	82	48
	<.005			
140.	I always talk over what I am going to do with my parents.	.002	68	34
125.	A good education will help you get ahead in the world.	.005	100	82
	<.05			
79.	Girls are just as smart as boys.	.02	80	56
127.	My father wants me to make up my own mind about what to do.	.05	80	60
131.	My mother usually knows where I am when I am not at home.	.03	86	66
60.	I can never save any money.	.02	68	42

* C, comparison group; D, delinquent group.

Table 46

Card Sort Statements on Which Significant Differences
between Mexican Delinquents and Nondelinquents Were Obtained

Statements answered "true" significantly more often by the delinquents:

No.	Content	p	% True C*	D*
	<.001			
123.	Sometimes I stay away from home overnight by myself.	.0002	8	46
27.	Mother is the real boss in our family.	.0006	38	76
31.	I smoked my first cigarette before I was ten years old.	.001	12	44
100.	I have always been my mother's favorite child.	.001	22	56
18.	My mother thinks she has to work too hard.	.001	26	62

Statements answered "true" significantly more often by the comparison group:

No.	Content	p	% True C*	D*
	<.005			
1.	I was happier when I was a small child than I am now.	.003	62	90
109.	My father gives up easily when things are hard to do.	.003	16	46
99.	Most boys will grow up to make more money than their fathers did.	.005	56	84
	<.01			
61.	Many of the boys I know would like to run away from home.	.009	30	58
54.	Sometimes I think I am an adopted son.	.01	10	32
17.	My mother treats me like a baby.	.01	24	50
	<.05			
107.	Young people are better drivers than older people.	.02	14	36
118.	My mother hates policemen.	.02	10	30
49.	My grandmother is always telling my father or my mother what to do.	.02	24	48
36.	My father acts like he is mad all the time.	.02	12	34
33.	My father always says to go ask mother—she's the boss.	.02	24	48
135.	Some people in our neighborhood are always making trouble.	.02	36	62
24.	Almost all my friends smoke.	.02	52	76
80.	Someone in my family has been in a car accident.	.02	30	54
122.	Sometimes I think my father is not very smart.	.03	22	44
119.	My father has a hard time making up his mind.	.03	18	40
95.	My mother says I do bad things just to make her feel bad.	.03	24	46
112.	When I get home I always tell my parents where I was and what I did.	.04	48	70
55.	Most girls only want you to spend money on them.	.04	46	68
63.	I often feel tired.	.04	30	52
70.	Sometimes when I am not feeling well I am cross.	.04	50	72

Statements answered "true" significantly more often by the comparison group:

No.	Content	p	C*	D*
	<.001			
53.	I can play a musical instrument.	.0006	68	30
	<.01			
52.	My folks treat me fair.	.008	90	66
	<.05			
19.	My father and mother often talk and laugh together.	.02	86	64
34.	My father spends most of his nights at home.	.05	88	70

* C, comparison group; D, delinquent group.

In view of the fact that significance tests were performed on all the 140 Card Sort items, it is quite likely that the tested probability level on some significance tests dropped below the .05 level simply because of chance fluctuations; indeed, it would be expected that 21 of the 79 differences that were significant at or beyond the .05 level occurred as a result of chance. The reader should keep this in mind in interpreting these tables and place the greatest reliance on the statements with the smallest p values and on statements that appear to reflect a common theme rather than an unusual one.

Another factor that should be considered in interpreting the data is the absolute percentage of the people in the delinquent and comparison samples who endorsed or rejected an item. While a statement may have been endorsed by significantly *more* delinquents than nondelinquents, this does not necessarily mean that a *majority* of the delinquents shared this sentiment. For example, one item that attained significance in all three samples was Item 123, "Sometimes I stay away from home overnight by myself." This item had a p value of .04 in the Anglo sample, .0006 in the Latin, and .0002 in the Mexican. Yet it was answered "true" by a majority of the delinquents only in the Anglo sample, in which 52 per cent endorsed it; in the Latin and Mexican samples only 38 per cent and 46 per cent, respectively, answered "true." It is therefore accurate to infer that this response was much more characteristic of delinquents than nondelinquents, but not that it characterized all or even most of the delinquents. Similarly, in the Anglo sample, the nondelinquents were significantly more likely ($p < .03$) to endorse Item 3, "I have many good friends." It would be a mistake to infer from this that most of the Anglo delinquents were friendless, however, because 84 per cent of them also answered this item "true." This happened to be a significantly smaller proportion than that found in the Anglo comparison group, in which 98 per cent endorsed the item. Therefore, it would appear that in the Anglo sample significantly more of the delinquents felt they didn't have many good friends, but this feeling could hardly be said to characterize the entire Anglo delinquent group.

Discussion

In an effort to bring some order to the data presented in Tables 44, 45, and 46, the content of the significant items was examined for common themes. Clusters of items reflecting several common themes could be identified.

DEVIANT BEHAVIOR

The first and least exciting cluster contained items relating to deviant behavior. Items significantly discriminating between one or more delinquent and comparison groups that could be assigned to this cluster included Items 24, 31, 80, 82, 104, 118, 123, and 135. Since no very deviant behavior was included in the 140-item list, these items referred to relatively mild things, such as smoking before age 10, staying out overnight, or not obeying one's parents. This cluster also included deviant behavior on the part of friends, relatives, and associates, such as being in a car accident, smoking, making trouble, helping cheat on homework, hating policemen, and so forth.

As might be expected, there were significant differences between delinquents and nondelinquents from all three ethnic samples on these items; in fact, three items, referring to smoking[6] and staying away overnight, attained significance in all three samples. The significant items indicated more deviant behavior on the part of the delinquents. If nothing else, this pattern reaffirms confidence in the veracity with which the boys sorted the statements.

Of the items that referred to deviant behavior on the part of elders, especially family members, it was noteworthy that no significant differences were found in the Anglo group. Only one item referring to parental deviance, which was quite mild in nature ("My mother does my homework for me when I can't do it"), was found to be significant in the Latin group. However, three items of this sort, in-

---

[6] These particular items afford another good example of the danger of making causal inferences from correlational data. Given the highly significant association between smoking one's first cigarette before age 10 and later delinquent behavior, we might be led to infer that in addition to cancer, heart disease, and other illnesses, cigarette smoking also causes delinquency. It is, of course, more likely that the early smoking was the result of delinquent tendencies. When more plausible associations arise, such as between parental rejection and delinquency, it will be helpful to recall that, just as smoking may come from delinquency and not vice versa, so, too, rejection may stem from the delinquent's behavior. In terms of the data and the inferences that may be drawn from them, the logical status of both propositions is the same.

cluding such strong statements as "My mother hates policemen," were found in the Mexican sample.

AUTHORITY PROBLEMS

The second cluster of Card Sort items consisted of items that appeared to reflect a common theme of authority problems: feelings that parents and other adults are untrusting, unfair, impossible to please, or angry most of the time. Included in this general category were Items 5, 17, 36, 52, 74, 89, 95, and 127. The Anglo delinquents and nondelinquents did not have many significant differences on this cluster of items. The Anglo delinquents did answer "true" more often to Item 74, "My mother does not like the way I act," which 50 per cent endorsed, and to Item 89, "Grownups are usually too hard on children," which 34 per cent of the delinquents agreed with, but otherwise there were no significant differences on these items.

The Latin and Mexican samples, however, showed more significant differences between the delinquents and nondelinquents in response to these items. The Latin delinquents were also more likely to feel that grownups are too hard on children (38% endorsement), and also indicated, "My mother scolds me no matter what I do" (34%), and "My father acts like he is mad all the time" (24%), while the nondelinquent Latins were significantly more inclined to indicate "My father wants me to make up my own mind about what to do" (80%). The Mexican delinquents were also significantly more likely to indicate that their father acted as if he were mad all the time (34%), but also signified difficulties with their mothers, as indicated by the statements "My mother treats me like a baby" (50%) and "My mother says I do bad things just to make her feel bad" (46%). The nondelinquent Mexicans, on the other hand, were significantly more likely to feel that "My folks treat me fair" (90%).

Thus, on items primarily reflecting intrafamilial authority problems, the Latin and Mexican samples were more likely to show significant differences between delinquents and nondelinquents than was the Anglo. Possibly this might be related to the more important role the family plays in Mexican culture.

In all samples, as might be expected, the direction of the differences indicated that the delinquents were more likely than the nondelinquents to feel picked on and persecuted, so that no matter what they did it would be regarded as wrong. This was consistent with the pattern noted in the literature, particularly in the studies of Andry (1962), Nye (1958), and Becker et al. (1959).

DISRESPECT OF THE FATHER

The next cluster of items to be examined dealt with the general theme of identification with and respect for the father. There were a number of items on which significant differences were found that related to this theme, including Items 4, 7, 27, 33, 36, 49, 109, 119, and 122. The general tenor of these statements was that the father is a weak, rather ineffectual person with little authority in the household. He is frequently angry, worries about losing his job, gives up easily, and defers to the mother and to the grandparents on important decisions. He is seen as having a difficult time making up his mind and is regarded as not being very smart.

Interestingly enough, this matrix of items differentiated between the delinquents and nondelinquents in the Latin and Mexican samples but not in the Anglo. On only one of these nine items did the Anglo delinquents answer "true" significantly more often than the Anglo comparison subjects. However, on five of the nine the Latin delinquents answered "true" significantly more often than the Latin comparison group, and on seven of the nine the Mexican delinquents did so. Thus, it appeared that the Latin and Mexican delinquents rebelled against one of the most fundamental tenets of Mexican culture, namely, that the father, the *jefe de la casa,* must be accorded respect, and that he is the embodiment of all those attributes a young man should wish to emulate. It is particularly interesting that this pattern differentiated between the delinquent and comparison groups not just in the Latin group, where some contempt for a father who may not speak good English or who may be somewhat "Old Country" and out of touch with the new culture might be expected, but even more so among the Mexican nationals. Apparently, disrespect for the father, as well as for other authorities, strikes to the heart of Latin and Mexican delinquency. Whether it is a symptom of a basic rebellious attitude or a condition that precedes and possibly contributes to the delinquent adjustment, cannot of course be answered.

This finding is particularly interesting in the light of Maslow and Diaz-Guerrero's speculations on the cause of delinquency. They stated:

If there is no adult value system, then a child or adolescent value system will be embraced. . . . Juvenile delinquency . . . is an example of such an adolescent value system. . . . The value system, insofar as it involves principles of law, order, justice, and judgments of right and wrong, is communicated primarily by the father. . . . To the extent that the father has no value system, or is uncertain or ineffectual about it, to that extent will his children be thrown back on their own resources. (Maslow and Diaz-Guerrero, 1960, p. 239)

Maslow and Diaz-Guerrero suggested that the reason for a higher delinquency rate in the United States than in Mexico stems from the differences in paternal authority between the two countries. "The Mexican father, although often physically absent, is, however, always psychologically present, . . . whereas the American father is much more physically present but is more apt to be a psychological nonentity" (Maslow & Diaz-Guerrero, 1962, p. 230).

The present data are consistent with their hypotheses, insofar as a close association was found between the breakdown of respect for the father and the occurrence of delinquency in the two samples with Mexican cultural roots. Why wasn't a similar pattern found in the Anglo sample? On the basis of Maslow and Diaz-Guerrero's paper, one might speculate that contempt for the father is so universal among Anglos that there could not be significant differences between delinquents and nondelinquents. They wrote, "Even when the American father wants to impose discipline, he is usually regarded as a sadist by his children, because most other fathers in the neighborhood set a more indulgent standard" (Maslow & Diaz-Guerrero, 1962, p. 230).

In order to determine if this was the case, the Card Sort responses of the Anglo sample were examined to see whether both the delinquent and comparison groups were highly contemptuous of the father. Inspection of the data indicated that this was not the case. In the Anglo sample, it was rare for more than 30 per cent of either the delinquents or the nondelinquents to answer these items in a disrespectful direction, and the median frequency of endorsement was only 23 per cent. This was very close to the pattern found in the Mexican and Latin comparison groups; however, the delinquents in these latter groups were approximately twice as likely as the nondelinquents to endorse these items. Thus, it was the Mexican and

Latin delinquents and not the Anglo nondelinquents whose response patterns were atypical.

There is no immediately apparent explanation for this failure to find as much paternal disrespect among the Anglo delinquents. The sociological data, it will be recalled, did not indicate that either the composition of the home or the amount of family cohesiveness was substantially better for the Anglo delinquents, nor does it appear to be the result of defensiveness on the Card Sort Test, for the Anglo delinquents were willing to endorse other socially undesirable items. While data from the Cartoon Test and Picture-Story Test may further illuminate this area, the most that can be concluded at this stage of analysis is that paternal disrespect and lack of identification seem to be most closely associated with delinquency in families in which paternal authoritarianism is emphasized.

ATTITUDES TOWARD THE MOTHER

An interesting aspect of the data is that while a major theme of disrespect for the father was found, no such pattern was obtained for the mother, despite the fact that there were items on the Card Sort Test that would have enabled negative feelings toward the mother to be expressed. While the delinquents did indicate they felt their mothers criticized, complained, and nagged, still, real disrespect for the mother never emerged. This is consistent with the observations made in other studies that delinquent boys are closer to their mothers than to their fathers (Andry, 1962; Bandura & Walters, 1959). Indeed, the Mexican delinquents endorsed the item "I have always been my mother's favorite child" significantly more often than did the Mexican comparison group (56% vs. 22%), and the majority of the delinquent Latin boys (68%) indicated that they wished they could be like their mothers, a sentiment shared by only 38 per cent of the nondelinquent Latins.

No clear cluster of attitudes toward the mother comparable to that found for the father was obtained. However, a number of items scattered over a number of clusters dealt with various perceived attributes of the mother. These included Items 4, 5, 17, 18, 27, 47, 74, 95, 100, 104, 118, and 131. From an examination of the content of these items, several factors become apparent. First, significant differences on these maternal items were most common in the Mexican sample. The Mexican delinquents described their mothers as overprotective, and indicated that the mothers were the real bosses in the family. The mother also appeared to them to be a rather nagging woman, complaining about having to work too hard and accusing her boy of engaging in delinquent behavior just to make her feel bad. At the same time 30 per cent indicated she hated policemen.

The Latin delinquents indicated that they would like to be like their mothers; while their mothers scolded them no matter what they did, their mothers also did their homework for them when they were unable to. Members of the Latin comparison group indicated their mothers knew where their sons were when they were not at home and that their mothers didn't care what their sons did, which could be interpreted as either an attitude of trust, a willingness not to interfere on vocational choice, or a display of rejection.

The Anglo delinquents and nondelinquents differed the least in their reported attitudes regarding their mothers. Not too surprisingly, the Anglo delinquents indicated that their mothers didn't approve of the way they acted, while the nondelinquent Anglos indicated their mothers usually knew their whereabouts.

The data thus suggested that the delinquents' attitudes toward their mothers were considerably more ambivalent than their attitudes toward the father. Mother was seen as overprotective but rejecting, scolding, but against authority herself. The picture was consistent in some respects to the "double bind" of the schizophrenic child or with Adelaide Johnson's (1949) notion of "superego lucanae," with apparently socialized parents obtaining unconscious gratification from their children's rebellions.

If we may speculate for a moment on the possible origins of these patterns and the reason they were most prevalent among the Mexicans and Latins, it could be that they have their roots in the effects of a broken home in Mexican society. It will be recalled from Chapter 3 that the traditional Mexican family was oriented around the family's unquestioning obedience of and respect for the father as the *jefe de la casa*. It will also be recalled that broken homes, in which the mother was perforce the head of the household, were significantly more common among the Mexican delinquents, as, indeed, they were in all three samples.

The Mexican or Latin boy growing up in a father-absent household is confronted with a situation in which the mother is the dominant figure in the household but in which society's contempt for the woman has undermined her effectiveness. Moreover, the mother is apt to be overprotective and, in her own bitterness, to teach cynical and antisocial attitudes to her son; Hoffman (1961) has shown that the dominant mother is apt to be derogatory toward the father so that the son learns disrespect for the father and has trouble identifying with him. This, of course, is conducive to delinquent behavior and other forms of psychopathology. While such patterns are not confined to Mexico, the great reliance that Mexican culture places on the father as the primary agent of socialization in the home (Maslow & Diaz-Guerrero, 1960), as well as the greater social acceptability of the female-dominated household in the United States, should combine to make the effects of father absence more severe in the Mexican or Latin family than in the Anglo. If so, this could explain the fact that the Card Sort data suggested that delinquency is more closely associated with disrespect of the father and ambivalence toward the mother among Latins and Mexicans than among Anglos.

In a similar analysis, focused on Italian immigrants, Rubenfeld (1965) has speculated how the feudal peasant father, frustrated economically and politically by secular and church authorities, might assume the authoritarian role within the walls of his own home, taking out his frustrations on his family. The women would turn against the men in such a situation and covertly encourage the hostility and rebellion of the sons against their fathers. But, while supporting this rebellion, the ambivalent mother would also be encouraging continued dependency on her, with consequent difficulty for the sons' assuming a normal male identity (Rubenfeld, 1965, pp. 248–249). While this analysis is based on speculations about the effect of European peasant traditions, the sociopolitical conditions described are similar to those found among lower-class Mexicans today. If Rubenfeld's analysis is accurate, it would help explain the rather crystallized disrespect toward the father coupled with ambivalent attitudes toward the mother. Such a situation could also interfere with the adolescent boy's achieving a stable, integrated masculine identification. This is perhaps epitomized by the fact that 68 per cent of the Latin delinquents endorsed Item 4, "I wish I could be like my mother." As we have noted repeatedly, such difficulties are felt by many to lie at the heart of the excessive masculinity that results in delinquency.

DISRESPECT OF ELDERS

There was also a small cluster of items reflecting a theme of generalized disrespect for elders. Statements that fell into this cluster included Items 101, 107, and 134. As was the case with the items indicating disrespect for the father, these items significantly differentiated delinquents from nondelinquents in the Latin and Mexican samples, but not in the Anglo. The Latin delinquents endorsed Item 101, "I am ashamed of the way my parents behave," and Item 134, "My grandfather and grandmother are too old to know much," significantly more often than did the Latin comparison group, while the Mexican delinquents were significantly more likely to agree to Item 107, "Young people are better drivers than older people," than were their nondelinquent peers.

Since respect for elders in general and the father in particular is one of the cardinal precepts of traditional Mexican culture, these responses indicate considerable cultural alienation on the part of the Latin delinquents and, to a lesser extent, the Mexican delinquents. They were consistent with the pattern of social alienation noted in other studies of delinquents.

FAMILY COHESIVENESS

The next cluster of items to be discussed reflected a broad theme made up of several subthemes. The major theme was one of generalized discontent with the family situation, reflected by items indicating wishes to escape from the family milieu, feelings of depression and rejection, an inability to communicate with the parents, and a lack of warmth and pleasure in each others' company by the members of the family. This overall theme could fit easily into the Gluecks' general concept of familial cohesiveness. All three ethnic groups endorsed items reflecting significant differences in these feelings, but they tended to be most common among the Anglo sample.

Escape

The subtheme of escape was common to all three groups. In each group the delinquents endorsed Item 61, "Many of the boys I know would like to run away from home," significantly more often than did the nondelinquents, with the percent of "true" responses ranging from a low of 26 per cent for the Latin delinquents to a high of 58 per cent for the Mexican delinquents; 76 per cent of the Anglo delinquents also endorsed Item 14, "I will be glad when I am old enough to join the armed forces."

Feelings of Rejection

Themes of depression or reported feelings of emotional rejection were also common to all three samples. The Anglo and the Mexican delinquents both answered "true" to Item 54, "Sometimes I think I am an adopted son," significantly more often than did their respective comparison groups, while 68 per cent of the Latin delinquents and 90 per cent of the Mexican delinquents endorsed Item 1, "I was happier when I was a small child than I am now"; 26 per cent of the Latin delinquents also indicated "true" to Item 6, "No one but me remembers my birthday," an exquisite sign of rejection in Latin culture, and, as noted above, 34 per cent also felt, "My mother scolds me no matter what I do." There were no items indicating that the nondelinquents in any sample felt significantly more rejected than the delinquents.

Intrafamilial Communication

Another subtheme that can be included in the overall theme of low family cohesiveness is one reflecting inability or unwillingness to confide in parents. Items 83, 112, 131, 136, and 140 reflected this subtheme. This particular feeling appeared to differentiate the delinquents from the nondelinquents in the Anglo sample more so than in the Latin and Mexican samples. The Anglo delinquents responded "true" significantly more often to Items 83, "I always keep my troubles to myself," and 136, "The boys I know usually try to keep grownups from finding out what they do," while the Anglo comparison group answered "true" significantly more often to Items 131, "My mother usually knows where I am when I am not at home," and 140, "I always talk over what I am going to do with my parents."

In the Latin sample the comparison group also answered "true" significantly more often to these last two items. In the Mexican sample, however, there was no tendency for the delinquents to indicate that they were less willing to communicate with their parents. On only one of the five items in this cluster, Item 112, "When I get home I always tell my parents where I was and what I did," was there a significant difference between the Mexican delinquents and nondelinquents, and, surprisingly, it was the delinquents who were more likely to endorse it. On the other four items in this cluster, the differences, while not significant, were in the expected direction. Since the p level of the difference was only .04 and since the reversal is so contrary to the general pattern, it is likely that this was one of the chance differences that may occasionally occur.

By and large, the results from this cluster of items suggested that, among the Anglos, the delinquents indicated significantly less willingness to confide in their parents and keep them informed as to their whereabouts. This is also true to some extent of the Latin delinquents, but not of the Mexicans.

Intrafamilial Dissension vs. Warmth

The next major subcluster of items reflecting on family cohesiveness consisted of six items, 9, 18, 19, 34, 36, and 51, that reflected whether the family milieu was perceived as warm, enjoyable, and harmonious, or instead was marked by quarreling, bitterness, and acrimony.

In the Anglo sample, 30 per cent of the delinquents answered "true" to Item 9, "My parents quarrel and fight much of the time," 46 per cent indicated that they agreed with Item 51, "My parents do not seem to have much fun," and, as noted before, 30 per cent endorsed Item 36, "My father acts like he is mad all the time." This rate of endorsement was two to three times as great as that for the Anglo comparison group and was significant in each case.

In the Mexican sample, 62 per cent of the delinquents, as compared with only 26 per cent of the nondelinquents, indicated agreement with Item 18, "My mother thinks she has to work too hard," and 34 per cent with Item 36, "My father acts like he is mad all the time." The nondelinquent Mexican boys, on the other hand, indicated that their home was a happier place; 86 per cent answered "true" to Item 19, "My father and mother often talk and laugh together," and 88 per cent to Item 34, "My father spends most of his nights at home."

Thus, in both the Anglo and Mexican samples, the delinquents apparently viewed home as a place where the family members experienced significantly less pleasure and joy in each others' company and instead indicated it was more likely to be characterized by resentment and quarreling. This was less true in the Latin sample, although the delinquents did agree with Item 36, "My father acts like he is mad all the time," significantly more often than did the nondelinquents.

One final item that fell under the general heading of family cohesiveness did not fit neatly into any of the subclusters defined above —Item 48, "My father always gives his pay check to mother." This item was endorsed by twice as many of the Anglo comparison group (48%) as the Anglo delinquents (24%).

Thus, a number of items referred directly or indirectly to the cohesiveness of the family home, a variable whose importance to delinquency was underlined by the Gluecks' findings as well as those of other investigators. In the present study, several aspects of family cohesiveness could be studied with the Card Sort Test: the desire to escape from the family scene, the amount of perceived emotional rejection, the degree to which the boys reported confiding in their parents, and the general atmosphere of warmth as opposed to recrimination in the family. In all three ethnic samples the delinquents were significantly higher than the comparison groups on items reflecting escapism and feelings of emotional rejection. The Anglo and Latin delinquents, but not the Mexican, indicated that they confided in their parents less than the nondelinquents did; the Anglo and Mexican delinquents and, to a lesser extent, the Latin delinquents indicated that they perceived their homes as being marked by more hostility and less warmth than did the nondelinquents. These data thus indicated that the association between lack of family cohesiveness and delinquency, which was noted in the other studies reviewed, has cross-cultural generality.

ECONOMIC ATTITUDES

Another cluster of items were those dealing with economic themes. Included in this cluster were Items 7, 21, 53, 60, 67, 94, and 99.

It would be expected from the sociological literature that, on economic items differentiating between delinquents and nondelinquents, the delinquents would probably manifest greater pessimism regarding their chances of success and more themes reflecting present economic hardship. The likelihood of much difference in the endorsement of items reflecting hardship would, of course, have been minimized by the fact that the delinquent and comparison groups were from the same economic levels.

While differences between the delinquent and comparison groups on economic items were found in all three ethnic samples, they were most common among the Latins, the only minority group studied. In the Latin sample, 52 per cent of the delinquents endorsed Item 7, "My father worries about losing his job," as compared with only 20 per cent of the nondelinquents. The delinquents thus appeared more insecure. On the other hand, the greater optimism of the Latin comparison group was displayed by significantly more frequent "true" responses to Item 67, "Some day I expect to have an expensive car," which 94 per cent of the nondelinquent Latins endorsed, as compared with 62 per cent of the delinquents, and Item 94, "A son expects to have a better job than his father," with which 82 per cent of the nondelinquents but only 48 per cent of the delinquents agreed.

Only one economic item discriminated the Anglo delinquents and nondelinquents, Item 21, "Our house is very crowded," which, as would be expected, the Anglo delinquents endorsed significantly more often.[7] In the Mexican sample, two items reached significance: Item 53, "I can play a musical instrument," which might reflect somewhat greater affluence, was answered "true" by 68 per cent of the comparison group but by only 30 per cent of the delinquents. Item 99, "Most boys will grow up to make more money than their fathers did," was endorsed by 84 per cent of the delinquents but by only 56 per cent of the nondelinquents ($p < .005$), a reversal from the expectation based on the assumption of greater economic optimism among the nondelinquents. Perhaps on this item the nondelinquents' optimism was tempered by the possibility of implied disrespect of the father if this item were answered "true," a consideration that did not influence the delinquents, who had already indicated disrespect of their fathers on other items.

Another item that was difficult to interpret was Item 60, "I can never save any money." On this item, the Latin comparison group

---

[7] It will be recalled from Chapter 6 that the Anglo sample was the only one in which the delinquents were found to come from significantly larger families than the nondelinquents. This strengthens our confidence in the Card Sort data.

answered "true" significantly more often than the Latin delinquents. Whether this indicated a reversal in the pattern of greater economic discouragement among the delinquents, or reflected the greater concern of the nondelinquents over saving demonstrated on the Choices Test in Chapter 8, is difficult to say.

By and large, then, the responses to the economic items tended to indicate significantly greater feelings of economic insecurity and discouragement among the Latin delinquents than among the Latin nondelinquents. Differences in economic attitudes were less frequent among the other two ethnic samples. When found, they usually, but not invariably, suggested that the delinquents perceived more economic privation.

MINOR THEMES

The remaining clusters of significant items were quite small, usually containing only two or three items.

School and Education

One such theme was defined by two items dealing with attitudes toward school, Items 40, "I go to school only because I have to," and 125, "A good education will help you to get ahead in the world." The latter item also has relevance for the theme of economic optimism discussed above. Significant differences on these items were found only in the Latin sample, with 50 per cent of the delinquents endorsing Item 40, as compared with only 12 per cent of the nondelinquents ($p = .0006$), and 100 per cent of the nondelinquents agreeing with Item 125, as compared with 82 per cent of the delinquents ($p = .005$). The fact that these highly significant differences between the attitudes of the delinquents and nondelinquents were found only in the Latin sample reflects the pressure that is often placed on the Latin boy in an Anglo school. As we have noted, the Latin is often forced to choose between the demands of the school and those of his family. Often, by adolescence he has had to resolve a major conflict between the two. The negative attitudes expressed against both school and elders by the Latin delinquents suggests that many resolved the dilemma by rejecting both sets of demands.

While it is particularly hazardous to interpret a lack of significant differences, particularly in response to only two items, nevertheless, it should be pointed out that the data for the Anglos and Mexicans are not consistent with Cohen's notion that the lower-class delinquent boys' negative experiences in school are a (if not *the*) primary determinant of his delinquent identification.

Rules

The next cluster of two items dealt with rules. Item 29, "My father always makes me be home by ten o'clock at night," and Item 37, "Children under sixteen are too young to drive cars," were both answered "true" significantly more often by the Latin delinquents. Possibly, this is a reflection of greater culturally dissonant authoritarianism in the home of the Latin delinquents. It is noteworthy that it was the Latin delinquents who answered true to the item "My father wants me to make up my own mind about what to do" significantly less often than the nondelinquent Latins. However, *ad hoc* explanations for this pattern must remain highly speculative at best.

Peers

The final cluster of three items deals with feelings toward peers, particularly girls. On these items, 3, "I have many good friends," 55, "Most girls only want you to spend money on them," and 79, "Girls are just as smart as boys," significant differences were found on one (3) for the Anglos, on two (55 and 79) for the Latins, and on one (55) for the Mexicans. On these items, the delinquents indicated that they had fewer friends and manifested more disparaging and suspicious attitudes toward girls.

Summary of the Card Sort Results

The Card Sort Test shifted the focus from external characteristics of the various samples to their subjective perceptions of their familial and social environments. A number of studies on the objectively and subjectively determined differences between the familial and social patterns of delinquents and nondelinquents were reviewed. Certain common patterns were found despite numerous variations in design, procedure, and samples tested. For example, several investigations noted that the parents of delinquents are themselves more likely to engage in deviant behavior than are the parents of nondelinquents. Delinquents are likely to receive less affection from their parents, particularly the father, and to be the recipients of erratic, lax, or overly harsh discipline. They identify less with their fathers than do nondelinquent adolescents, and have problems with other authorities as well. The delinquents' homes are often marked by a lack of cohesiveness, with acrimony and dissension taking the place of warm ties of mutual respect, affection, and pleasure among family members.

In the Card Sort Test, each boy had an opportunity to sort 140 statements into those he agreed with or felt were true and those he disagreed with or felt were false. The number of delinquents and nondelinquents endorsing and rejecting each item was determined for each sample, and the significance of the differences in endorsement frequency was calculated. A procedure such as this has some obvious drawbacks. The first is that one is unsure whether the differences that emerge accurately reflect differences in the delinquents' and nondelinquents' environments or instead merely indicate distorted perceptions. More troubling is the fact that the results were not cross-validated on a new sample so that a number of items that attained statistical significance simply as a result of chance variation were undoubtedly included.

In inspecting the items that differentiated between the delinquents and nondelinquents in the present study, certain clusters of items expressing similar content were formed by rational inspection of the data. Among these clusters or common themes were groups of items reflecting (*a*) deviant behavior, (*b*) authority problems, (*c*) disrespect of the father, (*d*) attitudes toward the mother, (*e*) disrespect of elders, (*f*) familial cohesiveness (with subthemes of wishing to escape, feelings of emotional rejection by the parents, lack of intrafamilial communication, and dissension as opposed to warmth), (*g*) economic attitudes, and (*h*) miscellaneous subthemes manifested by a few items reflecting attitudes toward school, attitudes toward rules, and attitudes toward peers. These clusters of items are reviewed in Table 47, along with the number of items in each cluster on which the delinquent and nondelinquent members of each sample differed significantly.

It will be seen that while some themes were equally common in all three ethnic samples, other attitudes appeared to be confined more to just one or two of the ethnic samples. The delinquents in all three expressed significantly more deviant behavior and attitudes and less family cohesiveness. The Latin and Mexican delinquents were much more likely to express disrespect of the father, criticism

Table 47

Résumé of Card Sort Results: Number of Significant Items
in Each Cluster Differentiating Control and Delinquent Groups

Cluster	No. Items	Anglo	Latin	Mexican
Deviant behavior	8	4	4	6
Authority problems	8	2	4	4
Disrespect of father	9	1	5	7
Attitudes toward mother	12	2	5	8
Disrespect of elders	3	0	2	2
Family cohesiveness	18	9	7	10
Escape	2	2	1	1
Feelings of rejection	4	1	3	2
Lack of communication	5	2	2	3
Dissension vs. warmth	6	3	1	4
Economic attitudes	7	0	4	2
Miscellaneous School	2	0	2	0
Rules	2	0	2	0
Peers	3	1	2	1

of the mother, and disrespect of elders than were the Latin or Mexican comparison groups or both the Anglo delinquents and nondelinquents. The Latins, the only minority group, were also more pessimistic about economic matters and more negative regarding school;
however, they were less likely than the Anglo or Mexican delinquents to indicate that their homes were characterized by dissen-

sion. Perhaps status-discontent theories are more applicable to a minority group than are family-personality theories. This conjecture can be evaluated only through further research.

By and large, the results of the Card Sort Test were congruent with those of other studies. The delinquents deviated from the comparison groups in the directions that would be expected, displaying more misbehavior, greater authority problems, marked disrespect of the father and other elders, mixed attitudes toward the mother but little of the disrespect that characterized the perception of the father, less family cohesiveness, and more pessimistic economic attitudes.

CHAPTER 11

THE CARTOON TEST

It will be recalled from the discussion of general methodology that in the Cartoon Test each subject was presented with eight drawings, each of which showed a boy interacting with an adult, identified as the boy's father or mother, in a tense social situation. The eight drawings are reproduced in Figures 4 through 11. The task of the subjects was to indicate the adult's response in each situation.

This test was less direct than the ones already discussed. The subjects were not asked how their own parents would react in each situation, but instead how the parents of the boy in the cartoon would respond. If significant differences should be obtained, therefore, it would not be correct to conclude that the actual child-rearing practices of the delinquent and nondelinquent boys' parents differed. It would, however, be valid to conclude that the delinquents' and non-delinquents' perceptions of typical parental responses differed. As in the case of the Card Sort Test, however, some idea of the correspondence between subjective and objective reality can be determined by a comparison of the present findings with those in the literature.

"The Car"

PROCEDURES

The first cartoon to be discussed was called "The Car." As can be seen from Figures 4 and 5, this cartoon depicted a teen-age boy appearing before his father or his mother and announcing, "I want a car." As in all the cartoons, the subjects were instructed to indicate each parent's response.

The first step in the analysis of the data from this and other cartoons was an inspection of the responses to determine the best categories for classifying the large number of individual responses. As many categories as were needed to adequately describe the data were generated from this initial reconnaissance. Next, each individual test response was assigned to one of these preliminary categories. In the case of "The Car" cartoon, eight such modal response categories were used. These eight categories, and the number of responses from each group that fell into them, are described in Table 48.

Table 48

Perceived Responses to the Cartoon "The Car"

	FATHERS						MOTHERS					
	Anglo		Latin		Mexican		Anglo		Latin		Mexican	
Modal Responses	C*	D*	C	D	C	D	C	D	C	D	C	D
1. Too young, too small	15	26	16	25	17	12	24	20	26	23	19	12
2. Earn money, save	19	13	9	9	12	15	12	9	6	9	14	16
3. No money, can't afford a car	2	3	3	8	8	14	1	0	4	7	11	12
4. Temporizing, Christmas, later, conditional	5	2	5	1	7	4	3	2	5	4	2	4
5. Noncommittal, ask father (or mother)	1	2	3	2	2	1	2	12	3	2	3	3
6. Not responsible, no license, can't drive	4	0	10	2	2	1	5	4	5	1	0	0
7. Critical of boy	2	3	3	2	2	1	2	3	1	4	1	0
8. No (blunt refusal)	2	1	1	1	0	2	1	0	0	0	0	3

* C, comparison group; D, delinquent group.

Figure 4. The cartoon "The Car," father version.

Figure 5. The cartoon "The Car," mother version.

The next step in data analysis was to inspect the descriptive categories in an effort to derive broader, psychologically more meaningful, classes of response for statistical analysis. These response classes had to relate to meaningful theoretical issues while at the same time doing justice to the modal-response-generated categories. In the case of "The Car," four broad classifications were used:

Personalized Refusal

In these responses the parent evidenced concern for the boy's feelings in replying. Either some hope for possibly being given a car in the future was held out, or, in denying the request, the parent gave the boy a reason relating to his own capabilities to operate a car, his age, and so forth. Modal Response Categories 1, 4, and 6 in Table 48 were included in this classification (see Table 49).

Economic Excuse

Included in this classification were all responses in which the request was denied because of some external financial factor rather than the boy's capabilities and in which no hope was held out. Responses from Category 3, such as "We can't afford it," were included in this class. This particular category was so infrequent in the Anglo groups that it was dropped from the statistical analyses. However, it was included in the analyses of the data for the Latin and Mexican samples.

Save or Work

This classification was made up of responses in which the boy was told that if he wants a car it is up to him to save or earn the money for it. It is implied that if he does so, he will be allowed to purchase the vehicle. Responses in Category 2 made up this class.

Hostile or Disinterested Refusal

Responses in which the parent refused without giving any reason, responded in a noncommittal or hostile fashion, or passed the responsibility to the other parent were included in this class. This group was made up of Modal Response Categories 5, 7, and 8 in Table 48.

Chi-square analyses were then conducted in which the data for

Table 49

Statistical Analyses of Perceived Responses to the Cartoon "The Car"

| | FATHERS | | | | | | | |
Response Categories	Anglo C*	D*	Latin C	D	Mexican C	D	Overall C	D
Personalized refusal	24	28	31	28	26	17	81	73
Economic excuse	2[a]	3[a]	3	8	8	14	13	25
Save or work	19	13	9	9	12	15	40	37
Hostile or dis-interested refusal	5	6	7	5	4	4	16	15
Total	50	50	50	50	50	50	150	150
χ^2	1.33[a]		2.76		3.84		4.36	
p (two tail)	N.S.		N.S.		N.S.		N.S.	

| | MOTHERS | | | | | | | |
Response Categories	Anglo C	D	Latin C	D	Mexican C	D	Overall C	D
Personalized refusal	32	26	36	28	21	16	89	70
Economic excuse	1[a]	0[a]	4	7	11	12	16	19
Save or work	12	9	6	9	14	16	32	34
Hostile or dis-interested refusal	5	15	4	6	4	6	13	27
Total	50	50	50	50	50	50	150	150
χ^2	6.05[a]		2.80		1.08		11.48	
p (two tail)	<.05		N.S.		N.S.		<.01	

[a] Data for "economic excuse" not included in analysis because of infrequent cell entries.
* C, comparison group; D, delinquent group.

the delinquents and nondelinquents in each ethnic group were contrasted. Data for the perceived responses of the mothers and the fathers in the cartoons were treated separately. It was hypothesized that the delinquents would be more apt to attribute hostile or disinterested refusals to the parent figures, particularly the father, while the nondelinquent would be more likely to perceive the parents as using a personalized refusal or suggesting that the boy work for the car. This hypothesis was based on the findings in the literature reviewed in the preceding chapter: that the parents of nondelinquents are more affectionate toward their sons, manifesting more interest in their needs and spending more time with them, while delinquents' families are characterized by less cohesiveness, less parental concern, and less willingness to reason with the son.

RESULTS

The results of the statistical analyses (Table 49) showed no significant differences in the perceived responses of fathers. There were significant differences in the perceived responses of the mothers in the Anglo sample ($\chi^2=6.05$, $p<.05$) and in the overall analysis of the combined groups. In the Anglo sample the perceived responses of the mothers were in the predicted direction, with the "personalized refusal" and the "save or work" categories showing greater frequency of usage by the nondelinquents and the "hostile or disinterested refusal" category being more frequent among the delinquents. (As already noted, the "economic excuse" category was not used in this analysis, since only one of the 100 Anglos used this category in describing the maternal response.)

The overall analysis also showed significant differences in the hypothesized direction with the "personalized refusals" more common among the nondelinquent subjects and the "hostile or disinterested refusals" more frequent among the delinquents. There was no noteworthy difference in the "save or work" category.

Thus, while there were few significant differences in the responses to the first cartoon, the differences that were found were in the general direction predicted on the basis of studies of the differences between delinquents' and nondelinquents' families, with the nondelinquents' perceiving the mother as being more likely to temper the refusal with some logical reason or to hold out some hope for the future, and the delinquents' seeing the mother as being more likely to respond in a hostile or disinterested fashion. In the Anglo sample the nondelinquents also perceived the mother as being some-what more likely to suggest that the boy earn the money for the car himself.

"The Cigarette"

The second cartoon, "The Cigarette," illustrated in Figures 6 and 7, depicted a teen-age boy standing before his mother or father hold-ing a smoking object that should be recognized as a cigarette behind his back. The concealment of the cigarette was designed to suggest that smoking was a forbidden activity so that the perception of the parents' disciplinary tactics could be determined.

PROCEDURE

As can be seen from Table 50, the initial reconnaissance generated 13 modal response categories to be used in coding the data. In the statistical analyses these disparate responses were grouped into three broader and more meaningful classifications:

Reasoned Refusals

All responses in which the parent explained to the boy why he should not smoke were placed in this class. Included in this classi-fication were replies from Modal Response Categories 2, 5, 7, and 9 in Table 50, in which such varied explanations as the boy's youth, the harmfulness of smoking, the fact that it would place him in bad company, or the possibility that the cigarette was doped were given.

Punitive Refusals

In this classification were placed all those parental replies in which the boy was told to dispose of the cigarette for no reason except to avoid expressed or implied punishment for noncompliance. Responses from Categories 1, 4, 6, and 12 were included in this classification.

Irrelevant, Noncommittal, or Unclear Responses

The remaining responses were placed in this category. Included among them were responses in which the central issue of discipline over forbidden smoking was not addressed. Responses from Catego-ries 3, 8, 10, 11, and 13 in Table 50 were included in this class. These

WHAT DOES THE FATHER SAY?

Figure 6. The cartoon "The Cigarette," father version.

WHAT DOES THE MOTHER SAY?

Figure 7. The cartoon "The Cigarette," mother version.

Table 50

Perceived Responses to the Cartoon "The Cigarette"

	FATHERS						MOTHERS					
	Anglo		Latin		Mexican		Anglo		Latin		Mexican	
Modal Responses	C*	D*	C	D	C	D	C	D	C	D	C	D
1. Put it out, throw it away, give it back	6	6	14	16	9	15	11	12	12	17	9	14
2. You're too young	10	3	9	11	3	4	6	9	12	10	8	3
3. Where get it? Who gave it? Why?	5	5	4	4	8	9	5	6	4	9	8	8
4. You are forbidden to smoke, does mother (or father) know?	4	3	3	1	2	10	5	5	3	3	3	9
5. You're in bad company	5	0	2	0	12	3	6	1	5	0	11	4
6. You will be punished	6	8	8	3	4	4	2	0	0	3	2	2
7. It is harmful	7	2	2	1	5	1	5	2	4	1	4	3
8. Noncommittal or approving	5	6	3	5	1	0	3	2	1	0	1	0
9. You shouldn't accept, perhaps it is doped	1	2	2	5	2	2	3	2	4	2	1	0
10. Failed to recognize cigarette	1	12	1	0	0	0	1	7	0	2	0	0
11. I'm going to tell father (or mother), suspicious, doubts boy's word	0	2	2	0	2	1	3	2	4	1	2	3
12. Don't smoke at home or before parents or relatives	0	1	0	3	2	0	0	1	1	1	1	3
13. Not before you can buy your own	0	0	0	1	0	1	0	1	0	1	0	1

* C, comparison group; D, delinquent group.

responses, however, were not included in the subsequent statistical analyses, because the central issue of discipline was not addressed.

As was the case with "The Car" cartoon, it was expected that the delinquents would indicate that the parents were more likely to respond with "punitive refusals," while the nondelinquents would be more likely to respond with "reasoned refusals."

RESULTS

The results of the statistical analyses are presented in Table 51. The differences between the perceived responses of fathers in the

Table 51

Statistical Analyses of Perceived Responses to the Cartoon "The Cigarette"

| | FATHERS | | | | | | | |
| | Anglo | | Latin | | Mexican | | Overall | |
Response Categories	C*	D*	C	D	C	D	C	D
Reasoned refusals	23	7	15	17	22	10	60	34
Punitive refusals	16	18	25	23	17	29	58	70
Total	39	25	40	40	39	39	118	104
χ^2	4.69		0.21		7.63		7.46	
p (two tail)	<.05		N.S.		<.01		<.01	

| | MOTHERS | | | | | | | |
| | Anglo | | Latin | | Mexican | | Overall | |
Response Categories	C	D	C	D	C	D	C	D
Reasoned refusals	20	14	25	13	24	10	69	37
Punitive refusals	18	18	16	24	15	28	49	70
Total	38	32	41	37	39	38	118	107
χ^2	0.55		5.25		9.68		12.86	
p (two tail)	N.S.		<.025		<.005		<.001	

* C, comparison group; D, delinquent group.

delinquent and comparison groups were significant in the analyses of the Anglo ($\chi^2 = 4.69$, $p < .05$), Mexican ($\chi^2 = 7.63$, $p < .01$), and overall data ($\chi^2 = 7.46$, $p < .01$), but not in the analysis for the Latin sample ($\chi^2 = 0.21$, N.S.). All the significant differences were in the hypothesized direction, with the "reasoned refusal" being more common among the nondelinquent groups and "punitive refusals" more common among the delinquents.

The differences between the perceived responses of the mother were highly significant in the analyses of the Latin ($\chi^2 = 5.25$, $p < .025$), Mexican ($\chi^2 = 9.68$, $p < .005$), and overall data ($\chi^2 = 12.86$, $p < .001$), but not in the analysis for the Anglo sample ($\chi^2 = 0.55$, N.S.). Once again, the differences were in the predicted direction.

The data for this cartoon thus offered convincing support for the hypothesis that the delinquents would be significantly more likely to perceive the reaction of parents to a teen-age boy's illicit smoking as being more punitive and less reasoning than the nondelinquents. This finding is consistent with, and offers cross-cultural generality for, the notion that delinquents generally perceive parents as being more punitive than do nondelinquents.

Of course, it is impossible to state from the present data whether this subjective perception is accurate or not. External observations in studies such as the Gluecks' and Reckless' would indicate that it may well be. Even so, it is still impossible to determine which came first, the parental punitiveness or the delinquency. Is delinquency a boy's response to excessive punishment, or is strict discipline a parent's response to excessive acting out? It is perhaps interesting to recall that one of the Card Sort items, No. 31, "I smoked my first cigarette before I was ten years old," was answered "true" significantly more often by the delinquents in all three samples. This might suggest that punitiveness about smoking is something with which many of the delinquent boys have had firsthand experience. In the case of smoking before the age of 10, it is likely that the behavior provoked the punitive response and not vice versa. On a deeper level, of course, it could well have been parental punitiveness that inspired a spirit of rebelliousness resulting in early smoking. While we shuttle to and fro weaving speculative webs, the fact that the lack of affection noted by many investigators could inspire bids for attention like early smoking should not be overlooked. Thus, it may be, as the present data suggest, that delinquents experience more punitiveness at the hands of their parents, but the exact role such punitiveness may play in the causal cycle is difficult if not impossible to ascertain. It could be a response to delinquent behavior, it could be a condition that incited delinquent behavior, or it could be a parental reaction unconsciously sought by the delinquent whose other bids for signs of concern or affection have failed. It is more than likely that in different cases or at different times in a single case, punishment could function in all of these ways.

"The Police"

It will be recalled from the review of the literature in Chapter 10 that various investigators, particularly McCord and McCord (1958) and Robins (1966), have noted that antisocial behavior on the part of the parents was associated with later criminality in the son, while Reckless, Dinitz, and Murray (1957) noted that the parents of "good boys" in a high-delinquency area made a positive effort to teach their children socially approved attitudes. Similarly, in the present study some of the Card Sort statements indicated that the delinquents in some samples, notably the Mexican, agreed more frequently with items that indicated their parents had antisocial attitudes. For example, 30 per cent of the Mexican delinquents endorsed the statement "My mother hates policemen." The greater incidence of marital instability among the delinquents' parents noted in Chapter 6 could be interpreted as evidence of poorer socialization.

The next two cartoons were designed to yield data indicative of the boys' perceptions of parental socialization. The first, "The Police," which showed a teen-age boy informing his father or mother that there is a policeman at the door (Figures 8 and 9), was specifically aimed at parental attitudes toward authority figures.

PROCEDURE

As might be expected, the responses to this cartoon clearly showed that none of the boys perceived the parent figures as being enthusiastic over the appearance of a policeman at the door. The initial reconnaissance indicated the responses could be placed into eight modal classifications (see Table 52). The coded data were then grouped into three broader response categories for statistical analysis:

Figure 8. The cartoon "The Police," father version.

Figure 9. The cartoon "The Police," mother version.

Table 52

Perceived Responses to the Cartoon "The Police"

	FATHERS						MOTHERS					
	Anglo		Latin		Mexican		Anglo		Latin		Mexican	
Modal Responses	C*	D*	C	D	C	D	C	D	C	D	C	D
1. Noncommittal, show him in	25	11	27	20	26	12	18	11	13	18	15	11
2. Brusque, what does he want?	14	21	13	13	6	14	17	10	14	8	15	19
3. Suspicious, what have you done now?	11	9	9	14	13	17	10	16	14	17	12	13
4. Irrelevant, he's probably selling tickets, who sent for the police?	0	2	1	1	4	2	3	1	1	4	3	5
5. No answer	0	6	0	0	0	0	1	9	3	1	0	0
6. I hope your father isn't in trouble, tell him I'm not here	0	1	0	2	1	2	0	2	3	0	1	1
7. Tell him to wait for your father	0	0	0	0	0	0	1	1	2	2	4	0
8. Don't let him in	0	0	0	0	0	3	0	0	0	0	0	1

* C, comparison group; D, delinquent group.

Noncommittal Responses

Included in this category were ordinary civil responses that did not indicate a particularly negative, guilty, or evasive attitude. The responses in Category 1 constituted this classification.

Brusque or Suspicious Responses

Responses that showed less courtesy, in which the parent was depicted as attempting to avoid the policeman or in which the parent suspected a family member of wrongdoing were included in this classification. These answers were in Categories 2, 3, 6, and 8.

Other

Into this classification fell responses that could not easily be classified in either of the above two classes. These included irrelevant responses, ones in which no answer was given, and ones in which the policeman was asked to wait for the husband. Few responses fell into this classification and it was not included in the statistical analyses.

It was hypothesized that in response to this cartoon the delinquent group would be more likely to depict the mother or father as giving a "brusque or suspicious response," while the nondelinquents would be more likely to depict the parents as giving the more civil "noncommittal response."

RESULTS

This hypothesis was generally confirmed for the perceived responses of the father but not those of the mother (Table 53). For the fathers' reactions, significant differences in the predicted direction were obtained for the Anglos ($x^2=5.43$, $p<.02$), Mexicans ($x^2=9.69$, $p<.005$), and the overall analysis ($x^2=15.16$, $p<.001$). The differences for the Latin sample were also in the predicted direction but were not significant ($x^2=2.00$, p [two tail] $<.20$).

No such trends were noted in the perceived responses of the mother, however. In studying the data to determine, if possible, the reasons for this difference, it was noted that among the delinquent groups there was little difference between the responses attributed to the mothers and the fathers. There was a change in the nondelinquent groups, however, with the father seen as giving more "noncommittal" and fewer "brusque or suspicious" responses than the mother. When tested, this difference between the nondelinquents' responses to the father and mother figures was found to be insignificant. Since this difference does not appear reliable, no attempt will be made to interpret it.

The results of the cartoon "The Police" were thus consistent with data in the literature that indicate antisocial attitudes on the part of parents are likely to be associated with delinquency. While no differences were found in the perceived responses of the mothers, significantly more antagonism to authority was attributed to the fathers by the delinquents. Since most authorities agree that the

Table 53

Statistical Analyses of Perceived Responses to the Cartoon "The Police"

| | FATHERS | | | | | | | |
| | Anglo | | Latin | | Mexican | | Overall | |
Response Categories	C*	D*	C	D	C	D	C	D
Noncommittal	25	11	27	20	26	12	78	43
Brusque or suspicious	25	31	22	29	20	36	67	96
Total	50	42	49	49	46	48	145	139
χ^2	5.43		2.00		9.69		15.16	
p (two tail)	<.02		N.S.		<.005		<.001	

| | MOTHERS | | | | | | | |
| | Anglo | | Latin | | Mexican | | Overall | |
Response Categories	C	D	C	D	C	D	C	D
Noncommittal	18	11	13	18	15	11	46	40
Brusque or suspicious	27	28	31	25	28	34	86	87
Total	45	39	44	43	43	45	132	127
χ^2	1.29		1.44		1.53		0.33	
p (two tail)	N.S.		N.S.		N.S.		N.S.	

* C, comparison group; D, delinquent group.

identification with the father is one of the most crucial variables in a boy's conscience formation and since so many studies have found the relation between the father and son to be closely associated with the development of delinquency, this is a particularly noteworthy finding.

"The Wallet"

The final cartoon related to the values of the parents even more closely. In this cartoon, depicted in Figures 10 and 11, a teen-age

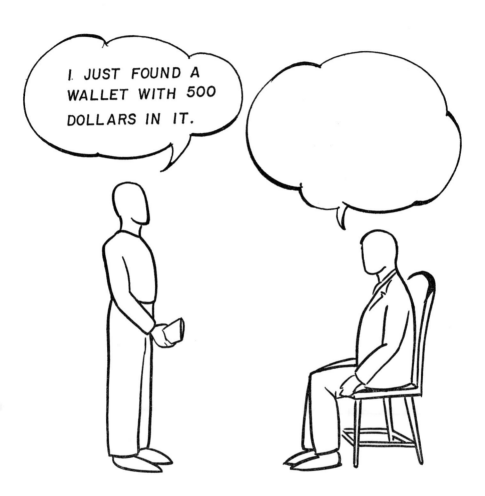

WHAT DOES THE FATHER SAY?

Figure 10. The cartoon "The Wallet," father version.

Figure 11. The cartoon "The Wallet," mother version.

boy was shown coming to his mother or father with a wallet containing 500 dollars (or pesos), which he had just found. The subjects had to indicate what the parent figure would advise in this situation.

PROCEDURE

As might be expected, there was considerably less diversity in the responses to such an overt test of the perceived parental value system. As can be seen in Table 54, only five modal response categories were needed to code the replies, and the overwhelming majority of the parents were depicted as recommending that the boy return it.

The individual response categories were combined into three broader classifications for analysis:

Social Responses

Included in this classification were all those replies in which the parent did the socially approved thing and advised the boy to return the wallet to its owner. As noted above, the majority of the responses in all groups fell into this category.

Table 54

Perceived Responses to the Cartoon "The Wallet"

| | FATHERS | | | | | | MOTHERS | | | | | |
| Modal Responses | Anglo | | Latin | | Mexican | | Anglo | | Latin | | Mexican | |
	C*	D*	C	D	C	D	C	D	C	D	C	D
1. Return it to owner	43	31	42	31	41	39	36	31	39	29	40	34
2. Noncommittal, see if anybody wants it	4	7	7	14	4	3	12	6	8	13	3	5
3. Keep it	3	0	1	3	2	4	1	3	1	2	3	7
4. No answer	0	11	0	1	0	0	1	8	1	3	0	0
5. Did you steal it?	0	1	0	1	3	4	0	2	1	3	4	4

* C, comparison group; D, delinquent group.

Unsocial Responses

In this classification were those replies in which the parent was depicted as advising the boy to keep the wallet and money, as well as those responses in which the boy was advised to postpone returning the wallet to see if anybody wanted it.

Other

In this category were responses that could not be placed in either of the above classifications, including those cases in which no reply was given and in which the parent asked the boy if he had stolen the wallet.

It was hypothesized that the delinquents, either through projection of their own antisocial tendencies or because of the fact that their parents might indeed be more antisocial, would be more likely to depict the parental response as being "unsocial," while the nondelinquents would be more likely to depict the parents as responding with statements in the social classification.

RESULTS

No significant differences were obtained in the Anglo and Mexican samples (see Table 55). In the Latin sample, however, the father was depicted by the delinquents as being significantly more likely to make an unsocial response. The differences for the mother in the Latin sample also approached significance ($\chi^2 = 2.80$, $p < .10$), using a two-tail test, and would have attained an acceptable level of significance ($p < .05$) had a one-tail test been made, which would have been legitimate, since a directional hypothesis had been used. The overall analysis was significant for the fathers, but only a noteworthy trend was obtained for the mothers. By and large, then, the data for the Latin sample supported the hypothesis, while those for the Anglo and Mexican samples did not.

There is no immediately apparent explanation for the fact that the predicted results were obtained for the Latin samples but not the others. In an earlier chapter discussing the Offenses Test, however, the data appeared to support the notion that, possibly because of cultural conflict, the Latin sample had greater conflict over values or anomie than the others.

The fact that the overall analysis indicated that the delinquents

Table 55

Statistical Analyses of Perceived Responses to the Cartoon "The Wallet"

	FATHERS							
	Anglo		Latin		Mexican		Overall	
Response Category	C*	D*	C	D	C	D	C	D
Social response	43	31	42	31	41	39	126	101
Unsocial response	7	7	8	17	6	7	21	31
Total	50	38	50	48	47	46	147	132
χ^2	0.28		4.77		0.10		3.88	
p (two tail)	N.S.		<.05		N.S.		<.05	

	MOTHERS							
	Anglo		Latin		Mexican		Overall	
Response Category	C	D	C	D	C	D	C	D
Social response	36	31	39	29	40	34	115	94
Unsocial response	13	9	9	15	6	12	28	36
Total	49	40	48	44	46	46	143	130
χ^2	0.17		2.80		1.72		2.50	
p (two tail)	N.S.		<.10		N.S.		<.12	

* C, comparison group; D, delinquent group.

were more inclined to attribute antisocial responses to the fathers than to the mothers is consistent with the pattern of paternal disrespect noted in the Card Sort data, as well as with the results obtained on the preceding cartoon, "The Police."

Summary of the Cartoon Test Results

The Cartoon Test was designed to determine how the subjects would perceive parent figures reacting in a series of four tense and rather challenging social situations involving an interaction with a teen-age son. The situations included a boy stating he wanted a car, a boy trying to conceal a cigarette, a boy announcing that there was a policeman at the door, and a boy saying he had found a wallet with a large amount of money in it.

In response to the request for the car and the concealment of the cigarette, almost all the parents were seen as disapproving. The data were analyzed to determine what differences, if any, the form of this disapproval took. Those significant differences that were found indicated that, as had been predicted, the nondelinquents perceived the parents as being more likely to explain why he should not smoke or have the car, while the delinquents more often perceived the parent as giving an abrupt, punitive, unexplained refusal. It thus appeared that the delinquents perceived the parent figures as being more arbitrary and unreasonable and less willing to spend the time necessary to communicate fully with their sons. Whether or not this is an accurate reflection of the actual home situation cannot be determined, but it is consistent with the findings on the Card Sort Test, in which the delinquents indicated they felt there was less cohesiveness and communication in their homes.

Of the eight significant differences found in the responses to the first two cartoons, five were found for the mother figure and three for the father figure. It would thus appear that the delinquents and nondelinquents differed slightly more in their perception of the mother's disciplinary role than the father's.

The next two cartoons were evaluated in terms of the social or antisocial nature of the perceived parental responses. It was found that, when significant differences did exist, the delinquents were more likely to depict the parents as acting in a suspicious, brusque, or evasive manner when a policeman arrived at the door and as more likely to keep or to postpone returning a wallet full of money. This was also consistent with predictions made on the basis of other studies in the literature.

On these latter cartoons, all five of the significant differences were found in the perceived responses of the fathers. The perception of the mother's value judgments did not differ significantly from delinquent to comparison groups. This finding further emphasized the importance of the values of the male identification figure that have been noted in other studies. Both the Card Sort Test and the Cartoon Test have thus pointed to the cross-cultural generality of the fact that the father is probably the crucial agent of socialization for adolescents.

Overall, about 40 per cent of the differences tested on the Cartoon Test attained statistical significance and all were in the predicted directions. The number of significant differences appeared to be about equally divided among the three ethnic samples, both in the responses to the first two cartoons, which tapped disciplinary techniques, and to the second two cartoons, which tested perceived parental values. This pattern indicated that differences in the perceptions of parents by delinquents and nondelinquents are not tied to Anglo culture, but instead appear to be general throughout the three cultures explored in the present sample. This, along with the results of the Card Sort Test, strengthens the case for cross-cultural validity of some of the patterns observed by other investigators who have explored the differences between delinquents and nondelinquents in a single culture.

CHAPTER 12

THE PICTURE-STORY TEST

Methodological Problems of the Symonds and Other Projective Tests

The Symonds Picture-Story Test consists of 20 pictures of adolescents in various situations. The subject is asked to make up a story about each picture, which the examiner writes down.

The basic advantage as well as the major disadvantage of projective tests like the Symonds is the fact that the subject is free to respond as he wishes. There are no limitations on the length or the type of the story he may tell. Usually, the story will be strongly influenced by the nature of the scene depicted on the card and by the constraints imposed by the testing situation. Nevertheless, the subject can, if he wants, tell any story that he wishes, whether it is appropriate or not. Thus, the opportunities for individual variations in response are maximized, but at the penalty of increased difficulties in the coding, analysis, and interpretation of the data.

Research with the Thematic Apperception Test (TAT), the first such story projective test to gain wide use, has indicated that a host of factors influence the content of apperception test stories. They include the picture depicted, the examiner's manner and personality, the subject's perception of the testing situation, the subject's needs and motives (both conscious and unconscious), the relative strength of competing drives, the subject's inhibitions against expressing certain themes, and the subject's verbal fluency. Lindzey has discussed some of the assets and hazards of the use of the TAT in cross-cultural research:

One of the advantages of the TAT is that it can be administered with only a modicum of special training, and, unlike the Rorschach, the examiner need not be intimately familiar with the technique of analysis to be employed subsequently. The richness of the response data elicited provides a relatively satisfactory basis for a wide variety of different kinds of analysis. The thematic material contained in the stories permits the interpreter to make inferences concerning many different dispositions and conflicts, and a great deal can be learned concerning the subject's psychological world and his relations with others, as well as with his physical world. Furthermore, the widespread use of this technique, in addition to the special forms that have been developed, makes clear that a good deal is known about its operation in a number of special settings.

The test appears to be sensitive to depth or unconscious factors, but at the same time it clearly reflects conscious factors and situational determinants, so that under appropriate circumstances it may provide information concerning all of these types of variables. The test activity is a relatively natural one for almost all subjects, and thus it is usually easy to explain and to elicit co-operation. The absence of a single, widely accepted, objective scoring system has led to a healthy approach to the instrument, in which the method of analysis employed is not accepted as God-given and beyond criticism and furthermore it is usually constructed in such a manner as to maximize the interests of the particular investigator.

On the other hand, the data collected by the instrument are ponderous and difficult to subject to analysis. Furthermore, the absence of a simple, objective scoring system means that the individual employing the instrument often spends dozens of hours in analysis for every hour spent in the collection of data. The fact that the instrument is responsive to dispositional, situational, and fleeting personal determinants means that it is difficult for the interpreter to be certain whether a given test characteristic reflects an enduring personal characteristic or a transient state. The entire test procedure rests upon complex linguistic skills so that for subjects who, because of education or intelligence, find it difficult to manipulate verbal symbols the test is relatively inappropriate. When individuals from a different culture are studied, it is difficult to interpret their stories with confidence because of the differences in the language which they employ. (Lindzey, 1961, pp. 72 and 73)[1]

These comments apply to the Symonds as well as the TAT. Projective techniques, such as the Symonds, were devised and are used

[1] From *Projective Techniques and Cross-Cultural Research* by Gardner Lindzey. Copyright © 1961 by Appleton-Century-Crofts, Inc. Reprinted by permission of Appleton-Century-Crofts, Division of Meredith Corporation.

primarily in clinical situations for the detailed diagnosis of the individual client. In such settings, each response is thoroughly studied, hypotheses are developed and checked against other data already known about the individual, and, eventually, a unique personality description emerges. When dealing with large masses of projective test data, however, a different strategy must be adopted. The present investigation was concerned with group rather than individual differences; therefore, it was necessary to devise an objective scoring system that would allow rich, complex data to be coded, quantified, and compared in a reliable and meaningful fashion. As Lindzey has stated (1961, pp. 162–163):

. . . it is generally agreed that responses to projective techniques are controlled by a variety of determinants, only a small number of which are likely to be of strategic interest to any single investigator. Thus, in part, projective-technique responses are determined by: temporary affective states, stimulus factors, response sets, ability and performance factors, definition of the testing situation, situational factors, and the relation between examiner and subject. At least as important as all of these specific determinants is the contribution of random or chance factors . . .

How is the analyst to winnow the meaningful and stable grain of his response data from the random chaff? In the case of group comparisons, most common in cross-cultural applications of projective tests, the typical method will necessitate transformation of the response data into some numerical form and the application of more or less conventional statistical techniques for testing distribution differences.

While some psychologists feel that such quantification irreparably distorts projective test data, Lindzey has argued that quantification is essential if meaningful comparisons are to be made in cross-cultural research (1961, p. 170):

In spite of this resistance to quantification, there seems little doubt that if we define this term broadly enough, we can argue strongly that all serious investigators must resort to some type of quantification. By defining this term broadly, I mean simply that "yes-no" or "presence-absence" applied to a particular attribute or configuration shall be considered a form of quantification.

Administration of the Picture-Story Test

The Picture-Story Test was usually administered as the second test of the second psychological examination, immediately after the

Card Sort Test. As noted above, the examiner simply asked the subject to look at each picture and make up a story about it. The subject was requested to tell what was going on in the pictures, what the people were saying, and how they felt about it. The examiner then wrote down the subject's response in longhand, as close to verbatim as possible.

Only four of the 20 Symonds Picture-Story cards were used in the present investigation. The chosen cards were A-4, A-7, B-1, and B-6. Card A-4 "shows an older man paying out money in bills to a young man" (Symonds, 1949, p. 53). The older man has a rather cross or angry expression. Picture A-7 depicts a woman facing a teen-age boy. The woman's face is solemn, her speech seems to be of a serious nature. The boy, unsmiling, listens attentively. In Picture B-1 a young man with clenched fist and firmly set jaw marches determinedly out the front door and into the street. There are no other persons present. The last, Picture B-6, reveals an extremely dejected-looking man sitting in a chair. He gives no evidence of being about to leave or to change his position. Nothing can be made out from the background, except that, since there seems to be a door leading to the outside, the man must be sitting in a room.

Scoring the Picture-Story Test

All stories that were told in Spanish were translated into English. All scoring was done by a single individual, Mrs. Carl Rosenquist, according to the procedures outlined below. Mrs. Rosenquist re-scored many protocols until she was satisfied with the reliability of her scoring.

The most common method of scoring thematic tests consists of identifying the "hero" or central character of each story and then identifying the needs that he apparently expresses in his behavior and the forces that impinge on him from others in the environment. This relatively sophisticated form of analysis requires considerable time and skill. Another common and less costly form of analysis is simply to classify stories according to whether certain themes, such as those of aggression, achievement, or affiliation, are present, without worrying about which character expresses them. This is more reliable, but one wonders whether lumping together as "need aggression" one story in which a parent hits a child and another in which a child hits a parent is conceptually valid. The scheme that was devised for coding the present data was designed to permit the identification of both the potentially meaningful story elements and the behavior of certain key figures in the stories.

SCORING STORY ELEMENTS

The story elements selected for investigation were fairly gross. Included was an evaluation of the overall story atmosphere as pleasant, neutral, or unpleasant; the identification of pleasant, unpleasant, and grossly antisocial events in the various stories; and the identification of pleasant or unpleasant economic events. These characteristics are explained in more detail below:

Story Atmosphere

An overall evaluation of the general tone of each story was made and the story was classified as pleasant, unpleasant, or neutral. The number of stories of each type told by the members of each group in response to each card was then determined.

Pleasant, Unpleasant, and Antisocial Situations

The various events and situations in each story were classified into three basic categories. The first consisted of pleasant, desirable, or happy situations. These included references to having a good time, being happy, or enjoying oneself (see Table 56 for a more detailed list of characteristics). This category also included socially desirable behavior or feelings, such as confession or remorse for misdeeds.

The second category consisted of unpleasant, undesirable, or unhappy situations. Included in this behavior were worrying, unpleasant emotions, and socially undesirable behavior, such as bad manners, cursing, and the like. Seriously antisocial behavior, such as fighting or serious crimes, was not included in this category. Because pleasant and unpleasant events were not mutually exclusive, it was possible for a single story to be scored as having both elements within it. However, it was not necessary for every event in a story to be placed into one category or the other, since many neutral events were present.

The third category consisted of aggressive, antisocial, or very unpleasant events. Included in this category were references to stealing, fighting, narcotics, and jail.

For each individual, the number of events falling into each of these categories was determined for each card. From these data, the total number of events in each category was determined for each of the six groups on each of the four cards. A record was also kept of the number of stories having one or more events or situations in each category. Thus, if a boy told a story on Card A-4 that contained three distinctly antisocial events, one unpleasant event, and no pleasant situations, he would be recorded as having three antisocial events and one antisocial story, one unpleasant event and one unpleasant story, and no pleasant events or stories on that card. The score for his group on that card would consist of the sum of these scores for all 50 individuals.

As we shall see below, the ideal method of statistical analysis would have used the individual data to compute means and standard deviations. Unfortunately, it was these individual data that were lost. What remained was the sum of the number of events for each group in each category for each card and the total number of stories for each group in each category on each card. This resulted in serious problems in the analysis of the data.

Pleasant and Unpleasant Economic Situations

Because differences in feelings about economic opportunities have played a central role in a number of theories of delinquency, the stories were also examined for references to pleasant or unpleasant economic situations. The exact nature of these events is spelled out in greater detail in Table 57. Once the individual stories were scored, the data were treated in the same fashion as the data for the pleasant, unpleasant, and antisocial events, with the total number of pleasant and unpleasant economic events and stories being determined for each group in response to each card. After the loss of the individual data, only these group data remained for analysis.

These data were then used to determine whether the delinquents and nondelinquents in each sample differed significantly in the general tone of their stories, in the number of pleasant or desirable, unpleasant or undesirable, or extremely unpleasant or antisocial events or stories. They were also used to determine if there were significant differences in the number of pleasant and unpleasant economic instances or stories.

No specific hypotheses were made regarding the direction in which the delinquents and nondelinquents would differ. The in-

Table 56

Situational Analysis of the Picture-Story Test

Pleasant, Desirable, Happy Situations	Unpleasant, Undesirable, or Unhappy Situations	Aggressive, Antisocial, or Very Unpleasant Situations
"Good time"	Sadness	Stealing
Good friends	Seriousness	Fighting
Recreation—movies, dancing, date	Worrying	Dope peddling
Happiness	Thinking about difficulties	Robbing
Thinking about pleasant things	Fatigue	"Getting someone"
Going out for fun, recreation, pleasure	Indolence	Killing
Seeking help, advice	Depression	Jail or detention
Being nice	Interference	In trouble (serious)
"Nice appearance," even if for court or other unpleasant situation	Punishment by parents	Run away
Dressing up, even if for court or other unpleasant situation	Bad company	
Confession	Living by self	
Church	Hate	
Talking, visiting	Slovenly or careless appearance	
Inviting person in	Anger	
Eating	Getting caught	
Remorse	"Square"	
Industry	Problem	
Dependability	Bad manners	
Kindness	Cursing	
Honesty	Doing something wrong	
Helpfulness	Be alone (escape from situation)	
Education	Want to be alone	
Future success	In trouble (minor)	
Counseling	Fear	
	Going out to escape situation	

Table 57

References to Economic Events in the Stories

Pleasant	Unpleasant
Getting a job	Poverty
Keeping a job	Clothing or furnishings indicating
Getting a raise	poverty
Earning money	Inadequate food
Money	Lack of money
Riches	Losing job
Buying things	
Giving gifts of money	
Fathers or mothers getting or keep-	
ing a job	
Having or getting enough money	
for food	
Having or getting enough money	
for clothes	
Anticipation of future job	
Anticipation of future wealth	
Anticipation of future car	
Anticipation of future house	
Anticipation of future adequate or	
better house	

vestigators had the general expectation that the milieus of the delinquents were probably more unpleasant than those of the non-delinquents, but we were unwilling to predict that this would be reflected in more unpleasantness or less pleasantness on the Picture-Story Test. Authorities differ on the relation that is to be expected between events in apperceptive material and events in the real world —some hold that the apperceptive world is a direct counterpart of the real world and others argue that it is just the opposite. According to the latter interpretation, which is based on the assumption that apperceptive tests tap unconscious rather than conscious functioning, a person with many aggressive responses would be evaluated as probably being relatively nonaggressive in his everyday behavior; on the other hand, the former interpretation would suggest that persons with many aggressive responses on the test are likely to be quite aggressive in their typical behavior, as well.

A good deal of research has considered the question of whether the relation between projective test data and overt behavior is direct or inverse. Much of this has focused on the relation of aggressive test content and overt aggression. In a recent article, Megargee and Cook (1967, p. 48) summarized some of the findings of these investigations as follows:

1. Authorities differ as to the relationship which should be expected between projective test scores and overt behavior, some holding that it should be direct and others that it should be inverse.

2. Empirical studies have generally found either no significant relationships or significant direct ones. The notion of significant inverse relations between projective test measures and overt aggression has received little empirical support (Lindzey & Tejessey, 1956).

3. There is a great deal of diversity in the findings reported. A number of factors apparently influence the relation between projective tests and overt aggressive behavior. These include: (a) internal inhibitions against the expression of aggression as measured by inhibitory forces within the test protocol (Mussen & Naylor, 1954; Pittluck, 1950) and by maternal attitude toward aggressive behavior (Lesser, 1957; Weatherly, 1962); (b) the guilt which the subject feels (Saltz & Epstein, 1963); (c) social class differences (Mussen & Naylor, 1954); (d) the degree to which the stimulus material "pulls" an aggressive response (Haskell, 1961; Kagan, 1956; Murstein, 1963, 1965); (e) external factors in the testing situation which might influence the level of response (Megargee, 1964b; Rosenzweig, 1950); (f) the criterion of aggression used (Haskell, 1961); and (g) whether the aggressive act is a product of excessive or inadequate controls (Megargee, 1966c).

It was because of such complexities in the relation between test data and overt behavior that the present investigators were unwilling to attempt to specify in advance the direction of any differences that might be obtained. Indeed, the contradictory nature of the findings in the literature could present problems in the interpretation of any such significant differences. As Lindzey has pointed out, however, this problem can be minimized if findings are interpreted in the light of the data that have already been gathered about the various groups (Lindzey, 1961, p. 172):

. . . it is clear that the interpreter of projective tests cannot assume safely that his interpretations automatically refer to some single level of behavior . . .

. . . unless the investigator has available a good deal of information from sources other than projective techniques which makes clear whether or not a given motive or disposition is expressed overtly, he is poorly advised to assume that the motives expressed in projective-test response are necessarily linked to any single domain or level of behavior. This indicates once again the strategic superiority of the investigator who is able to interpret his projective-technique responses against a rich background of supplementary information.

SCORING BEHAVIOR OF KEY FIGURES

In addition to identifying certain elements of the stories to analyze, attention was given to the roles attributed to certain key figures in the various stories. Through this analysis it was hoped that some idea of the differences, if any, in the way delinquents and non-delinquents view various people, could be determined.

Surveying the data, it was found that a number of characters entered into the 1,200 stories. A list of the most common characters appears in Table 58. The first step in this phase of the scoring consisted of recording all the characters, in addition to the boy who was the central figure, who entered into the story. The next step was to determine what these various characters did, in the hope that this might give an inkling to the role such figures played in the life of the storyteller.

Four types of behavior were selected for study:

1. *Offering counsel or advice.* In each story those characters who offered counsel or advice to the boy were identified and the number doing so was recorded.

2. *Reprimanding or scolding.* The second aspect of behavior that was investigated was verbal discipline, such as scolding or reprimanding. For each group of subjects, the figures who engaged in such behavior in the stories were identified and the number recorded.

3. *Administering punishment.* Thirdly, the figures who actually were seen as punishing the boy by any method, such as restrictions, deprivation of privileges, or corporal punishment, were identified.

4. *Figures to whom responsibility or obligation was shown.* The final aspect that was thought worthwhile to investigate was the

Table 58

List of Characters Appearing in the Stories

1. Family members (unspecified)
2. Parents
3. Mother
4. Father
5. Grandmother
6. Grandfather
7. Aunt
8. Uncle
9. Female adult, otherwise unidentified
10. Male adult, otherwise unidentified
11. Teacher
12. Police
13. Judge
14. Employer
15. Boss in illegal activities
16. Pastor or priest
17. Older people, otherwise unidentified
18. Older sisters
19. Older brothers
20. Younger sisters
21. Younger brothers
22. Siblings, unspecified
23. Boy other than central figure
24. Girl
25. Girl friend
26. Boy friend
27. Friends
28. Gang leader
29. Gang member
30. Accomplice
31. Others

number and identity of the figures to whom the boy was perceived as being obliged or responsible.

Statistical Analysis of the Data

Before the results of the Picture-Story Test are discussed, some of the statistical problems encountered in the analysis of the data will be reviewed. It has already been noted that before the data analysis was completed, some of the data were lost in the course of the senior author's move. Among the lost data were the Picture-Story Test protocols and the individual scores. This loss made it impossible to compute the number of pleasant, unpleasant, or antisocial stories told by any given individual; similarly, it was impossible to compute the total or mean number of such events in the stories told by an individual over the course of the four cards. Summary data of the performance of each *group* on each card were available and from these it was possible to calculate the number of stories with these various elements in them told by each group as a whole. However, without variance estimates, which could be determined only from the individual data, no parametric significance tests could be carried out. This problem arose in the analysis of all the Picture-Story scores.

It was therefore necessary to resort to nonparametric techniques, such as the binomial and chi-square tests, to determine the significance of differences in frequencies of various types of responses. However, it was impossible to conduct a chi-square or binomial test analysis of the pooled data over all four cards, for this involved repeated measurements that were obviously not independent. Therefore, the group results for each individual card had to be subjected to independent statistical analyses. While this was a statistically valid procedure, it resulted in four times as many significance tests being performed as would otherwise have been the case. Moreover, those tests that were performed were carried out on data that were perforce less reliable, using statistical tests that were less powerful, particularly in view of the small cell entries that were often found. The net effect was probably to reduce the proportion of significant findings, on the one hand, and to make more suspect those results that did attain significance, on the other.

While analyzing the cards separately left much to be desired, there was one advantage that deserves mention. Analyzing the results for each card independently allowed the investigators to observe any differences in the effects of the different stimulus cards. For example, it would be interesting if there should be significant differences between the delinquents and nondelinquents in the number of stories in which unpleasant events occur in response to Card A-4, which showed a boy and an adult man usually seen as the father, but not in response to Card A-7, which showed a boy with an adult woman usually seen as the mother.

Results and Discussion

ANALYSES OF STORY EVENTS AND ATMOSPHERE

Story Atmosphere

As noted above, the general atmosphere of all the stories was classified as pleasant, neutral, or unpleasant. For the purpose of statistical analysis, the neutral category was dropped out, and chi-square analyses performed to determine if the delinquent and non-delinquent groups differed significantly in the relative proportion of stories with pleasant and unpleasant atmosphere that they told. The groups' responses to each card were individually analyzed because of the statistical problems noted above. The results are presented in Table 59.

The data in Table 59 show that there were no significant differences or noteworthy trends in the relative frequency of pleasant and unpleasant stories told by the delinquent and nondelinquent members of the Anglo and Mexican samples. In the Latin sample, however, significant differences were found for two of the four pictures. On Card A-4, which depicted a man holding currency and a boy with an outstretched hand, the delinquents had a significantly higher ratio of pleasant to unpleasant stories ($\chi^2 = 5.62$, $p < .02$). Even more pronounced differences ($\chi^2 = 11.23$, $p < .001$) in the same direction were found for the stories told in response to Card B-1, which depicted a boy with clenched fists striding from a building.

Because of the problems noted above, it is difficult to interpret this finding. It could be that the Latin delinquents had pleasanter environments and therefore tended to tell pleasanter stories. The data we have reviewed thus far, however, make this unlikely. Most of the data have indicated that the Latin delinquents lived in surroundings distinctly less pleasant than those enjoyed by the nondelinquents, even when they were not incarcerated. It could be hypothesized that what was obtained on the stories was a wish-fulfilling fantasy: since the delinquents had more difficult lives they projected the desire for a better lot into their stories. To explain the

Table 59

Number of Stories with Pleasant and Unpleasant Atmospheres

Card	Story Type	Anglo		Latin		Mexican	
		C*	D*	C	D	C	D
	Stories with pleasant atmosphere	5	5	6	12	18	20
A-4	Stories with unpleasant atmosphere	18	25	32	14	20	14
	Total	23	30	38	26	38	34
	χ^{2a}	0.01		5.62		0.94	
	p (two tail)	N.S.		<.02		N.S.	
	Stories with pleasant atmosphere	7	6	11	23	13	10
A-7	Stories with unpleasant atmosphere	18	26	12	14	19	17
	Total	25	32	23	37	32	27
	χ^{2a}	0.26		1.19		0.08	
	p (two tail)	N.S.		N.S.		N.S.	
	Stories with pleasant atmosphere	3	1	3	16	11	9
B-1	Stories with unpleasant atmosphere	31	39	34	19	23	27
	Total	34	40	37	35	34	36
	χ^{2a}	0.47		11.23		0.17	
	p (two tail)	N.S.		<.001		N.S.	
	Stories with pleasant atmosphere	1	0	1	0	4	2
B-6	Stories with unpleasant atmosphere	42	44	39	38	34	32
	Total	43	44	40	38	38	34
	χ^{2a}	0.00		0.01		0.08	
	p (two tail)	N.S.		N.S.		N.S.	

[a] All chi-square values corrected for continuity when expected value ≤ 10.
* C, comparison group; D, delinquent group.

fact that only the Latin sample had significant differences, it would be necessary to assume that either they had a more difficult time or they were more prone to resort to fantasy as a defense, or both. Another alternative is that some factor in the relationship between the examiners and the Latin delinquents, possibly an eagerness to please or increased defensiveness by the respondents, was responsible for the results.

In any case, for whatever reason, it was clear that none of the delinquent samples told stories that were significantly *more* unpleasant in atmosphere than the comparison groups' and, on the contrary, the Latin delinquents told significantly pleasanter stories. The interpretation of this must wait until more results of the Picture-Story Test have been analyzed before it can be evaluated.

Stories with Pleasant Events; Number of Pleasant Instances

In addition to the overall evaluation of the story atmosphere, the number of pleasant events and the number of stories in which such events took place were recorded. By analyzing these data quite apart from whether or not these stories also contained unpleasant or antisocial events, a clearer picture of differences that may have been submerged in the global evaluation of atmosphere could be obtained. A story with many pleasant events and an equal number of unpleasant events of equal magnitude might have received an overall atmosphere rating of "neutral," while a story with only one pleasant event but no unpleasant ones might have been judged to have a "pleasant" atmosphere on an overall basis.

The data for the number of *stories* with and without pleasant events were first analyzed by means of chi-square. The results are presented in Table 60. None of the 12 tests attained statistical significance, nor were any consistent noteworthy trends found.

The data for the number of pleasant *instances* occurring in the stories of each group were next analyzed. These data were valuable insofar as they provided a measure of intensity, but they were considerably less reliable than the data on the number of stories. One problem was that a subjective decision had to be made as to what constituted one as opposed to two distinct pleasant events. For another, the data could be strongly influenced by one or two individuals who might have told lengthy stories with a great many such instances. With no individual data available, it was of course im-

Table 60

Number of Stories in Which Pleasant Events Occur

Card	Story Type	Anglo C*	Anglo D*	Latin C	Latin D	Mexican C	Mexican D
	Stories with pleasant events	12	14	19	22	31	26
A-4	Stories with no pleasant events	38	36	31	28	19	24
	Total	50	50	50	50	50	50
	χ^{2a}	0.21		0.37		1.02	
	p (two tail)	N.S.		N.S.		N.S.	
	Stories with pleasant events	37	35	44	41	43	39
A-7	Stories with no pleasant events	13	15	6	9	7	11
	Total	50	50	50	50	50	50
	χ^{2a}	0.20		0.31		0.61	
	p (two tail)	N.S.		N.S.		N.S.	
	Stories with pleasant events	22	15	22	34	42	39
B-1	Stories with no pleasant events	28	35	28	16	8	11
	Total	50	50	50	50	50	50
	χ^{2a}	2.10		0.58		0.26	
	p (two tail)	$<.20$		N.S.		N.S.	
	Stories with pleasant events	10	7	20	15	33	32
B-6	Stories with no pleasant events	40	43	30	35	17	18
	Total	50	50	50	50	50	50
	χ^{2a}	0.28		1.10		0.04	
	p (two tail)	N.S.		N.S.		N.S.	

a All chi-square values corrected for continuity when expected value ≤ 10.
* C, comparison group; D, delinquent group.

possible to determine to what extent the response tendencies of a few individuals influenced the results.

The data for the number of instances were tested using the binomial test (Siegel, 1956). Under the null hypothesis it was assumed that the number of pleasant instances in the stories told to a given card would be equally distributed between the delinquent and nondelinquent subjects. Since no a priori hypotheses had been made, two-tail tests were used throughout.

No significant differences were found in the number of pleasant instances on any of the four cards in the Anglo and Latin samples. However, there was a tendency on two cards for the nondelinquent Anglos to have more pleasant instances, and a slight trend in the same direction for the nondelinquent Latins (see Table 61).

In the Mexican sample significant differences were found in the responses to Cards A-7 ($p=.034$) and B-1 ($p=.022$). In both cases the comparison group had the higher number of pleasant instances, the same trend noted in the responses of the Anglo and Latin samples. Interpretation was made difficult, however, by the fact that a strong trend ($p=.073$) in the opposite direction was found for Card A-4. Not only was this trend different in direction from the others already noted, but also it was in response to the "father" card, on which one would expect the delinquents to relate fewer pleasant instances. To be sure, this difference did not attain accept-

Table 61

Binomial Analyses of Differences in the Number of Pleasant Instances

	Anglo			Latin			Mexican		
Card	C[*]	D[*]	p (two tail)	C	D	p (two tail)	C	D	p (two tail)
A-4	21	20	N.S.	30	41	N.S.	66	91	.073
A-7	89	67	.091	80	84	N.S.	187	147	.034
B-1	44	28	.077	47	56	N.S.	128	93	.022
B-6	16	18	N.S.	34	21	N.S.	76	87	N.S.

[*] C, comparison group; D, delinquent group.

able levels of statistical significance; however, it did serve as a warning against any sweeping interpretations that the investigators might otherwise have made.

The two significant findings were, as noted, in the direction that indicated more pleasant instances in the stories of the nondelinquent group. This finding was consistent with the results of the Card Sort Test and the sociological data, which by and large indicated more pleasant milieus and family backgrounds among the nondelinquents in general and the Mexican nondelinquents in particular. These data must still be approached with some caution, however, since the results for the global ratings of story atmosphere were in the opposite direction.

Stories with Unpleasant Events; Number of Unpleasant Instances

Whereas no significant differences in the number of stories with pleasant events were found in the preceding analysis, significant differences were obtained in the analysis of the number of stories in which unpleasant events took place. The Latin comparison group was significantly higher in the number of stories with unpleasant events told in response to Cards A-4 ($\chi^2=6.99$, $p<.01$) and B-1 ($\chi^2=12.40$, $p<.001$). There was a slight tendency for them to have more unpleasant stories on the other two cards as well. However, in the Anglo and Mexican samples no significant differences were obtained (see Table 62).

When the number of unpleasant instances was analyzed, the discrepancy between the Latin sample and the other two became even more marked. The Latin comparison group had significantly more unpleasant instances in their stories to Cards A-4 ($p=.002$), A-7 ($p=.023$), and B-1 ($p=.0001$), and a noteworthy trend ($p=.075$) on Card B-6 (see Table 63).

These highly significant differences were in contrast to the results for the Anglos, for whom no significant differences were found; however, the disparity with the Mexican sample was even more striking. While no significant differences were found on three cards, on Card A-7 the Mexican *delinquents* had significantly more unpleasant events in their stories. The magnitude of this difference ($p=.0005$) was such that it could not be easily dismissed as a random fluctuation of the data. Thus, there were significantly more unpleasant events and stories in the protocols of the Latin comparison group;

Table 62

Number of Stories in Which Unpleasant Events Occur

Card	Story Type	Anglo C*	Anglo D*	Latin C	Latin D	Mexican C	Mexican D
	Stories with unpleasant events	29	27	27	14	26	27
A-4	Stories without unpleasant events	21	23	23	36	24	23
	Total	50	50	50	50	50	50
	χ^{2a}	0.16		6.99		0.04	
	p (two tail)	N.S.		<.01		N.S.	
	Stories with unpleasant events	39	37	32	26	34	40
A-7	Stories without unpleasant events	11	13	18	24	16	10
	Total	50	50	50	50	50	50
	χ^{2a}	0.22		1.48		1.87	
	p (two tail)	N.S.		N.S.		N.S.	
	Stories with unpleasant events	38	43	40	23	34	36
B-1	Stories without unpleasant events	12	7	10	27	16	14
	Total	50	50	50	50	50	50
	χ^{2a}	1.04		12.40		0.00	
	p (two tail)	N.S.		<.001		N.S.	
	Stories with unpleasant events	47	47	46	43	45	44
B-6	Stories without unpleasant events	3	3	4	7	5	6
	Total	50	50	50	50	50	50
	χ^{2a}	0.00		0.41		0.00	
	p (two tail)	N.S.		N.S.		N.S.	

[a] All chi-square values corrected for continuity when expected value ≤ 10.
* C, comparison group; D, delinquent group.

Table 63

Binomial Analyses of Differences in the Number of Unpleasant Instances

Card	Anglo			Latin			Mexican		
	C*	D*	p (two tail)	C	D	p (two tail)	C	D	p (two tail)
A-4	46	43	N.S.	45	18	.002	54	58	N.S.
A-7	89	76	N.S.	63	39	.023	83	134	.0005
B-1	105	111	N.S.	98	40	.0001	89	109	N.S.
B-6	131	126	N.S.	112	93	.075	185	159	N.S.

* *C*, comparison group; *D*, delinquent group.

for the other samples no significant differences were usually found, but the one highly significant difference that was found was in the opposite direction.

In order to evaluate this puzzling state of affairs, let us briefly review the results thus far. For the Anglo sample, no significant differences were obtained on story atmosphere, the number of pleasant stories and events, or the number of unpleasant stories or events on any card. For the Latin sample, it was found that the nondelinquents had story atmospheres that were more unpleasant than those of the delinquents, and more unpleasant stories and unpleasant events within these stories. No differences in the number of pleasant stories or events were found. For the Mexican sample, it was found that the nondelinquents had significantly more pleasant events and significantly fewer unpleasant events in their stories.[2] There appear to be two possible alternative explanations for this pattern. One is that the personality dynamics that differentiate the delinquents from the nondelinquents in the Latin and Mexican samples differed funda-

[2] To decrease the tedious repetition of qualifying phrases, this summary has been oversimplified. Only the significant findings have been reviewed; the number of individual cards on which significant findings were found has not been specified.

mentally. The second explanation is that the personality structure did not differ, but the approach to the test did, possibly as a result of differences in the setting or the examiners, or the interpretation of the task by the subjects. As further data are analyzed it will be necessary to determine the reliability of this trend and examine the data closely in an effort to determine which of these explanations is more likely.

Stories with Extremely Unpleasant or Antisocial Events;
Number of Extremely Unpleasant or Antisocial Instances

Antisocial events were defined as including references to stealing, fighting, getting in serious trouble, dope peddling, robbing, "getting someone," killing, running away, being jailed, or being put in detention. In short, fairly direct references to delinquent behavior and its consequences were subsumed under this category. Since the structured tests had avoided overt or direct references to delinquency lest undue defensiveness be aroused, the Picture-Story Test data provided one of the few sources of data with explicit references to delinquent behavior.

It has already been noted that a large body of research has accumulated regarding the relation between aggressive content on picture-story tests, usually the Thematic Apperception Test (TAT), and overt aggression in various groups. Much of the content included in the present category of antisocial behavior would be scored as aggressive content in most of the TAT scoring systems that have been developed. Therefore, the findings that have been obtained concerning the relation of thematic aggressive content and overt aggressive or antisocial behavior in other studies will be briefly reviewed before the results of the present investigation are examined.

Most of the studies that have been performed indicated that aggressive or antisocial people have more aggressive or antisocial content in their stories. Megargee (1966c, pp. 3–4) reviewed several studies of assaultive psychiatric patients or delinquents:

Purcell (1956) gave the TAT to three groups of army trainees referred for psychiatric study and found the most aggressive group to be highest in need Aggression (n Agg). Young (1956) also found high n Agg scores among her sample of institutionalized delinquents, while Mussen and Naylor (1954) found a significant positive relation between the amount of overt aggression displayed in detention and the amount of *n* Agg in a sample of juvenile delinquents.

Stone (1953) administered the TAT and Rorschach to three groups of military prisoners who differed in aggressiveness. The most aggressive group consisted of 31 men in prison for assaults or murders who had at least two prior offenses of this type. . . . He found that on the TAT the most aggressive group manifested significantly more aggression than did the other two.

In a study by Megargee and Cook (1967), the TAT protocols of 76 juvenile delinquents detained for offenses ranging from incorrigibility to first degree homicide were scored on several TAT aggressive content scales. The scores were related to 11 criteria of overt aggressive behavior. The relationships between the TAT scales and most of the criteria, including the offenses with which the boys were charged, were insignificant. Those relationships that were statistically significant all showed the more antisocial boys to have higher TAT aggressive content scores.

Other studies have examined the relation between apperceptive test aggressive content scores and overt aggression in samples of "normals" of various ages from a variety of socioeconomic backgrounds. As noted above, these investigations have found that a number of factors influence the nature of the relation between the test scores and overt aggression (Megargee, 1966b, 1967; Megargee & Cook, 1967). In samples of delinquents, however, the results have been fairly clear: delinquents have higher aggressive content scores when significant differences have been found. On the basis of this prior research, it would be expected that the delinquent groups would tell more stories containing more antisocial material than would the comparison groups.

The results of the analysis of the number of stories in which antisocial events occurred are presented in Table 64. Significant differences were found in the Anglo and Mexican samples, but not the Latin. In the Anglo sample, significant differences were found between the number of stories with antisocial elements told by the delinquents and nondelinquents in response to Card B-1 ($\chi^2 = 5.88$, $p < .02$). As would be expected from the literature reviewed above, the delinquents had the higher number of stories with antisocial themes. A similar trend in this direction was noted in the responses

Table 64

Stories in Which Antisocial Events Occur

Card	Story Type	Anglo C*	D*	Latin C	D	Mexican C	D
	Stories with antisocial theme	3	9	7	3	17	20
A-4	Stories without antisocial theme	47	41	43	47	33	30
	Total	50	50	50	50	50	50
	χ^{2a}	2.37		1.00		0.39	
	p (two tail)	<.15		N.S.		N.S.	
	Stories with antisocial theme	1	6	2	3	11	22
A-7	Stories without antisocial theme	49	44	48	47	39	28
	Total	50	50	50	50	50	50
	χ^{2a}	2.46		0.00		5.47	
	p (two tail)	<.15		N.S.		<.02	
	Stories with antisocial theme	9	20	11	5	15	25
B-1	Stories without antisocial theme	41	30	39	45	35	25
	Total	50	50	50	50	50	50
	χ^{2a}	5.88		1.86		4.17	
	p (two tail)	<.02		N.S.		<.05	
	Stories with antisocial theme	6	13	8	4	22	31
B-6	Stories without antisocial theme	44	37	42	46	28	19
	Total	50	50	50	50	50	50
	χ^{2a}	2.34		0.85		3.25	
	p (two tail)	<.15		N.S.		<.10	

[a] All chi-square values corrected for continuity when expected value ≤ 10.
* C, comparison group; D, delinquent group.

to the remaining three cards. On these three cards the delinquents produced from two to six times as many stories with antisocial themes as did the nondelinquents; the chi-square values ranged from 2.34 to 2.46 with the associated two-tail p values $<.15$.

The data for the Mexican sample were similar to those of the Anglo, save that the differences between the delinquent and comparison groups were more pronounced. Not only was a significant difference ($\chi^2=4.17$, $p<.05$) obtained on the responses to Card B-1, but there was also a significant difference in the responses to Card A-7 ($\chi^2=5.47$, $p<.02$). In both cases, the data showed a higher incidence of antisocial stories in the delinquents' protocols. A noteworthy trend in this direction was also obtained for the Mexicans' stories on Card B-6 ($\chi^2=3.25$, p [two tail] $<.10$). This latter trend would have reached acceptable levels of statistical significance had we permitted ourselves a one-tail test of our directional hypothesis.

The data for the Latin sample did not indicate any statistically significant differences. The nonsignificant differences that did occur showed the Latin comparison group telling slightly more antisocial stories than the Latin delinquents. This continued the unusual trend noted in the analysis of the data on the number of stories with unpleasant events.

The results of the analysis of the number of antisocial instances were similar, except that on this variable it was the Anglos who had the most pronounced differences. As can be seen from the data in Table 65, the binomial test indicated that the delinquent Anglos' stories had significantly more antisocial instances than those of the nondelinquents in response to Cards A-4 ($p=.004$), A-7 ($p=.001$), and B-1 ($p=.003$). In the Mexican sample, the nondelinquents significantly exceeded the delinquents only in response to Card B-1, but that difference was highly significant ($p=.0001$). None of the differences for the Latin sample were statistically significant.

Thus, the results for both ethnic majority groups, the Anglos and the Mexicans, were consistent with those found in the literature, showing more antisocial material in the stories of the delinquents than the nondelinquents. As no such differences were found for the Latin sample, the tendency for the Latin sample to respond differently from the other two samples was continued. The direction of this difference suggested that possibly the Latin delinquents re-

Table 65

Binomial Analyses of Differences in the Number of Antisocial Instances

	Anglo			Latin			Mexican		
Card	C*	D*	p (two tail)	C	D	p (two tail)	C	D	p (two tail)
A-4	5	20	.004	8	4	N.S.	38	50	N.S.
A-7	1	15	.001	2	4	N.S.	36	45	N.S.
B-1	10	30	.003	14	7	N.S.	33	75	.0001
B-6	15	23	N.S.	12	6	N.S.	74	84	N.S.

* C, comparison group; D, delinquent group.

sponded more defensively than the delinquents in the other two groups. Since they were the only delinquents to be examined by someone from a different ethnic background, this might have had an inhibiting effect. The hypothesis of defensiveness is supported by an inspection of Tables 62, 63, 64, and 65, reporting the data on unpleasant and antisocial themes, which indicate that while the results for the nondelinquent Latin groups were similar to those for the other comparison groups, the Latin delinquents' stories showed a consistently lower incidence of such themes than did those of the other delinquent groups.

Stories with Pleasant Economic Events;
Number of Pleasant Economic Instances

The effects of poverty and limited chances for economic success have occupied a central place in many theories of delinquency causation. Cloward and Ohlin (1960) have stressed the discontent that results when a person who aspires to upward mobility is confronted with a situation in which the legitimate chances for success are few. Given models who demonstrate that illegitimate or illegal means to wealth are more effective, the person may turn toward crime and delinquency. Cohen (1955) has suggested that the profit motive may not play as important a role as some theorists would hold, particularly in "senseless" or profitless crimes, such as vandalism. Nevertheless, he felt that a discrepancy between aspirations and the means to achieve them in school and in the market place may still be powerful motivating forces. The looting and burning of stores that has accompanied riots in poverty ghettos of Detroit, Los Angeles, Washington, and other cities, while ignited by racial tensions, was no doubt fueled by economic frustrations as well.

Because of the possible importance of economic factors in causing delinquency, all references to economic events in the stories were scrutinized and classified as pleasant, neutral, or unpleasant.[3] The investigators were particularly interested in indications that the delinquents' and nondelinquents' picture stories might reflect significant differences in economic optimism or pessimism.

The analysis of the number of stories with pleasant economic references indicated that there were no significant differences between delinquent and nondelinquent groups in any sample (see Table 66). Pleasant economic stories were frequent in all samples in response to Card A-4, which showed a man handing money to a boy. On the less suggestive cards the Mexican subjects told many more stories with pleasant economic references than did their Latin and Anglo counterparts. This might have been the result of sampling differences, but it might also have been a function of differences in the Mexicans' personalities or the greater poverty to be found in Mexico.

Significant differences were obtained in the analysis of the number of pleasant economic instances (see Table 67). In the Latin sample, the delinquents' stories to Card B-1 had significantly more pleasant economic instances than did those of the nondelinquents ($p=.021$). The Mexican sample, however, had significant differences in the opposite direction, with the comparison subjects' stories having significantly more pleasant instances in response to the same card ($p=.0014$). Thus, the trend for opposite results to be found in the Latin and Mexican samples was continued.

No firm inferences can be drawn from these findings, because such a small proportion of the differences were significant. However, it is odd that of all the groups it was the Latin delinquents who had a

---

[3] While the neutral category was necessary for accurate coding, it was of little theoretical interest; therefore, only the data for the pleasant and unpleasant categories were analyzed for presentation.

Table 66

Number of Stories in Which Pleasant Economic References Occur

Card	Story Type	Anglo C*	Anglo D*	Latin C	Latin D	Mexican C	Mexican D
	Stories with pleasant economic references	34	37	40	31	37	42
A-4	Stories without pleasant economic references	16	13	10	19	13	8
	Total	50	50	50	50	50	50
	χ^{2a}	0.44		0.39		1.51	
	p (two tail)	N.S.		N.S.		N.S.	
	Stories with pleasant economic references	2	2	1	1	16	15
A-7	Stories without pleasant economic references	48	48	49	49	34	35
	Total	50	50	50	50	50	50
	χ^{2a}	0.00		0.00		0.05	
	p (two tail)	N.S.		N.S.		N.S.	
	Stories with pleasant economic references	1	6	11	14	27	19
B-1	Stories without pleasant economic references	49	44	39	36	23	31
	Total	50	50	50	50	50	50
	χ^{2a}	2.46		0.48		2.58	
	p (two tail)	N.S.		N.S.		N.S.	
	Stories with pleasant economic references	3	4	2	7	20	13
B-6	Stories without pleasant economic references	47	46	48	43	30	37
	Total	50	50	50	50	50	50
	χ^{2a}	0.00		1.95		2.22	
	p (two tail)	N.S.		N.S.		N.S.	

[a] All chi-square values corrected for continuity when expected value ≤ 10.
* C, comparison group; D, delinquent group.

Table 67

Binomial Analyses of Differences in the Number of Pleasant Economic Instances

	Anglo			Latin			Mexican		
Card	C*	D*	p (two tail)	C	D	p (two tail)	C	D	p (two tail)
A-4	53	54	N.S.	63	50	N.S.	129	117	N.S.
A-7	2	2	N.S.	3	3	N.S.	34	27	N.S.
B-1	1	6	N.S.	11	26	.021	58	28	.0014
B-6	3	8	N.S.	4	10	N.S.	40	26	N.S.

* C, comparison group; D, delinquent group.

significantly higher incidence of pleasant economic events in their stories. As a rebellious low-status minority group, it would appear likely that the Latin delinquents had experienced the most status discontent. Yet it was not reflected in their stories. This pattern was, of course, consistent with the trend already noted for the Latin delinquents to have more pleasant and less unpleasant material in their stories. It was suggested above that this might be the result of increased defensiveness by the Latin delinquents. However, while the relation of defensiveness to antisocial material is obvious, it is less apparent how this would influence pleasant economic references.

Stories with Unpleasant Economic Events;
Number of Unpleasant Economic Instances

The stories were also coded to indicate the number of unpleasant economic events, such as losing a job, and the number of stories reporting such happenings. It was hoped that this might measure pessimism about economic matters in some degree. Of the 12 statistical analyses of the number of stories with unpleasant economic references told by the various groups, only one achieved statistical significance (see Table 68). In the Latin group, significantly more stories with unpleasant economic references were told to Card A-4 by the members of the comparison group ($\chi^2 = 4.99$, $p < .05$). This

Table 68

Number of Stories in Which Unpleasant Economic References Occur

Card	Story Type	Anglo C°	D°	Latin C	D	Mexican C	D
	Stories with unpleasant economic references	21	15	26	15	26	24
A-4	Stories without unpleasant economic references	29	35	24	35	24	26
	Total	50	50	50	50	50	50
	χ^{2a}	1.56		4.99		0.16	
	p (two tail)	N.S.		<.05		N.S.	
	Stories with unpleasant economic references	1	1	4	2	10	14
A-7	Stories without unpleasant economic references	49	49	46	48	40	36
	Total	50	50	50	50	50	50
	χ^{2a}	0.00		0.18		0.88	
	p (two tail)	N.S.		N.S.		N.S.	
	Stories with unpleasant economic references	2	3	4	6	19	15
B-1	Stories without unpleasant economic references	48	47	46	44	31	35
	Total	50	50	50	50	50	50
	χ^{2a}	0.00		0.11		0.71	
	p (two tail)	N.S.		N.S.		N.S.	
	Stories with unpleasant economic references	8	10	15	13	22	19
B-6	Stories without unpleasant economic references	42	40	35	37	28	31
	Total	50	50	50	50	50	50
	χ^{2a}	0.07		0.20		0.37	
	p (two tail)	N.S.		N.S.		N.S.	

a All chi-square values corrected for continuity when expected value ≤10.
° C, comparison group; D, delinquent group.

continued the trend in the Latin sample for the delinquents to tell more pleasant stories and nondelinquents more unpleasant stories.

Only one of the analyses of the relative number of unpleasant economic instances in the stories attained significance (see Table 69). The nondelinquent Anglos told stories with twice as many unpleasant events as did the delinquents on Card A-4 ($p=.03$). In the other analyses of the Picture Stories that have been discussed thus far, the few significant differences that were found in the Anglo group consistently indicated a higher incidence of unpleasant or antisocial stories or events in the stories of the delinquents. The present findings reversed this trend.

All in all, the analyses of the economic material in the Picture-Story Test did not indicate any major consistent differences between the delinquents and the nondelinquents in their perceptions of economic opportunities or limitations. Only four of the 48 statistical tests had a probability less than .05; on these four tests the direction of the findings was inconsistent and confusing, with the Latin and Anglo nondelinquents having more unpleasant material, and the Mexican nondelinquents and Latin delinquents having more pleasant material. The primary conclusion to be made is that the results did not offer any support to the notion that delinquents are characterized by significantly greater pessimism or discontent regarding

Table 69

Binomial Analyses of Differences in the Number of Unpleasant Economic Instances

	Anglo			Latin			Mexican		
Card	C*	D*	p (two tail)	C	D	p (two tail)	C	D	p (two tail)
A-4	32	16	.03	35	22	N.S.	49	53	N.S.
A-7	1	3	N.S.	5	2	N.S.	20	29	N.S.
B-1	3	3	N.S.	5	11	N.S.	32	34	N.S.
B-6	8	15	N.S.	20	20	N.S.	34	36	N.S.

* C, comparison group; D, delinquent group.

economic matters. In view of the problems associated with apperceptive test data, this cannot be taken as disproving any theoretical position, but by the same token it certainly does not offer any support either.

Effects of Verbal Fluency

In interpreting the results reported thus far, some readers may well be curious about the possible influence of differences in verbal fluency. Some people give longer responses to projective stimuli than others and these differences in response length are capable of influencing the scores of projective techniques (Megargee, 1966a; Zubin, Eron, & Schumer, 1965). It is certainly plausible that longer stories might have more pleasant or unpleasant events than short stories. If so, the obtained Picture-Story differences could be artifacts of differences in response length or verbal fluency.

In order to evaluate this possibility, the number of words in each story was counted. The protocols of the Mexican sample were counted in the original Spanish. The mean number of words used by each group in response to each card is presented in Table 70. Without individual variance estimates, obtainable only from the lost individual data, it was of course impossible to test the significance of the differences between the means. However, it is clear from an inspection of the data that in all but one case the mean

Table 70

Mean Number of Words in the Stories

Card	Anglo		Latin		Mexican	
	C*	D*	C	D	C	D
A-4	28	31	31	21	77	73
A-7	25	27	29	24	84	82
B-1	23	29	30	22	37	37
B-6	23	30	30	24	79	40

* C, comparison group; D, delinquent group.

numbers of words used by the delinquent and comparison subjects were almost identical. The exception to this was the responses of the Mexican sample to Card B-6. Here the Mexican comparison subjects responded with a mean of 79 words, while the delinquents used on the average only 40 words per story. This could have led to an increased number of events in the stories of the Mexican comparison group compared with the delinquents. However, a review of the data in Tables 59 through 69 indicated that on no comparison was there a significant difference between the Mexican delinquents and nondelinquents in response to this card. Therefore, it seems safe to conclude that the differences obtained between the delinquents and nondelinquents in the various analyses were not artifacts of differences in verbal fluency.

ANALYSES OF FIGURES IN VARIOUS ROLES

The second major series of analyses was concerned with the perception of the role of various story characters, as indicated by the behavior in which they were engaged in the story. As noted above, four areas of behavior or action of theoretical importance were singled out for study. These were advising or counseling, scolding or reprimanding, administering punishment, and being the recipient of feelings of responsibility or obligation. On each card, the attitude or behavior of each figure toward the boy who was the central character in the picture stories was evaluated. Stories involving supporting characters in various roles were, of course, more common in the responses to Cards A-4 and A-7, in which a teen-age boy was shown with an adult man or woman, than they were in the responses to Cards B-1 and B-6, in which the boy was depicted alone. Still, it was possible for other characters to figure in stories told about the latter two cards. For example, in response to Card B-6, which depicted a boy sitting in a chair staring at the floor, a subject might respond, "This is a boy who has gotten in trouble at school and he doesn't know what to do. He's sitting and wondering what to do. He goes to his father and his father tells him to go to the teacher and tell her he is sorry." In such a case, the father would be scored as offering advice or counsel, even though no one who could be interpreted as a father figure was pictured.

As noted above, a wide variety of figures entered into the 1,200 stories that were told. The stories were surveyed to determine the characters most frequently engaging in the behaviors selected for analysis. For example, the figure most frequently seen as offering advice on Card A-4 was the father; the most frequent advisors on Card A-7 were the mother, father, and teacher. Occasionally, other infrequently mentioned figures, such as an aunt, uncle, priest, and so on, would be depicted in an advisory or counseling role. In such cases, this was tallied under the heading "other." The raw tabulations of the figures most frequently seen in each of the four roles on each of the four cards are presented in Tables 71, 72, 73, and 74.

It had originally been hoped that the data could be analyzed in such a way as to permit a comparison of the perceived behavior of various individual characters, or, at least, comparisons of family figures with nonfamily figures, or authority figures with nonauthority figures. However, the infrequency with which any one character was perceived of as engaging in most of these acts made such subdivisions of the data impossible. Therefore, no attempt was made in the analyses to differentiate the specific figures in the different roles.

Instead, the total number of people depicted as functioning in a certain role in the stories of the delinquent members of a sample was compared with the total number seen in that role by the nondelinquents. This first analysis thus represented a rather global effort to compare the world view of the delinquents and nondelinquents —the extent to which they depicted others as "good guys" or "bad guys," as helping or as harsh—in their stories. If the results of this rather global analysis had been sufficiently encouraging, other finer and more discrete analyses would have been attempted. However, the data did not indicate that these would be fruitful.

Binomial tests were used to analyze the data. The assumption was made that, of the total number of characters perceived as engaged in a particular form of behavior on a given card, the delinquents and nondelinquents should each perceive half under the null hypothesis ($P=Q=.5$). The statistical test computed the exact two-tail probability of any deviations from an even division between the delinquent and nondelinquent groups in each sample and overall.

The results are presented in Table 75. It can be seen that the null hypothesis proved to be quite correct. None of the 64 significance tests indicated a significant difference between a delinquent and a comparison group. Inspection of the frequencies showed there were no consistent or noteworthy trends for differences between the

Table 71

Story Characters Described as Offering Advice or Counsel

Card	Character	Anglo C*	Anglo D*	Latin C	Latin D	Mexican C	Mexican D
	Mother	0	0	0	0	0	0
A-4	Father	3	4	5	0	2	2
	Other	1	1	0	1	1	3
	Mother	20	23	34	25	23	22
A-7	Father	1	0	2	0	0	1
	Teacher	2	1	1	0	1	0
	Other	5	2	0	4	1	2
	Parents	0	0	0	0	1	0
B-1	Mother	0	0	0	0	2	3
	Father	0	0	0	0	0	2
	Parents	0	0	0	0	0	1
B-6	Mother	1	0	0	1	0	2
	Father	1	0	0	0	1	2
	Other	0	0	0	0	0	2

* *C*, comparison group; *D*, delinquent group.

groups. Either lower-class delinquent and nondelinquent adolescents perceive others in about the same way, or the differences that may exist are not manifested in stories told in response to these pictures under these conditions. In view of the Card Sort data and the responses to the Cartoon Test, the second explanation would appear to be the more likely.

Table 72

Story Characters Described as Reprimanding or Scolding

Card	Character	Anglo C*	Anglo D*	Latin C	Latin D	Mexican C	Mexican D
	Parents	0	0	0	0	0	1
	Mother	0	0	2	0	0	1
A-4	Father	0	3	0	0	1	1
	Police	0	0	0	0	1	0
	Other	0	1	1	0	0	0
	Parents	0	0	0	0	1	0
	Mother	8	6	5	6	7	12
A-7	Father	0	1	0	0	0	1
	Teacher	1	2	0	1	0	0
	Other	1	0	2	2	1	0
	Parents	0	0	1	0	0	1
B-1	Mother	0	0	0	0	1	4
	Father	0	1	0	0	0	1
	Other	1	0	1	0	0	0
	Parents	0	1	1	1	0	1
	Mother	0	1	0	1	1	0
B-6	Father	0	0	0	1	0	0
	Teacher	0	0	0	0	1	0
	Other	0	1	1	0	0	1

* C, comparison group; D, delinquent group.

References to the Father

It will be recalled that the relationship between a boy and his father has been singled out as being of crucial importance as a factor contributing to delinquency. Generally, the better the father-

Table 73

Story Characters Described as Administering Punishment

Card	Character	Anglo C*	Anglo D*	Latin C	Latin D	Mexican C	Mexican D
A-4	Father	0	0	0	1	1	1
	Police	0	0	0	0	0	1
A-7	Parents	1	0	0	0	1	0
	Mother	0	2	1	0	2	0
	Father	0	0	0	0	0	1
	Teacher	0	0	1	0	1	1
	Other	0	0	0	0	1	0
B-1	Parents	1	1	0	0	2	0
	Father	0	0	0	0	1	1
	Police	0	0	0	0	1	1
	Other	0	0	0	0	2	0
B-6	Parents	0	0	0	0	2	0
	Mother	1	0	1	1	0	0
	Father	0	0	0	0	2	2
	Police	0	0	0	0	0	1
	Other	1	2	2	1	0	0

* C, comparison group; D, delinquent group.

Table 74

Story Characters toward Whom Responsibility or Obligation is Owed

Card	Character	Anglo		Latin		Mexican	
		C*	D*	C	D	C	D
	Parents	0	0	1	0	1	2
A-4	Mother	0	0	0	1	2	4
	Other	0	0	0	0	0	1
	Family	0	0	0	0	3	2
	Mother	0	2	0	0	1	6
	Police	0	0	0	1	0	0
A-7	Other	0	0	0	0	1	1
	Family	0	0	0	0	2	0
	Male adult	0	0	0	0	2	0
	Parents	0	0	0	1	2	0
	Mother	0	0	0	0	1	1
B-1	Police	0	0	0	1	0	0
	Other	0	0	0	0	0	2
	Family	0	0	0	0	3	6
	Male adult	0	0	0	0	2	1
	Parents	0	0	0	0	1	3
	Mother	0	0	1	0	0	1
B-6	Father	0	0	0	0	0	2
	Police	0	0	0	1	0	0
	Family	0	0	1	0	2	0

* C, comparison group; D, delinquent group.

Table 75

Number of Figures Seen in Various Roles

Role	Card	Anglo C*	Anglo D*	Anglo p (two tail)	Latin C	Latin D	Latin p (two tail)	Mexican C	Mexican D	Mexican p (two tail)	Overall C	Overall D	Overall p (two tail)
Figures offering advice or counsel	A-4	4	5	N.S.	5	1	N.S.	3	5	N.S.	12	11	N.S.
	A-7	28	25	N.S.	37	29	N.S.	25	25	N.S.	90	79	N.S.
	B-1	0	0	N.S.	0	0	N.S.	3	5	N.S.	3	5	N.S.
	B-6	2	0	N.S.	0	1	N.S.	1	7	.07	3	8	N.S.
Figures reprimanding or scolding	A-4	0	4	N.S.	3	0	N.S.	2	3	N.S.	5	7	N.S.
	A-7	10	9	N.S.	7	9	N.S.	9	13	N.S.	26	31	N.S.
	B-1	1	1	N.S.	2	0	N.S.	1	6	.12	4	7	N.S.
	B-6	0	3	N.S.	2	3	N.S.	2	2	N.S.	4	8	N.S.
Figures administering punishment	A-4	0	0	N.S.	0	1	N.S.	1	2	N.S.	1	3	N.S.
	A-7	10	9	N.S.	2	0	N.S.	5	2	N.S.	17	11	N.S.
	B-1	1	1	N.S.	0	0	N.S.	6	2	N.S.	7	3	N.S.
	B-6	2	2	N.S.	3	2	N.S.	4	3	N.S.	9	7	N.S.
Figures to whom responsibility or obligation is shown	A-4	0	0	N.S.	1	1	N.S.	6	9	N.S.	7	10	N.S.
	A-7	0	2	N.S.	0	1	N.S.	6	7	N.S.	6	10	N.S.
	B-1	0	0	N.S.	0	2	N.S.	8	10	N.S.	8	12	N.S.
	B-6	0	0	N.S.	2	1	N.S.	3	6	N.S.	5	7	N.S.

* C, comparison group; D, delinquent group.

son identification, the less likely that the boy will become delinquent. One measure of identification is the number of references to a figure on an apperceptive test. Bach and Bremer (1947) found that children with antisocial or psychopathic tendencies gave significantly fewer references to the father in doll play. Therefore, the number of references to the father in response to each of the four cards was examined. It was hypothesized that the delinquents' stories would have significantly fewer such references.

These data are summarized in Table 76. The significance of differences was tested with one-tail binomial tests. It can be seen that on none of the cards did the delinquents give significantly fewer references to the father.

Summary

Although projective tests are notoriously difficult to administer and score reliably or to interpret validly, they have been widely used in cross-cultural research. In the present study the subjects were asked to tell stories about four cards from the Symonds Picture-Story Test. After the Spanish protocols had been translated, the tests were first scored according to certain key elements or situations that appeared in the stories. These elements included the atmosphere of

Table 76

Number of References to the Father

	Anglo			Latin			Mexican		
Card	C*	D*	p (one tail)	C	D	p (one tail)	C	D	p (one tail)
A-4	20	28	N.S.	33	22	N.S.	24	25	N.S.
A-7	0	4	N.S.	1	1	N.S.	9	7	N.S.
B-1	0	3	N.S.	1	2	N.S.	7	9	N.S.
B-6	2	5	N.S.	3	3	N.S.	12	6	N.S.

* C, comparison group; D, delinquent group.

the stories, the occurrence of pleasant, unpleasant, and extremely unpleasant or antisocial events in the stories, and the incidence of references to pleasant or unpleasant economic events or situations.

There were relatively few significant differences between the delinquent and nondelinquent Anglos. The two Anglo groups differed significantly only on the incidence of antisocial or extremely unpleasant events in their stories, with the delinquents having a significantly higher proportion of stories containing such elements and, also, significantly more such events in the responses to three of the four cards. This finding was consistent with other studies that have reported a higher incidence of such material in delinquents' TAT scores. There were no significant differences in the atmosphere of the Anglos' stories, the incidence of pleasant or mildly unpleasant events or stories, or the rate of pleasant or unpleasant economic events. This could mean that there were no differences between the two Anglo groups in their general world view or economic milieu, or simply that while there may have been such differences they were not reflected in the apperceptive test material.

More significant differences were obtained in the Mexican sample than in the Anglo. When significant differences were found, their direction indicated that the nondelinquent Mexicans told stories in which more pleasant and fewer unpleasant or antisocial events took place. They were also characterized by more pleasant economic instances in their responses to the cards.

The pattern for the Latins differed from that observed for the other two samples, for among the Latins the delinquent group told the more positive stories. On the cards for which significant differences were obtained, it was the delinquents rather than the nondelinquents who told stories with a more pleasant tone, with fewer unpleasant or antisocial events, and with a more optimistic economic outlook. There was no immediate explanation for this reversal in the Latin sample aside from the possibility that being tested by a non-Latin may have resulted in much more defensiveness among the Latin delinquents. In any case, this shift in pattern severely limits any generalizations we might have been tempted to make on the basis of the results for the Anglos and Mexicans.

The second phase of data analysis consisted of identifying certain key characters in the stories and determining the frequency with which they were depicted in various roles, such as offering counsel or advice or administering punishment. No significant differences were found in the roles or behavior attributed to the various figures in the stories by the delinquents and nondelinquents. There were also no differences in the identification of the subjects with their fathers, as measured by the number of references to fathers within the stories.

CHAPTER 13

THE PHYSICAL EXAMINATION

Biological theories of criminality have a long history. One of the first such theories was formulated by Cesare Lombroso in 1876. In his first statement of his theory, Lombroso proposed that criminals could be recognized by distinctive physical characteristics or stigmata, such as an asymmetrical cranium, an apelike chin, a flattened nose, or animal-like pouches in the cheeks (Sutherland & Cressey, 1966; Vold, 1958). These characteristics were thought to identify people who were more primitive or savage, both in constitution and behavior.

It was natural that the *Zeitgeist*, or spirit of the times, in the late nineteenth century should have produced a biological theory of criminality. Franz Gall (1758–1828) and Johann Spurzheim (1776–1832) had maintained that there was a close link between brain functioning and behavior, suggesting that specific parts of the brain were responsible for specific behavioral traits. They hypothesized that the relative development of these brain areas could be diagnosed by inspecting the skull: a bump indicated that one part and its associated behavior was strongly developed, and a dent meant that an area and the trait controlled by it were underdeveloped. While never fully accepted, this study of "phrenology" achieved great popularity throughout the remainder of the nineteenth century; *The Journal of Phrenology* was born in 1823 and didn't die until 1911 (Boring, 1950).

Charles Darwin's *Origin of Species*, published in 1859, further emphasized man's biological nature. In the *Expression of the Emo-*

tions in Man and Animals, published in 1872, Darwin went on to propose that aspects of human emotional reactions depended upon the inheritance of behavior that was useful in animals but not in man. For example, he regarded the curling of the lip into a sneer as a remnant of the baring of the teeth by carnivorous animals (Boring, 1950, p. 472). Sigmund Freud's work in the late nineteenth and early twentieth centuries further emphasized the biological bases of behavior. Thus, while criminologists of the mid-twentieth century are inclined to look back at the work of Lombroso and the Italian School with condescension, if not contempt, Lombroso's work was clearly in the mainstream of the nineteenth-century thought and research, for many other eminent scholars were also seeking direct links between innate physiological structure and behavior. Indeed, while it is still fashionable for criminologists to adopt a purely environmentalist stance, research on brain chemistry and brain function, work on DNA and RNA, and recent progress in behavioral genetics (Fuller & Thompson, 1960; McClearn, 1964) indicate that extreme environmentalism soon will have to be modified and an interactionist approach adopted.

Unlike many theorists, Lombroso tested his hypotheses through empirical research using anthropological measurements made on samples of Italian criminals and comparison groups of soldiers. The adequacy of such a comparison group is, of course, questionable, since soldiers are usually superior physical specimens. Nevertheless, the use of any comparison group is commendable.

Later, Goring (1913) conducted a careful large-scale study in which the measurements of 3,000 English criminals were compared with those of large groups of civilians. Members of the Royal Engineers, university undergraduates, and hospital patients made up the bulk of the comparison samples. On the basis of this research, Goring arrived at the following general conclusion (1913, p. 173):

> In the present investigation we have exhaustively compared, with regard to many physical characters, different kinds of criminals with each other, and criminals, as a class, with the law-abiding public. From these comparisons, *no evidence has emerged confirming the existence of a physical criminal type, such as Lombroso and his disciples have described.* Our data do show that physical differences exist between different kinds of criminals: precisely as they exist between different kinds of law-abiding people. But, when allowance is made for a certain range of probable

variation, and when they are reduced to a common standard of age, stature, intelligence and class, etc., these differences tend entirely to disappear. Our results nowhere confirm the evidence, nor justify the allegations, of criminal anthropologists. They challenge their evidence at almost every point. In fact, both with regard to measurements and the presence of physical anomalies in criminals, our statistics present a startling conformity with similar statistics of the law-abiding classes. The final conclusion we are bound to accept until further evidence, in the train of long series of statistics, may compel us to reject or to modify an apparent certainty—our inevitable conclusion must be *that there is no such thing as a physical criminal type.*

According to Sutherland and Cressey (1966, p. 128), "Goring's work is generally accepted as having demolished the early Lombrosian view that criminals are characterized by certain stigmata and constitute an inferior biological type."

However, E. A. Hooton, a Harvard anthropologist, attempted to resurrect Lombroso's theory. Never one to mince words, he attacked Goring's work as follows (Hooton, 1939b, pp. 16–17 *passim*):

Charles Goring was a medical officer in the English prison service, who published in 1913 a work entitled "The English Convict." This book has been commonly regarded as a final refutation of Lombroso's theories pertaining to criminal type—especially by criminologists who have not read it, or have been unable to understand it. . . .

Goring was frankly and violently prejudiced against Lombroso and all of his theories . . .

Impelled by his moral convictions, Goring used his statistical genius to distort the results of his investigation to conformity with his bias. He was quite unable to emulate the Walrus in divorcing his scientific procedure from his social sentiments. The following are his principal methods of perverting evidence: a specious and unjustifiable use of statistical devices for the purpose of reducing and minimizing physical differences actually observed between different classes of criminals or between criminals and non-criminals; the practice of impugning the accuracy and validity of his original data only when the results fail to conform to his bias; the use of comparative data which are really not comparable at all, having been derived from populations which are ethnically diverse from his criminals and which have been studied by different techniques; his selection of anthropometric measurements and observations which have never been considered criminologically important, and his neglect of those which have been regarded by criminal anthropologists as the most significant;

his disregard of the ethnic and even racial heterogeneity of his series, which consists not only of English, Welsh, and Scotch, but even of a smattering of other races and nationalities.

Hooton's primary objection was to Goring's use of techniques similar to analysis of covariance or partial correlation that enable investigators to determine the difference between criminals and noncriminals on a variable like height while statistically holding constant some other variable, such as age or intelligence, on which the groups may vary. The present investigators are inclined to question the legitimacy of this objection.

Hooton (1939a) examined 13,873 American criminals and contrasted them with a control group of 3,203 noncriminals, composed of 1,976 college students, firemen, policemen, and hospital patients, and 1,227 mental hospital patients. His principal report concerned the differences among native whites of native parentage, who constituted 4,212 of the criminals and 613 of the noncriminals. Hooton and his associates compared these groups on a number of anthropological indices. They summarized some of the characteristics that significantly differentiated the native white criminals from the controls as including, "Deficiencies of age, weight, chest breadth, head circumference, upper face height, nose height, ear length" (Hooton, 1939a, p. 305). Moreover, the following morphological variations were noted among the criminals (Hooton, 1939a, p. 305):

Excess of straight hair, deficiencies of low waves, deficiencies of blue eyes and homogeneous irides, excesses of submedium cheek fullness and of submedium gonial angles, deficiency of marked overbite, excess of submedium roll of helix, deficiency of medium and pronounced, [sic] deficiency of medium necks and excess of long, thin necks.

From data like these Hooton drew a number of conclusions, such as (1939a, p. 308):

Our information definitely proves that it is from the physically inferior element of the population that native born criminals of native parentage are mainly derived. My present hypothesis is that physical inferiority is of principally hereditary origin; that these hereditary inferiors naturally gravitate into unfavorable environmental conditions; and that the worst or weakest of them yield to social stresses which force them into criminal behavior.

He further concluded (Hooton, 1939a, p. 309):

Crime is the resultant of the impact of environment upon low grade human organisms. It follows that the elimination of crime can be effected only by the extirpation of the physically, mentally, and morally unfit, or by their complete segregation in a socially aseptic environment.

Hooton's study was widely criticized (Vold, 1958; Sutherland & Cressey, 1966). As might be expected, his sampling procedures were attacked. His control group has been described as "a fantastic conglomeration of noncriminal civilians" (Vold, 1958, p. 64) and as "worthless as a sample of the noncriminal population" (Sutherland & Cressey, 1966, p. 129). Moreover, critics have pointed out that convicted prisoners are a selectively biased sample that is not representative of the total criminal population.

A particularly weak point is the fact that Hooton did not present any adequate independent criteria of what constitutes physical inferiority. Assuming, for example, that the excess of straight hair noted above was not the result of biased sampling, and that if the study were cross-validated it would still be found to differentiate criminals and civilians, who is to say that straight hair is a sign of degeneracy or inferiority? Hooton's reasoning appears to be circular. If a sign characterized criminals it was regarded as a mark of inferiority, since criminals are known to be inferior; the presence of this "sign of inferiority" was then used to support the original notion that criminals are inferior.

Another drawback to the study was the fact that Hooton overlooked differences between civilians from different locales and from different walks of life that equalled or exceeded those between the criminals and the civilians. Since he made no effort to correct for such differences, his findings could have been the result of uncontrolled regional or occupational differences (Vold, 1958). Here the use of some of Goring's statistical techniques would have strengthened Hooton's study.

Finally, although Hooton asserted that physical differences were the product of heredity, he did not present any data to support this claim. While the genotype undoubtedly influences the phenotype, prenatal and postnatal environmental factors also play a major role in determining physical characteristics. Diet, health, and exercise are only a few of the nongenetic factors that are major determinants of many physical variables.

More recently, Sheldon (1949) has attempted to relate delinquency to physical constitution. Sutherland and Cressey (1966, pp. 130–131) have critically described this work as follows:

> Sheldon has more recently made another attempt to differentiate criminals from noncriminals in respect to somatotype. He found three somatotypes—the endomorphic which is round and soft, the mesomorphic which is round and hard, and the ectomorphic which is thin and fragile—and claimed that three temperamental types and three psychiatric types are closely related with their somatotypes. After making a study of 200 young adults in a Boston welfare agency, whom he described as "more or less delinquent," he concluded that delinquents are different from nondelinquents in their somatotypes and in their related temperamental and psychiatric types. Also he assumed that these differences are in the direction of inferiority and that the inferiority is inherited. His data, in fact, do not justify the conclusion that the delinquents are different from the nondelinquents in general, the conclusion that the difference if it exists indicates inferiority, or the conclusion that the inferiority if it exists is inherited. On the contrary, he found that body types of these delinquents are much like those of business and military leaders and of psychiatrists. He had no criterion of inferiority. His only evidence of inheritance was that sons resemble their parents, and this similarity obviously may be due to social experience rather than heredity. The Gluecks have used the logic of Kretschmer and Sheldon in a study of juvenile delinquents. Like Sheldon, they have adopted a system characterized by a noted physical anthropologist as a "new Phrenology in which the bumps of the buttocks take the place of the bumps on the skull."

Many of those who have investigated the physical differences between delinquents and nondelinquents have explicitly or implicitly assumed that evidence of such differences would support the notion that delinquency is inherited. Hooton's comments have already been cited; Sheldon (1949) attacked the uncontrolled breeding of the past that led to the delinquency of the present and suggested that in the absence of a world-wide program of controlled breeding or contraception a thermonuclear war might be the only solution. Once again we must re-emphasize that even if clear-cut, consistent physical differences between delinquents and nondelinquents should be established, it would not prove delinquency and criminality to be inherited. It has already been pointed out how environmental factors can influence physique; such environmental factors could also influence behavior. Moreover, genotypically determined physical characteristics can also affect environment by influencing the reactions of others and by expanding or limiting opportunities that are available (Anastasi, 1958). Sex, for example, is undoubtedly genetically determined. However, much of what is regarded as "masculine" or "feminine" behavior is determined not by the sex chromosomes, but by tribal taboos and cultural role prescriptions. Similarly, more mesomorphs may be found among the ranks of the delinquents simply because their physique is such that they are more apt to win fights and thus be rewarded for aggressiveness than is the ectomorph or endomorph. Thus, the phenotype, which is only partly determined by the genotype, can influence behavior indirectly by establishing different reinforcement probabilities. If lawful relations between crime and physique were to be established, all these alternative explanations would have to be ruled out before a direct causal link between genotype and delinquency could be tenable.

Another approach to the investigation of physiological factors and delinquency has been through the study of the health of delinquents and nondelinquents. Some theorists investigated this dimension in order to establish the biological inferiority of delinquents; others, with an environmentalist orientation, did so to determine if the delinquents had perhaps been more frustrated or handicapped by poor health or nutrition.

Burt (1944) stated: "Most repeated offenders are far from robust; they are frail, sickly and infirm . . . In London I find that defective physicals are, roughly speaking, one and a quarter times more frequent among delinquent children as they are among nondelinquent children from the same schools and streets." It is, of course, impossible to determine if this was a cause of delinquency or the effect of Borstal confinement. Burt's general conclusion was that the health of most delinquents was not seriously impaired relative to that of nondelinquents nor were the differences between them substantial.

Sutherland and Cressey (1966, p. 131) reported that the 1905 Massachusetts census found an excessive amount of lameness and deafness among offenders. They also state that optometrists have reported a much greater incidence of defective vision among delinquents. It could be, as the optometrists suggested, that the consequent physical irritation and difficulties in reading drive children into delinquency. Another possibility is that a person who is nearsighted, hard of hearing, or lame is more likely to be caught by the police.

Healy and Bronner (1936) compared 105 delinquents with their nondelinquent siblings and found that there had been a greater incidence of physical illness and developmental problems among the delinquents at an early age, but only minor differences were found when the subjects were examined during adolescence. The fact that these investigators also found a markedly higher incidence of neurotic behavior disorders, nail-biting, and enuresis among the delinquents also suggests the possibility that at least some of the early health problems, such as frequent illness, difficult toilet training, fussiness in infancy, and underweight in childhood, could have been of psychophysiological origin. If so, both the health difficulties and the delinquency could have had a common cause instead of one causing the other.

Glueck and Glueck (1950) included a medical examination in their study of 500 delinquents and 500 matched controls. The medical findings for the two groups were quite similar and the Gluecks concluded (Glueck and Glueck, 1950, p. 181):[1]

> Summarizing the findings of the medical examination of the delinquents and non-delinquents, we see that the view that delinquents are in poorer health than non-delinquents receives no support. Very little, if any, difference exists between the physical condition of the two groups as a whole.

Similarly, Robins' (1966) longitudinal study of 500 children seen in a child-guidance clinic found no significant differences in histories of physical illness, birth difficulties, or injuries between those who became sociopaths and the other patients who did not.

Thus, while some investigators have found a greater incidence of illness and physical defect among delinquents and criminals, others

---

[1] It should be noted that these findings refer only to the medical examination for evidence of physical disease or defect. There was also an anthropological examination, based on photographs, which revealed a number of significant differences in body size and shape.

have not. Even when such differences are found, it is usually difficult to interpret them. As has been pointed out, the illness might cause the delinquency or the delinquency might cause the defect, or both the defect and the delinquency might have a common cause, such as parental neglect. The chain of causation may be direct, as in the case of a criminal wounded in a holdup, or indirect, as in the case of a person with crossed eyes who is ridiculed by classmates and who consequently associates with a delinquent fringe group. Whatever the relation between physical disability and crime, it is clear that, while physical illness or defect may be an explanation for some crimes by some individuals, it cannot be considered a general explanation for crime, as some have hoped. Even studies that have demonstrated significantly more illness among a group of delinquents or criminals than among a group of controls have typically shown only a minority of the criminal group to be so afflicted. For example, serious visual defects were three times more common among the delinquents than the controls in Healy and Bronner's study; nevertheless, only 17 per cent of the delinquent sample had such defects.

One problem that has plagued much of the work on physical abnormalities and delinquency has been finding appropriate control groups. This was particularly true of the work investigating Lombroso's theories, in which soldiers or college students were contrasted with prisoners or in which felons from one region were compared with noncriminals from another. Since different ethnic groups are known to differ in height and weight, careful controls over ethnic background are necessary if valid results are to be obtained. However, such controls have often been lacking. Because social class, region, and ethnic background were fairly well controlled in the present study, it seemed that the inclusion of a medical examination might well shed valuable light on some of these unresolved issues.

Procedures

Each boy in the study was examined by a medical doctor. The medical examination was limited to physical characteristics that could be observed quickly with the use of only the simplest equipment and that might be expected on an a priori basis to be significant in the process of adjustment. The first criterion was dictated

by the practical limitations under which the study operated. Since
many examinations took place in schools, it was felt that half an
hour was as much time as could be devoted to the physical examination. Financial limitations precluded the use of laboratory tests or
of diagnostic instruments too heavy, cumbersome, or expensive to
be readily available in the schools. The physicians were supplied
with a watch, a scale, and a ruler and were expected to provide a
stethoscope and a sphygmomanometer. The characteristics chosen
under the second criterion included those likely to be easily observable in social situations and those that might be expected to
affect the individual's performance, particularly in competitive activities, such as school work or sports. Under the first heading came
such traits as height, weight, and deformities; under the second,
defects of vision, hearing, and circulation. The items to be included
were selected with the aid and advice of a physician, then included
in a physical examination form[2] designed to be filled out completely
by the doctor in the course of the examination.

Arrangements were made to have the examination administered
by a physician who would see each boy alone in a private room. The
nature of the examination was explained to the boy and he was
then requested to strip to the waist. A few of the boys were somewhat uncooperative, but none refused to be examined.

The first medical examination was given in July, 1959, and the
last in May, 1961. The locales varied widely, including a number
of schools in San Antonio and various institutions for delinquents
within Texas, not to mention the examinations given in Mexico. As
a result, a total of four different physicians served on the project
during the course of the investigation. The number of subjects in
the various groups seen by each of these men is presented in Table
77. It is likely that the criteria for normality and disorder varied
somewhat from one physician to another, particularly on the more
ambiguous and subjective items such as "disfigurements of the face"
or "posture." On the more strictly medical items, such as the "condition of the tonsils" or "blood pressure," reliability seemed quite
adequate.

These interexaminer differences would not have presented any
particular problem if the four examiners had each seen an equal

_____
[2] See Appendix 5 for the physical examination form.

Table 77

Number of Subjects in Each Group Examined by Each Physician

Physician	Anglo		Latin		Mexican	
	C*	D*	C	D	C	D
A	50	24	50	14	0	0
B	0	0	0	0	50	50
C	0	15	0	36	0	0
D	0	11	0	0	0	0

* C, comparison group; D, delinquent group.

number of subjects from all six groups, or even an equal number from the delinquent and comparison groups within each ethnic sample. While all the Mexican subjects were examined by a single physician, time and geography prevented such systematic sampling of the Anglo or Latin samples. As a result, examiner differences could have contributed to systematic differences being found on some of the more subjective items.

Occasionally, the examining physicians failed to record anything in the space after a query like "condition of lungs." In some cases the physicians meant this to indicate that there was no abnormality, or, in the case of a variable like "number of missing teeth," to indicate that there were no missing teeth. However, it could also mean that the physician had simply neglected to make the required observation or had forgotten to make the proper entry. Since there was no way to determine what the physician had intended, the tabulator classified all such entries as "no information." It is for this reason that on a few analyses the number of observations was less than 50 in a group. However, in no case were there less than 44 in a group and it was rare for more than one or two cases to fall into this category.

Results

The results of the physical examination will be presented one variable at a time. The first set of data to be presented will concern general aspects of the body, such as height, weight, state of nutrition, and general development. Next, data regarding the head will be presented and discussed. This will include the shape of the skull, disfigurements of the face, and the number of carious and missing teeth. This will be followed by data regarding the condition of the trunk and limbs, including bodily deformities, posture, and the condition of the arms and legs. Next the condition of the skin will be presented, followed by data regarding specific organ systems, including adenoids, tonsils, lungs, and circulatory system. Finally, the sensory systems will be discussed, and data regarding visual and auditory acuity and visual defects presented. For each variable, salient findings from the literature will be presented, followed by a presentation and discussion of the results of the present investigation.

GENERAL PHYSICAL VARIABLES

Height

In the search for physical characteristics that might differentiate criminals and noncriminals, it is natural that height would be extensively investigated. Not only are data regarding height and weight readily available from medical examinations conducted on newly arrived prison inmates, but also it can be argued that the shorter person is "inferior" so that height has been regarded as an index of physical inferiority.

Vold (1958) reported data from an anthropological study by August Drähms conducted in 1900, in which the heights of 2,000 inmates of Elmira Reformatory, 2,000 inmates of San Quentin, and an unreported number of Amherst College students were compared. The mean height of the Amherst students was 67.9 inches, as compared with 66.7 inches for the Elmira inmates and 66.8 inches for the San Quentin inmates. Vold also reported the results of a study by Frances Kellor in 1901 in which she reported the mean height of a group of 55 white women students as being 26 mm. greater than that of a group of 60 white women criminals.

While Goring (1913) found few significant differences in his study of the English convict, he did find that the mean height of his sample of convicts was less than that of his control group. Goring interpreted this as indicating an hereditary inferiority on the part of the criminal; however, the representativeness of his control sample, which included a substantial number of Royal Engineers, can easily be questioned.

Hooton (1939a) contrasted his sample of native white criminals with civilians examined in his and other studies. He found the criminals to be significantly shorter, with a mean difference of 1.02 cm.; the mean height of his criminal sample was also less than the mean height of samples of Americans reported in other studies. The major criticisms of Hooton's study have already been noted.

East (1946) studied the physical characteristics of 4,000 English adolescent offenders at Wormwood Scrubs Boys' Prison from 1930 to 1936. Contrasting recidivists with first offenders, he found no significant differences in stature.

In a study that was far better controlled than most of those reviewed thus far, Glueck and Glueck (1950) compared the height of their 500 delinquent subjects with that of their 500 matched controls and found the difference to be insignificant. The nondelinquents were slightly taller, but the mean difference was only 0.41 inches.

The results of the present study are presented in Table 78. In each of the three ethnic groups the delinquents were slightly shorter; in none of the groups was the difference statistically significant. When the data were combined and the overall difference between the de-

Table 78

Height in Inches

	Anglo		Latin		Mexican		Overall	
	C*	D*	C	D	C	D	C	D
x̄	67.34	66.54	65.22	64.02	64.54	63.62	65.70	64.73
σ	3.45	4.65	3.52	3.10	3.71	2.87	3.56	3.63
N	50	50	50	50	50	50	150	150
t	0.98		1.81		1.39		2.37	
p (two tail)	N.S.		N.S.		N.S.		<.02	

* C, comparison group; D, delinquent group.

linquents and nondelinquents tested, the difference did prove to be statistically reliable ($t=2.37$, $p<.02$). The direction of this difference was consistent with those reported by other investigators, with delinquents being almost a full inch shorter.

It has been noted that Goring and others have interpreted similar phenotypic data as indicating genetic inferiority of the criminal. This is only one of a number of possible interpretations. Height is certainly influenced by heredity. However, it would be highly dubious to argue from this alone that delinquency is hereditary. Outlining the deductive steps will illustrate the logical flaws in this argument:

Proposition 1.   Height is influenced by genotype.
Proposition 2.   Convicted criminals are significantly shorter than noncriminals.
Proposition 3.   Shorter people are biologically inferior.
Conclusion: Criminality is a result of hereditary biological inferiority.

Even supposing one were rash enough to agree to all the propositions, it is clear that the conclusion does not necessarily follow.

Others may use these data to support an environmental deprivation interpretation of delinquency. The logical steps here are no better:

Proposition 1.   A poor environment can result in shorter stature.
Proposition 2.   Delinquents are shorter than nondelinquents.
Conclusion 1:   The delinquents have a poorer environment.
Proposition 3.   Poor environments can cause delinquency.
Conclusion 2:   The shorter stature of the delinquents proves that their delinquency was the result of a poorer environment.

A similar analysis would demonstrate that an interpretation of delinquency as a reaction formation against feelings of inferiority induced by shorter stature is equally speculative.

Turning to another aspect of the data, we see that the results illustrated the interaction of genetic and environmental factors on height, as well as the importance of ethnic and regional controls in physiological studies. The data in Table 78 clearly showed the Anglos to be the tallest, followed by the Latins, with the Mexicans shortest in stature.[3] Genetic differences were probably responsible for much of the difference between the Anglos and Latins, who shared the lower-class San Antonio environment but who probably stemmed from separate gene pools. Environmental differences, however, were probably one of the major determinants of the fact that the Latins living in the United States were taller than the Mexicans living in Monterrey. (This interpretation is supported by the work of Goldstein [1943] who found similar differences between Mexican-Americans and Mexicans, and who also noted that the North American-born children of Mexican-born immigrants were significantly taller than their parents.)

These differences between the ethnic samples highlight the importance of adequate controls for ethnic origin and for region in the study of physiological and anthropological phenomena. While a consistent difference was found between the delinquents and nondelinquents, the absolute amount of this difference was quite small relative to the differences in height noted between the ethnic and regional groups. Biased sampling could easily produce major differences.

The present data, which stem from what the investigators feel are reasonably well-controlled samples, indicated that the finding consistently noted in the literature for criminals to be shorter than noncriminals is probably a reliable difference that has cross-cultural generality. However, the absolute magnitude of this difference was slight and large numbers of subjects were needed before it attained statistical significance.

Weight

Although it is much more subject to environmental influences and variations as a result of diet, as well as to systematic changes with age, weight has also been extensively studied. The expectation of most investigators has been that delinquents or criminals would be lighter than normal control groups, either because of inherited biological inferiority or because of economic privation. Most, but not all, studies have obtained data supporting this expectation.

[3] Because of sampling differences already noted, it is not strictly valid to compare the different ethnic samples. Nevertheless, an analysis of variance that was surreptitiously made on the data regarding stature indicated that the ethnic group differences were highly significant ($F = 17.89$, $p < .001$).

Vold (1958) reported the results of a study conducted by Kellor in 1901 that obtained results in the opposite direction. Kellor found that her sample of 60 white female criminals had a mean weight of 129 pounds, as compared with 124 pounds for her sample of 55 white women students. Vold did not report how close in age the two samples were, an unfortunate omission, since weight is likely to increase with age. If the criminals were in prison it is likely that they had a starchier diet and less exercise than the students, and this, too, could have increased the average weight.

Goring (1913) found that weight was one of the few variables that reliably differentiated his English convicts from the control groups. With the exception of those criminals convicted of fraud, his criminal groups weighed three to seven pounds less than his civilian contrast groups. Hooton's (1939a) data were in agreement with Goring's in this respect, showing an 11.7-pound difference between his criminal and civilian groups. Hooton noted that this difference could be an artifact of the younger age of his criminal sample, so he compared the weights of those criminals and civilians between the ages of 35 and 39. Even with age thus controlled, he found the criminals to be significantly lighter. Vold (1958) has pointed out that this difference in weight is meaningful only if the diet is known and standardized, particularly if this difference is used to support the notion of innate differences. Hooton, of course, could not control diet nor has any other investigator in this area, with the possible exceptions of East (1946) and Healy and Bronner (1936).

These latter investigators both studied physical differences among juvenile, as opposed to adult, criminals. Healy and Bronner (1936), it will be recalled, contrasted 105 delinquents with their nondelinquent siblings. Insofar as both groups were living in the same households, it can be assumed that the diets of the two groups were comparable. They reported that 12 per cent of the delinquent siblings had a history of being very underweight in childhood, in contrast to only 5 per cent of the nondelinquent siblings. East (1946) compared first offenders and recidivists in an English institution for delinquents. He found no difference in weight between first and second offenders; third offenders, on the other hand, were somewhat heavier, in contrast to most of the findings thus far. However, this difference was not significant when age differences were controlled. When East compared the weight of his 4,000 delinquents with the norms for employed males and artisans in London and other large towns, he found no significant differences.

Finally, the Gluecks (1950) found their delinquent sample to have a somewhat higher mean weight (112.09 lbs.) than their nondelinquent sample (109.21 lbs.). While this difference did not attain acceptable levels of statistical significance (Critical Ratio = 1.83, p [two-tail] = .067), it was still a noteworthy trend, particularly since it was in the opposite direction from that generally expected. The Gluecks noted that the younger delinquents were lighter in weight but that the weight of the older delinquents exceeded that of the older controls. These and other physical data suggested a delayed pubertal growth spurt on the part of the delinquents. Since Jones and Bayley (1950) have found that early-maturing boys are better adjusted and more esteemed by their peers than late maturers, it would not be surprising to find more late-maturing boys among the ranks of the delinquents.

The investigations of weight differences in the literature have thus indicated that adult male criminals tend to be lighter than various noncriminal contrast groups. Female and adolescent male offenders, on the other hand, tend to be heavier than the contrast groups when significant differences are found. The studies by Healy and Bronner and by the Gluecks suggested that the delinquents might have been relatively underweight in childhood or before puberty and later equalled or exceeded the contrast groups in middle or late adolescence.

The mean weights of the various groups in the present investigation are presented in Table 79. In all three samples, the comparison groups were heavier on the average than were the delinquents. The difference in mean weight was 11.4 pounds in the Latin sample, 7.0 in the Anglo, and only 1.2 in the Mexican. In the Latin sample this difference attained statistical significance ($t = 2.29$, $p < .025$), as it did in the overall analysis of the combined groups ($t = 2.44$, $p < .02$). If we were to adopt Hooton's reasoning, we would infer from this that the data indicated that among Latins delinquency stems from innate biological inferiority. Being more environmentally oriented, we prefer to look to possible differences in diet or exercise for an explanation. If the diet and the amount of exercise provided in the Mexican institution in which all the Mexican delinquents were confined were similar to that received by the nondelinquent Mexicans

Table 79

Weight in Pounds

	Anglo		Latin		Mexican		Overall	
	C*	D*	C	D	C	D	C	D
$\bar{x}$**	135.50	128.50	128.10	116.70	118.30	117.10	127.30	120.77
σ**	23.32	26.11	29.94	18.55	23.71	14.26	25.84	20.24
N	50	50	50	50	50	50	150	150
t	1.41		2.29		0.31		2.44	
p (two tail)	N.S.		<.025		N.S.		<.02	

* C, comparison group; D, delinquent group.
** $\bar{x}$, mean; σ, standard deviation.

at home, there would probably be little difference between the Mexican delinquents and nondelinquents. On the other hand, if the diet in the Texas institutions were less fattening or if the Texas delinquents had more exercise than their free-world peers, they might be lighter.

In any case, the present data are similar to those reported for adult male criminals in the literature but discrepant with those reported for juvenile delinquents. This is particularly true with respect to the Gluecks' research, in which the Massachusetts Anglo delinquents were noted to be somewhat heavier. The diversity of these findings points up the wisdom of not using weight data, which are influenced by so many variables, as the basis for far-reaching conclusions about the causes of delinquency.

Nutrition

The nutritional state of offenders has been investigated much less than height and weight. Some may attribute this to the fact that, unlike height and weight, these data are not routinely collected; others, who are less charitable, might suggest that many physical investigators have a hereditary bias and the discovery of significant nutritional differences might be evidence for environmental influences that they would prefer to ignore. However, we prefer to believe that the failure to investigate nutritional state has been a result of the difficulties associated with measuring or rating this variable. A trained physician is obviously required, and even then a rather subjective estimate must be made that may vary from rater to rater. Moreover, a global appraisal without expensive laboratory tests is not really an adequate test of nutrition. People may appear quite robust but still be suffering from anemia, calcium deficiencies, or other nutritional difficulties.

Scholars who have taken note of nutritional differences have generally focused on adolescent offenders. Their general conclusion has been that delinquents are more likely to be poorly nourished than nondelinquents. These conclusions are, of course, no better than the adequacy with which other factors are controlled. Burt's (1944) observation that the English delinquents he studied appeared less robust and more poorly nourished has already been noted. East (1946), in his review of research on the relation of physical factors to criminal behavior, noted two studies of nutrition as follows (East, 1946, p. 26):

> Verner Wiley, in 1930, reported to the London County Council on 803 children (696 boys and 107 girls) admitted to Ponton-road place of detention. The group showed "a very marked inferiority in respect of nutritional state and physical make-up when compared with the average London children as met with in the age group examinations."
>
> In an investigation into Juvenile Delinquency in the Liverpool area J. H. Bagot found among the delinquents and the general school population the most significant difference was a considerably greater amount of subnormal nutrition among the delinquents. He considered that there might be some reason to think that inferior health is an important factor in causing delinquency.

The results of the present investigation are presented in Table 80. No noteworthy nutritional differences were found between the delinquent and comparison groups in the Anglo or Latin samples, despite the fact that significant weight differences had been obtained in the latter sample. In the Mexican sample a highly significant difference was noted; 64 per cent of the comparison group were judged to have "excellent or good" nutrition as compared with only 40 per cent of the delinquent group ($\chi^2 = 7.89$, $p < .005$).[4]

[4] It will be recalled that a single physician examined all the Mexican subjects, so these differences were not an artifact of interexaminer differences.

Table 80

State of Nutrition

Rating	Anglo C*	Anglo D*	Latin C	Latin D	Mexican C	Mexican D	Overall C	Overall D
Excellent or good	33	29	28	30	34	20	95	79
Fair, poor, or very poor	16	19	19	19	16	30	51	68
Total	49	48	47	49	50	50	146	147
χ^2	0.51		0.00		7.89		3.90	
p (two tail)	N.S.		N.S.		$<.005$		$<.05$	

* C, comparison group; D, delinquent group.

The lower nutrition of the Mexican delinquents is consistent with some of the other data that have been reported. While the mean income levels of the delinquents and nondelinquents were almost identical in the Anglo and Latin samples, it will be recalled from Chapter 6 that the average income of the fathers of the Mexican delinquents was only 84 per cent of that of the nondelinquents' fathers. Further corroboration comes from a reanalysis of the data of the Choices Test. If the Mexican delinquents had significantly poorer nutrition than the Mexican comparison group, while there were no differences in nutrition in the other samples, one might then expect them to indicate they would buy food more often. To test this hypothesis, the data from Table 28, regarding how the members of the various groups would choose to spend 25 cents or 20 centavos, were reviewed. The number of subjects in each group choosing to buy food, candy, or soft drinks was extracted, and the differences were tested with the binomial test. It can be seen from the data in Table 81 that the Mexican delinquents did indeed choose to buy food significantly more often than did the nondelinquent Mexicans, while in the Anglo sample there was no difference and in the Latin sample the opposite trend was noted.

It is interesting to note that the Mexican subjects differed with respect to nutrition despite the fact that there was no difference in weight. Average weight coupled with below-average nutrition could be the result of a starchy institutional diet combined with inadequate opportunity to exercise. Thus, the data regarding nutrition could indicate economic deprivation but they could also indicate the effects of confinement subsequent to delinquent acts. Further research on the association of nutrition and delinquency in non-institutionalized Mexican samples would be desirable, particularly since the findings would be quite relevant to economic privation theories of delinquency.

General Development

"General development" was meant to summarize the overall developmental status and health of each individual, relative to the norms for boys of his age and background. A number of quite diverse observations in the literature are relevant to this general variable.

In 1925 Burt studied the development of 197 delinquent boys and girls aged five to 18. Consistent with the later research of Jones and Bayley (1950), he noted that delinquency in the boys was likely to be associated with delayed development and small size, while for girls the opposite pattern was found, with early sexual development and large size being related to delinquency. He indicated that abnormal development was probably a cause of delinquency in 12 per cent of the boys and 5 per cent of the girls.

East (1946) reported the results of a study carried out by Rhodes in 1936 for the Oldham Council for Mental Health. According to East, Rhodes found 18.8 per cent of the offenders were of above-

Table 81

Binomial Comparison with Respect to Spending 25 Cents or 20 Centavos on Food

	Anglo		Latin		Mexican	
	C*	D*	C	D	C	D
Number buying food	20	20	23	15	17	33
p (two tail)	N.S.		N.S.		<.024	

* C, comparison group; D, delinquent group.

average physique, 48.9 per cent were normal, and 32.2 per cent were below average. (The criterion for abnormality in this investigation was a deviation of the ratio of height:weight by more than 5 per cent from the anthropometric ratio given in the Board of Education Medical Report.)

Goring (1913) exhaustively studied the health records and the causes of mortality of his sample of English convicts and compared them with similar data for noncriminals. On the basis of this research he concluded (Goring, 1913, p. 228):

> In the main, the present investigation, dealing with three very different kinds of material—(a) statistics of good health and delicacy, observed in English convicts; (b) statistics of sickness amongst all prisoners during the last decennium; and (c) statistics of death from old age amongst the inmates of all State prisons during the past 23 years—in the main, this exhaustive inquiry indicates that there is no relation between a healthy or delicate constitution *per se* and the committing of crime; and that the coefficient of correlation between these conditions is .07: a value which shows that, if anything, the criminal is healthier on the whole than is the law-abiding subject.

Goring also observed that burglars, who constituted 90 per cent of his criminal population, and arsonists were "puny in their general bodily habit" compared with other criminals and the population at large.

Healy and Bronner (1936) noted a number of salient differences in their comparison of delinquent and nondelinquent siblings. First, in regard to sexual development, of the 105 delinquents, four were very premature in sexual development and five were retarded. Only one nondelinquent's sexual development was abnormal. Thus, marked deviations in the onset of sexual development were nine times more likely to be found among the delinquents than among their nondelinquent siblings.

Secondly, Healy and Bronner found that the general health of the delinquents as children was much poorer. While 75 of the 105 nondelinquent boys had a history of distinctly good health, this could be said of only 44 of the delinquents; while only eight of the nondelinquents had a history of many illnesses or of severe illness, this was true of 28 of the delinquents.

The most marked differences, however, occurred in the area of physical problems that are related to emotional difficulties. Hyperactivity and extreme restlessness was noted in 46 of the delinquents but none of the nondelinquents; similarly, 22 of the delinquents were noted to have been enuretic after the age of eight, but only four of the nondelinquents had this problem. Thus, Healy and Bronner's data indicated that developmental abnormalities, a history of poor health, and symptoms of possible emotional disturbance were much more common among delinquents than among their nondelinquent siblings.

There was much less difference in the current health status of the subjects, however. Interpreting their results, Healy and Bronner (1936, p. 57) pointed out:

> It can be seen . . . that many more of the delinquents than of the controls had been subject to interference with healthy normal development. The relationship however between health conditions and behavior tendencies is not easy to determine. One might speculate, for example, about the significance of severe illness—as consequent to the disease was there organically caused irritability or restlessness, or was the child spoiled or overprotected on account of illness, or did he through illness acquire specially demanding and selfish attitudes?

The Gluecks (1950) also obtained developmental data that were consistent with Healy and Bronner's results. While no significant difference was found between the present health status of their 500 delinquents and 500 matched control subjects at the time of testing, the past histories of the two groups did differ on several variables. The Gluecks found that the delinquents had been more susceptible to contagion ($p<.05$) and had had more recurrent colds of the head or chest ($p<.02$). Even more noteworthy were the facts that 59.6 per cent of the delinquents had been extremely restless, as compared with only 30.0 per cent of the controls ($p<.01$), and that 28.2 per cent of the delinquents had been enuretic, as compared with only 13.6 per cent of the controls ($p<.01$). These findings were strikingly similar to those of Healy and Bronner. Interpreting them, the Gluecks noted the impossibility of determining whether these childhood problems were reactions to environmental events or if they reflected differences in physiologic-temperamental constitution. In either case, they noted the data indicated that even in early childhood the delinquents had been "more difficult" children than the nondelinquents.

Robins (1966) compared child guidance clinic records of patients who as adults were diagnosed as sociopathic personalities with the clinical records of other patients with different diagnoses, and found no significant differences in the history of physical illness. When this study is considered in conjunction with those of Healy and Bronner and Glueck and Glueck, it suggests that early developmental and health problems may be associated with an increased rate of disturbance, of which delinquency is but one possible manifestation. Significant differences in early history may be found between delinquents and nondelinquents but not between delinquents and other disturbed children.

While few studies have investigated "general development" as a single global variable, the developmental data from a number of studies thus suggest that juvenile delinquency is associated with a history of developmental difficulties, including deviations from the norm in time of maturation, poor health, physical signs of emotional difficulties, an undersized or puny physique, and a generally lower amount of stamina or resistance to infection. These difficulties may be common to other forms of behavior disturbance as well.

In the present study, the physicians were simply asked to record their impresssion of each child's general development (see the Physical Examination Form in Appendix 5). This allowed them a wide latitude in response. The various individual comments were coded as "above average," "average," and "below average," according to the following scheme:

Above average: good, *bueno*, above average.

Average: normal, N, *normal*,[5] average, medium, medium built-tall built.

Below average: fair, below average, under, slightly underdeveloped, obesity, *regular*.

The resulting data were then analyzed by means of chi-square. The results of these analyses are presented in Table 82. It can be seen that significant differences between the delinquents and nondelinquents were obtained in every sample. However, the direction of these differences was not uniform.

---

[5] In order to avoid alarming any boys who might look on as the physical examination form was filled out, the physician in Mexico used the Spanish word *normal* to indicate "average" and the Spanish word *regular* to indicate "below average."

Table 82

General Development

Development	Anglo		Latin		Mexican	
	C*	D*	C	D	C	D
Above average	22	31	12	28	22	5
Average	21	8	22	14	26	42
Below Average	6	10	12	6	2	3
Total	49	49	46	48	50	50
χ^2	8.36		11.10		14.68[a]	
p (two tail)	<.02		<.005		<.001	

* C, comparison group; D, delinquent group.

[a] Table collapsed by combining "average" and "below average" categories because of low cell entries in latter; χ^2 based on collapsed table.

In the Anglo sample more of the delinquents were rated as "above average"; however, more were also rated as "below average." More nondelinquents fell into the "average" category. These differences were statistically significant ($\chi^2 = 8.36$, $p < .02$).

Since there were more delinquents in the "below average" category as well as more who were "above average," it would be an overstatement to interpret these data as unequivocally showing the delinquent group's general development to be superior to that of the nondelinquents. However, it was certainly abundantly clear that their health was not inferior to that of the comparison group subjects, as might have been expected from the literature.

The results were less equivocal for the Latin sample. Here the delinquents clearly predominated in the "above average" category, while the nondelinquents were overrepresented in the "average" and "below average" categories. The data for the Latin sample thus clearly indicated that the delinquents were significantly better developed ($\chi^2 = 11.10$, $p < .005$).

How might the discrepancy between these results and those reported in the literature be explained? First, it should be recalled that most of the studies in the literature, particularly the more recent ones like that of the Gluecks (1950), indicated significant differences in early developmental history but no significant differences in present status. Secondly, those studies that did report differences in the present developmental status of the delinquents were conducted during the first quarter of the twentieth century. Even if the controls can be assumed to have been adequate (which may not always have been the case), a number of major changes in social welfare programs have taken place since these studies were conducted. The Latin and Anglo subjects in the present study were all born between 1943 and 1948 and raised in San Antonio, Texas. Thus, they developed in a time and in a place where public health and welfare services were much better than those in which Goring's (1913) English convicts or Burt's (1944) juvenile delinquents were raised. Indeed, with their more unstable family backgrounds (see Chapter 6), it is quite possible that the delinquents' families received more public assistance and health care than did those of the nondelinquents, who may have come to the attention of the authorities less often. These improvements in lower-class environment may have been responsible for the failure to find significantly poorer development among the delinquents in this and other fairly recent studies.

To the extent that social service programs were less well developed in Monterrey than in San Antonio during the period from 1945 to 1960, it would be expected that this pattern would be lessened or even reversed, with the delinquents having poorer development. If the earlier observations were accurate, the more the environmental conditions in Mexico resembled those that obtained at the time of the early studies, the more it would be expected that the results would be similar.

Turning to the data for the Mexican sample, it can be seen that the development of the nondelinquents was rated as being significantly better than that of the delinquents ($\chi^2 = 14.68$, $p < .001$). In the comparison sample, 44 per cent of the nondelinquents but only 10 per cent of the delinquents were rated as "above average" in development. More of the delinquents were rated as "average" or "below average." These results are consistent with those for nutrition, in which no difference was found between the delinquents and nondelinquents in the Anglo or Latin samples, but the Mexican delinquents were found to be significantly poorer (Table 80).

These data on general development were thus consistent with the speculation that differences in public health and assistance programs might be responsible for the differences that have been observed in studies of the general health and development of delinquents. Whether or not this explanation is accurate, the temporal and regional differences in the data regarding general physical condition, height, weight, nutrition, and development indicate that it is unwise to base any far-reaching theory of delinquency on data that might show delinquents to be inferior to nondelinquents. While some studies and some samples may show delinquents to be inferior with respect to some variables, the present data make it quite clear that other samples tested at other times or in other places may well yield opposite results. When this occurs, as it has in the present investigation, it is clear that flat assertions, such as "Crime is the resultant of the impact of environment upon low grade human organisms" (Hooton, 1939a, p. 309), are untenable as general explanations. No doubt some, and perhaps many, individual criminals or delinquents are physically unfit, and this might play a role in the delinquency of some of these individuals. However, innate biological inferiority is inadequate as a general explanation for crime.

HEAD AND TEETH

The head, the most visible part of the body, has long been of interest to researchers. It has already been noted how the nineteenth-century phrenologists hypothesized that behavioral traits would be represented in the shape of the skull. Lombroso continued this tradition when he suggested that the atavistic reversal to a more primitive type that led to much criminal behavior would be manifested by various facial anomalies.

More recent investigators have continued to be interested in the head, not because it might indicate inherited criminality, but because facial disfigurements might lead to social rejection, which in turn could cause delinquency. While the Italian School studied dental characteristics because Lombroso hypothesized that abnormal dentition was a primitive characteristic, more recent investigators use the number of cavities or missing teeth as an index to possible physical neglect or inadequate hygiene. While the reasons have varied, the net effect has been continuing research on the characteristics of the heads and teeth of criminals for almost a century.

Disfigurements of the Face

In describing the facial characteristics of the criminal type, Lombroso focused on characteristics that he thought resembled the pattern found in primitive savages. Included in his list of facial characteristics were facial asymmetry, twisted noses, overly large cheeks or jawbones, excessively large or small ears, receding or excessively long chins, an abundance of wrinkles, and swollen, fleshy, or protruding lips (Vold, 1958). Goring (1913) studied facial symmetry, protrusion of the chin, facial breadth, facial length, and facial index, and concluded that there were no significant differences in facial characteristics between criminals and noncriminals. Hooton (1939a) found no significant difference in facial asymmetry or in chin form between criminals and civilians. Contrary to Lombroso's prediction, he found significantly *less* wrinkling of the cheeks among criminals. Hooton's criminals were characterized by more protruding ears and more sloping foreheads.

Apart from the theoretical significance of facial disfigurements as possible indications of organic inferiority, some scholars have commented on the role such characteristics might play in social rejection or isolation, which in turn might lead to behavior disorders. Banay (1943) has pointed to the role physical disfigurement can play in a number of behavior disorders, including crime. According to Bloch and Flynn (1956), Karl Menninger suggested that plastic surgery might be quite therapeutic in a number of cases; consistent with this, the rate of parole violations among 376 inmates who had facial surgery prior to release from Statesville Penitentiary in Illinois was less than 1 per cent, in marked contrast to a statewide parole violation rate of 17 per cent. As Bloch and Flynn pointed out, it is impossible to determine to what extent this improvement was the result of the change in appearance and to what extent it resulted from the mere fact that society was concretely demonstrating its concern for the individual criminal's welfare. In either case, these findings are consistent with the notion that facial disfigurement can play a vital role in individual cases of criminality.

The data regarding facial disfigurements in the present investigation are presented in Table 83. Gross inspection of the data showed that there were no significant differences between the delinquent and comparison groups in any sample or overall. Of the 295 boys on whom information was available, facial disfigurements were observed in eight nondelinquents and seven delinquents. These results did not provide any support for the Lombrosian hypothesis or for the notion that facial disfigurements are a major cause of delinquency, although they could be a factor in some cases.

Condition of the Teeth: Number of Caries and Number Missing

The dental condition of criminals and delinquents has also been investigated since Lombroso suggested that abnormal dentition was a sign of the physical criminal type. It would be highly questionable to attribute dental abnormalities solely to heredity in view of the many environmental factors that can influence tooth condition and development, such as diet, presence of fluorides in the water supply, and physical trauma. However, the issue of making inferences regarding heredity from dental data has never arisen, since investigators have rarely found significant differences between delinquents and nondelinquents.

Table 83

Disfigurements of the Face

Disfigurement	Anglo C*	D*	Latin C	D	Mexican C	D	Overall C	D
None	47	43	43	47	50	50	140	140
Acne	0	0	2	0	0	0	2	0
Moonfaced	1	6	4	1	0	0	5	7
Cleft lip	1	0	0	0	0	0	1	0
No information	1	1	1	2	0	0	2	3

* *C*, comparison group; *D*, delinquent group.

Hooton (1939a) investigated the tooth wear, the number of caried teeth, the number of lost teeth, and the bite of his criminal and civilian samples. By and large, Hooton found the criminals to have significantly better teeth. They had fewer cavities, fewer missing teeth, and less tooth wear. These data were clearly inconsistent with Hooton's theory that the criminal is an inferior biological organism. Unlike many of the variables Hooton investigated, the criteria for inferiority in dental condition are neither arbitrary nor ambiguous. However, Hooton pointed out that his criminal sample was younger than the civilian sample and, therefore, would be expected to have better teeth. He concluded that the significant differences he had obtained were "almost certainly attributable to the younger mean age of the criminals" and, despite his data to the contrary, that "there were virtually no general differences between the criminals and the civilians in the condition of teeth" (Hooton, 1939a, p. 240).

Healy and Bronner (1936), on the other hand, found poorer teeth among their delinquents. They noted that 27 of their 105 delinquents had "at least some badly carious teeth" in contrast to only 19 of the nondelinquent siblings. However, according to the present investigators' calculations, this difference was not significant ($\chi^2 =$ 1.78, $p < .20$). The Gluecks (1950) also investigated the incidence of carious teeth, as well as the incidence of improperly developed or crowded teeth. They found no significant differences between the delinquents and nondelinquents.

In the present study, the physicians recorded the number of carious teeth and the number of missing teeth for each boy. These data are presented in Tables 84 and 85. It can be seen that the results of the present cross-cultural investigation are consistent with those reported in the literature. No differences were found between the delinquent and comparison groups in the various samples in the number of carious or missing teeth. Although not reported in the tables, overall comparisons were also computed and were also found to show no significant differences.

Since tooth condition is clearly a product of both heredity and environment, these negative findings should be comforting to partisans on both sides. Those who cling to a biological theory of delinquency can use the absence of differences in tooth condition (which is known to be influenced by environment) to support their

Table 84

Incidence of Carious Teeth

Carious Teeth	Anglo C*	Anglo D*	Latin C	Latin D	Mexican C	Mexican D
None	25	24	26	25	27	26
One	3	9	11	8	7	10
Two	3	3	9	6	6	6
Three	1	3	2	5	4	5
Four	15	8	1	1	4	1
Five	1	1	0	1	1	1
Six	2	1	1	0	0	0
Seven	0	1	0	0	0	1
Eight or more	0	0	0	0	1	0
No information	0	0	0	4	0	0
$\bar{x}$**	1.78	1.48	0.90	0.96	1.20	1.06
σ**	2.03	1.90	1.25	1.30	1.74	1.52
N	50	50	50	46	50	50
t	0.77		0.23		0.42	
p (two tail)	N.S.		N.S.		N.S.	

* C, comparison group; D, delinquent group.
** $\bar{x}$, mean; σ, standard deviation.

claim that environmental differences are relatively unimportant;
similarly, environmentalists can argue that the failure to find differences in this variable (which is known to be influenced by
heredity) contraindicates the notion that delinquency is a result of
innate biological inferiority.

TRUNK AND LIMBS

Perhaps because they are generally clothed and less visible than
the face, the condition of the trunk and limbs has been investigated
much less by criminologists and anthropologists. Nevertheless, physical deviations in this area could be associated with delinquency
almost as readily as facial deviations. Nutritional inadequacies can
affect the growth and development of the bones of the legs and
arms. The psychological effect of a curved spine is probably no less
than that of a cleft palate.

Bodily Deformities

Lombroso suggested that bodily deformities would be among
the stigmata characterizing the born criminal. He listed a number

Table 85

Incidence of Missing Teeth

Missing Teeth	Anglo		Latin		Mexican	
	C*	D*	C	D	C	D
None	40	35	34	29	39	40
One	6	7	9	8	9	2
Two	2	4	6	8	2	7
Three	0	1	0	1	0	0
Four	2	2	1	1	0	1
Five	0	1	0	0	0	0
No information	0	0	0	3	0	0
$\bar{x}$**	0.36	0.62	0.50	0.66	0.26	0.40
σ**	0.90	1.19	0.86	0.98	0.53	0.88
t	1.14		0.85		0.97	
p (two tail)	N.S.		N.S.		N.S.	

* C, comparison group; D, delinquent group.
** $\bar{x}$, mean; σ, standard deviation.

of representative deformities, such as overly long (apelike) arms, or an odd number of ribs or nipples. Other scholars, for example, Banay (1943), have discussed the role that deformities of the body may play in causing emotional problems of which crime may be one manifestation.

The Gluecks (1950) studied abnormalities of the bony skeleton and found no significant differences between their delinquent and nondelinquent samples; similarly, they found no significant differences in the number of acquired motor handicaps. After studying a number of various remediable and irremediable defects (including sensory, glandular, and other defects, as well as trunk defects), the Gluecks concluded that the delinquents had significantly fewer defects than did the nondelinquents; 74.9 per cent of the nondelinquents had one or more such defects, as compared with only 62.7 per cent of the delinquents ($\chi^2 = 17.21$, $p < .001$). The major difference was in remediable defects. This led the Gluecks to believe that the medical attention afforded the delinquents at the institutions in which they were confined may have been largely responsible for the difference noted.

The Gluecks also investigated the bodily constitutions of their subjects. Photographs of each subject were projected on a screen and an anthropologist measured a number of body dimensions. Several anthropological indices were computed from these measurements and from the records of height and weight. These included 21 lateral body ratios, that is, the ratio of the breadth of the body at one point to its breadth or depth at another, and 15 ratios of height to the breadth of the body at various points. These data were then examined for evidence of bodily disproportions, such as a chest too narrow for the width of the shoulder or a head too large for the chest. When the incidence of such excessive deviations from the norm in the delinquent and nondelinquent samples was compared, it was found that by and large the delinquents were significantly less disproportionate than the nondelinquents. Moreover, this was found at all age levels. The Gluecks stated that this "evidently comprises a deeply-anchored somatic difference between the delinquents and the controls" (1950, p. 192). The most noteworthy aspect of these data was that they were in the opposite direction from that which would be expected on the basis of the Lombrosian hypothesis and Hooton's later theories.

In the present study, no anthropological measurements were made. Instead, the physicians noted the presence or absence of the grosser sorts of deformities that can be detected by the inspection of a trained medical observer. The results of these observations are presented in Table 86. As it was obvious that no significant differences separated the groups, no statistical tests were carried out. The data thus supported the Gluecks' data, in that the delinquent was not found to be inferior; unlike the Gluecks' results, however, there was no indication of any superiority on the part of the delinquents.

Posture

Posture is much more difficult to measure or quantify than many other physical or anthropological variables. This may be one reason why it has not been studied extensively in criminological investigations.

Healy and Bronner (1936) included posture in their investigation; they found that three of the 105 delinquents had very poor posture but none of the nondelinquent siblings did. The difference was, of course, too small to be statistically significant.

Table 86

Bodily Deformities

Deformity	Anglo C*	D*	Latin C	D	Mexican C	D	Overall C	D
None	45	46	45	47	50	50	140	143
Chest	1	1	4	1	0	0	5	2
Obesity	1	0	0	0	0	0	1	0
Emaciation	2	1	0	0	0	0	2	1
Limbs limited in movement	0	1	1	0	0	0	1	1
No information	1	1	0	2	0	0	1	3

* C, comparison group; D, delinquent group.

Table 87

Ratings of Posture

Rating	Anglo C*	D*	Latin C	D	Mexican C	D	Overall C	D
Normal	40	43	45	43	50	50	135	136
Poor	9	6	5	5	0	0	14	11
No information	1	1	0	2	0	0	1	3

* C, comparison group; D, delinquent group.

While Hooton (1939a) did not investigate posture per se, he did study the incidence of sloping shoulders in his samples. He found that many more criminals had pronounced shoulder slope, while the civilians for the most part had only a moderate shoulder slope. He also investigated the relation of shoulder slope to age and found that the younger subjects had a higher incidence of sloping shoulders. Despite the fact that the criminal group was younger than the civilian group, Hooton nevertheless felt that the disparity in shoulder slope was too great to be accounted for by age alone. He therefore concluded that this was one of the basic differences between criminals and civilians.[6]

In the present study, the physicians rated the posture of the subjects. On the basis of their reports the subjects were classified as having either normal posture or poor posture. The results are presented in Table 87. It was obvious from an inspection of the data that there were no significant differences between the delinquent and nondelinquent groups. The present findings thus failed to confirm those of other studies that suggested delinquents might have poorer posture than nondelinquents.

Condition of Arms and Legs

Very little has been reported in the literature regarding the relative condition of the limbs in delinquents and nondelinquents. The

[6] It is interesting to compare this with Hooton's reasoning on the confounding of age and dental defects (above, and Hooton, 1939a, p. 240).

most salient bit of data that the present investigators have been able to uncover is the aforementioned Massachusetts Census Report of 1905, which indicated an excessive amount of lameness among offenders (Sutherland & Cressey, 1966). In view of the widespread prescription of baseball and other sports as an antidote to delinquency, it is rather surprising that the hypothesis of delinquency being caused by physical inability to take part in such activities has not been investigated more thoroughly.

In the present study, each of the four limbs was classified as normal or limited in movement. The data for the arms are presented in Table 88 and the results for the legs in Table 89. It was clear that there were no significant differences between the delinquents and nondelinquents in any of the ethnic samples or overall.

These findings make it clear that abnormalities of the trunk or limbs are not generally associated with delinquency. Indeed, such disabilities are so rare that it would be surprising to find them significantly associated with delinquent behavior. However, it should be pointed out that the failure to find general associations does not

Table 88

Condition of Arms

Condition	Anglo		Latin		Mexican		Overall	
	C*	D*	C	D	C	D	C	D
Right arm:								
Normal	50	47	49	50	50	48	149	145
Limited in movement	0	0	0	0	0	0	0	0
No information	0	3	1	0	0	2	1	5
Left arm:								
Normal	49	46	49	50	50	50	148	146
Limited in movement	1	1	0	0	0	0	1	1
No information	0	3	1	0	0	0	1	3

* C, comparison group; D, delinquent group.

Table 89

Condition of Legs

Condition	Anglo C*	D*	Latin C	D	Mexican C	D	Overall C	D
Right leg: Normal	48	47	46	50	50	49	144	146
Limited in movement	1	1	0	0	0	1	1	2
No information	1	2	4	0	0	0	5	2
Left leg: Normal	47	47	47	50	50	50	144	147
Limited in movement	1	1	1	0	0	0	2	1
No information	2	2	2	0	0	0	4	2

* *C*, comparison group; *D*, delinquent group.

mean that such abnormalities cannot play a significant role in an individual case. For example, a recent news story discussed the case of a 17-year-old boy who pleaded guilty to larceny. When he was 12 he had had his right arm completely severed from his body and successfully replaced. It is possible that this accident was a major factor in his subsequent behavior problems. However, it would be manifestly absurd to attempt to substantiate this hypothesis by comparing the rates of successfully replaced severed arms among large samples of delinquents and nondelinquents.

SKIN

While skin condition has not received much attention from criminologists, the emotional problems associated with skin disorders have been well documented by developmental psychologists, particularly those concerned with adolescence. There is little doubt that physical appearance in general and the appearance of the skin in particular are extremely important problems in the eyes of adolescents. Frazier and Lisonbee (1950) documented this in a survey of

580 tenth-grade boys and girls. They found skin condition to be one of the major worries of their sample; for example, 51 per cent of the boys and 82 per cent of the girls expressed concern over the presence of pimples and blackheads. According to Cole and Hall (1966, p. 125):

> Pimples and boils are not merely infections; they are emotional hazards. Probably nothing so embarrasses an adolescent as a rash, an outbreak of pimples, or some other distressing skin condition . . . Such conditions make a pupil feel that he is not normal and never will be, that his appearance is offensive to others, that he will be rejected if he makes advances, that he is an outcast.

Moreover, this is likely to produce a vicious circle, for emotional disturbances, in turn, can result in acne (Garrison, 1965).

Given this close interrelation between skin conditions, social acceptance, and emotional problems, it would be natural to suppose that a greater incidence of skin disorders might be found among delinquent adolescents. The data, however, do not support this assumption. Glueck and Glueck (1950) investigated the incidence of dermatitis, eczema, psoriasis, acne, impetigo, and other miscellaneous skin conditions, such as boils, birthmarks, and shingles, among their delinquent and nondelinquent samples. There was no significant difference between the groups on any of the individual conditions save psoriasis, which was more common among the nondelinquents ($p < .02$). There was no noteworthy difference in the overall incidence of skin disorders—23.0 per cent of the delinquents and 23.5 per cent of the nondelinquents suffered from some form of skin disorder.

In the present study, the examining physicians noted any abnormalities of the skin on the physical examination form. As can be seen from Table 90, these notes included a variety of skin disorders, such as acne, impetigo, dermatitis, and fungus infections; in addition, some physicians took the opportunity to comment on other deviations from the norm, such as tattoos or hairiness. In the statistical analysis the relative incidence of skin diseases was compared, with those subjects in the "tattooed" or "hairy" categories deleted.[7]

---

[7] Tattoos were deleted because they are obviously a reflection of the personality and not the physiology of the individual. However, it should be noted that Lombroso listed excessive tattooing as one of the signs of the atavistic criminal.

Table 90

Condition of Skin

| | Anglo | | Latin | | Mexican | |
Condition	C*	D*	C	D	C	D
Normal	35	35	30	45	41	45
Acne	0	2	3	0	0	0
Impetigo	14	4	11	2	6	3
Dermatitis	0	1	0	0	1	0
Fungus infection	0	0	0	0	2	2
Hairy	0	0	4	0	0	0
Tattooed	0	5	1	2	0	0
No information	1	3	1	1	0	0

* C, comparison group; D, delinquent group.

The results of this analysis are presented in Table 91. In each of the three groups, more cases of skin disorder were noted among the nondelinquents than among the delinquents. This difference was statistically significant in the Latin sample ($\chi^2=10.09$, p [two tail] $<.005$) as well as in the overall analysis ($\chi^2=11.88$, p [two tail] $<.001$).

Goring (1913) found more criminals to be tattooed than the general public, but maintained that the relationship between crime and tattooing disappeared when other variables related to tattooing, such as age, intelligence and military service, were allowed for. Hooton (1939a) also found tattooing to be more common among criminals and, as might be expected, scored Goring for his attempt to "explain away" the difference. East (1946) reported that in 1901 he examined 500 English convicts and found 43 per cent to be tattooed. This appeared to him to be a smaller percentage than was common in the military at that time. In the present sample, eight boys were tattooed, of whom seven were delinquents. This difference was significant (p [one tail] $= .035$).

Table 91

Statistical Analyses of Skin Disorders

Condition	Anglo C*	Anglo D*	Latin C	Latin D	Mexican C	Mexican D	Overall C	Overall D
Normal	35	35	30	45	41	45	106	125
Skin disorder	14	7	14	2	9	5	37	14
Total	49	42	44	47	50	50	143	139
χ^2	1.20		10.09		0.75		11.88	
p (two tail)	N.S.		<.005		N.S.		<.001	

* C, comparison group; D, delinquent group.

Thus, there were significant differences in the incidence of skin disorders, but not in the expected direction. It had been expected that because of the association of skin disease with emotional problems the delinquents would have more skin problems, but the opposite was the case. These findings are not too different from those of the Gluecks. It therefore appears that delinquents definitely do not have a higher incidence of skin disorders. The present investigators are not willing to take the next logical step, however, and assert that they are therefore better adjusted. There are too many data in this and other studies that indicate otherwise.

INTERNAL ORGANS: ADENOIDS, TONSILS, THYROID, AND LUNGS

Condition of the Adenoids

Both Healy and Bronner (1936) and the Gluecks (1950) investigated the incidence of nasal obstructions in their samples, but neither pair of investigators found any relation between nasal obstructions and delinquency. Healy and Bronner (1936) found six cases of nasal obstruction in their delinquent sample and two in their nondelinquent; the Gluecks reported 72 cases in their delinquent sample and 69 in the nondelinquent. The Gluecks also investigated the extent of upper respiratory system pathology and found 71 cases in the delinquent sample and 74 cases in the contrast group.

In the present investigation, the condition of the adenoids was classified as "normal" or "obstructed." No significant differences were noted between the delinquents and nondelinquents in either the Anglo or Mexican samples (see Table 92). However, 12 per cent of the Latin delinquents had nasal obstructions compared to none of the Latin comparison group (x^2 [corrected] $=4.43$, p [two tail] $<.05$). While this difference was statistically significant, it is questionable how meaningful it is. In view of the large number of significance tests that have been performed and the relatively small number of individuals with obstructed adenoids, it would probably be a mistake to place any great importance on this finding unless it appears to be part of a general pattern. Since the major differences thus far have shown the Latin delinquents to be superior in general development and skin condition, although somewhat inferior in weight, the significantly higher incidence of nasal obstructions does not appear to be part of a general pattern of physical illness.

The generally higher incidence of nasal obstructions found among the Mexican sample is also noteworthy. While the rate of nasal obstructions in the Latin and Anglo samples was 5.6 per cent, the rate in the Mexican sample was 18 per cent; this difference was

Table 92

Condition of Adenoids

Condition	Anglo C*	Anglo D*	Latin C	Latin D	Mexican C	Mexican D	Overall C	Overall D
Normal	41	43	50	44	40	36	131	123
Obstructed	0	4	0	6	10	7	10	17
Total	41	47	50	50	50	43	141	140
χ^{2a}	1.96		4.43		0.04		1.79	
p (two tail)	N.S.		$<.05$		N.S.		N.S.	

* C, comparison group; D, delinquent group.
a Chi-square corrected for continuity.

probably a result of the fact that Monterrey is much drier and dustier than San Antonio.

Condition of the Tonsils

The Gluecks (1950) and Healy and Bronner (1936) also investigated the incidence of diseased tonsils in their samples. Healy and Bronner found that 20 of their 105 delinquent boys had markedly enlarged or diseased tonsils, in contrast to only 12 of the 105 nondelinquent sibs. The present investigators' calculations indicate that this difference was not statistically significant ($\chi^2 = 2.36$, $p < .20$). The Gluecks found no noteworthy difference: 12 per cent of their delinquent sample and 13 per cent of their comparison sample had enlarged or diseased tonsils.

In the present investigation, the boys' tonsils were classified as "normal," "reddened or enlarged," or "removed." A significant difference was found between the Anglo delinquents and nondelinquents ($\chi^2 = 12.04$, $p < .005$). The incidence of reddened or enlarged tonsils was identical in the two groups; however, the nondelinquent Anglos were much more likely to have had their tonsils removed, while the

Table 93

Condition of Tonsils

Condition	Anglo C*	Anglo D*	Latin C	Latin D	Mexican C	Mexican D	Overall C	Overall D
Normal	16	29	36	38	19	28	71	95
Reddened or enlarged	13	13	12	9	27	22	52	44
Removed	21	6	2	3	1	0	24	9
Total	50	48	50	50	47	50	147	148
χ^2	12.04		0.19[a]		2.07[a]		10.96	
p (two tail)	<.005		N.S.		N.S.		<.005	

* C, comparison group; D, delinquent group.
[a] Chi-square based on "normal" and "reddened or enlarged" categories only; "removed" category deleted from analysis because of low cell entries.

Anglo delinquents were more likely to have normal tonsils (see Table 93).

The most parsimonious explanation for this pattern is simply that more of the Anglo comparison group had had tonsilitis as children and hence more had had tonsillectomies. However, if we permit ourselves to indulge in speculation for a moment, it is possible to make an *ad hoc* explanation that, while less parsimonious, is in better accord with theories of delinquency. A tonsillectomy is rarely a mandatory operation and a fair amount of parental discretion enters into the decision as to whether it will be performed. If the rate of tonsillitis was *not* higher in the Anglo comparison group, then these data would indicate that the nondelinquent Anglos' parents were more willing than the delinquents' parents to spend the extra money for an operation to ensure their children's health. According to this line of speculation, the greater number of tonsillectomies in the Anglo comparison group would thus be a sign of greater parental concern. However, there are no data available to support the assumption of an equal rate of tonsillitis.

Tonsillectomies were conspicuously fewer in the Latin and Mexican samples, probably because of diminished income, fatalism, and a distrust for hospitals and surgical procedures (Madsen, 1964; Rubel, 1966). Because of the infrequency of removed tonsils, the statistical analysis was confined to a comparison of the incidence of normal versus reddened or enlarged tonsils. No significant differences between the delinquent and comparison groups were found in the Latin and Mexican samples.

The overall analysis showed a significant difference, with the comparison subjects having a higher incidence of tonsils that were removed or reddened and enlarged, and the delinquents a higher incidence of normal tonsils ($\chi^2 = 10.96$, $p < .005$). The significance of this analysis can be traced to the differences in the number of delinquents and nondelinquents who had tonsillectomies. In order to determine if there was a significant difference in the condition of the tonsils among those subjects who had not had them removed, a second 2×2 chi-square analysis was performed on the overall data with the "removed" category deleted. This analysis was not significant ($\chi^2 = 3.33$, $p < .10$). However, the trend toward healthier tonsils in the delinquent group, even when the subjects who had had tonsillectomies were omitted, was noteworthy.

The present overall results thus indicated that the delinquents were more likely to have normal tonsils. This is the opposite of what would be expected if the delinquents were biologically or environmentally inferior. In the Anglo sample the nondelinquents were much more likely to have had tonsillectomies. This could indicate significantly better health on the part of the Anglo delinquents; a more speculative possibility is that the nondelinquents' parents were more willing to have tonsillectomies performed on their children.

Condition of the Thyroid

With the discoveries of the effects of the endocrine glands on behavior, there arose a "biochemical" or "endocrinological" school of criminology, which sought to attribute most, if not all, crime to endocrinological malfunctions. Among those who have sought to explain criminal behavior in terms of endocrinology were Berman (1921), who posited endocrinological personality types, and Schlapp and Smith (1928), who went so far as to state: ". . . most crimes come about through disturbances of the ductless glands in the criminal and through mental defects caused by endocrine troubles in the criminal's mother . . ." (1928, p. 28).

According to Vold (1958), Berman attempted to support these theories with a study in which 250 Sing Sing inmates were compared with a control group of normal noncriminal males from New York City. In this study, according to Vold, Berman reported two to three times as much glandular disturbance among the criminals as among the controls. However, Vold reports that a series of "carefully conducted and fully reported research studies" at the New Jersey State Home for Boys failed to confirm Berman's findings.

The thyroid gland is one of the endocrine glands that can have powerful effects on development and behavior. According to Podolsky (1955), an excess of thyroxin has been found in Sing Sing inmates convicted of murders, grand larceny, fraud, forgery, rape, and assault and battery.

Most criminologists (Bloch & Flynn, 1956; Caldwell, 1965; Tappan, 1960; Vold, 1958) do not deny that the endocrine glands can play a role in behavior; however, they feel that the members of the "endocrinological school" have been guilty of vast oversimplification and reductionism in their attempts to prove that endocrine malfunction is the primary, and possibly the only, cause of crime. Even in cases where there may be endocrine pathology, the glandular criminologists have underemphasized the complexity of the relation between biochemistry and behavior. Bloch and Flynn (1956), for example, cite Levy's carefully conducted study of the basal metabolism of problem children in which it was found that the hyperactive problem children had a lower basal metabolism than the hypoactive children, just the opposite of what had been expected. The Gluecks' (1950) research gave no support to the notion that glandular disturbances are among the primary causes of crime or delinquency. To be sure, their medical examination revealed that 32.9 per cent of the delinquents suffered from some glandular abnormality, but it also indicated that this was true of 34.3 per cent of the nondelinquents. Regarding the thyroid, only 1.8 per cent of the delinquents, as compared with 2.8 per cent of the nondelinquents, displayed evidence of any thyroid disturbance.

In the present investigation, there was even less indication of thyroid malfunction being associated with delinquent behavior. Each subject, delinquent and nondelinquent, for whom information was available was evaluated as normal in thyroid functioning. In fairness to the endocrinological school it should be pointed out that in both the Gluecks' study and the present one these diagnoses were made without benefit of laboratory tests; nonetheless, the results offered no support to the glandular hypothesis.

Condition of the Lungs

In his massive study of the English convict, Goring investigated the incidence of various diseases in his criminal and civilian samples. Among these were several diseases of the lungs. He found no relation between crime and the incidence of tuberculosis or pneumonia. He did note that criminals were less likely than civilians to be suffering from chronic bronchitis and emphysema. The Gluecks found no significant differences in the extent of impaired pulmonary function in their delinquent and control samples.

The data regarding the condition of the lungs in the present sample are presented in Table 94. Two Mexican delinquents were suffering from bronchitis; the remaining 295 subjects for whom reports were obtained were all classified as normal. There were thus no intergroup differences worthy of note.

Table 94

Condition of Lungs

Condition	Anglo		Latin		Mexican		Overall	
	C*	D*	C	D	C	D	C	D
Normal	50	48	49	50	50	48	149	146
Bronchitis	0	0	0	0	0	2	0	2
No information	0	2	1	0	0	0	1	2

* C, comparison group; D, delinquent group.

THE CIRCULATORY SYSTEM

Pulse and Blood Pressure

Goring (1913) found a negative relation between circulatory disorders and crime. The incidence of "Apoplexy, &c" correlated −.12 with criminality, while the incidence of "other diseases of the heart and blood vessels" correlated −.13 with criminality. Goring interpreted this as indicating that chronic disease suppresses crime, since a sick person is "physically prevented from pursuing a criminal calling." The Gluecks (1950) found that 3.0 per cent of their delinquent sample had marked or slight evidence of cardiac disease as compared with 3.8 per cent of the nondelinquents.

Several circulatory measurements were employed in the present study. The first of these was pulse rate. After the initial pulse rate was determined, the boys were asked to exercise vigorously. Originally, it had been intended to have each boy do 10 push-ups; however, in the course of experimentation it was found that a considerable proportion of the boys could not do 10 push-ups without resting once or twice. Squatting was therefore substituted. Immediately after this exercise, the pulse rate was again determined; after a minute had passed for recovery, the pulse was taken a third time.

The data for pulse rate are presented in Table 95. The initial pulse rate for all groups was within the normal range. The Latin delin-

Table 95

Circulatory System Results

Variables		Anglo C††	Anglo D††	t	Latin C	Latin D	t	Mexican C	Mexican D	t
Pulse Rate										
Before exercise	x̄†	82.44	81.37		76.04	80.84		71.32	71.32	
	σ†	10.02	11.83	0.45	8.09	12.21	2.18*	9.46	11.25	0.00
	N	50	36		45	44		50	49	
Immediately after exercise	x̄	107.26	101.30		102.44	103.81		87.56	88.47	
	σ	12.54	12.18	2.18*	11.98	13.49	0.50	12.11	11.65	0.38
	N	49	36		45	42		50	49	
One minute after exercise	x̄	86.64	82.33		79.03	82.33		76.18	76.24	
	σ	10.28	11.62	1.64	8.19	11.05	1.50	9.09	12.02	0.02
	N	34	36		34	42		50	49	
Blood Pressure										
Systolic	x̄	103.36	116.95		103.36	103.52		114.36	117.80	
	σ	16.97	15.16	4.10***	15.59	18.38	0.04	12.28	11.08	1.47
	N	50	44		50	42		50	50	
Diastolic	x̄	56.52	69.75		53.60	51.76		68.10	73.84	
	σ	17.99	12.50	4.18***	15.58	15.86	0.55	11.12	13.10	2.36**
	N	50	44		50	42		50	50	

* p (two tail) < .05.
** p (two tail) < .02.
*** p (two tail) < .0001.
† x̄, mean; σ, standard deviation.
†† C, comparison group; D, delinquent group.

quents, however, had a significantly higher initial pulse than the Latin comparison group. Possibly, they were more anxious regarding the examination. The differences between the other groups were not significant.

The pulse rate immediately after exercise was significantly higher for the Anglo comparison group than for the Anglo delinquents ($t=2.18$, $p<.05$). This could indicate that the nondelinquent Anglos were in somewhat poorer physical condition, which would be consistent with the data on general development (Table 82), or that they responded more faithfully to the physician's instructions to exercise vigorously. The differences in the other samples were not significant.

One minute after exercise the mean pulse rate in all groups had recovered to a point where it was only a few beats higher than the initial rate. There were no significant intergroup differences.

Systolic and diastolic blood pressures were also measured and are presented in Table 95. In the Anglo sample, the delinquents were significantly higher on both measures of blood pressure ($p<.0001$). The diastolic blood pressure of the Mexican delinquents was also significantly higher than that of the Mexican comparison group ($t=2.36$, $p<.02$). This could indicate a higher degree of arousal in the delinquents in these two samples. Perhaps they found the examination more threatening; possibly, the delinquents were readier to respond emotionally.

These findings are also consistent with the hypothesis advanced by Funkenstein, King, and Drolette (1957) that overt aggression, such as is often found among delinquents, might be associated with norepinephrinelike reactions to the sort of sustained stress that is involved in a physical examination. If this notion is correct, it might be expected that the delinquents would have higher diastolic blood pressure readings than the nondelinquents, as was the case in the Anglo and Mexican samples (Hokanson, 1961). This is not consistent with the differences in systolic blood pressure that were also found. While the present data on the circulatory system are not conducive to a simple clear-cut interpretation, nevertheless, the data do indicate that further work on the autonomic reaction patterns of delinquents and nondelinquents in different cultures would be profitable.

There is no need to list in detail the many problems that defective vision or hearing can cause a child, particularly when they are un-detected and uncorrected. Because success in school and in society depends on communication and the ability to absorb and act on in-formation, visual or auditory defects can handicap the child tremen-dously. The frustration and bewilderment that such handicaps may produce could easily find expression through antisocial acting out.

Visual Acuity

The relation between eyesight and crime has been fairly well in-vestigated. Goring (1913) studied the eyesight of 996 English con-victs. He classified 21 per cent as having "indifferent" eyesight, 19 per cent as having "fair" eyesight, and 59 per cent as having "good" eyesight. East (1946) found that 12.5 per cent of the 4,000 adoles-cent offenders he examined at Wormwood Scrubs had bad or im-paired vision. Sutherland and Cressey (1966, p. 131) reported that the 1905 Massachusetts Census indicated "that blind persons were not over-represented in the delinquent and criminal population . . .," hardly a surprising finding considering the difficulties a blind person would have in pursuing a criminal career. However, they also noted (Sutherland & Cressey, 1966, p. 131):

> Optometrists have reported wide difference between the delinquents and school children in respect to defective vision, and offer the explana-tion that children with defective vision are more likely to become delin-quent because of the physical irritation caused by defective vision and because of the difficulty in reading, which drives them into truancy and gang activities.

Healy and Bronner (1936) reported that 17 of the 105 delinquents they studied had more than slightly defective vision, as compared with only six of their nondelinquent siblings. The present investiga-tors' calculations indicate that this difference was statistically signifi-cant ($\chi^2 = 5.91$, $p < .02$).

In the present investigation, the physicians indicated whether the subjects' vision in each eye was "20/20" (normal), "better than 20/20," "less than 20/20," "corrected by glasses," or so poor that he "sees light only." These data are reported in Table 96.

The data in Table 96 were next dichotomized into "20/20 vision or

Table 96

Visual Acuity

Eye	Acuity	Anglo C*	Anglo D*	Latin C	Latin D	Mexican C	Mexican D
Right	Better than 20/20 vision	3	0	2	4	0	0
	20/20 vision	44	41	41	40	50	50
	Less than 20/20 vision	3	5	6	3	0	0
	Corrected by glasses	0	3	0	0	0	0
	Sees light only	0	0	1	0	0	0
	No information	0	1	0	3	0	0
Left	Better than 20/20 vision	4	0	2	4	0	0
	20/20 vision	44	40	42	39	50	49
	Less than 20/20 vision	2	6	6	4	0	0
	Corrected by glasses	0	3	0	0	0	0
	Sees light only	0	0	0	0	0	0
	No information	0	1	0	3	0	1

* C, comparison group; D, delinquent group.

better" and "less than 20/20 vision." Chi-square analyses were then performed on the data for the right eye, left eye, and both eyes. The results of these analyses are presented in Table 97. It can be seen from this table that there were no differences in the reported visual acuity of the delinquents and the nondelinquents in either the Latin or Mexican samples.[8] In the Anglo sample, there was a nonsignificant tendency for more delinquents to have poorer vision in the right eye

[8] With one exception, all of the Mexican sample was classified as 20/20. The reader who has been studying the tables in this chapter may have noticed a tendency for the Mexican sample to be rated as having fewer defects than the others. This trend was most apparent in the visual data. It is likely that this was because Dr. B., who examined all of the Mexican sample, was more tolerant of minor deviations.

and also the left eye; when both eyes were considered, this trend attained significance ($\chi^2=3.91$, $p<.05$). These data for the Anglo sample, indicating poorer vision among the delinquents, were thus consistent with those reported by Healy and Bronner.

Visual Defects

The incidence of observable visual defects in delinquents has also been studied, but these studies have not indicated any significant differences. Healy and Bronner (1936) investigated the incidence

Table 97

Statistical Analyses of Visual Acuity

Eye	Acuity	Anglo C*	D*	Latin C	D	Mexican C	D	Overall C	D
Right	20/20 or better	47	41	43	44	50	50	140	135
	Less than 20/20	3	8	7	3	0	0	10	11
	Total	50	49	50	47	50	50	150	146
	χ^{2a}	1.72		0.81		0.00		0.33	
	p (two tail)	N.S.		N.S.		N.S.		N.S.	
Left	20/20 or better	48	43	44	43	50	50	142	136
	Less than 20/20	2	6	6	4	0	0	8	10
	Total	50	49	50	47	50	50	150	146
	χ^{2a}	1.30		0.11		0.00		0.07	
	p (two tail)	N.S.		N.S.		N.S.		N.S.	
Both	20/20 or better	95	84	87	87	100	100	282	271
	Less than 20/20	5	14	13	7	0	0	18	21
	Total	100	98	100	94	100	100	300	292
	χ^{2a}	3.91		1.00		0.00		0.34	
	p (two tail)	<.05		N.S.		N.S.		N.S.	

* C, comparison group; D, delinquent group.
a Chi-square corrected for continuity.

of slight and marked strabismus in their delinquent and nondelinquent samples. They found no noteworthy differences. The Gluecks (1950, p. 176) investigated the incidence of strabismus, nystagmus, left-eyedness, myopia, hyperopia, astigmatism, eye injury, and other defects, such as amblyopia, color blindness, corneal opacity, and cataracts. They found no significant differences for any of these individual categories of defects, or for the overall rate of defects in their delinquent and nondelinquent samples.

The various types of visual defects noted in the present study are reported in Table 98. This table was then collapsed and a statistical test was made comparing the number of subjects in each group with and without visual defects. The results of these analyses are presented in Table 99. There were no significant differences in the reported incidence of visual defects in the Anglo and Mexican samples. In the Latin sample and in the overall analysis, however, significantly more visual defects were reported among the nondelinquents. Thus, the data on visual defects clearly indicated that delinquency was not associated with an increased rate of visual defects.

Table 98

General Defects of Vision

Defect	Anglo		Latin		Mexican	
	C*	D*	C	D	C	D
None	34	39	36	42	49	50
Astigmatism	0	5	2	1	0	0
Myopia	5	1	3	1	1	0
Myopia and astigmatism	0	0	0	1	0	0
Other	5	3	7	0	0	0
No information	6	2	2	5	0	0

* C, comparison group; D, delinquent group.

Table 99

Statistical Analyses of Visual Defects

Defect	Anglo C*	D*	Latin C	D	Mexican C	D	Overall C	D
No defect	34	39	36	42	49	50	119	131
Some defect	10	9	12	3	1	0	23	12
Total	44	48	48	45	50	50	142	143
χ^2	0.05[a]		4.50[a]		0.00[a]		4.03	
p (two tail)	N.S.		$<.05$		N.S.		$<.05$	

* C, comparison group; D, delinquent group.
[a] Chi-square corrected for continuity.

Auditory Acuity

Hearing has also received its share of attention over the years. Sutherland and Cressey (1966) reported that the 1905 Massachusetts Census indicated an excessive amount of deafness among criminal offenders. Likewise, Goring (1913), comparing his data on hearing with those reported for Scottish medical students by another investigator, noted more impaired hearing in his criminal sample. However, after limiting the comparison to criminals of the same age as the students and estimating the probable effect of socioeconomic differences, Goring concluded that, other things being equal, there probably would not be an excessive amount of defective hearing among criminals. East (1946) reported that 4 per cent of the 4,000 adolescent offenders at Wormwood Scrubs had bad or impaired hearing. Without a comparison group, however, this finding cannot be properly evaluated. Similarly, Bloch and Flynn (1956, p. 137) reported that, "Slawson, on the basis of rather specialized samples, concluded that delinquents suffered from a higher rate of visual and auditory defects than nondelinquents."

Healy and Bronner (1936) compared delinquent and nondelinquent siblings on the incidence of otitis media and moderately defective hearing; the nondelinquents were slightly higher on both variables. The Gluecks also compared the incidence of otitis media and slight or marked deafness in their samples and found no significant differences.

In the present study, the incidence of subnormal auditory activity in the right ear, left ear, and both ears of the delinquent and nondelinquent subjects was compared. The results are presented in Table 100. No significant differences were noted in the Anglo and Latin samples. However, the Mexican delinquents had a significantly higher incidence of impaired hearing than did the nondelinquent

Table 100

Statistical Analyses of Auditory Acuity

Ear	Acuity	Anglo C*	Anglo D*	Latin C	Latin D	Mexican C	Mexican D	Overall C	Overall D
Right	Normal	48	46	49	47	50	46	147	139
	Subnormal	2	3	1	2	0	4	3	9
	Total	50	49	50	49	50	50	150	148
	χ^{2a}	0.00		0.00		2.34		2.24	
	p (two tail)	N.S.		N.S.		N.S.		N.S.	
Left	Normal	49	45	49	47	50	47	148	139
	Subnormal	1	2	1	2	0	3	2	7
	Total	50	47	50	49	50	50	150	146
	χ^{2a}	0.00		0.00		1.37		1.95	
	p (two tail)	N.S.		N.S.		N.S.		N.S.	
Both	Normal	97	91	98	94	100	93	295	278
	Subnormal	3	5	2	4	0	7	5	16
	Total	100	96	100	98	100	100	300	294
	χ^{2a}	0.18		0.19		5.33		6.21	
	p (two tail)	N.S.		N.S.		$<.025$		$<.02$	

* C, comparison group; D, delinquent group.
a Chi-square corrected for continuity.

Mexicans. Largely because of this significant difference in the Mexican sample, the overall comparison of all three samples also attained statistical significance.

While the delinquents did have a significantly higher incidence of impaired hearing, it should be pointed out that the absolute rate of subnormal hearing was extremely low. Subnormal hearing can hardly be considered to be closely associated with delinquency, particularly when the present data are considered in the context of the generally negative results reported in the literature.

Summary of the Results of the Medical Examination

The present chapter has reviewed the data regarding physical differences between offenders and nonoffenders in the literature and has presented the findings of the medical examinations of the Anglo, Latin, and Mexican delinquents and nondelinquents. The review of the literature has shown that a great deal of research, much of which was rendered suspect by problems in the selection of control groups or interpretation of the data, has focused on the physical characteristics of the criminal. These studies have generally fallen into two broad groups. The first group was concerned with testing the hypothesis that criminality results from innate biological predispositions that are also manifested in the physical appearance of the individual. If this theory is correct, the criminal should be biologically inferior to the noncriminal, and many studies have sought evidence for such inferiority.

The second group of studies has explored the health of criminals and delinquents, not because this might be an indication of inherited criminality, but simply because defective hearing, malnutrition, and the like might be part of a matrix of environmental factors that could result in criminal behavior.

The results permit several conclusions to be drawn. First, there was no systematic evidence of basic biological inferiority of the delinquents in the Anglo and Latin samples. For the most part, no significant differences were found. When significant differences were obtained they were as likely to show the delinquents to be superior as inferior. By the same token, there was little evidence that medical problems were a major factor associated with delinquency. The health and development of delinquents and nondelinquents in the Anglo and Latin samples was approximately the same in most areas.

When differences were found, they frequently showed the delinquents to be superior.

The results of the Mexican sample deviated somewhat from those of the other two in that all the significant differences showed the delinquents to be inferior to the comparison group. However, the importance of this consistent finding dwindles in the light of the fact that only four of the 30 differences tested in the Mexican sample attained statistical significance at the .05 level. Moreover, at least two of the four differences—the significantly poorer nutrition and the significantly poorer general development of the Mexican delinquents —could have been an artifact of the diet at the Escuela Prevocacional, at which the entire Mexican delinquent group was incarcerated.

If the differences in height, weight, nutrition, and development that were found in the various comparisons were not artifacts of institutionalization, they could indicate environmental deprivation. This in turn could have resulted in less stamina and impaired ability to compete effectively in school or in sports. One difficulty with this chain of ex post facto reasoning is the fact that in the Latin sample it was the delinquents rather than the nondelinquents who were assessed as being superior in general development, and there was a similar pattern in the Anglo sample as well. Given this finding, it is possible to start another chain of speculation to the effect that the physically superior boy is rewarded for aggression and hence may develop habits that lead to delinquency. If we confined ourselves to one sample and to one or two of these variables, it would be tempting to make such speculations; however, given the total data matrix, we can see that such interpretations of one segment of the data are inconsistent with other segments.

There were, however, some physical differences not strictly connected with health or illness that might be more meaningful. The data indicated that the delinquents were more likely to have subnormal hearing, and, in the Anglo sample, impaired vision. Such sensory difficulties could cause problems in school and in associating with peers, which might influence personality and social development. Further research should be conducted to cross-validate this finding.

Another interesting finding was the highly significant differences between the blood pressure and pulse rate of some of the delinquent and nondelinquent groups. The direction of the differences suggested that there might be a higher level of arousal or a lower threshold for emotionality in the delinquents. Some of the data were consistent with speculations about autonomic reaction patterns in the literature. Further research on the physiological indices of emotionality in delinquents and nondelinquents might be quite fruitful.

With these exceptions, the general findings of the present study, in conjunction with those already in the literature, suggest that the search for concurrent physical correlates of criminal behavior is not likely to justify the time and expense involved. The regional and ethnic differences that were often found served to highlight the need for extremely careful sampling procedures in such research. Frequently, these differences far outweighed those found between delinquents and nondelinquents. While differences in examiners and sampling could have influenced some of the more subjectively rated variables, similar differences were also found on such objective measures as height, weight, and pulse rate. It was particularly interesting that on these latter variables the Anglo and Mexican samples were at opposite poles, with the Latin sample in between. This medical finding reinforced in an unexpected fashion the selection of the Latin sample as one that would share characteristics of both the Anglo and Mexican samples.

PART III

The Problem in the Light of the Results

CHAPTER 14

RÉSUMÉ OF THE FINDINGS

The reader who has patiently followed us in our microscopic examination of the data may now find himself too overburdened with details to make much sense of the results. Before attempting to integrate the data or draw any general conclusions, it would be best to briefly review the significant findings for each ethnic sample in a more macroscopic fashion.

Anglos

SOCIOLOGICAL INVESTIGATION

The sociological investigation indicated that there was more marital instability among the families of the delinquents than among the families of the nondelinquents. The delinquents' parents were significantly more likely to have been divorced ($p<.001$), and the delinquents showed a strong tendency to be less likely to live with both natural parents ($p<.06$).[1]

The sibling patterns that differentiated the Anglo delinquents and nondelinquents differed from those found to characterize the other two samples. The Anglo delinquents had significantly more siblings than did the Anglo nondelinquents ($p<.001$). However, there was no difference in birth order between the two groups.

The data regarding church attendance showed that the Anglo delinquents attended church significantly less regularly than did the

[1] All p levels reported in this chapter are two tail.

nondelinquent Anglos ($p<.001$). The delinquents' fathers ($p<.001$) and mothers ($p<.001$) also attended church significantly less regularly than the nondelinquents' parents. There were no significant differences in denominational preferences.

When the socioeconomic status of the fathers' jobs was evaluated, it was found that the delinquents' fathers had jobs significantly lower in socioeconomic status than those held by the nondelinquents' fathers ($p<.05$). However, the opposite pattern was noted in the Latin sample.

The analysis of the educational achievement of the Anglo sample showed that the Anglo delinquents' grade level was significantly lower than that of nondelinquent Anglos ($p<.005$). The mothers of the Anglo delinquents had also left school earlier than the mothers of the nondelinquents ($p<.005$), and there was a trend in this direction for the fathers as well.

PSYCHOLOGICAL TEST RESULTS

On the Wechsler Intelligence Scales the Anglo delinquents obtained significantly lower Verbal ($p<.005$) and Full Scale IQs ($p<.05$). There was no significant difference in Performance IQ. This pattern, which was consistent with those reported in the literature, was repeated in the Latin sample but reversed in the Mexican sample.

The Anglo delinquents' Performance IQs were significantly higher than their Verbal IQs ($p<.005$), as is usually the case. A similar trend for the comparison group suggested that this could at least in part be an artifact of lower-class status.

The first part of the Choices Test asked the subjects how they would dispose of various sums of money ranging from 25 cents to 200 dollars. The responses of the Anglo sample showed that there were significant differences between delinquents and nondelinquents regarding the smaller sums of money, but not the larger, less realistic sums. For the smaller amounts, the nondelinquents were significantly more likely than the delinquents to spend the money on school supplies or save it, while delinquents were more likely to spend the money on clothes, cigarettes, candy, and so forth. This was interpreted as indicating that the delinquents were less willing to defer immediate need gratification in favor of some future goal. The Anglos showed no significant difference in the other Choices Test items.

On the Offenses Test the data indicated significant agreement between the Anglo delinquents and nondelinquents on the mean rank order of 10 different transgressions. On only one of the 10 offenses were the delinquents' rankings significantly more variable than those of the nondelinquents. This latter finding was interpreted as indicating that there was no more value confusion or anomie among the Anglo delinquents than among the nondelinquent Anglos.

On the Card Sort Test, there were many items on which the Anglo delinquents and nondelinquents showed significant disagreement. Several broad trends were apparent. The delinquents endorsed significantly more items indicating deviant or antisocial behavior on the part of themselves and their associates. Relatively few differences occurred between the Anglo delinquents and nondelinquents on the clusters of items reflecting authority problems, disrespect of the father, or attitudes toward the mother. This was one of the most noteworthy differences between the Anglo sample and the other two. The results of the Anglo sample agreed with those of the Latin and Mexican samples in indicating significantly less family cohesiveness among the delinquents' families. In the Anglo sample this lack of cohesiveness was manifested primarily by wishing to escape, reports of dissension in the home, and lack of communication between family members. The Card Sort results of the Anglos differed from those in the Latin sample in that there were no significant differences in the clusters of items dealing with economic attitudes, school, or rules.

On the Cartoon Test more Anglo delinquents depicted mothers as being hostile and disinterested toward their sons' requests ($p<.05$). Fathers were seen by the delinquents as being significantly more punitive and less inclined to reason with a child ($p<.05$), and also as being more antisocial in their attitudes toward the police ($p<.02$).

The only major difference between the Anglo delinquents and nondelinquents on the Picture-Story Test was that the delinquents told significantly more stories with antisocial themes on one card ($p<.02$) and related stories with significantly more antisocial or extremely unpleasant events in response to three cards ($p<.004-.001$). There were significantly fewer unpleasant economic instances ($p<.03$) in the delinquents' responses to one card.

MEDICAL EXAMINATION

Relatively few significant differences were evident between the Anglo delinquents and nondelinquents on the medical examination. The data indicated that the delinquents were superior to the nondelinquents in general development ($p<.02$) and that they were more likely to have normal tonsils and less likely to have had tonsillectomies ($p<.0001$). The Anglo delinquents had a lower pulse rate after exercise ($p<.05$) and higher diastolic ($p<.001$) blood pressure. They also had poorer visual acuity ($p<.05$).

Latins

SOCIOLOGICAL INVESTIGATION

The Latin delinquents' families were also found to have more marital instability than those of the nondelinquent Latins. The present marital status of more of the Latin delinquents' parents was listed as "unmarried, separated, divorced or deserted," while more of the nondelinquents' parents were "married and living together" or "deceased." No significant differences were found between the Latin delinquents and nondelinquents in the composition of the family home, the divorce rates of either parents, or the date of the present marriage or divorce.

The number of siblings and the relative proportion of older and younger brothers and sisters were also investigated. On both measures the pattern for the Latin sample resembled that of the Mexican sample more than the Anglo. There were no significant differences between the delinquents and nondelinquents in the number of siblings. However, there was a strong trend for the nondelinquents to have a higher ratio of older to younger sisters ($p<.06$) and older to younger siblings in general ($p<.10$).

The data regarding church attendance were the same for the Latins as for the Anglos. Significantly more regular church attendance was reported for the nondelinquents ($p<.001$), and for the nondelinquents' fathers ($p<.001$) and mothers ($p<.001$). However, there was no association between delinquency and denominational preference.

The analysis of the socioeconomic ratings of the fathers' occupations showed the delinquents' fathers to have jobs with significantly higher status than those held by the nondelinquents' fathers ($p<.001$). This finding was the opposite of what had been found in the Anglo sample.

The Latin delinquents resembled the Anglo delinquents in having a significantly lower grade level in school than did the subjects in their comparison group ($p<.001$). There was also a strong tendency for both the fathers and the mothers of the Latin delinquents to have left school earlier than had the parents of the nondelinquent Latins ($p<.07$).

PSYCHOLOGICAL TEST RESULTS

The results of the Wechsler Intelligence Scales, which were individually administered to the Latin subjects in English by Anglo examiners, were similar to those found in the Anglo sample and to most studies reported in the literature. The delinquents obtained significantly lower Verbal ($p<.001$), Performance ($p<.005$), and Full Scale ($p<.001$) IQs. As might be expected in a bilingual sample, both the delinquent and nondelinquent Latins obtained Performance IQs that were significantly higher than their Verbal IQs. The pattern of subtest scores was for the most part consistent with the patterns that have been reported in the literature.

On the Choices Test the results for the Latin sample once again resembled those of the Anglos. There were no significant differences in the manner in which the delinquent and comparison groups indicated they would dispose of larger sums of money ($20.00 or $200.00), but in regard to smaller sums (25¢ or $2.00) more delinquents indicated they would buy clothes or spend the money immediately on some pleasurable purchase, while more nondelinquents said they would spend the money on school supplies or save it ($p<.05$ and $<.005$).

Unlike the Anglos, the Latin delinquents and nondelinquents also differed significantly on their choice of places to go ($p<.001$). The delinquents were more likely to choose a distant place, while the nondelinquents favored visiting friends or going to the movies. The delinquents were also more likely to endorse going home, but this was probably an artifact of institutionalization.

The final Choices Test item asked what sort of work the boys would like to do when they grew up. There had been no significant differences on this item in the Anglo sample. However, significant differences were found among the Latins. More Latin delinquents chose a skilled trade, while more nondelinquents chose a profession ($p<.02$). This was consistent with other studies, which have shown delinquents to have lower aspirations than nondelinquents.

The data from the Offenses Test showed a significant correlation between the Latin delinquents and nondelinquents on the mean ranking of the various offenses, although the Rho of .81 was the lowest of the three samples. On the basis of culture conflict theory it was predicted that the Latin delinquents would manifest the greatest amount of anomie or value confusion, and indeed the Latin delinquents were found to be significantly more variable in their ratings than the Latin comparison group, or, for that matter, any of the other five groups, on six of the ten offenses.

On the Card Sort Test the Latin delinquents were significantly more likely to endorse items reflecting mildly deviant behavior patterns among themselves, their associates, and their families. In this respect they resembled the Anglo and Mexican samples. They were also more likely to endorse items indicating authority problems, disrespect of the father and other elders, and ambivalent attitudes toward the mother. In this respect the Latin sample differed from the Anglo sample, in which the delinquents and nondelinquents had not differed strongly on these items. Instead, the pattern resembled that found in the Mexican sample, in which even more extreme disrespect was found to characterize the delinquents.

Like the other two samples, the Latin delinquents indicated that their families were less cohesive than the nondelinquents'. In the Latin sample this was manifested primarily by feelings of rejection, although the delinquents also indicated that there was a lack of communication in their families.

Unlike the other two samples, the Latin delinquents and nondelinquents differed on items that indicated the delinquents felt more economically insecure, more pessimistic about educational and occupational opportunities, and more negative toward school; they also had more problems relating to peers. It would appear likely that this matrix of items indicated the Latin delinquents had not managed to cope as successfully with the special problems facing members of alien minority groups as had the nondelinquent Latins.

On the Cartoon Test more Latin delinquents depicted the mother figure as being punitive, while more nondelinquents indicated she would be inclined to reason with the child ($p<.025$). This was the same behavior pattern that the Anglo had attributed to the father. More Latin delinquents also portrayed the father figure as recommending socially disapproved actions ($p<.05$). There was a noteworthy trend in this direction for the mother as well ($p<.10$). The Latin sample was the only one in which a trend such as this was noted for the mothers. The delinquents' attribution of more antisocial behavior to the fathers was found in all three samples, however.

On the Picture-Story Test the responses of the Latin sample were in marked contrast to those of the Mexican sample. The analysis of the story atmosphere showed the delinquents' stories to have a significantly pleasanter tone than those of the nondelinquents on two of the four cards ($p<.02$–.001). While there were no significant differences in the number of pleasant events, it was found that the Latin delinquents told fewer stories with unpleasant events on two of the four cards ($p<.01$–.001) and had significantly fewer such instances in their responses to three of the four cards ($p<.02$–.0001), with a strong trend in this direction ($p<.07$) on the fourth card as well. This was just the opposite of the pattern found in the Mexican sample, as was the finding that the Latin delinquents' stories to one card had significantly more pleasant economic instances ($p<.02$), while there were significantly fewer unpleasant economic stories told about another card ($p<.05$). The exact meaning of these reversals is difficult to determine, particularly since the data are also internally inconsistent. For example, the pleasanter economic themes in the delinquents' stories are in contrast to the greater economic insecurity they manifested on the Card Sort Test.

MEDICAL EXAMINATION

The pattern of significant differences on the medical examination was mixed, with the delinquents being significantly healthier on some measures and below par on others. The delinquents were found to be lighter in weight than the nondelinquents ($p<.025$), but they were also evaluated as superior in their general development ($p<.01$). They were found to have a significantly lower incidence of skin disorders ($p<.005$) and visual defects ($p<.05$), but they also had a significantly higher incidence of obstructed adenoids ($p<.05$). Their pulse rate before exercise was significantly higher than that of the comparison group ($p<.05$). Unlike the other two samples, there were no significant differences in the systolic or diastolic blood pressure readings of the Latin delinquents and nondelinquents.

Mexicans

SOCIOLOGICAL INVESTIGATION

As was the case in the other two samples, there was greater marital instability in the families of the Mexican delinquents. The analysis of the present marital status of the parents showed that more of the delinquents' parents were unmarried, separated, divorced, or deserted ($p<.005$). More of the nondelinquents were living with both natural parents ($p<.005$).

In a subanalysis it was found that among those boys with broken homes, half the delinquents were living with a natural parent and a stepparent, while the nondelinquents were all living with a single natural parent ($p<.05$). This finding supported the hypothesis advanced by other investigators that adding a stepparent to a broken home often results in more tension and behavior pathology.

In analyzing the sibling patterns in the Mexican sample it was found that there were no significant differences in the number of siblings. However, significantly higher ratios of older to younger brothers ($p<.001$), older to younger sisters ($p<.005$), and older to younger siblings in general ($p<.001$) were found among the nondelinquent Mexicans. In the Mexican family older siblings act as quasi-parents to the younger siblings. The data suggested that this increased familial supervision might deter delinquency. This hypothesis was supported by the fact that no such pattern was found in the Anglo sample, in which there is no such tradition, while a strong but nonsignificant trend in this direction was found with the Latins, among whom this family tradition has weakened.

The same differences in religious patterns were obtained among the Mexicans as had been found in the other two samples, namely, significantly more regular church attendance on the part of the nondelinquent boys ($p<.001$) and their mothers ($p<.001$) and fathers ($p<.001$), with no significant differences in denominational preference evident.

No significant differences in the socioeconomic status of the fathers' occupations were found. Significant differences were found in the educational attainment of the boys and their parents, however. As was the case in the other samples, the delinquents were found to have a significantly lower grade level than the nondelinquents ($p<.001$). In addition, the Mexican delinquents' fathers were found to have left school significantly earlier ($p<.01$) (replicating a strong trend in the Latin sample), as had their mothers ($p<.01$) (replicating a significant difference in the Anglo sample and a strong trend in the Latin).

PSYCHOLOGICAL TEST RESULTS

The results of the Wechsler Intelligence Scale in the Mexican sample were quite different from the patterns found among the Anglos and Latins. While the results of the other samples, as well as those of most of the studies in the literature, had shown the nondelinquents' IQs to be significantly higher than those of the delinquents, the opposite pattern was found in the Mexican sample. No differences were found in Verbal IQ, but on the Performance and Full Scale IQs the Mexican delinquents were significantly higher than the nondelinquents ($p<.001$). This was the result of the extremely low Performance scores obtained by the nondelinquent Mexicans. Indeed, their Performance IQs were significantly lower than their Verbal IQs ($p<.001$), reversing the pattern found in all the other groups. It appeared likely that this reversal was the result of some sort of sampling bias but no definitive explanation could be found.

On the first part of the Choices Test, highly significant differences were found between the Mexican delinquents and nondelinquents in how they would dispose of sums of money ranging from 20 centavos to 20 pesos. In every case more nondelinquents chose to save the money or spend it on school supplies or a gift for mother, while more delinquents chose to spend it on immediate pleasurable consumption or clothes ($p<.001$). These differences were in the same direction as, but more pronounced than, those found in the other two samples.

The delinquents and nondelinquents also differed in their choice of places to go ($p<.01$). However, the pattern of preferences differed from those found in the other samples and did not appear to be related to any theories regarding delinquent behavior.

There was also a significant difference in the work that the delinquent and nondelinquent Mexicans indicated they would like to do when they grew up ($p < .005$). Skilled trades were selected by 80 per cent of the delinquents, while the professions were chosen by 71 per cent of the nondelinquents. A similar, although less extreme, pattern had been found in the Anglo and Latin samples.

On the Offenses Test there was a highly significant correlation between the mean rankings of the ten offenses by the Mexican delinquent and comparison groups ($r = .98$). There was no tendency for the delinquents to be more variable in their ratings than the nondelinquents, as had been found in the Latin sample. This further supported the hypothesis that the Latin delinquents' highly variable ratings reflected anomie.

As was the case in both the Anglo and Latin samples, the Mexican delinquents' Card Sort responses suggested that they and their friends and relations engaged in more deviant behavior than did the nondelinquents; however, in the Mexican sample this pattern was stronger than it had been in the other two.

The most important aspect of the Mexicans' Card Sort results was the fact that the delinquents' statements indicated much more disrespect toward the fathers and other elders and authorities than was found among the nondelinquents. The fathers especially were seen as weak, passive, and not very smart. This pattern was even more marked than it had been in the Latin sample. Apparently, among those raised in the paternalistic authoritarian Mexican family, disrespect of elders is much more closely associated with delinquent behavior than is the case among those raised according to the more laissez-faire or democratic Anglo pattern.

The ambivalent attitudes toward the mother noted in the Latin sample were also found to an even greater extent among the Mexicans. Individual Card Sort responses indicated that perhaps one key to this ambivalence lay in the mother as assuming a dominant but overprotective role in the family, as well as providing an antisocial example in certain respects. One possible explanation for these patterns was the effect of father absence in Mexican culture, in which strong reliance on the father is coupled with contempt toward women.

As in the other samples, the Card Sort data for the Mexican sample indicated less cohesiveness in the delinquents' families. This was manifested primarily by the endorsement of items reflecting quarreling and dissension as opposed to warmth and respect between family members. The Card Sort results also indicated that a lack of communication was more prevalent among the delinquents' families.

Items reflecting feelings of economic insecurity, negative attitudes toward school, and problems with peers did not differentiate the delinquents from the nondelinquents to any great extent. In this respect the results for the Mexicans resembled those for the Anglos more than the Latins. This supported the notion that the prevalence of these items among the Latins was primarily the result of the Latin delinquents' failure to resolve adequately the problems confronting members of underprivileged minority groups.

On the Cartoon Test more delinquents depicted the father figure ($p<.01$) and the mother figure ($p<.005$) as being punitive, while more nondelinquents portrayed them as reasoning with the child. The delinquents also depicted the father as more antisocial in his attitude toward authority ($p<.005$). These differences were similar to those observed in the other two samples and had been anticipated on the basis of previous studies in the literature.

The responses of the Mexican subjects to the Picture-Story Test resembled the pattern found in the Anglo sample more closely than that found among the Latins. The nondelinquents' stories in response to two of the four cards had significantly more pleasant events than did those of the delinquents ($p<.03–.02$). By the same token, the nondelinquents had significantly fewer unpleasant events in response to one of the cards ($p<.005$). This last finding was exactly opposite the pattern found in the Latin sample, as was the finding that the nondelinquents told stories with significantly more pleasant economic instances in response to one card ($p=.0014$). Like the Anglo delinquents, the Mexican delinquents told significantly more antisocial stories in response to two of the cards ($p<.05–.02$) and had significantly more antisocial events in their responses to one of the cards ($p=.0001$). This pattern, too, differed from the Latin samples, in which no significant differences in antisocial events or stories were found.

Why the Picture-Story results for the Mexican and Anglo samples should differ so from those for the Latins was not immediately apparent. Since the test results suggested greater optimism for the Latins, it seemed possible that the reversals might have been the result of increased defensiveness by the Latin delinquents, possibly because they were tested by non-Latin examiners. However, no particular signs of defensiveness were noted on other techniques, such as the Card Sort Test. By and large, in the absence of consistent patterns in the Picture-Story Test data, it seemed advisable not to make any far-reaching conclusions based on them.

MEDICAL EXAMINATION

Unlike the results for the other two samples, the medical data were consistent in showing the Mexican delinquents to be less physically fit. They were rated as being significantly poorer in nutrition ($p<.005$), inferior in general development ($p<.001$), and as having poorer auditory acuity ($p<.025$). The delinquents were also evaluated as having a significantly higher diastolic blood pressure ($p<.05$).

CHAPTER 15

CONCLUSIONS AND IMPLICATIONS

The basic problem that the present study confronted was the cross-cultural generality of patterns of delinquency. Juvenile delinquency is ultimately defined by the local representatives of middle-class society. Despite this, would characteristics that have been found typical of delinquents in the Northeastern United States also apply to delinquents in the Southwestern United States or in Mexico? Are the personality dynamics of the delinquent who is a member of an underprivileged minority group different from those of delinquents who are members of the dominant ethnic group? Are the attitudes and family backgrounds of lower-class juvenile delinquents in Anglo, Latin, or Mexican society significantly different from those of other members of the lower class who are not known to be delinquent?

In addition to their theoretical significance, the answers to these questions could have considerable practical importance. If few differences were found between delinquent and nondelinquent members of the lower class in the various societies, it could be inferred that the best method of preventing juvenile delinquency would be through a broad attack on the basic problems and attitudes of the lower class itself. If significant differences between delinquents and nondelinquents were found, however, it would indicate that specific solutions to the problems of delinquency prevention and treatment should continue to be sought. If quite different social, familial, or personality patterns were found to characterize the delinquents in the different cultural groups, or if the results of the present study should have little in common with those in the literature, it would imply that there was little likelihood that the programs developed in one area would, with minor adjustments, prove effective in a different cultural milieu.

Relation of the Results to the Expected Patterns

On the basis of our review of the literature, certain broad expectations of the patterns that would differentiate the delinquents from the nondelinquents were derived in Chapter 4. Some of these expectations dealt with characteristics of the individual delinquents and others with patterns that might be found in their families. Since most of these expectations were derived from studies conducted in the Northeastern United States, it seemed likely that the Anglo sample would conform most closely to these patterns, followed by the Latin sample, which shared both Anglo and Mexican traditions, with the Mexican sample being the most different.

CHARACTERISTICS OF THE INDIVIDUAL DELINQUENT

Attitudes toward Parents and Authorities

The first major expectation was that the delinquents would have more antagonism against authorities in general and against the father in particular. The instruments most likely to elicit these attitudes were the Card Sort Test, the Cartoon Test, and the Picture-Story Test. No significant differences in the role behavior of any figures were found for any of the samples on the Picture-Story Test. However, the other two instruments did indicate significantly greater attitudes of disrespect and antagonism and the ascription of more antisocial attitudes to the fathers by the members of the delinquent groups. This was more pronounced in the responses of the Mexican and Latin delinquents than among those of the Anglo delinquents.

The cross-cultural differences in this pattern suggested that the more the culture stresses the father's role in the family, particularly at the expense of the mother's, the more closely will attitudes of paternal disrespect be associated with delinquency. Maslow and Diaz-Guerrero (1960) emphasized the importance of culturally sanctioned paternal authoritarianism in inhibiting delinquency. However, if this authority is lacking, perhaps because of the absence of the father from the home, then the failure of the patriarchal culture to provide approved alternative socializing influences might make the father-absent home more conducive to delinquency than would otherwise have been the case. This hypothesis should be tested by further research comparing the association between father absence and antisocial behavior in societies that differ in the amount of culturally prescribed patriarchal authoritarianism.

Additional research is also required to clarify the reason for the strong association between paternal disrespect and delinquency in the Latin and Mexican samples. The simplest explanation is that this disrespect helps cause the delinquency. According to this hypothesis, the child learns negative attitudes toward his father, perhaps because the mother undermines the father-son relationship or because the father is not present in the home. These negative attitudes make it difficult for the boy to establish an adequate identity and may lead to hypermasculine behavior that gets the boy into trouble with the law.

While this explanation is the most plausible one, it is also possible that it was the delinquency that caused the disrespect. According to this speculation, the child for some reason or another developed a rebellious, defiant, antisocial attitude. One symptom of this is delinquent behavior; another is paternal disrespect. The great value placed on respect for the father in the Latin and Mexican cultures would induce the antisocial Mexican boy to attack this particular institution more than the Anglo delinquent, who lives in a culture in which the father's role is less central.

Longitudinal research is required to explore these alternatives properly. If the first alternative is accurate, then attitudes of disrespect should manifest themselves before a delinquent identification develops; if the second hypothesis is correct, the attitude toward the father should not deteriorate until after signs of rebellion have appeared.

Most research has shown that delinquents' attitudes toward the mother are more positive than their attitudes toward the father. This pattern was found to apply across cultures in the responses to the Card Sort and Cartoon Tests. However, attitudes toward the mother appeared to be rather ambivalent among the delinquents in the present investigation. This was particularly true in the Latin and Mexican samples, suggesting a complex interaction between cultural values and attitudes toward the father and the mother. It will be recalled that in the typical Mexican family the mother is regarded almost as if she were sacred. Women in general, however, are held in poor regard, and the woman who masculinizes herself is disparaged. The Mexican woman who is forced by circumstances to become head of a household and raise male children, as were 52 per cent of the Mexican delinquents' mothers, is thus placed in an extremely difficult position. It is likely that her son, in addition to the problems in identification faced by any fatherless adolescent boy, would also have more difficulty maintaining his respect for his mother in the face of this social disapproval than would a boy raised in Anglo society, where the mateless mother's position is more socially accepted. Further cross-cultural research on the parental attitudes of Mexican and Anglo boys in broken homes would clarify this issue.

World View

A second broad expectation was that the delinquents would have a more negative world view, that is, they would see others as being more hostile and rejecting and they in turn would be more suspicious. There was some evidence for this in the data for all three samples. These attitudes were reflected in Card Sort items, which distinguished delinquents from nondelinquents, in Cartoon Test responses, in which more delinquents depicted parents as being hostile, suspicious, or disinterested, and in the Anglos' and Mexicans' Picture-Story Test responses, which showed delinquents telling stories with significantly more antisocial or extremely unpleasant themes. While different sorts of responses were symptomatic of this negative world view in different samples, there was no evidence that it was stronger in one sample than in the others.

Values

The third expectation was that the delinquents would have more antisocial values and attitudes. This was a difficult area to assess adequately, for defensiveness could easily distort the replies. It is the rare interviewer who can learn whether a teen-age delinquent really thinks it is wrong to "borrow" a car for a few hours or to hit someone who has insulted him. Moreover, the defensiveness aroused by questions of this sort could well influence responses to other more neutral items. For this reason, it was necessary to skirt the area of value judgments rather circumspectly. As a result, relatively few data were collected that were directly relevant to this issue.

The data most closely related to this question were the results of the Offenses Test. This instrument showed substantial agreement between the delinquent and nondelinquent group in each sample on the rank order of 10 quite heterogeneous transgressions. However, this procedure was so crude it could only have reflected gross differences in values. The Offenses Test did show significant differences in the variability of ratings between delinquents and nondelinquents in the Latin sample, but not in the other two, thus indicating that differences in value judgments did exist in the Latin sample, at least. These differences appeared to support the notion that value confusion might be engendered by the strain of having to live according to two different sets of social mores and that the inability to resolve this dilemma adequately could be associated with delinquent behavior.

On the Card Sort Test the delinquents in all three samples acknowledged more mildly deviant behavior, such as late hours, smoking, or disliking policemen, on the part of themselves, the members of their families, and their associates. The data also indicated that in all three samples the delinquents attended church significantly less regularly than did the nondelinquents. While these behavior patterns cannot be considered antisocial, they could perhaps be symptomatic of somewhat less socialized attitudes and values. Although much more research is necessary in this area, the results of these preliminary findings would indicate that the observation that the values of delinquents and nondelinquents differ does have cross-cultural generality. Further research on this subject is currently under way. The junior author and Mr. Angel Velez-Diaz are currently conducting a cross-cultural study in which lower-class criminals and noncriminals in Puerto Rico are being asked to rate the seriousness of 141 different offenses, using the procedures developed by Sellin and Wolfgang (1964). Another fruitful approach would be to compare the moral judgments of delinquent and nondelinquent children, using a modification of the approaches devised by Jean Piaget. Participant-observation methods might reveal that delinquents and nondelinquents who agree on whether a given act is right or wrong may disagree on the extent to which extenuating circumstances justify various transgressions.

Achievement

Fourth, it was expected that there would be significant differences between the delinquents and the nondelinquents in the general area of achievement. It was hypothesized that the actual level of present achievement of the nondelinquents would be higher than that of the delinquents, that the nondelinquents would have more of the personal abilities necessary for achievement, and, finally, that the nondelinquents would have more of the attitudes required for achievement in a society dominated by middle-class values.

The best criterion of achievement level was the grade level attained in school. This was significantly higher for the nondelinquents in every sample, thus confirming the cross-cultural generality of the first expectation.

The first criterion of achievement ability was intelligence, as measured by the Wechsler Scales. From the findings reported in the literature it was predicted that the delinquents would have significantly lower Verbal IQs than the nondelinquents. It was also expected that the delinquents' Verbal IQs would be lower than their Performance IQs, indicating they had less aptitude for the abstract reasoning and conceptual abilities that are rewarded in the classroom than for more concrete manual tasks. It will be recalled that the Anglo and Latin samples conformed to this pattern, but that there was a reversal in the Mexican sample.

Another quality important for achievement in middle-class society is the ability to think in terms of the future rather than the present and to defer immediate need gratification in favor of long-term goals. This is a quality conspicuously lacking among most delinquents. The results of the Choices Test indicated that this was true in the present study as well, not only among the Anglos but also among the Latins and Mexicans. By and large, then, with the exception of the intelligence test results in the Mexican sample, the data indicated that the observation that delinquents have fewer of the attributes necessary for vocational or academic success in middle-class society was found to have cross-cultural generality.

Turning to attitudes associated with achievement, it was expected that the delinquents would be more negative toward school, that they would have less ambition, as reflected by lower aspirations, and that they would manifest more economic insecurity and pessimism. It seemed likely that the first of these factors, negativism toward school, would be particularly characteristic of the delinquents in the Latin sample, in view of special conflicts confronting a Latin boy in an alien Anglo school (see Chapter 3).

Contrary to this expectation, negativism toward school was not particularly apparent in the results for any sample. Few of the picture stories dealt with attitudes toward school or teachers, nor did hostility toward school, education, or teachers emerge as a major theme in the Card Sort Test. It did appear as a minor theme, however, and it is noteworthy that it was confined to the Latin sample, in which the greatest differences in school attitudes had been expected. These data suggested that negativism toward school is not a fundamental characteristic distinguishing the delinquent from the nondelinquent when both are members of the lower class.

It is possible that by asking if the delinquents were significantly more negative toward school we were asking the wrong question. Perhaps we should have asked if the *nondelinquents* were more *enthusiastic* about school. The research on lower-class mores reviewed in Chapter 3 indicated that many scholars have found antipathy toward school widespread in lower-class society, and some have indicated that it is the "college boy" orientation that is unusual among lower-class Anglos and Latins (Heller, 1966; Whyte, 1955). There was evidence that enthusiasm for education was significantly more common among the nondelinquents in all three samples. For example, the Choices Test indicated that eight times as many nondelinquents valued education enough to say that if they had 25 cents they would spend it on school supplies rather than on candy or some other treat.

Further research aimed specifically at exploring scholastic attitudes is needed to supplement these data. If it is true that delinquents and nondelinquents differ not in negativism but in enthusiasm toward school, the difference would be more than semantic. It would imply that instead of examining the school system to determine what forces drive boys away from school and toward delinquency, we should instead examine it to determine what there is that gets some lower-class boys interested in learning, and then ask how these positive features could be emphasized so that more boys can become actively involved in the educational process.

The next aspect of achievement motivation was aspiration level.

As we saw in Chapter 2, theorists like Merton (1957) and Cloward and Ohlin (1960) have argued that differences between aspirations and the means available to achieve them are a major cause of delinquency. Others have disagreed with this viewpoint. Rubenfeld (1965) cited data that indicated the aspiration level of delinquents is lower than that of nondelinquents and argued that Cloward and Ohlin overemphasized the importance of vocational opportunities in causing delinquency.

The Choices Test data regarding aspiration level indicated that the nondelinquents in the Latin and Mexican samples did have significantly higher aspirations than the delinquents. There was a nonsignificant trend in this direction among the Anglos as well. These data are consistent with those cited by Rubenfeld (1965). Their relevance to status-discontent theory is not clear cut, however. If the delinquents' aspirations have always been closer to a level they could reasonably expect to attain, then it would pose serious problems for theories emphasizing status discontent. However, it is possible that the lower ambitions of the delinquents represent a downward revision of their original goals. If so, they could be a symptom of the very discouragement described by Merton and by Cloward and Ohlin. Longitudinal research on the developmental changes in aspiration level is required to resolve this issue.

Another attitudinal factor related to achievement is the amount of perceived economic insecurity. Economic insecurity involves not only worries about current financial problems but also pessimism over future opportunities. Although no significant differences were apparent in income level between the delinquents' and nondelinquents' families in the three samples, the psychological tests suggested that there were significant differences between the delinquents and nondelinquents in the Latin and Mexican samples in feelings of economic security and optimism. The lower aspiration levels that we have just discussed could be interpreted as one manifestation of greater pessimism among the delinquents. Items on the Card Sort Test also indicated that the Latin delinquents and nondelinquents felt more economically deprived. The data from the Picture-Story Test were, as might be expected, rather muddled, with more unpleasant economic themes evident among the Mexicans but the reverse trend found among the Latins.

By and large, then, the test data indicated an association between delinquency and economic insecurity in the Latin and Mexican samples, but not in the Anglo. This is noteworthy, for, of the three samples, the Anglo sample had the highest income level and faced the fewest obstacles in the path to economic success, since they were confronted by neither the discrimination facing the Latins nor the generally low standard of living found in Mexico. This suggests that the relation between economic insecurity and delinquency is found only when there are realistic obstacles in the path of economic advancement. To this extent, the data, while fragmentary, were consistent with the arguments of Merton and of Cloward and Ohlin.

Even if these rather tenuous associations should be reliable, the causal connections are far from clear. The question of why there is not more status discontent among the more ambitious nondelinquent Latins and Mexicans, who presumably share the same economic disadvantages, remains unanswered. Rubenfeld (1965) has suggested that the rate of school failure is a crucial factor. Additional follow-up studies controlling the various possible factors, such as father absence, school failure, and ability level, are needed to determine the precise way in which individual factors identified as potentially significant in the present study interact with one another.

To recapitulate the data relating to achievement, most of the hypotheses were confirmed. As expected, the delinquents had a lower level of attainment than the nondelinquents, they were by and large less able to achieve on middle-class terms, and they had fewer of the attitudes generally associated with academic and vocational success.

Physical Characteristics

The last area in which individual differences between delinquents and nondelinquents were explored was that of physical fitness. While some authorities would predict that delinquents would be less fit, either because of biological inferiority or environmental deprivation, the present investigators doubted that there would be noteworthy physiological differences. For the most part, we found little in the data to dissuade us from this view. Of the 90 physical differences tested for statistical significance, only 16 had probability levels lower than .05. The absolute magnitude of many of the statistically significant differences did not suggest that the variables in question were likely to be of great practical importance. Moreover, the Anglo and Latin delinquents were judged superior as often as they were rated less fit. It seemed likely that the physical variables that did significantly differentiate delinquents and nondelinquents, such as visual acuity in the Anglo sample, would probably be important only in interaction with other variables, such as inability to afford glasses.

The one physiological variable that did appear to warrant further investigation was blood pressure. Highly significant differences in diastolic blood pressure were obtained that were consistent with speculations by physiological psychologists as to the patterns of autonomic arousal that might differentiate those who express emotions, such as anger, from those who suppress them. If, as so many have suggested, there are constitutional differences between delinquents and nondelinquents, it appears to the present investigators that such differences are most likely to be found in the area of autonomic responsivity to stress. Most theories of delinquency are stress theories: they single out some source of stress, such as status discontent, school problems, poverty, or family difficulties, and suggest that this stressor may be a cause of delinquency. Empirical studies like the present one may demonstrate a reliable association between this stressful factor and delinquency. However, these associations are always less than perfect, and the question is never resolved why some people in this stressful situation do not become delinquent, while others who are not exposed to the source of stress do. It is possible that the study of individual differences in the autonomic reactions to various forms of stress could provide some clues as to why similar stimuli have such different effects on different individuals.

DIFFERENCES BETWEEN THE FAMILIES OF DELINQUENTS AND NONDELINQUENTS

Family Cohesiveness

Our survey of the literature indicated that the families of the delinquent and nondelinquent groups might also differ in various ways. The first broad expectation was that the families of the delinquents would be less cohesive than the families of the nondelinquents. The least cohesive homes are broken homes, ones in which the parents do not live together or in which children do not live with the parents. This is particularly true if the home has been broken by the inability of the family members to live together amicably rather than by some external factor, such as military service or the death of a parent. Marital stability was evaluated in a number of ways, and it was found that significantly more of the delinquents in each sample came from unstable or broken homes. The nature of the typical broken home varied from sample to sample. Divorce was most common among the Anglos, while illegitimacy was most common among the Mexicans. Broken homes resulting from parental death were not associated with delinquency.

Marital stability is not the only measure of family cohesiveness, of course. A home might be formally intact, yet torn by suspicion and dissension. While no external observations of the quality of family life were made, there was little doubt that the delinquents perceived their homes as being much less cohesive. We have already discussed the Latin and Mexican delinquents' disrespect of their fathers and their ambivalence toward their mothers. There were other indications, as well, that there was less warmth and cohesiveness in the delinquents' homes. In every sample the Card Sort responses indicated that more delinquents wanted to leave home, that more delinquents felt rejected, and that fewer delinquents confided in their parents. Moreover, the Card Sort data indicated that within the delinquents' families there was less communication and more quarreling and dissension. Thus, despite the different social, political, and economic factors that the Anglo, Latin, and Mexican samples had to confront and the different cultural milieus in which they lived, the same lack of cohesiveness that has been found to be associated with delinquency in studies of urban Anglo delinquents, such as the Gluecks' (1950), was found to characterize all three of the present delinquent groups as well. This cross-cultural generality was particularly important in the case of the Latin sample, for it demonstrated that their deviant behavior was not solely a result of external social pressures.

Parental Attitude toward Children

A second factor closely related to cohesiveness is the general attitude of the parents toward the child. Is the child valued as an individual with his own needs and personality? Or is the parents' behavior toward him determined primarily by their own needs and convenience? Without interviewing or assessing the parents directly, it was impossible to assess this dimension adequately. However, indirect indications were available. Probably the most relevant information came from the Cartoon Test, in which it was found that significantly more nondelinquents in the Anglo sample depicted the parent figures as reasoning with a child and explaining to him why a certain course of action was necessary. This attitude was in contrast to the hostility or indifference that more of the Anglo delinquents attributed to the parent figures. Similar trends were found in the other samples. Some of the Card Sort items indicated that the delinquents were more likely to see their parents as being hostile or nagging, and we have already noted that the delinquents felt more rejected. On the other hand, there were no significant differences on the Picture-Story Test.

A less reliable source of data that could possibly relate to parental attitudes came from the results of the medical examination. It will be recalled that in the Anglo sample significantly more of the non-delinquents had had tonsillectomies. It is possible that this could indicate greater concern for the health of their children on the part of the nondelinquent Anglos' parents. However, it could also mean that the nondelinquent Anglos had simply had more tonsillitis. Similarly, the significantly greater incidence of poor nutrition among the Mexican delinquents could be taken as a sign of parental neglect, but it could also have been the result of inadequate institutional diets. In connection with this, it should be pointed out that there were no significant differences in the number of decayed or missing teeth, which is one of the better physiological signs of neglect.

Thus, while there were some indications that the delinquents' parents might have been somewhat less concerned about their children than were the parents of the nondelinquents, particularly in the Anglo sample, no strong differences were found between the delinquent and nondelinquent groups in this regard.

Discipline

A third familial factor that has been identified as being associated with delinquency is the nature and quality of parental discipline. It will be recalled that studies like the Gluecks' and Reckless' indicated that delinquents' fathers and mothers were likely to be more erratic in their discipline, being punitive in some respects and lax in others. However, the studies of lower-class Anglo culture reviewed in Chapter 3 indicated that this sort of pattern was fairly common throughout the lower class and was perhaps not specific to delinquency.

Some data relevant to this issue were gathered in the present study. The Card Sort responses made it evident that the delinquents in all three samples regarded their parents as being overly strict and impossible to please. While the truth of these attitudes is impossible to assess, it does indicate that this attitude, which is so common among Anglo delinquents, is not limited to North American culture.

The responses to the Cartoon Test were more revealing. In all three cultures more delinquents depicted one or both of the parents as using threats of punishment when confronted with undesirable behavior, while more nondelinquents indicated the parents would reason with their sons. Not only were these data obtained on a measure that was less likely to be distorted by dissimulation, but also the results are consistent with those reported in other studies, in which parents and offspring were interviewed directly about disciplinary practices.

The Card Sort responses indicated that the delinquents' parents were less likely to be aware of their sons' whereabouts or behavior. This was probably a result of the delinquents' being less willing to confide in their parents, a finding reminiscent of Bandura and Walters' (1959) observation that the parents of aggressive delinquents discourage dependency or closeness in their sons.

The sociological investigation rather unexpectedly provided additional findings relevant to discipline. It was found that there was a significantly higher ratio of older to younger siblings among the nondelinquents in the Mexican sample. A similar trend was noted in the Latin sample, but no such pattern was evident among the Anglos. It will be recalled from Chapter 3 that the older siblings in the traditional Mexican household assume an important role in the supervision and discipline of their younger brothers and sisters. The fact that the nondelinquents had more older siblings suggests that this extra supervision may serve to inhibit delinquency. While further research is necessary to test this interpretation, it indicates that the study of sibling relationships and delinquency would be almost as important as the investigation of parent-child relationships and delinquency, at least in the Mexican family.

By and large, then, the results of the present study were consistent with those of other investigations that have found delinquents to come from homes with less adequate supervision and more inconsistent discipline, with greater reliance on punitive techniques and less use of reasoning.

Socialization of the Parents

It will be recalled from Chapter 2 that a number of studies demonstrated that delinquents' parents were likely to be criminal or to exhibit other forms of deviance, such as alcoholism or promiscuity. While no direct measures of criminal behavior were available for the parents, data were available from which the socialization of the parents in the various samples could be inferred. One such indicator has already been discussed in the section on family cohesiveness, namely, the higher incidence of divorce, desertion, and illegitimacy among the parents of the delinquent boys. Another indication of socialization is church attendance, and it will be recalled that in every sample the parents of the nondelinquents were found to attend church significantly more regularly than did the delinquents' parents. Finally, it was noted that the delinquents' parents had left school earlier than the nondelinquents'.

The Card Sort Test included items reflecting parental values, such as attitudes toward police, doing a boy's homework for him, and getting into auto accidents; on these items the delinquents in the Latin or Mexican samples had significantly higher rates of endorsement than did the nondelinquents.

It was on the Cartoon Test that the most relevant data regarding the sons' perceptions of parental values were obtained. Two cartoons depicted situations that called for an indication of parental values; in all three samples it was the delinquent group that had significantly more members depicting the parent as making a less-socialized response in the situations.

A definitive cross-cultural study of parental values and delinquency would necessitate the direct assessment of the parents themselves. Such research should be undertaken. One fruitful approach would be to ask the parents of delinquents and nondelinquents in various cultures to resolve various ethical dilemmas and explain their reasoning.

The data from the present study indicated that the delinquents in all three cultures perceived their parents as being less socialized, and, insofar as marital instability, scholastic achievement, or church attendance are measures of socialization, the objective data corroborated this perception.

Achievement Level of the Parents

The final area in which differences between the parents of the delinquents and nondelinquents was expected was in the degree to which they would provide conditions in which the children could develop achievement motivation. One datum relevant to this expectation was the achievement level of the parents. In the Anglo and Mexican samples the grade level of one or both of the delinquents' parents was significantly lower than that of the nondelinquents', and a strong trend in this direction was found for the Latins as well.

The socioeconomic status of the fathers' jobs is also relevant. These results were mixed, with the Anglo delinquents' fathers having significantly lower-status jobs, no difference being found in the Mexican sample, and the Latin delinquents' fathers having significantly higher-status jobs. By and large, these bits of data are consistent with the notion that the lower achievement of delinquents is a learned familial pattern.

Implications of the Results

The most important finding of the present investigation was that, despite the many differences between the three cultural groups, the same basic factors differentiated the delinquents from the nondelinquents in all samples. While there were differences in emphasis, the similarities far outweighed the differences. This means that delinquency cannot be ascribed to fundamentally different factors in the different cultures sampled. Mexican, Latin, and Southwestern Anglo delinquency are basically the same. It is not valid to ascribe the Latins' delinquency to culture conflict, for example, or the Mexicans' to poverty. This may be disappointing to the reader who is seeking a new or different explanation of delinquency, but for those of us who are searching for lawful regularities in behavior it comes as a relief. These similarities indicate that the patterns found in one ethnic group are for the most part generalizable to other ethnic groups, which suggests that theoretical explanations derived in one sample could well apply to others. If the findings for the Anglo

sample had differed considerably from those reported for other Anglo samples in the literature, or if the patterns in the Latin or Mexican samples had been quite different from those found in the Anglo,
our hopes for finding general patterns or deriving broad theoretical
principles would have been dashed.

To be sure, some important differences were found among the
various ethnic samples. The data indicated, however, that these differences were not primarily a result of differences in ethical values
as some have suggested. Instead, it was the cultural differences in
family patterns and child-rearing methods that appeared to lie at
the root of the differences that were obtained. In particular, the emphasis on authoritarian paternalism in Mexico seemed to foster a
pattern of delinquency in which disrespect of parents and other
authorities was a central aspect.

The fact that so many highly significant differences were found
between the delinquents and nondelinquents in all three samples
was also of major importance, for it indicated that the differences
noted in some other studies were not simply artifacts of comparing
lower-class delinquents with middle-class nondelinquents. While
some of the patterns noted for delinquents are more common in
lower-class culture, important differences still remain between delinquent and nondelinquent members of the lower class.

THEORETICAL IMPLICATIONS

Turning to the implications of the data for theories of delinquency, there was no evidence that delinquency was the result of innate
or environmentally caused physiological inferiority, defective glands,
or mental deficiency. While some of these variables may be factors
in certain individual cases, they were clearly not generally associated with delinquent behavior.

By and large, the differences that did emerge favored environmental theories of delinquency in general and familial theories in
particular. This could have been partly a result of the research design that eliminated social-class and neighborhood differences as a
systematic source of variance. Lower-class status probably constitutes a major pressure toward deviance, although studies of the frequency of unreported delinquency among middle-class youth (Short
& Nye, 1958) suggest its apparent importance has been exaggerated.
However, even given a broad class-associated pressure toward devi-

ance, it appears that differences in the family are crucial in determining whether or not a lower-class boy does in fact become delinquent. Marital instability, a lack of mutual respect and affection among family members, indifferent or hostile parents, a passive or absent father, and lack of achievement motivation or asocial behavior on the part of the parents all appeared to increase the likelihood that a lower-class boy would become delinquent. The opposite factors, such as an intact home or parents who will reason and explain things to a child, as well as adequate supervision and consistent discipline by the parents or older siblings, appeared to decrease the likelihood that a boy would be delinquent.

In terms of some specific theories, there was little evidence that culture conflict was a major cause of delinquency in the Latin sample. To be sure, there were indications of more anomie in the Latin delinquent group, as we would expect from Thorsten Sellin's (1938) analysis. However, the fact that the same familial and behavioral patterns found in the Anglo and Mexican delinquents also characterized the Latin delinquents indicated that culture conflict was not a sufficient explanation for delinquency in the Latin sample. Other things being equal, the added stress of living in two cultures may have constituted a pressure toward deviance, but this alone did not cause delinquent behavior. Indeed, the problem of being a "have-not" in a "have" country appeared to be more stressful for the Latins than the problems of differing values.

There was also little support for Cohen's (1955) view that delinquency grows out of problems encountered in the school setting. There was little evidence that the delinquents were significantly more negative toward school than were the nondelinquents, although there was evidence that more of the nondelinquents were enthusiastic or strongly positive toward school. In fairness to Cohen, it should be pointed out that he was focusing on a specific form of delinquent behavior, gang vandalism, and not on delinquency as broadly defined in the present study. Moreover, by confining the present investigation to members of the lower class, most if not all of whom would be likely to experience problems in adjusting to school, according to Cohen's analysis, we were minimizing the chance of finding the differences in school attitudes that might be predicted from Cohen's theory.

The study did provide evidence consistent with Sutherland's differential-association theory. The indications that the delinquents' parents had achieved less and were less socialized, as well as the data suggesting that the delinquents' associates engaged in more delinquent behavior, were what would be expected on the basis of Sutherland's position.

The implications of the data for Cloward and Ohlin's (1960) and Merton's (1957) theories of discrepancies between opportunities and ambitions were less clear. Possibly, this is because it is not clear what sort of patterns would be predicted on the basis of these theories. The delinquents were found to have lower aspirations, which opponents of position-discontent theories might interpret as disproving the hypothesis that there is more discontent among lower-class delinquents. On the other hand, this lower aspiration level could be viewed as a symptom of discouragement resulting from obstacles to economic advancement. It has already been noted that the group facing the biggest obstacles, namely, the Latin delinquents, did appear to manifest the most economic insecurity and pessimism, although even here the data were mixed. As was the case with Cohen's theory, using delinquents and nondelinquents living in the same neighborhood could have minimized the apparent influence of position discontent.

None of the tests directly assessed individual psychopathology. The test most closely resembling such clinical instruments, the Picture-Story Test, did not indicate any major or consistent differences between the delinquents and nondelinquents. Alienation from one's family is associated with most forms of psychopathology, and the Card Sort results did indicate that such feelings were more common among the delinquents in all three cultures. On the basis of Maslow and Diaz-Guerrero's (1955) research, one might hypothesize that more psychopathology would be found in the Mexican sample, since it would appear from their theory that delinquency is more infrequent and hence more of a deviation from the norm in Mexico. There was some support for this notion in the data, particularly in the Card Sort material relating to attitudes toward the parents. However, these were suggestive data at best and cannot be considered a real test of this hypothesis in the light of possible sampling differences and the absence of more definitive measures of psychopathology.

While the familial data were not directly related to theories that delinquency stems from individual psychopathology, they were quite consistent with the personal-control and containment theories offered by such scholars as Reiss (1951), Nye (1958), and Reckless (1961), all of whom emphasized the importance of familial factors in socialization.

Turning to multiple-factor approaches, the data were consistent with the position that delinquency is the result of complex interaction of many individual factors. In almost every area examined— intelligence, family setting, physical fitness, impulsivity, and so on— significant differences were found between delinquents and nondelinquents. However, a great deal more research must be done before this multiple-factor *approach* can be considered a multiple-factor *theory*. It is not enough to identify various factors that are reliably associated with delinquency within a given culture, or even across cultures as in the present investigation. Each factor must be subjected to closer scrutiny to determine *how* it interacts with other variables. Given that antisocial parents are conducive to deviance, does the school operate to increase or decrease the likelihood of a boy becoming delinquent, or does this in turn depend on social class, intelligence, visual acuity, and the like? Only by detailed research charting the parameters of the various factors to determine how they accentuate or minimize each other's influence will it be possible to predict delinquent behavior in advance rather than explaining it after the fact. Such predictive power is essential for any theory.

To do this, it will probably be necessary to focus first on different subtypes of delinquent behavior rather than dealing with the phenomenon of delinquency as a whole. Broad studies like the present one will have to be supplemented with smaller, more carefully controlled field and laboratory investigations aimed at determining the way two or three of the important factors interact in various forms of delinquent behavior. When research has advanced to the point where multiple regression equations predicting delinquency can be constructed, or flow charts specifying exactly how important factors like class, family, and school operate in defined situations can be devised, then what is now a multiple-factor approach will be advanced to the point where it can be referred to as a multiple-factor theory.

This is a difficult, complex, long-term task, but it can be done.

Reckless' studies have charted the interaction between personality traits and the effects of living in a high-delinquency neighborhood (Scarpitti, Murray, Dinitz, & Reckless, 1960). Earlier, studies by the McCords investigated the interaction of such factors as parental values and affection for the child. With the advent of high-speed electronic computers with large memory cores it is now possible to construct mathematical models that will specify the interaction of various factors once the basic data charting these parameters are collected. While the magnitude of this task is great, it is our conviction that the attempt to raise multiple-factor approaches to the level of theory will be more fruitful in the long run than efforts to create simpler theories that arbitrarily eliminate potentially significant variables.

PRACTICAL IMPLICATIONS

The similarity between the patterns of delinquency in the three samples suggests that programs of prevention and rehabilitation proven successful in one area or with one group could be applied to other groups in other areas with reasonable hopes for success. This is a most encouraging finding. If each sample had been unique, it would have implied that solutions to the problems of that sample would probably not be applicable to other delinquent groups. It would have suggested that there was little chance of developing general principles for working with delinquent boys.

The fact that significant differences were found between the delinquent and nondelinquent groups after the neighborhoods had been matched indicated that the problem of delinquency is not the same as the problems of poverty or lower-class culture. This means that programs aimed at solving the problems of poverty cannot be expected to eliminate delinquency. Delinquency prevention must take on the task of coping not only with poverty, which undoubtedly does constitute a pressure toward deviance, but also with those other factors that help determine whether or not a poor boy becomes delinquent. Poverty can be cured with money, but money alone is not likely to prevent delinquency. Extrapolating from the data, it would appear that programs aimed at restoring the integrity and independence of the family would have the most beneficial influence. Broad family programs like "Project Know How" (Parker & Dunham, 1968)—which is designed to prepare preschool children for first grade, starting at age one or two, to teach their mothers the basic fundamentals of home economics and human relationships, to train the fathers so that they can support their families on their earnings, and to enhance the health of all the family members— should have much more success than welfare programs that merely enable the family to survive to repeat the same maladaptive patterns in successive generations.

The consistency of the data from the present study, as well as research with various prediction devices (Briggs & Wirt, 1965), indicates that it is possible to identify high-risk groups—boys of whom a large proportion might be expected to become delinquent without some form of intervention. Delinquency prevention efforts should focus on such groups. It will be recalled that the more authoritarian the culturally approved family pattern, the more delinquency was associated with a breakdown of family cohesiveness and rebellion against the parents. From this we might hypothesize that for potential delinquents from ethnic groups with a tradition of a strong patriarchal family, such as Latins or Italians, casework that includes the parents might be most effective. Such casework requires a delicate approach lest the counselor undermine rather than bolster the parents' effectiveness. In the long run, however, such a family-centered approach is likely to be more economical, since all the children in the family may benefit from the intervention. In cultural groups that do not have the tradition of a strong effective family, however, it might be better to focus on the individual delinquent and his peer-group interactions.

Cross-cultural Research and Delinquency

It seems appropriate for us to conclude with some reflections on the place of cross-cultural research on delinquency. There is no doubt that a cross-cultural investigation involves infinitely more problems in data collection, reduction, and interpretation than does a mono-cultural study with the same number of subjects and variables. The fact that over 10 years elapsed from our first pilot studies to the completion of this final report is ample evidence of these difficulties. Is such cross-cultural research worth the time, effort, and money?

As with most of the questions we have posed for ourselves, the answer is not a simple "yes" or "no" but an equivocal "sometimes."

The investigation of some independent variables will always require cross-cultural designs. For example, in the present report we have formulated several hypotheses about the relation of delinquency to paternal authoritarianism. To test these hypotheses adequately would require the use of cultural groups in which the socially defined role of the father differs. Similarly, studies of the relation of values to delinquency will probably require different groups with different value orientations.

Apart from such specialized investigations, routine cross-cultural research to determine the generality of patterns of delinquency does not appear to be as urgently needed as it did when the present investigation was launched. If major cultural differences had been found between the cultural groups in the present study, then continued cross-cultural research would have appeared necessary to determine the generality of each new observation about delinquents made in any given cultural group. However, since the present investigation gave us no cause to suspect that the juvenile delinquent in one ethnic group is radically different from the delinquent in another ethnic group, it appears more important at this stage to devote research efforts to the task of determining how the various factors that have been identified as being associated with delinquency interact with one another. Such research can be done most efficiently using but a single ethnic group. When such studies have charted the basic parameters, then it would be important once again to conduct a major cross-cultural investigation to determine the generality of these interactions.

Appendices

1. The Boys Individually
2. Statements Used in the Reading Test
3. Frequency Distributions for the Offenses Test
4. Statements Marked "True" in the Card Sort Test
5. Physical Examination Form

APPENDIX 1

The Boys Individually

It seems appropriate to give the reader at least a slight notion of what the boys are like as persons, including, besides their reactions to the tests, the background of their families, the circumstances of their day-by-day existence, the behavior of their parents, the size and location of the houses they live in, and so on. For this purpose a series of vignettes has been prepared by the senior author, each dealing with a member of one of the six groups of boys encountered in the study. These descriptions are necessarily brief, yet they will, it is hoped, convey a sense of the humanness of the subjects and function in a limited way as a personal introduction and as the beginning of acquaintance.

Daniel McRae[1] (Anglo Nondelinquent)

In a six-room frame house at 3516 Waller Street, San Antonio, Texas, lives the McRae family. Identical in floor plan with hundreds of other houses in the subdivision, the McRae residence differs from the others only in that it has been recently painted and it has a weeping willow tree in the front yard. However, it also lacks the clutter of toys so common in the neighborhood, mainly, it may be presumed, because Frank, the

[1] All personal names used are fictional.

younger boy in the family, is already eight years old and is beginning to transfer his outdoor activities beyond the confines of his own home to the two vacant lots near the end of the street. The yard might have looked rather neat, were it not for the old Chevrolet in the driveway, which is nearly always in the process of being taken apart or put together by Daniel, the older boy, aged 16.

There is nothing distinctive about the house at 3516 Waller. When the McRaes bought it new about six years ago, they had shut their eyes to the monotony of similar houses that stood like soldiers stiffly at attention on both sides of the narrow street for block after block, whichever way one looked. They wanted a bigger and better house than the one they had been renting, and one located in a "better" neighborhood. These ends they had achieved, and they were satisfied. Most of the neighbors had numerous small children, but this did not disturb the McRaes; there had been even more children where they had lived before they moved to Waller Street.

The husband and father, Frank Daniel McRae, was born in a small town in northeast Texas. He left his home town for San Antonio immediately after graduating from high school and, except for a brief period of duty with the Coast Guard, he has lived in San Antonio ever since. He is a steady worker, employed by the city at a salary of $85 a week, which seems hardly enough to support the family at the apparent economic level on which they live.

Mr. McRae is a sociable man. He has several friends with whom he goes fishing and golfing on weekends. He seems contented with his job and his way of life. Mostly, his decisions have been quickly made, without undue contemplation, followed by action without regret. He is not the kind of man who looks backward in speculation as to what might have been. While in the service, he met his future wife at a public entertainment, fell in love with her, and married her shortly thereafter. Unfamiliar with the social position of Latin Americans in San Antonio, he hardly noticed that Dolores was of Mexican origin until after he had married her and met her relatives.

Mrs. McRae is about the same age as her husband, but has only an eighth-grade education. She seems, however, to be at least of his intellectual level in all other respects. She was born in a small town about fifty miles from San Antonio, to which she moved with her parents when she was six years old. Unlike a large part of the Latin population of the city, she is almost completely Americanized, preferring association with Anglos to members of her own ethnic group. She continues to belong to the Catholic Church and has brought up her two sons in this faith, but makes no effort to convert her husband, who still goes to the Methodist Church once in a while, apparently for the purpose of keeping himself convinced that he is a Protestant.

Dolores may be somewhat hampered in her efforts to move more fully in Anglo social circles by the presence of her mother, who lives with the family and still prefers Spanish to English in her conversation. She does not interfere in any noticeable way with the McRae's family affairs, but nevertheless may be responsible unconsciously for Mr. McRae's habit of leaving his wife out of his social life and spending many of his evenings away from home. Daniel has little to do with his grandmother and she, realizing that he wants to be identified with Anglos rather than with Latins, does nothing to embarrass him.

Everything seems to run smoothly in the McRae household. There are no quarrels, no harsh words, no crises. On the other hand, there is no warmth, not much intimate contact, and little demonstration of affection, except now and then by Mrs. McRae for her children. It seems as if everyone goes pretty much his own way, expecting and receiving but little beyond tolerance from the other members of the family. To the casual passerby the McRae home would seem to be nearly ideal, and in many ways it undoubtedly is. In any event, it appears to furnish a satisfactory background for the 16-year-old boy with whom we are primarily concerned.

Daniel is a well-developed boy, an inch or so over six feet in height, weighing 160 pounds. He stands erect and moves about without the awkwardness characteristic of many young teen-agers. Except when working on his car, he is clean and neat looking. These traits, together with his dark hair and eyes and the fine teeth he shows when he smiles, combine to make him unusually attractive. It is no wonder that he is popular with girls.

He is fond of his mother, but not excessively so. He does not regret the passing of his childhood or of the attention he consequently no longer receives. His mother is no longer his confidant, though he still recognizes in her a protector who will come to his aid at any time she may be needed. Her character, he states positively, is above reproach. Possibly one may detect in Daniel's emphatic approval of his mother a slight feeling of guilt for his disposition to disavow her, possibly for the same reason that he ignores his grandmother, namely, his desire to assure himself a place among the Anglos.

Perhaps this is also the reason Daniel prefers his father to his mother, though he would never boldly say so. Without being insistent, he attributes to his father every desirable trait, finding no fault with him whatever. The father obviously serves as a model for his son. Daniel says he wants to be like his father, but not like his mother. If he succeeds in conforming to the image he has of his father he will certainly become a man of the highest personal qualities. In only one respect does he hope to excel his father; he thinks he will make more money. However, this does not constitute a complaint; he says his father has always given him whatever he has needed in the way of spending money.

Daniel's school record is good. He was promoted to high school from the eighth grade with eight As, three Bs, and two Cs. He has not maintained this level in high school, having to date two As, 10 Bs, 14 Cs, and three Ds. He should perhaps be doing better, since his IQ, as indicated by various tests, is somewhere between 113 and 121. There is nothing to indicate that he is in any way maladjusted in school. He says he enjoys getting an education and his class attendance record proves it. In the seven semesters he has completed in high school he has never been tardy and has been absent only four days.

The question of his attending college was not discussed with him, though apparently he does not anticipate continuing his education after graduation next spring. His friends, many of whom are older than he, have already finished high school or have dropped out and are seeking jobs, not admission to college. Possibly their attitudes influence Daniel in his unconcern for the future. As to occupation, he says he once considered becoming a doctor, but has given up the idea. It is, of course, evident that he is not thinking of following the occupational example of his father. Finding something profitable to do may become a serious problem for Daniel when he faces up to it, which he will have to do after the end of school next June.

Meanwhile, the days pass happily. School imposes no hardship on him and his extracurricular activities are satisfying. He goes fishing with his father occasionally, and plays baseball and basketball with his schoolmates and other friends. He belongs to the Hi-Y. He attends the movies once in a while with a girl friend. One can hardly imagine a more nearly normal life for a high school senior. This normality is reflected in the several tests to which he, like all the other subjects in the study, were subjected.

The stories he told in response to the pictures of the Symonds Test indicate that the characters in the pictures have problems, but not serious ones. Thus, the main figure in Picture A-4 is identified as a man who has come to make a payment on a loan that he had contracted earlier. In Picture A-7 a boy is being corrected by his teacher for creating a disturbance in class. The teacher is hopeful that his misdemeanor will not be repeated. The story about Picture B-1 is given a time and place orientation, namely, the Civil War. Possibly this is a by-product of Daniel's interest in history. The problem presented is that of a servant who is dissatisfied with his status. The man in Picture B-6 is described as mentally retarded and consequently under mild confinement in an institution. Daniel's concept of the nature of mental retardation permits him to suggest that the man will some day be released from the institution.

It will be seen from these stories that Daniel falls in with the cheerless mood inspired by the pictures, but does not think of the actors as being in hopeless situations. He indulges in only the faintest suggestion of moralizing. There is no indication that he identifies himself with any of the actors.

In the Cartoon Test Daniel represents his parents as responding in a manner that might be described as in complete accord with the requirements of standard middle-class morality. The boy who finds the wallet is not suspected of theft by his parents, but is advised to turn the money over to the police. The boy with the cigarette is told that he is too young to smoke and that he should not have accepted the cigarette as a gift. The demand of the third boy for a car is met with the question of his driving ability and his sense of responsibility; he is reminded that he must earn the money to pay for it if he wants a car. The boy who reports a policeman at the door encounters calm, unfrightened parents who merely suggest finding out what the policeman wants.

Daniel's choices of ways to utilize money are nicely balanced between spending for recreation and utility, on the one hand, and saving, on the other. His arrangement of offenses on the Offenses Test is in complete accord with the notions of the investigators as to how they should be arranged. His drawings of the male and female figures are good, though he avoids the difficulty of drawing the boy's hand by putting it into a pocket. His comments on the latter drawing may quite possibly be taken as a rather modest self-evaluation. He said, "It's an ordinary guy. He's about the average teen-ager, about 16 years old. He's not real popular, just average."

There is little to add to this by way of conclusion. Daniel is, of course, hardly to be described as average. He is, on the contrary, so exceptional that he may be approaching the ideal held by middle-class society for its adolescents. Though belonging to a rather low-income family, with mixed-marriage parents, little affection in the home, and a resident grandmother, he nevertheless has reached the age of 16 without ever having been in trouble with his teachers or the police or, as far as we can tell, with anybody. It would appear that certain home conditions, often alleged to be the causes of delinquency, do not necessarily produce it even when present in multiple form. We could wish we had many more Daniel McRaes.

Edgar Piggott (Anglo Delinquent)

The Piggott family is on the brink of dissolution. Mr. Piggott left about six months ago, giving no indication of any intention to return, and Mrs. Piggott has filed suit for divorce. She assumes the divorce will be granted soon and optimistically looks forward to re-establishing the family by marrying a Mr. Lafferty, who has, so she says, shown a great deal of fatherly interest in her problem boy, Edgar. Without being explicit she conveys the impression that Mr. Lafferty is practically waiting at the church door for her to become his bride.

The present state of affairs is not the outcome of sudden change. It has been in the process of development for a long time, but even as recently as two years ago the Piggotts did not anticipate anything like the present crisis. It was at that time they bought the new six-room house they now occupy and an outfit of furniture to go with it. They have been making monthly payments on both the house and the furniture and so far have managed to deliver these payments on time, but there is serious question about the future. Although Mrs. Piggott has a job, her wages will scarcely feed the family and pay off the debts as well. She has given up her telephone and would like to sell the 1956 Chevrolet that stands as if permanently parked in the driveway. She is, of course, counting heavily on help from Mr. Lafferty. In response to a question, she says he's an old, old friend.

Harvey and Nellie Piggott started out auspiciously enough. Both were born in small towns in West Virginia, in families that provided them with limited educational and economic opportunities. Harvey finished the seventh grade; Nellie dropped out of the eleventh. They were married in 1940, when Harvey was eighteen and his bride was nineteen. The young husband had only a poorly paid job; nevertheless, they seemed happy enough at first. When the war came along, Harvey enlisted, and when the war was over and nothing better was in sight, he decided to make the Army his career. This led to the family's moving frequently as his assignments took him to various places and thus, it seems in retrospect, began the series of crises that led to the present disaster. Apparently, the Piggotts could not adjust to the itinerant life required by Harvey's occupation. They moved to San Antonio in 1955, then spent a year in the Far East, after which they returned to San Antonio. The expectation of remaining there a long time led them to buy the house they live in.

Had the Piggotts been adequately resourceful, they could no doubt have adjusted themselves to the frequent changes of residence and to the separations that must be endured by families in the armed forces. However, they were handicapped by lack of capacity for meeting family problems. Mrs. Piggott is a vacillating, uncertain person. She cannot make up her mind and keep it made up, nor choose a sensible course of action and stick to it. For example, though she now says she knew better, during a protracted absence of her husband in 1953 she allowed herself to enter into an affair with a man that resulted in her having an illegitimate child. The threatened rift was patched up by placing the child in an adoptive home, but Mrs. Piggott's relations with her husband were never quite the same afterward. She has no insight into or understanding of her difficulties. She would need, it seems, almost continuous counseling to keep to the role she should fill. One wonders how a person with so little general ability could secure and keep the job she now has. One wonders, also, how Mr. Lafferty can find her as interesting as she suggests. Her children, unfortunately, seem to have inherited all of her objectionable traits.

Her husband is different but quite as severely handicapped in character. He is ruthless, overbearing, and selfish. He beats all the members of his family whenever he is at home. Naturally they all hate him. About six months ago he was court-martialed for incest with his daughter Paula, then 12 years old. The evidence was not conclusive, though all the judges believe the charge was true. This event precipitated the final break between Piggott and his wife and led to the separation and the divorce proceedings.

The Piggotts have six children: Sandra, 17, engaged to marry Jerry Basford, who is in the Air Force; Sandra's twin brother, now in the Air Force; Edgar, aged 15; Paul and Paula, twins aged 13; and Albert, aged two. The older girl looks and acts like her mother; the younger one, Paula, resembles her brother in appearance and her mother in behavior, that is, she is completely passive, with no disposition to assert herself. She does not appear to have been affected in any way by her father's attack upon her, though, like the rest of the family, she hates him. Paul, her twin brother, has already begun a delinquent career, having been placed on probation for theft some months ago. Edgar, of course, is the big problem.

Born in Elkins, West Virginia, he is now 15 years and eight months old. Blue-eyed and fair-complexioned, he is healthy in appearance, but not handsome. With a height of five feet seven inches and a weight of 150 pounds, he gives the impression of being a little heavier than he ought to be. It cannot be said of him that he resembles a criminal or a delinquent. He has some tattoo marks on his arm, which he refuses to explain and which might be taken as indicative of deviancy, though this is admittedly slight evidence. His nails are bitten to the quick, but this might be merely the result of nervousness. However, his court record is little short of appalling.

As far as we know officially, his troubles began while the family was in

Baltimore, where Edgar, at the age of eight, was placed on probation. The next recorded episode occurred in Tokyo. According to the court history he ran away from home; the army became concerned about him and persuaded his father to have him examined by a psychiatrist, at whose report the father became enraged. Because of the father's attitude, it appears that nothing came of it. It is clear, however, that the court report does not tell the whole story. Edgar himself admitted to the interviewer that he cannot remember a time when he was not assigned to a probation officer.

What we may call the San Antonio series of difficulties began in March, 1956. Since that time Edgar has been arrested nine times, has been in and out of institutions four or five times, and has been continuously on probation. As a result of several expulsions, he has attended six different schools, all public, where his grades, when he stayed long enough to accumulate any, were, according to his mother, Cs and Bs. He was in the eighth grade when he was expelled from the Spring Valley School; in the Bexar County Boys School, which he attended later, he was in the seventh. According to the records of the latter, his grades, while he was there, ranged from C to F. It is apparent that his mother exaggerates his intellectual achievements. He has never gone to church nor held a job.

His reported offense in San Antonio was arson. He was charged with starting a fire in the Spring Valley Christian Church that resulted in damages amounting to $20,000. He has committed many offenses since, most of them felonies. After a number of commitments to the Bexar County Boys School, he was finally sent to Gatesville State School for Boys in December, 1960, where he is now.

What sort of boy is this Edgar Piggott, who has been in trouble so many times and who is so unresponsive to efforts made to change and improve his behavior? We have selected for presentation here some revealing incidents in his life and some of the results of the tests given to him. They provide, we believe, a fairly good answer to the question.

In April, 1956, there was a costly fire in the Spring Valley Christian Church. An investigation among the boys of the neighborhood led to Edgar Piggott as a suspect. It was soon learned that the boy had broken into the church, performed some acts of vandalism, stolen some ornaments, and then started a fire to cover up his offenses. Although he was not yet 12 years old, his actions showed considerable experience and skill in the art of burglary. In view of his youth, no punitive action was taken against him, but, because of the casual manner in which his acts were treated by his mother, a probation officer undertook an inquiry into conditions in Edgar's home. The officer received no cooperation at all from

Edgar's father and little from his mother. It was clear that the father accepted no responsibility for the discipline of his son; whatever control was to be exercised would have to be carried on by the mother. The conclusion reached was that Edgar's home life was so bad as to constitute a decided handicap to his future.

The court officer hopefully recommended that Mrs. Piggott be helped in her efforts to regulate her son's behavior. To this end it was planned to instruct her as to ways in which Edgar's position in the family could be made more secure and consistent. It was also suggested that, through counseling, the poor relationship now existing between Mrs. Piggott and her husband could be improved.

Unfortunately, Mrs. Piggott did not have the strength or stability of character necessary to profit by the assistance of the court worker. Her family continued to lead a chaotic existence; although she managed to hold her job, her children and housework were neglected. She failed utterly in her sporadic efforts to control Edgar's behavior. He paid no noticeable attention to her admonitions. Mr. Piggott's contribution was completely negative.

In August, 1958, Edgar, then 14 years old, turned up in Corpus Christi, where he promptly broke into a drive-in cafe, from which he took cigarettes, candy, food, and other items. A few hours later he made the acquaintance of a local delinquent of about his own age and an adult police character, Tom Sully. Together they broke into Carey's Cafe, taking more cigarettes, and later they burglarized a construction worker's shack from which they carried off a portable radio.

Arrested and taken to the Nueces County Detention Home, Edgar was at first unwilling to tell where he lived. He gave the impression that he was a shy, retiring boy who was extremely diffident about answering questions. Other evidence indicates that this attitude on Edgar's part was merely a pose, maintained only as long as he thought he could avoid telling the Corpus Christi authorities where he lived. When, after a couple of days it became evident to him that he would have to stay in the detention home until he told the truth, he admitted that he had hitchhiked from San Antonio, arriving in Corpus Christi only some six hours before he was arrested. He gave no plausible explanation as to why he had elected to come to Corpus Christi, nor why he had engaged in the burglaries, except that he wanted some of the things he had taken. Under repeated questioning he admitted that he had once set fire to a church, that he had stolen more bicycles than he could remember, and that he had many times been sent to the Bexar County Boys School. He also recalled that he had run away from home while he was living in Japan. He did not appear to have any guilt feelings or any great concern as to what would happen to him as a result of the offenses he had just committed.

After some difficulty the Juvenile Probation Office got in touch with Mrs. Piggott. She seemed relieved to hear of Edgar's whereabouts and kept asking when he would be sent home. She referred to his earlier offenses as minor pranks and refused to recognize the seriousness of his present trouble. It seemed not to occur to her that there was any problem at all, except that of Edgar's return to San Antonio, and she persistently argued that it was the duty of the Corpus Christi authorities to furnish Edgar with transportation. It soon became clear that no cooperation could be had from Edgar's mother; Mr. Piggott consistently refused to be interviewed on the subject. Arrangements were subsequently made to turn Edgar over to the San Antonio Juvenile Department. He was returned to his home, where he promptly resumed his career as a delinquent.

It might well be supposed that a boy so persistently delinquent might be suffering from mental defect or disease. To resolve this question he was given several psychological and psychiatric examinations; when he became an object of study in the delinquency project, he was given a series of tests, the results of which could also present us with some information as to his character and personality. The results are uniformly negative, that is, they show no stigmata, mental or physical, that point unmistakably to criminality. Yet they do show that Edgar is an unusual boy. This will become evident as we proceed.

Edgar was tested by means of the Wechsler-Bellevue Intelligence Scale for Adolescents and Adults, which indicated for him an IQ of 103. He was completely cooperative during the test, though he frequently became tired, saying he couldn't do it, but he responded well to encouragement. He showed no hesitation in answering questions, and his replies indicated a good understanding of social situations, as well as a disposition to utilize this knowledge for his own purposes. Like so many maladjusted boys, he scored higher on the Performance Scale than on the Verbal Scale, the difference being 21 points. He did especially poorly in the Digit Span and in Arithmetic and very well on Picture Arrangement and Picture Completion. In taking the test he worked slowly and gave up easily. References to car-stealing in his answers indicate the thoughts that ran through his mind. Almost all his reports on the Ink Blot Test were in terms of people or animals. He completed a sentence (Miale-Holsopple) "Parents would worry less if," by adding "I'd be good," and another, "It's easy to get into trouble when," by adding "you hang around bad company." "No one can repair the damage caused by," was completed by "fire." To "The best of mothers may forget that," he added "they're married";

to "The kind of animal I would most like to be," he added "a German Shepherd"; to "Nothing is harder to stop than," he added "smoking."[2]

In reply to questions as to how he would dispose of varying amounts of money, Edgar made no mention of saving; he would invariably spend the money for immediately consumable goods.

Edgar was given the "Draw-a-Person" Test twice, each time by a different interviewer. Both the two female figures and the two male figures strongly resembled each other, as if he had practiced repeatedly over an extensive period in an effort to produce identical figures. This was especially noticeable in the male figure, which depicted a dejected-looking man with a large face and bushy hair, looking to the right. The details are numerous and fairly accurate. In connection with one drawing he commented, "He is tall and needs a haircut. The boy ran away from home, because his father didn't like him. Needs a new pair of pants and a haircut." With respect to the other drawing he said, "Looks like a bum or something." We regret never having seen his father. We suspect there may be a resemblance between Mr. Piggott and the male figure drawn by his son.

Edgar strongly dislikes his father, thinks he is not very smart or very honest. However, he credits his father with many good qualities and wishes he could be like him. Edgar also wishes he could be like his mother, despite the dissimilarities between the parents. He finds no fault with her whatsoever. It is clear that, despite her shortcomings (which we know about from sources other than Edgar's reports), he likes her very much. Possibly the affection he feels for her is a result of his need for the affection denied him by his father. However, the relationship between the mother and son is not such as to enable her to influence the boy's behavior significantly.

This boy fully realizes that circumstances could be better for him than they are. He yearns for the happy days of childhood and at the same time is looking forward to the time when he will be old enough to join the Army. His occupational choice is centered on the military; he would like to be a law enforcement officer in the Air Force. He displays numerous inconsistencies in his replies to questions about himself. He says he does not like comics, yet reads comic books on crime whenever he has the opportunity. He claims to be a good sleeper, yet admits it is hard to go to sleep when you are lonely. If he had his life to relive, he says, he would keep out of trouble.

[2] From *The Projective Use of Incomplete Sentences* by J. W. Holsopple and Florence R. Miale (in press). Courtesy of Charles C. Thomas, publisher, Springfield, Illinois. Copyright © 1950 by Florence R. Miale and J. W. Holsopple.

Edgar's stories, told in response to Symonds Pictures, appear to be evoked by events in his own experience. In Picture A-4 he says "Looks like a boy getting his allowance. His father is mad at him, probably because he wants too much money." In Picture A-7, "It's a boy going to his mother and telling his troubles. The mother is not mad, but she is scared what his father will do." In Picture B-4, "A boy is going out of his home mad. He thinks everybody is against him and he's looking for a fight." In Picture B-6, "A boy that ran away from home. He's sitting there thinking about all the good things he had and how he shouldn't have run away from home."

One may wonder why a boy who so well diagnoses his own case does not reform. It appears that he fully recognizes the advantages of law-abiding behavior. The reason is probably to be found in the disgracefully poor home life made available to him. Yet, despite the experiences he has had at home, he would like to go there; he has several times commented on the unhappy state of boys who run away from home. Unfortunately for Edgar's future, it does not appear that the outlook is promising.

During the time consumed by the investigation there was no sign of Mr. Lafferty.

Mario Campos (Latin Nondelinquent)

The Campos home, which the family has been renting for many years, wears the dejected look of poverty. Dilapidated, unpainted, rickety, it lacks every amenity except electricity and a telephone. Each of the five small rooms has a 25-watt bulb dangling at the free end of a short piece of wire from the ceiling. There is no gas, no bath, no toilet, no water. The latter commodity has to be fetched from an outdoor hydrant half a block away. Charcoal or wood is used as fuel for cooking and probably also for such heating as is done. We wondered why, in the circumstances, there was a telephone. A gift from the four children who live away from home, it was explained; they want to be able to talk with their mother. The family has no car. When transportation is absolutely necessary, they call on one of the married children.

Gregorio Campos and his wife, Josefina, are old, 63 and 60, respectively, which by Latin standards is very old. They have been married for 33 years. Gregorio thinks perhaps he was married before, but his memory has gone from him, he says; he cannot be sure of anything that happened so long ago. Both members of the couple were born in San Antonio and have lived there all their lives. Josefina has never attended school and speaks no English. She has scarcely been outside the city and has been downtown only a few times. Her husband, Gregorio, is a carpenter. In search of jobs, he has been in some of the towns of South Texas. He appears to be healthy and strong despite his age and does not plan to retire soon. He earns from $35 to $40 per week. He speaks English fairly well though, like his wife, he has no formal education.

Gregorio spends but little time at home, in contrast to his wife, who hardly ever leaves it. His work keeps him away most of the time; for the rest he saunters around the neighborhood until he finds a group of men about his own age with whom he then stops to talk. He spends no money on recreation. He goes to church, but only rarely. His wife is not much of a church-goer, either, though she manages to attend when the occasion is important. Her chief recreational activity, if it can be so called, appears to be listening to the radio, which she keeps turned on constantly.

The Campos family has six children, four sons and two daughters. The daughters and the two older sons range in age from 28 to 32. All of them are married and all of them, their parents proudly assert, own the houses they live in. This may mean, of course, only that they have made the small down payment required and are keeping up with the monthly installments, though even this is no small achievement. It is obvious that the Campos parents are more than satisfied with the successes of their children. At home are the two younger sons, Felipe and Mario, aged 16 and 14, respectively. The older boy is attending the technical high school, the younger is in the seventh grade.

Mario, the main character in this sketch, is a wiry, dark-complexioned lad, with large brown eyes. He is five feet four inches tall and weighs 106 pounds. In general development he seems to be somewhat below average for his age. He has already lost four of his permanent teeth and, unless he receives dental attention promptly, will soon lose another. The interviewer feels like telling his parents they ought to do something about this until she recalls the amount of Mr. Campos' pay and that two teen-age boys have tremendous appetites.

Mario's score on the Wechsler is disappointing. He is personally so pleasant and cooperative that it seems he should do better. His English, however, is strongly accented and he has considerable difficulty expressing himself. As is so often the case with bilingual subjects, he does much better on the Performance Scale than on the Verbal Scale. And together they yield for him an IQ of only 78.

His school work, naturally, reflects his limited ability. He is two years behind most of the pupils of his age, but still seems to make more Ds than Cs. One might expect him to be discouraged with the slow progress he is making or, at least, that he would feel badly about his low grades. But not so. When asked which subjects he liked best he said "P.E.," but quickly corrected himself with "No, I like them all." On further questioning he insisted that he liked every course and every phase of school life, including all his teachers. "The teachers," he said, "are all good to me." His parents apparently are oblivious of the meaning of school grades and promotions. Could it be that his cheerful attitude toward what might be regarded as a poor performance is a reflection of the peace of mind that is his because of parental ignorance?

He has no unattainable occupational ambitions. In response to a question about what he would like to do when he is a grown-up, he referred to a brief part-time job he once had and said he would like to work in a furniture store. Nor does he yearn to visit far-off places. When asked where he would go if he could go anywhere he wanted to tonight, he answered without hesitation, "To a movie." Similarly, he would not splurge on luxuries if he had money. His only choices were saving and buying clothes.

Mario takes an unemotional and detached view of his parents, possibly because of the many years that separate their respective ages from his. He does not prefer one parent to the other. He thinks they love each other, since they get along with each other well, but he notes that they do not go anywhere together. The parents do not play with Mario, and he seems not to care. He does not share his troubles with them, nor do they seem to have any of their own. The family gathers regularly for meals and all of them eat together. They seem to be held together in a kind of loose camaraderie, basically a sort of symbiosis, which is a matter of convenience to all of them but does not require nor lead to any emotional involvement on the part of anyone concerned.

Mario describes his father as an easy-going, permissive man whose disciplinary hand rests ever so lightly on his youngest son. The father has never prescribed a curfew and rarely shows displeasure to Mario. The boy ascribes to his father all the standard acceptable attitudes and behavior patterns. Unlike many boys, he accepts the idea that old people are wise. On this basis it might be reasonable to say that Mario greatly admires his father but for the care he takes to say that he does not wish to be like him.

Mario's relationship with his mother is much the same. He describes her as a woman who does not nag or scold, who does not disapprove of him or become angry, who stands up for her son and asks his friends to visit him at his home. Mario enjoys being with her, but does not wish to be like her. She resembles her husband in that she seems to be completely permissive as far as Mario's behavior is concerned.

In speaking of himself, Mario appears to be completely contented. He has no nostalgia for childhood nor does he long to be old enough to escape from his present environment into the adventurous life of the army. He is not popular with girls, though he likes them well enough. He has many friends, most of them somewhat older than he. He enjoys playing football and baseball and going to the movies. He does not care very much for reading, but reads comic books when he has the opportunity. He can think of no complaints of the treatment he receives at home.

Mario's reactions to the Symonds Pictures are exceptional and since they reflect fairly well the easygoing level of his own life we give them in full. Picture B-6:

He is sleeping. He was reading a book and got sleepy. It was late in the night when he was reading the book. Morning came and he was still sleeping. His wife is making breakfast for him, she thinks he is awake and she is calling him. She knocks on the door, but he doesn't answer. She opens the door and sees him sleeping in the chair. She calls him but he doesn't answer. He is waking up and he goes to the bathroom to wash up and eats his breakfast. I think that's enough.

Picture B-1:

This is the same man. After breakfast he goes to work and as he is walking by the street he meets a lady and says 'Good morning' and continues to go to work. When he arrives his manager tells him he is late and if he is late once more he is going to be fired. He is working and he is a little sleepy. He sits down and he sleeps. The manager calls him but he is still sleeping. He wakes up and the manager is mad, and he goes back to work. After the manager is gone, he sits down again and goes to sleep. After work he wakes up and the manager tells him that if he sleeps again he will be fired.

Picture A-7:

After he comes home, his wife is telling him that he better go to sleep so he can wake up early so he won't be late for work. He goes to sleep, but he doesn't feel sleepy and tells his wife he is going to the movies and she argues with him. He goes out angry and she is warning him that he is going to get up late, but he goes. After two hours pass, he comes home and feels sleepy and goes to bed. In the morning he wakes up and sees the clock and he puts clothes on, doesn't eat, because he is late.

Picture A-4:

The manager is very angry and tells him he is going to give him another chance and then he starts working. After work the manager is paying him money. He tells him that this better not happen again and the man thanks him and tells him he won't be late again. He goes home with the money and tells his wife to fix something to eat, because he is hungry. He gives her the money. She is happy, because she knew that he was late for work and the manager didn't fire him.

Were he delinquent, it would be easy to rationalize Mario's derelictions by noting the poverty in his home, the absence of demonstrations of affection, the handicap of bilingualism and low mentality leading to poor school performance and presumably frustration. All these are present, yet Mario is a normal, happy, nondelinquent boy. ¿Por qué?

Ramón Rocha, Jr. (Latin Delinquent)

The first thing that strikes the reader of the Rochas' record is that, besides the son, Ramón, they have eleven daughters and live in a three-room house. The problem eases somewhat with the discovery that only the three youngest daughters, 15, nine, and four, live at home. The others, some of them married, live elsewhere, but all in San Antonio. The absent ones are all the offspring of an earlier marriage of Ramón Rocha, Sr. Even with only six persons in the house it is inadequate. The rooms are small and the structure is in poor repair. Considering that the house is located in a decaying area, the rent they pay seems excessive. The neighbors are, however, even poorer than the Rochas. No books or magazines are to be seen anywhere in the neighborhood. The main problem at the Rocha residence is where to sleep. The parents have one room, the girls another, leaving the kitchen for Ramón. Since there is not room for a bed, the boy has to make do with a thin mattress and two or three covers, which are rolled up and pushed under a bench during the daytime. The kitchen is the largest room in the house and consequently has to serve in several capacities. It is not only a kitchen, it is also a dining room and living room. Here is where Mrs. Rocha comes early in the morning to prepare breakfast; here also is where the person who is last to retire stays until the moment he goes to bed. Ramón never gets what he considers a full night's rest. As for privacy, it hardly exists for anybody in the Rocha home.

The father, Ramón Rocha, was born 54 years ago in a small town in South Texas, from which he was brought by his parents at an early age to San Antonio, where he has lived ever since. He went to the public schools of San Antonio for parts of four years, which was not enough to make reading English easy for him, and, unless compelled to by the circumstances, he never undertakes it. He speaks English fairly well, though with a strong accent. Most of his associates are Latins and most of the time he speaks Spanish, though, never having had any formal education in that language, he cannot read it. Orally fluent in two languages, he is illiterate in both.

He was married in 1925 to a woman who died about 12 years later, leaving him a widower with seven daughters. In 1939 he married Serafina González, who became the mother of Ramón and three other children, all daughters. Despite the fact that he had several dependents at the time, Rocha senior served in the army in World War II and soon after his return entered the occupation at which he is now engaged. Employed as a sheetmetal worker at one of the several United States Air Force bases near San Antonio, he earns $95 a week, enough, now that most of the children are self-supporting, to enable the family to live in comparative comfort. They have no telephone, but they do have a three-year-old Chevrolet in good repair.

Mr. Rocha is in good health, with an excellent work record. He seems to get along well with his fellow workers and his neighbors, but has the reputation of being strict to the point of harshness or even cruelty in dealing with his family.

His wife, Serafina, 15 years younger than her husband, has a couple of years more schooling than he, but seems no better educated. She lived with her parents until she was married, and has never been employed. She has proved to be wholly uncooperative in her dealings with the authorities when her son got in trouble and is regarded by them as unreliable, though it seems possible that she may not understand fully what is required of her. She seems confused and overwhelmed and helpless when discussing Ramón's problems, tending on the one hand to minimize them as trifles not worth her attention and on the other hand to deplore them as a crushing catastrophe. There is good reason to believe that she has less than normal intelligence.

The Rocha family belongs to the Jehovah's Witnesses Church and all the members are fairly regular in attendance.

Let us now have a look at the kind of boy produced by the kind of home and parentage we have described.

Known to his friends and family as Junguito (Junior), Ramón makes a really impressive appearance at the interview. His clothes are well-fitting, neat, and clean. His shoes are nicely polished, his hair combed. He greets the interviewer with a pleasant "Good morning, ma'am," followed by a quick and ready smile. He certainly does not look like a delinquent. Ramón is five feet four inches tall and weighs 111 pounds. He looks younger than he is, possibly because he is a good deal shorter than one expects a boy of his age to be. His complexion is described by the doctor as olive. No slighter word than handsome will adequately describe his general appearance.

According to his mother he was born in the Robert B. Green Hospital with a physician in attendance. The birth was normal, with no complications. Except as indicated below, Ramón has been in good health ever since he was born. He is now nearly 17 years old. At nine he had a tonsillectomy; at 10 he suffered a compound fracture of the left leg as a result of being hit by a car while he was riding his bicycle. He was in-capacitated for more than two months, but made a complete recovery. At the age of 14 he struck his head on a rock while diving into a swimming hole and nearly tore off his entire scalp. He spent some time in a hospital after this injury; later he received treatment at home from a doctor. The scars left after the replacement of his scalp are barely visible; they do not adversely affect his appearance in the slightest degree.

His mother has seized upon Ramón's head injury as an explanation for his deviant behavior. She says that he still suffers from it, that he is gradually becoming "hard-headed." She also states that during the last two months he has had a number of extremely severe headaches. He is not now receiving any medical attention, though it is possible that he needs it. Although he has the appearance of health, he nevertheless has a body temperature of 99 degrees.

According to Mrs. Rocha, Ramón used to do well in school. In view of his poor showing on the WISC, his IQ being 66, this seems quite unlike-ly. No official grades are available, because he has so frequently changed schools; the last two years or so he has been so objectionable that he has been repeatedly expelled. He has been variously charged with being in-solent, with disrupting classes, and with threatening to harm the football coach. He has been described as being antisocial and as a troublemaker. He is, of course, not now in school nor likely to be, since no school will admit him. He is said to have completed the eighth grade. His delinquent career, at least that part of it that has found its way into the records of the juvenile department, began only about a year ago, but includes several episodes.

A little more than a year ago a crisis and a change arose in the rela-tionships of Ramón's parents to each other, which may possibly have had some effect on the boy's behavior. A neighbor told Mr. Rocha that his wife was seeing another man. This may have been untrue; at any rate, she has steadfastly denied it. However, Mr. Rocha believed it and pro-ceeded to give his wife a series of cruel beatings. She has never quite forgiven him for this outrage, with the result that the couple has engaged in a good deal of quarreling since that time. Ramón's delinquencies began about the same time as the trouble between his parents. He sided with his mother and had some unhappy sessions with his father as a conse-quence.

The first charge levelled against Ramón was armed robbery in which he used a knife to threaten his victim. He was placed on probation, but was shortly thereafter apprehended a second time for a similar offense. This time, too, the judge let him off with probation. The third time, Ramón was found involved with a gang of four other boys in attempting to rob a man on the street. The members of the gang had no weapons and the victim managed to fight off his assailants. This time, however, the judge's patience was exhausted; he sent Ramón to Gatesville State School for Boys, where he is now.

This disposition of the case can be at least partly blamed on the parents, especially the mother. She refused to cooperate with the probation officers in keeping track of her son and seeing to it that he reported regularly to the probation office. The father managed to stay out of the picture, though he expressed himself as concerned and about to engage in an extensive reformation project for his son. He has bought a farm, to which he says he plans to send Ramón to work as soon as he is released from the reformatory. The plan may have some merit, though it is by no means certain that Ramón will fall in with it. Boys with an urban background are not often satisfied with the lonely isolation of the farm.

Some insight into the boy's character may be gained from noting his performance on the tests. As previously noted, he has an IQ of 66 according to the WISC. As is usual with maladjusted boys, his score on the Performance Scale was definitely higher than his score on the Verbal Scale. This result suggests not only that Ramón has not had enough of the right kind of teaching in school but also that he suffers from being unable to overcome the handicaps of his bilingual environment. In a situation less difficult he might have made a higher score on the WISC. However, his language handicap is undoubtedly one of his serious problems.

His answers on the Card Sort Test are in some cases contradictory. There is, for example, plenty of evidence that he dislikes his father and that, consequently, he relies on his mother alone for emotional security, yet in his answers he shows an ambivalence that is hard to understand in the circumstances. His arrangement of offenses indicates a very poor understanding of the meaning of the terms.

His performance on the Draw-a-Person Test is replete with detail, yet extremely infantile in the impression it conveys. The female figure looks much like a doll, and as if it had been drawn with the deliberate intent to create the likeness of a doll. Both figures are rather small, thereby adding further to the impression that Ramón is of low mentality.

Any evaluation of Ramón is of necessity inconclusive. There seems to be no way in which it can be confidently asserted that his problem is not due to his unhappy home life. The occurrence of his delinquency and the outbreak of quarreling between his parents seem to be more than a coincidence. On the other hand, it is difficult to believe that an otherwise normal boy will suddenly go berserk without a good reason. The question remains as to whether Ramón can be considered a normal boy. It is hard to forget his poor performance on the intelligence test and the possible damage done by the accident in the swimming hole.

José Paz González (Mexican Nondelinquent)

The family of José Paz González could well be described as extended, perhaps even as a clan or tribe. It includes the grandparents on both sides and numerous aunts, uncles, and cousins. Most of the adults are agricultural workers, who often make more or less lengthy trips into the farming areas around Monterrey. This results in frequent changes in the personnel of the households, with shifting of the children from one home to another, as the exigencies of the current employment situation may demand.

José's parents have their headquarters in a large and crowded neighborhood of low-income families. The streets are unpaved, crooked, and not wide enough for two vehicles to pass, which makes little difference, for only rarely does a truck or car venture to negotiate the ditches, ruts, and pits, which in fact constitute the streets. The area is poorly drained, so that when the occasional rains come to Monterrey most of the streets and many of the houses are flooded. Water and electricity are available, but only a few of the residents can afford them. Obviously, they can afford certain other purchases; there are 10 cantinas in the immediate vicinity of José's home.

The Paz residence, like most of the others, is of wood, apparently in slightly better repair than most. There are only two rooms, scantily furnished, but the house is supplied with both water and electricity. The rent is 150 pesos a month.

It is fortunate that at least some of the members of the family are often absent, for the household consists of the parents and nine children ranging in age from two to 16 years. Six of them are girls, aged four, eight, 10, 13, 14, and 15. José is 16 and has two brothers aged seven and two. When they are all at home for the night they pretty well fill up the two rooms. José's admission that the house is crowded sounds, in the circumstances, like an understatement.

The father of this large family, Pedro Paz, is a vigorous man of 38, a farmer who spends most of his time working on his farm, which is located southeast of Monterrey. Born in a rural village, Sr. Paz has never adjusted occupationally or otherwise to city life. This does not mean that he lacks intelligence. He has completed only four years of school, yet has learned to read well enough so that he has been able to make newspaper reading a major leisure time activity. He also enjoys an occasional movie. He says he is unable to estimate his income, since it varies with the size and quality of the crop and the market price, but it is obviously good, certainly much higher than that of most of his neighbors in the *barrio*, who work as ordinary unskilled laborers in the city.

His wife, Carmen González, aged 35, was born in a small town in Coahuila. She and her husband were married at ages 15 and 18, respectively. They lived in Matamoros, Tamaulipas, for seven years before moving to Monterrey. Their nearness to the United States did not apparently offer them much opportunity to acquire North American culture, for neither of them knows any English. Carmen finished only two years of school, not enough to enable her to read. When questioned about her employment of leisure time she says she spends it resting. She is in excellent health, though she says she once had an operation.

The children are all reported to be in good health, though their education, especially that of the girls, has been somewhat sketchy, owing to their frequent change of residence. José started to school in Matamoros, transferred to Monterrey, then returned to Matamoros to the home of an uncle, where he is continuing his education. He is taking a commercial course that currently includes accounting and typewriting. At the time this study was in progress he was on vacation at the parental home in Monterrey.

The physical examination showed José to be in all respects practically normal. He has four carious teeth and suffers from chronic pharyngitis, but these ailments are so common among boys of his class that their presence can scarcely be regarded as abnormal. The boy is five feet three inches tall and weighs 106 pounds, not an impressive set of measurements for a boy of 16. Yet he looks healthy, has a clear though dark complexion, and seems to have an abundance of energy. He was interested and cooperative throughout the examination.

In his response to the WISC he was atypical for the boys in the sample, in that he made a much higher score in the Verbal Scale than in the Performance Scale. His IQ for the combined scales was 71. Some doubt is cast on the validity of the test when one looks at this boy's school record. He has never had to repeat a year and appears to be doing reasonably well in his school work at present.

As might be expected from his low score on the Performance Scale, his drawings of persons were poor for one of his age. However, his comment on the male figure is of some interest as a revelation of his own ideals. "His name is Pedro Rosales. He is 23 years old. He is a workman. He works in the building trade. He went to school for six years. As to character he is honest and of rather happy disposition. Sometimes he is sad when he thinks about his work or about his family. His satisfaction comes from work. Nothing about it displeases him."

Further information on his understanding of the normal demands of

life come from his response to the Symonds Test. Three of his answers are
quoted verbatim:

Picture A-7:

He is the son of those wealthy parents who like to do evil things, because he
thinks that because they are rich he can do anything he pleases. He thinks
they have the money to take him out of any jail he may be in. Sometimes
his parents give him advice. His mother says to him, "Don't think that because
you are rich you can do whatever you please. Think before you do anything;
don't do anything just like that, foolishly." The boy understands everything he
is told, but thinks it is easy to do anything that pops into his head. One day he
wounded someone. His father, as a form of punishment and a warning said to
his wife, "This time we won't do anything for our son, because we are tired of
giving him advice and seeing him disregard it. So, what we are going to do is
to put him in a correctional school so he can conduct himself well and be good
instead of bad." Every day they would go and visit him at the school. Time
went by, the boy is almost a man when he leaves school, and he left with different ideas. He thinks about what he did and then his parents are satisfied to
see their son was no longer what he used to be in the past.

Picture B-1:

This is a young man who used to go out every night with his friends to wait at
the corner with them, just loitering. Sometimes his parents would tell him to
be very careful with his friends, because they could get him mixed up in something and then blame him for it. The boy takes their advice and no longer goes
out with them. He got himself a job. He would come home from work, eat
supper, and go to bed, and in the morning he would go to work. On Sundays
he went to a movie or to a dance. But he did not like to go accompanied by his
friends any more, because he realized it was better to go by himself, because his
friends could lead him into evil roads or vices, which he did not like.

Picture B-6:

This was a boy who would not obey his parents or his brothers. Sometimes he
would get drunk and not go home, or not go until the next day. They put him
to work. He wouldn't go; he'd rather go somewhere else. He didn't like his work;
he would leave and go out with his friends. He grew up and didn't know his
responsibilities. He thought about getting married, but he didn't know how to
work. His life was very difficult.

These responses indicate that verbally at least José has assimilated the
standards of behavior characteristic of the "good" boys in his culture.
There is nothing in his responses differentiating him from most of the
other boys in his group. Moralizing is nearly always found wherever the
response is long enough to permit it. This is generally true of the delinquents as well, though they nearly always include some accounts of
actual delinquency in their stories.

The relationship José maintains with his parents is indicated by his responses in the Card Sort Test. He wishes to be like his father, though he recognizes that his father is no paragon. The father worries about his income and does not always act intelligently. He is not strictly honest and is tolerant of misdeeds that do not result in apprehension, yet on the whole he favors obedience of the law. Though José is not satisfied with the amount of spending money he has been receiving, he concedes that his father is unselfish in providing for the family, that he always turns over the money he received to his wife. According to José, he spends very little money on himself. José expects to make more money than his father does.

José does not wish he could be like his mother. He feels he is too old to be the object of her demonstrations of affection, though he likes to be with her. She defends her children against outsiders, but requires obedience from them and keeps close watch on their behavior. It is apparent that José is pretty free from emotional dependence upon his parents. Perhaps this is a consequence of the fact that either they or he have been away from home a good deal of the time.

The parents get along with each other well enough, according to José. They go out together, they enjoy each other's company, they do not quarrel or argue. Yet José says he does not always approve of their actions. Apparently their lives seem pretty dull to him. They rarely go to church. They do not manage their financial affairs very well. Their son speaks of them much as if they were people he knows well but with whom he has little emotional involvement.

José's attitudes toward himself reveal him as a pretty normal boy. He thinks life was more pleasant for him when he was younger and it will be pleasant again when he becomes a little older. However, he does not feel unloved or neglected. He has never thought that perhaps he is an adopted son. His birthday is remembered, he sleeps well, he is popular with girls and likes them, collectively. He thinks an education will help one to success in life and goes to school to secure an education, not because he has to. He liked his first teacher. He has made a definite occupational choice; he wants to be a secretary. He likes movies, especially Westerns, and reads comics when he has the opportunity. Though not especially athletic, he is fond of baseball. He has been influenced a good deal by the rural life and background of his parents; he says if he had 200 pesos he would buy a piece of land. References to crime and criminals are totally absent from his responses to the various tests to which he was subjected.

He is, as is obvious, a fairly typical nondelinquent. Not too closely supervised by his parents, he has grown up for the most part in a neighborhood that might well spawn delinquents. Perhaps his exposure to rural life has saved him. No one can know, though it seems reasonable to predict that he has passed the age when he is likely to yield to the temptations of crime, that he is, in fact, pretty well set in his nondelinquent ways, and that he will become a law-abiding adult, content to accept whatever fate may hand him in the way of a job and other meagre rewards of life.

Ignacio Pacheco Gil (Mexican Delinquent)

The *barrio* (or neighborhood) where the Pacheco family lives provides as poor an environment for homes as can be imagined. There are no parks or playgrounds, nor any sanitary services whatever. The streets present a dismal aspect owing to the numerous drainage ditches, mud puddles, and garbage heaps of which they are largely composed. A few of the houses are of wooden construction; most of them are of adobe with ragged tin roofs. All of them are makeshift in that they have been constructed by do-it-yourselfers, the people themselves, who live there, few of whom have had any training whatever in the art of house-building. In spite of this environment the inhabitants as a whole are peaceful and law abiding, though, understandably, there are a good many criminals, mostly thieves, who steal not so much from viciousness as from necessity.

The Pacheco house is made of adobe and has in it three small rooms, arranged in a row from front to back. The hinges of the door to the outside are broken so that it is necessary to lift the door when opening or closing it. The furniture consists of the indispensable items only. Everything about the house is dilapidated. The occupants pay no rent, which is fortunate, for their income is both small and uncertain.

The founder of this family, Edmundo Pacheco, came originally from Mexico City, where he was born 43 years ago. He was married in 1942 to Gloria Gil, who bore him three sons and a daughter. They were poor from the beginning and became poorer as the number of children increased. Edmundo's earnings, derived from his work in a shoe repair shop, were too small to provide for his family. They moved from bad houses to worse ones, as they were evicted from one after another for nonpayment of rent, eventually ending up in an abandoned squatter's hut, which they repaired themselves. Not long after they had moved, Edmundo was apprehended for a murder he had committed in Mexico City many years earlier. The police took him there to be tried. Convicted, he is now serving a life term in prison. There is not at present any communication between him and the rest of the family.

The mother, 10 years younger than her husband, married him when she was 15. She had gone to school for five years. Left with four children to support she worked as a servant and occasionally as a prostitute. After a haphazard existence of two or three years, she entered into a free union with Manuel Torres that lasted until two years ago. Three children were added to the family during this period. Manuel's income as a chauffeur was insufficient to maintain so many persons; consequently, the Pacheco children sometimes lived for months as lodgers with various relatives. The free union came to an end when Manuel, tired and discouraged, deserted, leaving no address nor, of course, any provision for the support of the family. At the time of this study only one member of the family was employed, namely, the oldest daughter, aged 17, who works as a dancer in a low-class cabaret. This girl is the mother of an illegitimate child, the care of which requires that Gloria remain at home most of the time as a baby sitter. The older children wander around town looking for something of value that may be carried off and sold for a little money, which is promptly exchanged for food.

In this apparently hopeless home environment lives Ignacio Pacheco Gil, aged 16 years and three months. He is quite small for his age, five feet two inches tall and weighing 102 pounds. The physician reports in the physical examination that he has enlarged tonsils but no other serious physical defects, and may be classed as good looking. In his responses to the WISC he follows the usual pattern for boys of his kind, having a relatively high score on the Performance Scale and a much lower score on the Verbal Scale, the combination of which gives him an IQ of 79. He started to school at seven, had to repeat the first and second years, then, without finishing the second year, he dropped out, remaining so until about three years ago when he was sent to a school for delinquents. There he was again placed in the second year. The teachers in this school are said to be especially well qualified to teach boys like Ignacio. He says he likes all the teachers, but prefers the women to the men because they are less severe.

Ignacio's irregular school attendance may be accounted for in part by the irregularity of his home life. During a comparatively brief period he has lived with his parents, with his grandparents, with his mother and stepfather, with his mother alone, and with other relatives. On several occasions he stayed away from home, living by himself, no one knows how, for a month or more at a time.

Such an environment is not calculated to produce strong attachments between a son and his parents. The failure of such attachments to develop is well demonstrated by the mixed-up replies given by Ignacio in the Card Sort Test. He has some difficulty in determining whether the reference to the father should apply to his actual father or to the stepfather, but since he dislikes both of them, this may not make much difference.

The father, according to Ignacio, worries about losing his job, spends his nights away from home, gets mad easily, thinks only of himself, believes everyone is against him, and does not object to a little successful law-breaking. He is not regarded by his son as being very smart.

Ignacio's mother fares little better in her son's evaluation. She scolds, she does not care what he does, she does not stand up for him, she hates policemen, she tells Ignacio's father when he does something she doesn't like, and she does not usually know where her son is. Nevertheless, he is rather fond of her, though he has no wish to be like her. It can only be concluded that she has failed to establish herself firmly in Ignacio's esteem.

Ignacio observes that his parents argue and quarrel a great deal, that they do not laugh and talk together, nor do they go to parties or the movies together, nor do they seem to have much fun. Finally, they do not love each other. Ignacio ends up his evaluation by stating that he likes one parent more than the other; obviously, his mother has some slight hold on his affections despite all that has happened.

Growing up has brought no rewards to Ignacio. He says he was happier when a small boy and wishes he could be little again. Sometimes he thinks he is an adopted son. He recognizes the value of an education, but says he attends school only because he has to. He likes movies, but not baseball; he reads crime comics whenever he has the opportunity. He claims to be popular with girls and he may well be; certainly he is good looking enough and willing enough to accept whatever attention from girls that may come his way. He is definitely precocious and sophisticated in his sex interests. This is indicated in the female figure he produced in the Draw-a-Person Test, a figure apparently in short tights with the mammae clearly delineated. According to information given by Ignacio's aunt, he has definitely been involved in dealings with male homosexuals. This interest also is suggested in his drawings. The male figure shows a powerfully built man in trunks, with oversized biceps, his hands encased in boxing gloves. This drawing may also be interpreted as a wish fulfillment on Ignacio's part. Doubtless he often wishes he were a bigger and more masculine looking physical specimen than he actually is. As for his general sexual precociousness, this hardly indicates anything especially abnormal about him. The conditions prevailing in his home, where the difficulties of maintaining privacy must have brought him into close contact with various manifestations of sexual behavior from as far back as he can remember, could easily account for his attitudes. Also, he is, it must be recalled, 16 years old, with much experience among criminals, some of them much older than he.

From these associations, it is reported by his aunt, he has learned how to smoke marijuana and has repeatedly engaged in this practice over the past two years. He admits the charge, stating that he bought his supply of the narcotic from a man from Victoria, whose name he does not know. His more important offenses have been thefts. From the age of five or six he has had the habit of taking small objects of value and carrying them home to his mother, who never offered any objections to the practice. As long as the boy was small, the victims of his depredations, when they caught him in the act, were content to scold him and make him return the stolen articles. Repeated experience made him adept, however, so that he was rarely caught. More recently he has moved into what may well be called "big time" criminality. He belongs to a gang, the only object of which is to engage in theft. This gang includes several boys with nicknames typical of Mexican delinquents, like El Cazador (the Hunter) and El Palillo (the Toothpick). Ignacio is known to his friends as La Esponja (the Parasite). He admits to having committed a number of sizable thefts that were not discovered by the police. This good luck, however, could not last indefinitely. In the company of another boy he journeyed to Reynosa, Tamaulipas, where the pair broke into and took from a cash register the sum of 3,500 pesos. The boys were arrested. The major blame was attached to Ignacio's companion, who was sent to a reform school; Ignacio was set free. Some months later he stole 4,000 pesos, all of which he spent on a trip to Mexico City. Upon his return he was arrested and placed on probation. His most recent theft netted him 1,300 pesos, of which he gave 300 pesos to his mother, spending the rest for clothes and amusements. He is now in a reform school, where he was examined and interviewed as a subject of this study.

What kind of boy Ignacio is can be pretty well deduced from the account of his home, his family, and his criminal behavior. However, his reactions to the Symonds Pictures add something to our understanding of his attitude toward himself. Here is the story he told in response to Picture B-1:

This was a thief who was repenting from stealing, because his mother used to tell him not to go stealing, but he said that he couldn't break the habit, that this business of stealing was stuck on him. Finally, he became a notorious thief. He went from city to city, being caught by the police and put in jail in each city. After having gone far from his mother, he arrived home. His mother believed that he was returning home a hard-working man in order to live happily the rest of his life, but it wasn't true, for he came with the intention of stealing.

He robs a bank in the city where his mother lives and is sentenced for 38 years, leaving the prison when he was very old and when his mother had died and when nothing else was left now for him in this world. His conscience tormented him for having been a thief and he thought, "Why didn't I change so as not to make my mother suffer?"

And with respect to the male figure he produced in the Draw-a-Person Test, he remarked, apparently forgetting the prize-fighting stance of the figure, "This is a boy like me who goes out in the streets stealing and who left home saying he was going to work, but he could not give up his evil skill until he was stopped by the police. He was a prisoner for five years and when he got out he began to work and to save money. He married and established a home and lived happily with his family."

So it appears that he realizes well enough that he is on the wrong track and in his fantasies he sees himself turned at last into an industrious, law-abiding citizen, having what he never had, a happy home. But the chances of his reaching any such ideal seem remote.

APPENDIX 2

Statements Used in the Reading Test

1. A boat can cross the ocean in a few minutes.
2. A month is longer than a week.
3. Airplanes usually go faster than cars.
4. My mother cooks on the refrigerator.
5. Wheat and milk are foods that we get from animals.
6. Baseball bats are made of wood.
7. The cat is a three-legged animal.
8. Two and two make five.

APPENDIX 3

Frequency Distributions for the Offenses Test

Subjects' Ratings of Offense of Accidentally
Breaking a Window While Playing Ball

Rating	Anglo C*	Anglo D*	Latin C	Latin D	Mexican C	Mexican D
1 Most wrong	0	0	0	0	2	0
2	0	0	0	0	0	0
3	0	0	0	0	0	0
4	0	0	0	2	0	0
5	0	0	1	0	2	0
6	0	2	3	2	2	1
7	1	3	4	6	4	1
8	7	2	10	8	4	9
9	6	12	5	10	7	9
10 Least wrong	34	25	26	14	29	29
Total	48	44	49	42	50	49
x̄**	9.52	9.25	8.90	8.48	8.74	9.31
σ**	.82	1.11	1.39	1.56	2.12	.97

* C, comparison group; D, delinquent group.
** x̄, mean; σ, standard deviation.

Subjects' Ratings of Offense of Being Rude to Grandparents

Rating	Anglo		Latin		Mexican	
	C*	D*	C	D	C	D
1 Most wrong	0	0	0	2	1	1
2	0	0	1	0	1	6
3	3	0	3	3	4	4
4	0	1	0	1	5	3
5	4	2	3	4	4	6
6	9	4	12	13	6	8
7	9	8	7	7	6	10
8	9	10	3	1	10	5
9	13	11	10	7	7	5
10 Least wrong	1	8	10	4	6	1
Total	48	44	49	42	50	49
$\bar{x}$**	7.19	8.02	7.37	6.50	6.72	5.71
σ**	1.72	1.52	2.14	2.25	2.37	2.31

* C, comparison group; D, delinquent group.
** $\bar{x}$, mean; σ, standard deviation.

Subjects' Ratings of Offense of Breaking into a House
and Stealing Something

	Rating	Anglo		Latin		Mexican	
		C*	D*	C	D	C	D
1	Most wrong	0	0	0	2	1	6
2		0	2	1	1	7	7
3		11	12	11	3	19	14
4		28	27	22	8	8	14
5		7	3	14	9	5	5
6		1	0	1	3	5	3
7		1	0	0	2	2	0
8		0	0	0	3	2	0
9		0	0	0	2	1	0
10	Least wrong	0	0	0	9	0	0
	Total	48	44	49	42	50	49
	$\bar{x}$**	4.02	3.70	4.06	6.05	3.96	3.29
	σ**	.80	.66	.82	2.72	1.77	1.34

* C, comparison group; D, delinquent group.
** $\bar{x}$, mean; σ, standard deviation.

Subjects' Ratings of Offense of Carrying a Knife or Gun

Rating	Anglo C*	Anglo D*	Latin C	Latin D	Mexican C	Mexican D
1 Most wrong	0	0	0	0	0	0
2	0	0	0	5	5	6
3	1	5	8	15	4	9
4	4	2	8	7	10	5
5	26	28	19	10	9	10
6	9	4	7	4	6	7
7	6	4	1	0	7	12
8	1	1	5	1	3	0
9	0	0	0	0	3	0
10 Least wrong	1	0	1	0	3	0
Total	48	44	49	42	50	49
$\bar{x}$**	5.48	5.07	5.10	3.93	5.46	4.80
σ**	1.15	1.07	1.57	1.35	2.21	1.74

* C, comparison group; D, delinquent group.
** $\bar{x}$, mean; σ, standard deviation.

Subjects' Ratings of Offense of Failing to Stop at a Red Light

Rating	Anglo		Latin		Mexican	
	C*	D*	C	D	C	D
1 Most wrong	0	0	0	9	0	0
2	0	0	0	2	0	0
3	0	0	0	0	2	2
4	1	0	0	3	0	3
5	0	2	2	1	2	4
6	5	10	10	2	8	5
7	13	7	12	7	13	6
8	13	7	9	7	14	10
9	12	8	10	8	10	14
10 Least wrong	4	10	6	3	1	5
Total	48	44	49	42	50	49
$\bar{x}$**	7.85	7.89	7.67	5.93	7.34	7.47
σ**	1.26	1.60	1.42	3.18	1.45	1.92

* C, comparison group; D, delinquent group.
** $\bar{x}$, mean; σ, standard deviation.

Subjects' Ratings of Offense of Murder

Rating		Anglo		Latin		Mexican	
		C*	D*	C	D	C	D
1	Most wrong	30	34	25	21	35	29
2		18	10	23	16	11	12
3		0	0	1	3	2	5
4		0	0	0	1	2	2
5		0	0	0	0	0	0
6		0	0	0	0	0	0
7		0	0	0	0	0	0
8		0	0	0	1	0	1
9		0	0	0	0	0	0
10	Least wrong	0	0	0	0	0	0
	Total	48	44	49	42	50	49
	$\bar{x}$**	1.37	1.23	1.51	1.79	1.42	1.71
	σ**	.48	.42	.54	1.34	.75	1.23

* C, comparison group; D, delinquent group.
** $\bar{x}$, mean; σ, standard deviation.

Subjects' Ratings of Offense of Rape

Rating	Anglo C*	Anglo D*	Latin C	Latin D	Mexican C	Mexican D
Most 1 wrong	18	10	22	6	11	7
2	28	32	23	13	18	13
3	2	1	0	9	6	5
4	0	0	2	5	3	9
5	0	1	1	3	3	6
6	0	0	0	4	2	2
7	0	0	0	1	4	5
8	0	0	1	1	3	1
9	0	0	0	0	0	0
Least 10 wrong	0	0	0	0	0	1
Total	48	44	49	42	50	49
$\bar{x}$**	1.67	1.86	1.82	3.17	3.12	3.65
σ**	.55	.66	1.22	1.76	2.16	2.14

* C, comparison group; D, delinquent group.
** $\bar{x}$, mean; σ, standard deviation.

Subjects' Ratings of Offense of Shooting a BB Gun in the Park

Rating	Anglo		Latin		Mexican	
	C*	D*	C	D	C	D
Most 1 wrong	0	0	1	1	0	2
2	0	0	0	3	1	0
3	0	0	0	4	2	1
4	0	0	0	4	5	2
5	3	3	1	6	12	3
6	6	11	6	3	8	8
7	10	8	12	4	8	12
8	10	15	11	12	7	9
9	13	7	16	4	6	6
Least 10 wrong	6	0	3	2	1	6
Total	48	44	49	42	50	49
$\bar{x}$**	7.87	7.27	7.90	6.24	6.24	7.06
σ**	1.42	1.19	1.22	2.31	1.84	2.08

* C, comparison group; D, delinquent group.
** $\bar{x}$, mean; σ, standard deviation.

Subjects' Ratings of Offense of Staying Away from School

Rating	Anglo C*	Anglo D*	Latin C	Latin D	Mexican C	Mexican D
Most 1 wrong	0	0	1	1	0	2
2	0	0	0	1	0	0
3	0	0	0	0	0	0
4	1	0	1	1	3	1
5	8	2	4	1	5	2
6	17	12	9	7	7	8
7	8	14	13	7	4	3
8	8	9	10	7	5	11
9	4	6	8	9	16	15
Least 10 wrong	2	1	3	8	10	7
Total	48	44	49	42	50	49
$\bar{x}$**	6.71	7.18	7.18	7.62	7.82	7.71
σ**	1.41	1.17	1.67	2.07	1.89	2.05

* C, comparison group; D, delinquent group.
** $\bar{x}$, mean; σ, standard deviation.

Subjects' Ratings of Offense of Stealing a Car

Rating	Anglo		Latin		Mexican	
	C*	D*	C	D	C	D
Most 1 wrong	0	0	1	1	0	2
2	2	0	1	1	7	5
3	31	26	26	5	11	9
4	14	14	16	10	14	10
5	0	3	4	8	8	13
6	1	1	1	4	6	7
7	0	0	0	8	2	0
8	0	0	0	2	2	3
9	0	0	0	1	0	0
Least 10 wrong	0	0	0	2	0	0
Total	48	44	49	42	50	49
$\bar{x}$**	3.31	3.52	3.49	5.31	4.18	4.29
σ**	.65	.72	.84	2.02	1.55	1.64

* C, comparison group; D, delinquent group.
** $\bar{x}$, mean; σ, standard deviation.

APPENDIX 4

Statements Marked "True" in the Card Sort Test

Statement Number	Anglo		Latin		Mexican	
	Comparison Group	Delinquent Group	Comparison Group	Delinquent Group	Comparison Group	Delinquent Group
1	10	16	16	34	31	45
2	28	20	21	26	28	31
3	49	42	45	42	40	36
4	21	25	19	31	27	33
5	0	5	3	17	12	14
6	2	2	4	13	20	23
7	8	14	10	26	26	28
8	14	16	25	35	12	16
9	4	15	5	11	4	9
10	8	3	10	16	30	30
11	13	7	11	17	12	21
12	27	26	22	25	33	33
13	35	35	39	36	45	44
14	27	38	39	43	36	37
15	33	25	29	35	44	39
16	24	18	16	20	20	23
17	5	9	5	6	12	25
18	19	27	18	19	13	31
19	43	38	41	39	43	32
20	41	43	37	45	48	46
21	2	9	11	13	17	25
22	15	21	12	15	13	21
23	32	32	38	37	39	44
24	17	32	18	35	26	38
25	19	24	18	20	15	16
26	28	27	27	34	38	41
27	6	14	15	21	19	38
28	18	15	16	21	19	21

APPENDIX 4 (Continued)

Statements Marked "True" in Card Sort Test

	Anglo		Latin		Mexican	
Statement Number	Comparison Group	Delinquent Group	Comparison Group	Delinquent Group	Comparison Group	Delinquent Group
29	16	17	18	32	36	30
30	48	50	45	38	31	33
31	11	26	4	18	6	22
32	37	35	24	30	28	21
33	17	13	7	22	12	24
34	39	35	32	34	44	35
35	49	47	48	45	45	46
36	3	15	3	12	6	17
37	20	26	21	39	39	40
38	37	36	26	30	28	23
39	23	29	16	20	21	24
40	6	12	6	25	15	23
41	3	4	2	7	5	13
42	40	35	40	37	40	38
43	42	42	36	29	34	37
44	40	47	38	41	32	36
45	37	37	33	38	32	38
46	3	9	7	11	8	14
47	49	43	42	21	41	41
48	24	12	28	20	36	39
49	9	7	5	4	12	24
50	47	41	44	23	27	28
51	11	23	14	18	19	17
52	42	44	45	40	45	33
53	20	24	9	9	34	15
54	4	12	4	9	5	16
55	15	16	18	38	23	34
56	20	20	9	16	13	20
57	2	6	6	3	23	19
58	29	30	24	26	21	15
59	46	41	42	38	27	27
60	39	30	34	21	31	29
61	10	20	4	13	15	29

APPENDIX 4 (Continued)

Statements Marked "True" in Card Sort Test

	Anglo		Latin		Mexican	
Statement Number	Compari- son Group	Delin- quent Group	Compari- son Group	Delin- quent Group	Compari- son Group	Delin- quent Group
62	45	44	43	41	41	42
63	31	34	28	37	15	26
64	27	36	36	36	38	40
65	9	13	4	9	30	27
66	24	18	32	28	19	25
67	50	45	47	31	41	36
68	38	37	37	32	34	27
69	41	35	38	30	6	14
70	43	48	26	26	25	36
71	32	27	23	32	31	38
72	11	13	16	10	18	25
73	35	28	37	29	43	44
74	10	25	18	19	27	33
75	16	20	15	20	27	27
76	3	8	2	3	12	19
77	0	5	2	8	8	7
78	3	4	2	6	9	13
79	46	45	40	28	29	27
80	32	40	23	26	15	27
81	37	37	20	19	28	29
82	44	35	39	33	39	39
83	14	25	24	32	29	35
84	14	17	19	21	22	31
85	43	40	35	29	39	36
86	19	22	21	22	18	21
87	50	46	43	42	47	44
88	18	12	13	16	38	44
89	7	17	9	19	20	26
90	15	22	10	12	8	11
91	41	34	36	34	39	39
92	14	18	26	24	31	40
93	25	24	26	10	25	9
94	34	28	41	24	37	41
95	13	11	7	8	12	23

APPENDIX 4 (Continued)

Statements Marked "True" in Card Sort Test

Statement Number	Anglo		Latin		Mexican	
	Comparison Group	Delinquent Group	Comparison Group	Delinquent Group	Comparison Group	Delinquent Group
96	16	19	10	8	18	20
97	28	20	27	27	29	29
98	2	4	1	3	7	3
99	36	36	39	43	28	42
100	13	9	10	14	11	28
101	5	11	5	16	32	30
102	10	12	7	8	5	11
103	14	20	18	27	25	29
104	5	3	2	9	3	10
105	3	4	1	2	2	1
106	31	24	23	26	21	28
107	25	22	16	22	7	18
108	1	4	5	3	9	13
109	5	6	4	5	8	23
110	47	49	36	27	19	23
111	32	23	20	20	22	24
112	30	20	29	26	24	35
113	8	12	21	23	22	31
114	19	17	22	17	9	9
115	32	32	45	39	39	41
116	25	23	20	24	30	31
117	29	23	29	26	38	43
118	2	1	3	3	5	15
119	11	12	9	15	9	20
120	2	4	5	3	9	14
121	13	14	13	12	17	23
122	17	12	6	15	11	22
123	15	26	3	19	4	23
124	24	19	26	28	18	22
125	49	49	50	41	45	49
126	42	42	46	40	44	45
127	45	38	40	30	27	29
128	2	4	3	3	12	21
129	2	6	2	3	3	5

APPENDIX 4 (Continued)

Statements Marked "True" in Card Sort Test

Statement Number	Anglo		Latin		Mexican	
	Comparison Group	Delinquent Group	Comparison Group	Delinquent Group	Comparison Group	Delinquent Group
130	10	12	5	11	10	14
131	44	35	43	33	33	28
132	43	46	42	44	40	37
133	42	33	44	39	41	38
134	2	6	2	9	16	23
135	23	31	26	20	18	31
136	20	31	25	21	26	30
137	6	13	19	19	28	35
138	46	44	42	38	38	37
139	16	17	18	20	18	18
140	30	19	34	17	25	16

APPENDIX 5

Physical Examination Form

Name_____

Number_____School_____

Age_____B.D._____

Date _____

DEVELOPMENT:

    Height_____Weight_____Nutrition_____
    General description_____

HEAD:

    Skull contour_____
    Deformations_____

EYES:

    Vision R._____Defects of Vision_____
             L._____

EARS:

    Hearing R._____
             L._____

MOUTH:
    Teeth Crowded_____Hutchinson's_____
           Carious_____Missing_____

NOSE:
    Adenoids_____
    Throat_____
    Tonsils_____

NECK:

    Thyroid_____

THORAX:

    Heart_____B.P._____

    Circulation_____S.T._____B._____A._____

    Lungs_____

ARMS: R._____L._____

LEGS: R._____L._____

GENERAL APPEARANCE BY OBSERVATION:

    Posture_____

    Complexion_____

    Skin_____

    Deformities:

    Face_____

    Body_____

    Stigmata_____

    Physiognomy_____

    _____

    Estimate of Handsomeness_____

    _____

SYMPTOMS COMPLAINED OF ON QUESTIONING:

    Pain_____

    Other_____

GENERAL OBSERVATIONS:_____

_____

_____

_____

Signature of Person Giving Examination

REFERENCES

Adorno, T. W., Frenkel-Brunswik, E., Levinson, D. J., & Sanford, R. N. *The authoritarian personality.* New York: Harper, 1950.

Alexander, F., & Staub, H. *The criminal, the judge, and the public.* (Rev. ed.) New York: Collier Books, 1962.

Altus, W. D. Birth order and its sequelae. *Science*, 1966, *151*, 44–49.

Anastasi, A. Heredity, environment and the question "how"? *Psychological Review*, 1958, *65*, 197–208.

Anderson, B., & Gurley, R. *The juvenile offender and Texas law: A handbook.* (Rev. ed.) Austin: Hogg Foundation for Mental Health, 1966.

Anderson, H. H., & Anderson, G. L. Image of the teacher by adolescent children in seven countries. *American Journal of Orthopsychiatry*, 1961, *31*, 481–498.

Anderson, H. H., Anderson, G. L., Cohen, I. H., & Nutt, F. D. Image of the teacher by adolescent children in four countries: Germany, England, Mexico, United States. *Journal of Social Psychology*, 1959, *50*, 47–55.

Andry, R. G. Parental affection and delinquency. In M. E. Wolfgang, L. Savitz, & N. Johnston (Eds.), *The sociology of crime and delinquency.* New York: John Wiley, 1962. Pp. 342–352.

Ashley-Montagu, M. F. The biologist looks at crime. *The Annals*, 1941, *218*, 53–55.

Bach, G. R., & Bremer, G. Projective father fantasies of preadolescent, delinquent children. *Journal of Psychology*, 1947, *24*, 3–17.

Bacon, M. K., Child, I. L., & Barry, H. A cross-cultural study of correlates of crime. *Journal of Abnormal and Social Psychology*, 1963, *66*, 291–300.

Banay, R. S. Physical disfigurement as a factor in delinquency and crime. *Federal Probation*, 1943, *17* (January–March), 20–24.

Bandura, A., & Walters, R. H. *Adolescent aggression: A study of the influence of child-training practices and family interrelationships.* New York: Ronald Press, 1959.

Becker, W. C. Consequences of different kinds of parental discipline. In M. L. Hoffman & L. W. Hoffman (Eds.), *Review of child development research.* Vol. 1. New York: Russell Sage Foundation, 1964. Pp. 169–208.

Becker, W. C., Peterson, D. R., Hellmer, L. A., Shoemaker, D. J., & Quay, H. C. Factors in parental behavior and personality as related to problem behavior in children. *Journal of Consulting Psychology*, 1959, *23*, 107–118.

Berkowitz, L. *Aggression: A social psychological analysis.* New York: McGraw-Hill, 1962.

Berman, L. *The glands regulating personality.* New York: MacMillan, 1921.

Black, H. *They shall not pass.* New York: William Morrow, 1963.

Bloch, H. A., & Flynn, F. T. *Delinquency: The juvenile offender in America today.* New York: Random House, 1956.

Bloch, H. A., & Niederhoffer, A. *The gang: A study in adolescent behavior.* New York: Philosophical Library, 1958.

Block, J. *The challenge of response sets.* New York: Appleton-Century-Crofts, 1965.

Boehm, L. The development of conscience: A comparison of American children of different mental and socio-economic levels. *Child Development*, 1962, *33*, 575–590.

Boring, E. G. Intelligence as the tests test it. *The New Republic*, June 6, 1923, 33–35.

Boring, E. G. *A history of experimental psychology.* (2nd ed.) New York: Appleton-Century-Crofts, 1950.

Borow, H. Development of occupational motives and roles. In L. W. Hoffman & M. L. Hoffman (Eds.), *Review of child development research.* Vol. 2. New York: Russell Sage Foundation, 1966. Pp. 373–422.

Boston Juvenile Court, *Citizenship Training Group, Inc.* Pamphlet issued on the 25th anniversary of the Citizenship Training Group Program, Boston, 1961.

Briggs, P. F., & Wirt, R. D. Prediction. In H. C. Quay (Ed.), *Juvenile delinquency.* Princeton: Van Nostrand, 1965. Pp. 170–208.

Brill, H. Postencephalitic psychiatric conditions. In S. Arieti (Ed.), *The American handbook of psychiatry.* Vol. 2. New York: Basic Books, 1959. Pp. 1163–1174.

References

Bullock, P., & Singleton, R. The minority child and the schools. In Gowan & G. D. Demos (Eds.), *The disadvantaged and potential drop out.* Springfield, Ill.: Charles Thomas, 1966. Pp. 113–122.

Burt, C. *The young delinquent.* (4th ed.) London: University of London Press, 1944.

Burton, R. V., & Whiting, J. M. V. The absent father and cross-sex identity. *Merrill-Palmer Quarterly,* 1961, 7, 85–95.

Caldwell, B. N. The effects of infant care. In M. L. Hoffman & L. W. Hoffman (Eds.), *Review of child development research.* Vol. 1. New York: Russell Sage Foundation, 1964. Pp. 9-88.

Caldwell, R. G. *Criminology.* (2nd ed.) New York: Ronald Press, 1965.

Caplan, N. S. Intellectual functioning. In H. C. Quay (Ed.), *Juvenile delinquency.* Princeton: Van Nostrand, 1965. Pp. 100–138.

Castillo, C., & Bond, O. F. (Eds.) *The University of Chicago Spanish dictionary.* New York: Pocketbooks, 1950.

Cavan, R. S. *Juvenile delinquency.* Philadelphia: J. B. Lippincott, 1962.

Clausen, J. A. Family structure, socialization and personality. In L. W. Hoffman & M. L. Hoffman (Eds.), *Review of child development research.* Vol. 2. New York: Russell Sage Foundation, 1966. Pp. 1–53.

Cloward, R. A., & Ohlin, L. E. *Delinquency and opportunity: A theory of delinquent gangs.* Glencoe, Ill.: Free Press, 1960.

Cohen, A. K. *Delinquent boys: The culture of the gang.* Glencoe, Ill.: Free Press, 1955.

Cohen, A. K. Multiple factor approaches. In M. E. Wolfgang, L. Savitz, & N. Johnston (Eds.), *The sociology of crime and delinquency.* New York: John Wiley, 1962. Pp. 77–80.

Cole, L., & Hall, I. N. *Psychology of adolescence.* (6th ed.) New York: Holt, Rinehart & Winston, 1966.

Craig, M. N., & Glick, S. J. Ten years experience with the Glueck social prediction table. *Crime and Delinquency,* 1963, 9, 249–261.

Cropley, A. J. Differentiation of abilities, socio-economic status, and the WISC. *Journal of Consulting Psychology,* 1964, 28, 512–517.

Darcy, N. T. The effect of bilingualism on the measurement of the intelligence of children of pre-school age. *Journal of Educational Psychology,* 1946, 37, 21–44.

Davis, A., & Havighurst, R. J. Social class and color differences in child-rearing. *American Sociological Review,* 1946, 11, 698–710.

Diaz-Guerrero, R. Neurosis and the Mexican family structure. *American Journal of Psychiatry,* 1955, 112, 411–417.

Diaz-Guerrero, R. Sociocultural and psychodynamic processes in adolescent transition and mental health. In M. Sherif & C. W. Sherif (Eds.),

Problems of youth: Transition to adulthood in a changing world. Chicago: Aldine, 1965. Pp. 129–152.

Diaz-Guerrero, R., & Peck, R. F. Respeto y posición social en dos culturas. In *Sociedad Interamericana de Psicología, VII Congreso Interamericano de psicología.* México, D. F.: S. I. A., 1963. Pp. 116–137.

Dollard, J., Doob, L. W., Miller, N. E., Mowrer, O. H., & Sears, R. R. *Frustration and aggression.* New Haven: Yale University Press, 1939.

Douvan, E., & Adelson, J. The psychodynamics of social mobility in adolescent boys. *Journal of Abnormal and Social Psychology,* 1958, *56,* 31–54.

Douvan, E. & Gold, M. Modal patterns in American adolescence. In L. W. Hoffman & M. L. Hoffman (Eds.), *Review of child development research.* Vol. 2. New York: Russell Sage Foundation, 1966. Pp. 469–528.

East, W. N. Physical factors and criminal behavior. *Journal of Clinical Psychopathology,* 1946, *8,* 7–36.

Eckenrode, C. J. Their achievement in delinquency. *Journal of Educational Research,* 1949–50, *43,* 554–558.

Edmonson, M. S. A triangulation on the culture of Mexico. In M. S. Edmonson, G. Fisher, P. Carrasco, & E. R. Wolf, *Synoptic studies of Mexican culture.* New Orleans: Mid-American Research Institute, 1957. Pp. 201–240.

Edwards, A. L. *The social desirability variable in personality assessment and research.* New York: Dryden, 1957.

Erikson, E. H. *Childhood and society.* New York: W. W. Norton, 1950.

Ewing, R. C. Major historical themes. In R. C. Ewing (Ed.), *Six faces of Mexico: History, people, geography, government, economy, literature and art.* Tucson: University of Arizona Press, 1966. Pp. 1–63.

Flavell, J. H. *The developmental psychology of Jean Piaget.* Princeton: Van Nostrand, 1963.

Foster, G. M. *Tzintzuntzan: Mexican peasants in a changing world.* Boston: Little, Brown, 1967.

Frazier, A., & Lisonbee, L. K. Adolescent concerns with physique. *School Review,* 1950, *58,* 397–405.

Freud, S. Some character types met within psychoanalytic work: (III) Criminals from a sense of guilt. In J. Strachey (Ed.), *The standard edition of the complete psychological works of Sigmund Freud.* Vol. 14. London: Hogarth Press, 1957.

Friedlander, K. *The psychoanalytic approach to juvenile delinquency.* New York: International Universities Press, 1947.

Fuller, J. L., & Thompson, W. R. *Behavior genetics.* New York: John Wiley, 1960.

Funkenstein, D. H., King, S. H., & Drolette, M. W. *Mastery of stress.* Cambridge: Harvard University Press, 1957.

Garrison, K. C. *Psychology of adolescence.* (6th ed.) Englewood Cliffs, New Jersey: Prentice-Hall, 1965.

Glidewell, J. C., Kantor, M. B., Smith, L. M., & Stringer, L. A. Socialization and social structure in the classroom. In L. W. Hoffman & M. L. Hoffman (Eds.), *Review of child development research.* Vol. 2. New York: Russell Sage Foundation, 1966. Pp. 221–256.

Glueck, E. Efforts to identify delinquents. *Federal Probation,* 1960, *24* (2), 49–56.

Glueck, S., & Glueck, E. *Unraveling juvenile delinquency.* New York: Commonwealth Fund, 1950.

Glueck, S., & Glueck, E. *Physique and delinquency.* New York: Harper & Brothers, 1956.

Goldstein, M. S. *Demographic and bodily changes in descendants of Mexican immigrants.* Austin: Institute of Latin American Studies, 1943.

Gomez-Robleda, J. *Imagen del Mexicano.* México, D.F.: Secretaría de Educación Pública, 1948.

Goodenough, F. L. The Kuhlman-Binet test for children of preschool age: A critical study and evaluation. *Institute of Child Welfare Monographs,* No. 2. Minneapolis: University of Minnesota Press, 1928.

Goodenough, F. L., & Leahy, A. The effect of certain family relationships upon the development of personality. *Pedagogical Seminary and Journal of Genetic Psychology,* 1927, *34,* 43–71.

Goring, C. *The English convict: A statistical study.* London: His Majesty's Stationery Office, 1913.

Gottlieb, D. Youth subculture: Variations on a general theme. In M. Sherif & C. W. Sherif (Eds.), *Problems of Youth: Transition to adulthood in a changing world.* Chicago: Aldine, 1965. Pp. 28–45.

Gough, H. G. A sociological theory of psychopathy. *American Journal of Sociology,* 1948, *53,* 359–366.

Gough, H. G. *Manual for the California Psychological Inventory.* Palo Alto, Calif.: Consulting Psychologists Press, 1957.

Gregory, I. Anterospective data following childhood loss of a parent: Delinquency and high school dropout. *Archives of General Psychiatry,* 1965, *13,* 99–109.

Haskell, R. J., Jr. Relationship between aggressive behavior and psychological tests. *Journal of Projective Techniques,* 1961, *25,* 431–440.

Hathaway, S. R., & McKinley, J. C. *The Minnesota multiphasic personality inventory.* New York: Psychological Corporation, 1943.

Hathaway, S. R., & Monachesi, E. G. *Analyzing and predicting juvenile delinquency with the MMPI*. Minneapolis: University of Minnesota Press, 1953.

Hayner, N. S. Notes on the changing Mexican family. *American Sociological Review*, 1942, 7, 489–497.

Healy, W. W., & Bronner, A. F. *New light on delinquency and its treatment*. New Haven: Yale University Press, 1936.

Healy, W., & Bronner, A. F. Delinquency as a mode of adjustment. In R. G. Kuhlen & G. G. Thompson (Eds.), *Psychological studies of human development*. New York: Appleton-Century-Crofts, 1963. Pp. 574–583.

Hebb, D. O. *The organization of behavior*. New York: John Wiley, 1949.

Heller, C. S. *Mexican American youth: Forgotten youth at the crossroads*. New York: Random House, 1966.

Hemingway, E. *Death in the afternoon*. New York: Charles Scribner's Sons, 1932.

Hewitt, E., & Jenkins, R. L. *Fundamental patterns of maladjustment: The dynamics of their origin*. Springfield, Ill.: State Printer, 1946.

Hoffman, L. W. The father's role in the family and the child's peer-group adjustment. *Merrill-Palmer Quarterly*, 1961, 7, 97–105.

Hokanson, J. E. Vascular and psychogalvanic effects of experimentally aroused anger. *Journal of Personality*, 1961, 29, 30–39.

Hollingshead, A. B. *Elmtown's youth: The impact of social classes on youth*. New York: John Wiley, 1949.

Holtzman, W. H., Thorpe, J. S., Swartz, J. D., & Herron, E. W. *Inkblot perception and personality*. Austin: University of Texas Press, 1961.

Hooton, E. A. *The American criminal: An anthropological study. Vol. 1. The native white criminal of native parentage*. Cambridge: Harvard University Press, 1939. (a)

Hooton, E. A. *Crime and the man*. Cambridge: Harvard University Press, 1939. (b)

Hoskins, R. G. *Endocrinology*. New York: Norton, 1941.

Johnson, A. Sanctions for super-ego lacunae of adolescence. In K. R. Eissler (Ed.), *Searchlights on delinquency*. New York: International Universities Press, 1949.

Johnson, E. N. Application of the standard score I.Q. to social statistics. *Journal of Social Psychology*, 1948, 27, 217–227.

Jones, M. C., & Bayley, N. Physical maturing among boys as related to behavior. *Journal of Educational Psychology*, 1950, 41, 129–148.

Juvenile Delinquency Prevention Act of 1967. H. R. 6162. U.S., 90th Congress, 1st Session.

Kagan, J. Measurement of overt aggression from fantasy. *Journal of Abnormal and Social Psychology*, 1956, 52, 390–393. [Republished in E. I.

References 523

Megargee (Ed.), *Research in clinical assessment.* New York: Harper and Row, 1966.]

Kessler, J. W. *Psychopathology of childhood.* Englewood Cliffs, New Jersey: Prentice-Hall, 1966.

Kinsey, A. C., Pomeroy, W. B., & Martin, C. E. *Sexual behavior in the human male.* Philadelphia: Saunders, 1948.

Knetz, W. *An empirical study of the effects of selected variables upon the chi square distribution.* Washington, D. C.: American Institute for Research, 1963.

Kohlberg, L. Development of moral character and moral ideology. In M. L. Hoffman & L. W. Hoffman (Eds.), *Review of child development research.* Vol. 1. New York: Russell Sage Foundation, 1964. Pp. 383–481.

Kohn, M. L. Social class and parental values. *American Journal of Sociology,* 1959, *64,* 337–351.

Konopka, G. *The adolescent girl in conflict.* Englewood Cliffs, N. J.: Prentice-Hall, 1966.

Kraus, I. Sources of educational inspiration among working-class youth. *American Sociological Review,* 1964, *29,* 867–879.

Kvaraceus, W. C. Delinquent behavior and church attendance. *Sociology and Social Research,* 1944, *28,* 284–289.

Kvaraceus, W. C. *Juvenile delinquency.* What research says to the teacher, No. 15. Washington, D. C.: Department of Classroom Teachers and American Educational Research Association, National Education Association, 1958.

Kvaraceus, W. C. The broken home. In R. S. Cavan (Ed.), *Readings in juvenile delinquency.* New York: J. B. Lippincott, 1964. Pp. 181–182.

Lagunes, R. *El Wechsler para niños en México: Consideraciones psicológicas sobre adaptación.* Tesis profesional, Universidad Nacional Autónoma de México, D. F., 1965.

Lesser, G. S. The relation between overt and fantasy aggression as a function of maternal response to aggression. *Journal of Abnormal and Social Psychology,* 1957, *55,* 218–221. [Republished in E. I. Megargee (Ed.), *Research in clinical assessment.* New York: Harper & Row, 1966.]

Levin, M. M. Status anxiety and occupational choice. *Educational and Psychological Measurement,* 1949, *9,* 29–38.

Levine, M. Psychological testing of children. In L. W. Hoffman & M. L. Hoffman (Eds.), *Review of child development research.* Vol. 2. New York: Russell Sage Foundation, 1966. Pp. 257–310.

Levy, J. A quantitative study of behavior problems in relation to family constellation. *American Journal of Psychiatry,* 1931, *10,* 637–654.

Lindzey, G. *Projective techniques and cross-cultural research.* New York: Appleton-Century-Crofts, 1961.

Lindzey, G., & Tejessey, C. Thematic apperception test: Indices of aggression in relation to measures of overt and covert behavior. *American Journal of Orthopsychiatry,* 1956, *26,* 567–576.

Maas, N. Some social-class differences in the family systems and group relations of pre and early adolescence. *Child Development,* 1951, *22,* 145–152.

McCandless, B. R. *Children: Behavior and development.* (2nd ed.) New York: Holt, Rinehart & Winston, 1967.

McClearn, G. E. Genetics and behavior development. In M. L. Hoffman & L. W. Hoffman (Eds.), *Review of child development research.* Vol. 1. New York: Russell Sage Foundation, 1964. Pp. 433–480.

Maccoby, E. E., Gibbs, P. K., & the staff of the laboratory of Human Development, Harvard University. Methods of childrearing in two social classes. In C. B. Stendler (Ed.), *Readings in child behavior and development.* (2nd ed.) New York: Harcourt, Brace & World, 1964. Pp. 272–287.

McCord, J., & McCord, W. The effects of parental role model on criminality. *Journal of Social Issues,* 1958, *14,* 66–75.

McGehee, W., & Lewis, W. D. The socio-economic status of homes of mentally superior and retarded children and the occupational rank of their parents. *Journal of Genetic Psychology,* 1942, *60,* 375–380.

McGinn, W. N., Harburg, E., & Ginsburg, G. Perceptions of middle class Mexican and American males about parent-child and inter-personal relations. Unpublished mimeographed manuscript, 1963. Cited by R. Diaz-Guerrero, Socio-cultural and psycho-dynamic processes in adolescent transition and mental health. In M. Sherif & C. W. Sherif (Eds.), *Problems of youth: Transitions to adulthood in a changing world.* Chicago: Aldine, 1965.

McWilliams, C. *North from Mexico: The Spanish-speaking people of the United States.* (1st ed.) Philadelphia: J. B. Lippincott, 1949.

Madsen, W. *Mexican-Americans of South Texas.* New York: Holt, Rinehart, & Winston, 1964.

Maldonado-Sierra, E. D., Trent, R. D., & Fernandez-Marina, R. Three basic themes in Mexican and Puerto Rican family values. *Journal of Social Psychology,* 1958, *48,* 167.

Maslow, A. H., & Diaz-Guerrero, R. Delinquency as a value disturbance. In J. G. Peatman & E. L. Hartley (Eds.), *Festschrift for Gardner Murphy.* New York: Harper & Brothers, 1960. Pp. 228–240.

Medinnus, G. R. The development of a parent attitude toward education scale. *Journal of Educational Research,* 1962, *56,* 100–103.

Megargee, E. I. Assaultive behavior in adolescents. In P. L. Sullivan (Chm.), The treatment of aggression and violence in the American culture. Symposium presented at the American Psychological Association, Los Angeles, September, 1964. (a)

Megargee, E. I. The utility of the Rosenzweig Picture-Frustration Study in detecting assaultiveness among juvenile delinquents. Paper presented at the meeting of the Southwestern Psychological Association, San Antonio, April, 1964. (b)

Megargee, E. I. Assault with intent to kill. *Trans-action*, 1965, *2* (6), 27–31.

Megargee, E. I. The relation of response length to Holtzman Inkblot Technique scores. *Journal of Consulting Psychology*, 1966, *30*, 415–419. (a)

Megargee, E. I. (Ed.) *Research in clinical assessment.* New York: Harper & Row, 1966. (b)

Megargee, E. I. Undercontrolled and overcontrolled personality types in extreme anti-social aggression. *Psychological Monographs*, 1966, *80* (3, Whole No. 611). (c)

Megargee, E. I. Hostility on the TAT as a function of defensive inhibition and stimulus situation. *Journal of Projective Techniques and Personality Assessment*, 1967, *31*, 73–79.

Megargee, E. I., & Cook, P. E. The relation of TAT and inkblot aggressive content scales with each other and with criteria of overt aggressiveness in delinquents. *Journal of Projective Techniques and Personality Assessment*, 1967, *31*, 48–60.

Megargee, E. I., Cook, P. E., & Mendelsohn, G. A. The development and validation of an MMPI scale of assaultiveness in overcontrolled individuals. *Journal of Abnormal Psychology*, 1967, *72*, 519–528.

Megargee, E. I., Lockwood, V., Cato, J., & Jones, J. K. Effects of differences in examiner, tone of administration and sex of subject on scores of the Holtzman Inkblot Technique. In *Proceedings of the 74th Annual Convention of the American Psychological Association.* Washington, D. C.: American Psychological Association, 1966. Pp. 235–236.

Megargee, E. I., & Mendelsohn, G. A. A cross validation of 12 MMPI indices of hostility and control. *Journal of Abnormal and Social Psychology*, 1962, *65*, 431–438.

Merton, R. K. *Social theory and social structure.* Glencoe, Ill.: Free Press, 1957.

Miller, W. B. Lower class culture as a generating milieu of gang delinquency. *Journal of Social Issues*, 1958, *14*, No. 3, 5–19.

Miller, W. B. Implications of urban lower class culture for social work. *The Social Service Review*, 1959, *33*, 219–236.

Monahan, T. P. Family status and delinquency. *Social Forces*, 1957, *35*, 250–258.

Moore, B. M., & Holtzman, W. H. *Tomorrow's parents: A study of youth and their families.* Austin: University of Texas Press, 1965.

Murstein, B. I. *Theory and research in projective techniques (Emphasizing the TAT).* New York: John Wiley, 1963.

Murstein, B. I. Projection of hostility on the TAT as a function of stimulus, background and personality variables. *Journal of Consulting Psychology*, 1965, *29*, 43–48.

Mussen, P. H., Conger, J. J., & Kagan, J. *Child development and personality.* (2nd ed.) New York: Harper & Row, 1963.

Mussen, P. H., & Naylor, H. K. The relationships between overt and fantasy aggression. *Journal of Abnormal and Social Psychology*, 1954, *49*, 235–240. [Republished in E. I. Megargee (Ed.), *Research in clinical assessment.* New York: Harper & Row, 1966.]

National Advisory Commission on Civil Disorders. *Report of the National Advisory Commission on Civil Disorders.* New York: Bantam Books, 1968.

Nye, F. I. *Family relationships and delinquent behavior.* New York: John Wiley, 1958.

Parker, R. K., & Dunham, R. M. Project Know How: A comprehensive and innovative attack on individual familial poverty. In R. K. Parker (Ed.), *Readings in Educational Psychology.* Boston: Allyn & Bacon, 1968. Ch. 7.2.

Paterson, D. C., Ggerken, C. d'A., & Han, M. E. Revised Minnesota Occupational Rating Scales. In E. G. Williamson (Ed.), *Minnesota studies in student personnel work,* No. 2. Minneapolis: University of Minnesota Press, 1953.

Payne, D. E., & Mussen, P. H. Parent-child relations and father identification among adolescent boys. *Journal of Abnormal and Social Psychology*, 1956, *52*, 358–362.

Pearl, A. Youth in lower class settings. In M. Sherif & C. W. Sherif (Eds.), *Problems of youth: Transition to adulthood in a changing world.* Chicago: Aldine, 1965. Pp. 89–109.

Peck, R. F., & Diaz-Guerrero, R. Two core-culture patterns and the diffusion of values across their border. In Sociedad Interamericana de Psicología, *VII Congreso Interamericano de Psicología*, México, D. F.: S.I.A., 1963. Pp. 107–115.

Peterson, D. R., & Becker, W. C. Family interaction and delinquency. In H. C. Quay (Ed.), *Juvenile delinquency.* Princeton: Van Nostrand, 1965. Pp. 63–99.

Peterson, D. R., Quay, H. C., & Cameron, G. R. Personality and background factors in juvenile delinquency as inferred from questionnaire responses. *Journal of Consulting Psychology*, 1959, *23*, 395–399.

Pittluck, P. The relationship between aggressive fantasy and overt behavior. Unpublished doctoral dissertation, Yale University, 1950.

Podolsky, E. The chemical brew of criminal behavior. *Journal of Criminal Law and Criminology*, 1955, *45*, 675–678.

Pope, B. Socioeconomic contrasts in children's peer culture prestige values. *Genetic Psychological Monographs*, 1953, *48*, 157–220.

Purcell, K. The TAT and anti-social behavior. *Journal of Consulting Psychology*, 1956, *20*, 449–456.

Quay, H. C. (Ed.) *Juvenile delinquency*. Princeton: Van Nostrand, 1965. (a)

Quay, H. C. Personality and delinquency. In H. C. Quay (Ed.), *Juvenile delinquency*. Princeton: Van Nostrand, 1965. Pp. 139–169. (b)

Ramos, S. *Profile of man and culture in Mexico*. (Translated by P. G. Earle) Austin: University of Texas Press, 1962.

Reckless, W. C. *The crime problem*. (3rd ed.) New York: Appleton-Century, 1961.

Reckless, W. C., Dinitz, S., & Kay, B. The self component in potential delinquency and potential non-delinquency. *American Sociological Review*, 1957, *22*, 566–570.

Reckless, W. C., Dinitz, S., & Murray, E. Self-concept as an insulator against delinquency. *American Sociological Review*, 1956, *21*, 744–746.

Reckless, W. C., Dinitz, S., & Murray, E. The "good" boy in a high delinquency area. *Journal of Criminal Law, Criminology and Police Science*, 1957, *48*, 18–26.

Reiss, A. J., Jr. Delinquency as the failure of personal and social controls. *American Sociological Review*, 1951, *16*, 196–208.

Reiss, A. J. Social correlates of psychological types of delinquency. *American Journal of Sociology*, 1952, *17*, 710–718.

Rhodes, L. Anomie, aspiration and status. *Social Focus*, 1964, *42*, 434–440.

Robins, L. N. *Deviant children grown up: A sociological and psychiatric study of sociopathic personality*. Baltimore: Williams & Wilkins, 1966.

Robison, S. *Juvenile delinquency, its nature and control*. New York: Holt, Rinehart & Winston, 1960.

Rodríguez, R. A. Estudios psicológicos de validación cruzada del Wechsler (W.I.S.C.) y el Goodenough en escolares Mexicanos. Tesis para obtener el título del psicólogo, Universidad Autónoma de México, México, D.F., 1965.

Rodríguez, R. A., & Díaz-Guerrero, R. Algunos problemas en la adaptación del W.I.S.C. a México. In Sociedad Interamericana de Psicología, *Proceedings of the IXth Congress of the Interamerican Society of Psychology.* Miami Beach: S.I.A., 1964. Pp. 483–495.

Rosenow, C., & Whyte, A. H. The ordinal position of problem children. *American Journal of Orthopsychiatry,* 1931, *1,* 430–434.

Rosenzweig, S. The picture-association method and its application in a study of reactions to frustration. *Journal of Personality,* 1945, *14,* 3–23.

Rosenzweig, S. Levels of behavior in psychodiagnosis with special reference to the Picture-Frustration study. *American Journal of Orthopsychiatry,* 1950, *20,* 63–72. [Republished in E. I. Megargee (Ed.), *Research in clinical assessment.* New York: Harper & Row, 1966.]

Rubel, A. J. *Across the tracks: Mexican-Americans in a Texas city.* Austin: University of Texas Press, 1966.

Rubenfeld, F. *Family of outcasts: A new theory of delinquency.* New York: Free Press, 1965.

Salisbury, H. E. *The shook-up generation.* New York: Harper & Row, 1959.

Saltz, G., & Epstein, S. Thematic hostility and guilt responses as related to self-reported hostility, guilt and conflict. *Journal of Abnormal and Social Psychology,* 1963, *67,* 469–479.

Scarpitti, F. A follow up study of good boys in high delinquency areas. Master's thesis, The Ohio State University, 1959.

Scarpitti, F. R., Murray, E., Dinitz, S., & Reckless, W. C. The "good boy" in a high delinquency area: Four years later. *American Sociological Review,* 1960, *25,* 555–558.

Schlapp, M. G., & Smith, E. H. *The new criminology.* New York: Boni & Liveright, 1928.

Sellin, T. *Culture conflict and crime.* New York: Social Science Research Council, 1938.

Sellin, T., & Wolfgang, M. *The measurement of delinquency.* New York: John Wiley, 1964.

Sexton, P. C. *Spanish Harlem.* New York: Harper & Row, 1965.

Shaw, C. R., & McKay, H. D. *Juvenile delinquency in urban areas.* Chicago: University of Chicago Press, 1942.

Sheldon, W. H., et al. *Varieties of delinquent youth.* New York: Harper & Bros., 1949.

Sherif, M., & Sherif, C. W. *Reference groups: Exploration into conformity and deviation of adolescents.* New York: Harper & Row, 1964.

Sherif, M., & Sherif, C. W. The adolescent in his group in its setting II. Research procedures and findings. In M. Sherif & C. W. Sherif (Eds.), *Problems of Youth: Transition to adulthood in a changing world.* Chicago: Aldine, 1965. Pp. 295–329.

Short, J. F., Jr. Social structure and group processes in explanation of gang delinquency. In M. Sherif & C. W. Sherif (Eds.), *Problems of youth: Transition to adulthood in a changing world.* Chicago: Aldine Publishing Co., 1965. Pp. 155–188.

Short, J. F., Jr. Juvenile delinquency: The sociocultural context. In L. W. Hoffman & M. L. Hoffman (Eds.), *Review of child development research.* Vol. 2. New York: Russell Sage Foundation, 1966.

Short, J. F., Jr., & Nye, F. I. Extent of unrecorded juvenile delinquency. *Journal of Criminal Law, Criminology and Police Science,* 1958, *49,* 297.

Siegel, S. *Nonparametric statistics for the behavioral sciences.* New York: McGraw-Hill, 1956.

Simmons, O. G. Anglo-Americans and Mexican-Americans in South Texas. Unpublished doctoral dissertation, Harvard University, 1952.

Sletto, R. S. Sibling position and juvenile delinquency. *American Journal of Sociology,* 1934, *39,* 657–669.

Spicer, E. H. Ways of life. In R. C. Ewing (Ed.), *Six Faces of Mexico: History, people, geography, government, economy, literature and art.* Tucson: University of Arizona Press, 1966. Pp. 65–102.

Stagner, R. *Psychology of personality.* (3rd ed.) New York: McGraw-Hill Book Company, 1961.

Stephenson, R. M. Occupational aspiration and plans of 443 ninth graders. *Journal of Educational Research,* 1955, *49,* 27–35.

Stone, H. The relationship of hostile-aggressive behavior to aggressive content on the Rorschach and Thematic Apperception Test. Unpublished doctoral dissertation, University of California, Los Angeles, 1953.

Sutherland, E. H. *Principles of criminology.* (3rd ed.) New York: J. B. Lippincott, 1939.

Sutherland, E. H. Critique of Sheldon's *Varieties of delinquent youth. American Sociological Review,* 1951, *16,* 10–13.

Sutherland, E. H., & Cressey, D. R. *Principles of criminology.* (7th ed.) New York: J. B. Lippincott, 1966.

Symonds, P. M. *Manual for the Symonds Picture-Story Test.* New York: Bureau of Publications, Teacher's College, Columbia University, 1948.

Symonds, P. M. *Adolescent fantasy.* New York: Columbia University Press, 1949.

Tappan, P. W. *Juvenile delinquency.* New York: McGraw-Hill, 1949.

Tappan, P. W. *Crime, justice & correction.* New York: McGraw-Hill, 1960.

Terman, L. M., & Merrill, M. A. *Measuring intelligence.* Boston: Houghton, Mifflin, 1937.

Tuck, R. D. *Not with the fist: Mexican-Americans in a southwest city.* New York: Harcourt, Brace and Co., 1946.

Tuma, E., & Livson, N. Family socioeconomic status and adolescent response to authority. *Child development,* 1960, *31,* 387–399.

Vaillant, G. C. *The Aztecs of Mexico.* Bungay, Suffolk: Penguin Books, 1950.

Vold, G. B. *Theoretical criminology.* New York: Oxford University Press, 1958.

Walker, H. M., & Lev, J. *Statistical inference.* New York: Henry Holt & Co., 1953.

Wattenberg, W. W. Delinquency and only children: A study of a "category." *Journal of Abnormal and Social Psychology,* 1949, *44,* 356–366.

Wattenberg, W. W. Delinquent behavior and church attendance. *Sociology and Social Research,* 1950, *34,* 195–202.

Weatherley, D. Maternal permissiveness toward aggression and subsequent TAT aggression. *Journal of Abnormal and Social Psychology,* 1962, *65,* 1–5.

Wechsler, D. *The measurement and appraisal of adult intelligence.* (4th ed.) Baltimore: Williams and Wilkins, 1958.

Whiting, J. W. M. The cross-cultural method. In G. Lindzey (Ed.), *Handbook of social psychology,* Vol. 1. Reading, Mass.: Addison Wesley, 1954. Pp. 523–531.

Whyte, W. F. *Street corner society.* (Enlarged ed.) Chicago: University of Chicago Press, 1955.

Williams, W. C. The PALS Test: A technique for children to evaluate both parents. *Journal of Consulting Psychology,* 1958, *22,* 478–495.

Wirt, R. D., & Briggs, P. F. The meaning of delinquency. In H. C. Quay (Ed.), *Juvenile delinquency.* New York: Van Nostrand, 1965. Pp. 1–26.

Wortis, H., Bardach, J. L., Cutler, R., Rue, R., & Freedman, A. Childrearing practices in a low socio-economic group. *Pediatrics,* 1963, *32,* 298–307.

Yarrow, L. Separation from parents during childhood. In M. L. Hoffman & L. W. Hoffman (Eds.), *Review of child development research.* Vol. 1. New York: Russell Sage Foundation, 1964. Pp. 89–136.

Young, F. M. Responses of juvenile delinquents to the Thematic Apperception Test. *Journal of Genetic Psychology,* 1956, *88,* 251–259.

Zubin, J., Eron, L. D., & Schumer, F. *An experimental approach to projective techniques.* New York: John Wiley, 1965.

GLOSSARY OF COLLOQUIAL SPANISH AND
"TEX-MEX" WORDS AND PHRASES

barrio: that section of a North American town in which Mexican Americans live.

brujo: a witch or sorcerer. Unlike the *curandero*, the *brujo* engages in black magic and casts evil spells.

campesino: a peasant or farmer.

cantina: a bar or tavern.

casa chica: "little house." This term refers to the establishment in which the Mexican male keeps his mistress.

castigo de Dios: divine punishment.

chicano: a term used by Mexican Americans to refer to themselves.

chulo: a term used by Mexican Americans to refer to themselves.

compadrazgo: the institution of coparenthood through godparents.

compadre: a godparent who functions as a coparent for the child.

criollo: Creole; a person of pure Spanish blood born in America.

curandero: a healer or curer; a person who heals disease with a combination of herbal remedies, magic, and religion. The *curandero* is neither a doctor nor a witch.

empresario: manager or promoter; holder of a Mexican land grant in the early nineteenth century.

gringo: a disparaging term for a North American.

La Huelga: labor strike. This term is used to refer to the attempts to organize farm workers in the Rio Grande Valley.

inglesado: a Mexican American who has adopted North American cultural values or behavior.

jefe de la casa: literally, the chief of the house. This phrase denotes the position of the husband in the Mexican family.

machismo: masculine honor.

mal ojo: a folk disease caused by the glance of an evil eye or a spell cast by a witch.

mestizo: a person of mixed Spanish and Indian blood.

muchos huevos: literally "many eggs"; colloquially, "balls" or masculinity.

palomilla: male clique. *Palomilla* literally means moth and the term is applied to the male peer group because its ever changing membership is reminiscent of a group of moths fluttering around a light.

pelado: a derogatory term signifying a lower-class city bum.

peninsulares: people of pure Spanish blood born in Spain.

pulquería: a tavern selling pulque, the fermented juice of the maguey plant.

la raza: "the race"; all Latin Americans united by holy cultural and spiritual bonds.

santos: saints.

susto: "shock"; a folk disease caused by sudden confrontation with a supernatural being or by a natural narrow escape.

INDEX

Abbott, ———: 175
Adelson, J.: 52, 97
adenoids: condition of, as related to delinquency, 146, 386, 441
Adler, ———: 212
Adorno, T. W.: 44
aggression: muscular boys rewarded for, 14, 430; direction of delinquent, 29; excessive, of delinquents, 31; degree of, permitted toward parents, 36, 38; as related to class, 40, 41, 54, 56; as related to masculinity, 65, 85; greater degree of, in Mexican culture, 73, 77; as threat to middle-class teacher, 90; of Latins, causes trouble with law, 101–102; first-born children low in, 175; relation between frustration and, 200; family patterns related to, 271–272, 459; thematic tests scored in regard to, 337; scoring for, on Picture-Story Test, 338; meaning of responses expressing, on projective tests, 341–342, 354–355; as related to stress, 422
alcoholism. SEE psychopathology
Anderson, G. L.: 72
Anderson, H. H.: 64, 72
Andry, R. G.: 273–274, 293

Anglos: selected as research subjects, 6, 111, 117, 120–121, 123, 124, 129, 149; settle Texas, 7; as dominant cultural group, 8; Latins exposed to values of, 10; family patterns among, 33, 153, 155–156, 160–161, 163–164, 166, 167, 168–169, 173, 174, 177–183, 206, 207, 280, 302 n., 435, 438, 442, 444, 447, 449, 450, 457, 458–459, 463; defined, 34–35; Negro child-rearing practices compared to those of, 37; taverns not ritualized into life of, 42; prejudices of lower-class, 44; class differences in personality characteristics among, 45; compared to Puerto Ricans, 47 n.; Harlem children read about, 48; peer relationships among, 53, 76; conclusions of research on lower-class, 55–56; amount of empirical data on, 64; aggressiveness of, compared to that of Mexicans, 65; attitude of middle-class, toward sex, 66; focal concerns of lower-class, 67, 103; fatalism of lower-class, 69; racial prejudice of, 72; comparison of values of, with those of Mexicans, 73, 77; school adjustment of, 74; colonize South-

lated to delinquency, 274, 278; in polygamous societies, 279; statements about, on Card Sort Test, 280–285, 286, 287, 288, 289, 291, 292, 295–297, 299, 300, 301, 306, 321, 493, 496; fathers defer to, of delinquents, 293; overprotectiveness of, as related to delinquency, 295, 296; perception of, on Cartoon Test, 314–315, 318, 319, 324, 325, 326, 329, 330, 331, 332, 437, 440–441, 445; references to, on Picture-Story Test, 341, 344, 346, 366, 367, 368, 369, 370, 482, 492, 497–498; attitudes of, toward aggressive behavior, 342; endocrine troubles of, as related to criminality, 418; attitudes of Anglos toward, 437; cultural role stressed at expense of, 448; undermine father-son relationship, 449; "Project Know How" training for, 467; in case studies, 472–473, 476–477, 478–479, 480, 481, 482, 483, 484, 486, 487, 488, 489, 491, 493, 494–495, 496, 497; statements about, on Reading Test, 499

multiple-factor theories of delinquency: 28–30

Murchison, ———: 212

murder: in panorama of illegal behavior, 30; statistics on, 126; rated on Offenses Test, 145, 255, 256, 258, 264, 265, 266, 505; ratings of similar Sellin-Wolfgang item to, 262; as related to aggression, 355; as related to excess thyroxin, 418; by father in case study, 494. SEE ALSO killing

Murray, E.: study by, of "good" boys in high-delinquency neighborhoods, 277–279; on family patterns as related to delinquency, 321

Mussen, P. H.: 354–355

narcotics: children see buying of, 19; use of, as escape device, 24, 42; peddling of, in panorama of illegal behavior, 30; pushers of, shown in film, 48; use of, as related to socioeconomic class, 56; treatment for addiction to, 122; references to, on Picture-Story Test, 338, 340, 354

National Educational Television: report on Harlem school by, 48

Naylor, H. K.: 354–355

Negroes: arrests of, for sit-ins, 4; child-rearing practices of, 37–38; job opportunities for, 49; slave, 79; lynchings of, 80; segregation of, 81; civil rights organizations of, 86; educational aspirations of, 94; open opportunities for Latins, 96; percentage of, in San Antonio, 113; socioeconomic status of, 114; not included in present study, 117, 149; delinquent, in Bexar County, 120; religious affiliations of, 189

New Haven, Conn.: movie attendance in, as related to delinquency, 243 n.; lower-class aspirations in, 246, 248

New York City: Latin girl forbidden to study in, 95; questions about, on WISC, 214; glandular disturbance in, 418

Niederhoffer, A.: 23–24

Nisei: delinquency rate among, 254

Norway: study of birth order and delinquency in, 176

Nueces County Detention Home: 479

Nuevo León: choice of research site in, 7, 111, 149; lower-class culture in, 34; home headed by women in, 67; Monterrey capital of, 115; juvenile tribunal for, 121; difference in juvenile delinquency in, and in Texas, 122; manner of classifying and reporting crimes in, 127

Nuevo León, University of: 116

nutrition: as related to delinquency, 5, 16, 381, 386, 392–395, 400–401, 430, 446, 458; physicians' opinions of subjects', 150; as nongenetic factor, 379–380; relationship of weight to, 389, 390, 391–392; effects of, on

in high-delinquency neighborhoods, 277; contacts with, of "bad" boys in Columbus study, 278; statements about, on Card Sort Test, 282, 283, 284, 289, 291, 292, 296, 321, 451, 460; stories concerning, in Picture-Story Test, 344, 368, 369, 370, 497; criminals compared to, in physical characteristics, 378; thefts not discovered by, 497; mentioned, 498

Pomeroy, W. B.: 41

Pope, B.: 54–55

Positivist School: 209

poverty: as related to delinquency, 16, 18, 21, 22, 29, 31, 104, 148, 358, 359, 456, 461, 466; police patrols in areas of, 17; as related to social class, 55; more widespread in Mexico, 77; among Latins, 87, 114; amount of, in Monterrey, 116; cycle of, 200; as related to thrift, 229; references to, on Picture-Story Test, 341; in case studies, 482, 486. SEE ALSO socioeconomic status

projective tests. SEE Cartoon Test; Picture-Story Test; Rorschach Test; Thematic Apperception Test

"Project Know How": predicted success of, 466–467

prostitution: children exposed to, 19; in Harlem neighborhood, 48

psychopathology: as related to criminality, 4, 16, 22, 26–27, 28, 271, 382, 396–397, 464; alcoholism, 16, 122, 271, 460; rate of, in high-delinquency areas, 18; neurosis, 28, 273, 382; psychopathy, 28; psychosis, 56; depression, 56; juvenile court assigns treatment for, 122; subjects excluded because of, 123, 127, 149; sociopathy, 170–171, 382, 398; of siblings of delinquents, 171; as related to criminal guilt, 208; schizophrenia, 296; lack of identification with father conducive to, 297; relationship of physical factors to, 382, 398, 407, 411–412

P-TA: 50

Puerto Ricans: compared to Anglos, 47 n.

Puerto Rico: WISC standardized in, 136, 214–215, 221, 222, 224; research in, on relation of values to criminality, 451

Purcell, K.: 354

Quay, H. C.: on theoretical positions, 11; on time orientation of delinquents and nondelinquents, 226; study of family patterns by, 271–272, 273

Ramos, Samuel: 67–69, 90

rape: statutory, 4; multiple motivations for, 25; statistics on, 126; rated on Offenses Test, 145, 255, 256, 258, 264, 265, 506; Sellin-Wolfgang rating of, 262; relation of excess thyroxin to, 418

raza, la: meaning of term, 34. SEE ALSO Latins; Mexicans

Reckless, Walter C.: "containment" theory of, 28; study by, on relationship of neighborhoods to delinquency, 277–279, 466; on subjective perception of delinquents, 320; on family patterns as related to delinquency, 321, 458, 465

Regiomontanos: culture of, 116

Reiss, A. J., Jr.: attributes delinquent behavior to failure of controls, 27; influence of, on Reckless, 28; on relation of family patterns to delinquency, 465

religion: overtones of, in concept of *la raza*, 34; role of, in settlement of North America, 57; aspects of Mexican, 70–71; as related to *compadrazgo*, 75; classes share same, in Mexico, 77; as related to English-Spanish antipathy, 79; Latin attitudes toward, 88–89; influences divorce and remarriage, 156, 159, 164,

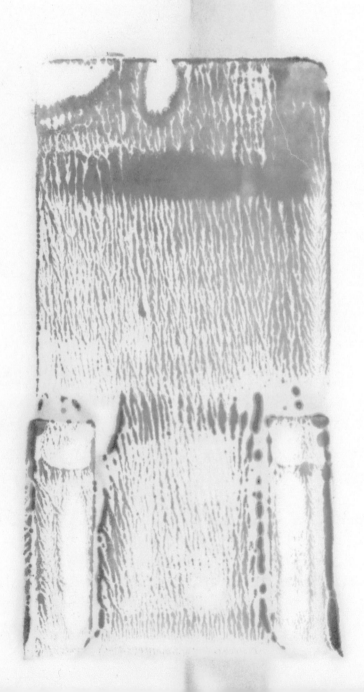